The
Chefs Reference
Guide

Master Chef Edition

Frederick J. Tiess ME, WCMC, CEC, CCA, FMP

Le Guild Culinaire

Published in Matthews North Carolina by

Le Guild Culinaire

Library of Congress Control Numbers: 2011919396, 2006930873, In Publication Data

Tiess, Frederick J.
     The Chefs Reference Guide- 1st Edition
     ISBN 0-9724642-9-8
     ISBN 978-0-9724642-9-1

     The Chefs Reference Guide- 2nd Edition-
     Master Chef Edition
     ISBN 0-9724642-7-1
     ISBN 978-0-9724642-7-7

                    Printed in the United States of America

Dedication

To the love of my life,
the butter to my bread,
my best friend - Beth

Table of Contents

ϕ Mental Mise en Place ϕ

Mise en Place: Fr. "Everything put in its place"

"Mise en place" is a French phrase that means *everything in its place*. This common professional phrase emphasizes the need to have all ingredients and equipment ready for the intended time of use. The introduction of this book is entitled "Mental Mise en Place". A successful cook is one who has <u>mentally prepared</u> before beginning preparation of a dish. Mental Mise en Place is comprised of three concepts: knowledge, skill, and repertoire.

Knowledge: Understanding an organized body of facts and principles through words, sensations, and observations.

The measure of a cook's culinary knowledge starts with his or her understanding of the relationship between cooking techniques, ingredients, and the desired outcome. A dish often begins with a creative thought that builds upon what is known so that the cook can discover what is possible. Creating a dish is really just an experiment. *The Chefs Reference Guide* presents over 1300 proven culinary experiments. These experiments can be used to understand the relationship between the ratio of ingredients. The understanding of these relationships is an essential first step in creating new concepts and dishes.

Skill: The ability gained though correct repetitive practice.

The most effective way to learn a new technique is through observation and practice. For a novice culinarian this involves an apprenticeship, a formal culinary education, or work experience. After a skill has been observed and practiced it needs to be refined through continued practice over a longer period of time. The mastering of some techniques may only take a few weeks, but the perfection of that technique may be a lifelong challenge. Skills are perishable; continued practice is the key to success.

Can you recall a dish that you really enjoyed from your past? Have you ever been to a restaurant where you ordered the same thing on two separate occasions and found that the dish you ordered was not as you had expected? Perhaps your second experience was an improper execution of the formula or recipe. This could have happened through a lapse in skill amongst the team of cooks, improper sequencing of the preparation or a formula mise en place issue. The consistency of preparation is critical because you ordered the dish the second time because you liked it the first time, your guests expect the same of you. A successful cook is one who can deliver a defined set of skills consistently therefore producing a consumable work of art every time. As chefs and cooks we are only as good as the last meal we prepared.

Repertoire: A list of what has been learned for the purpose of performance.

The Chefs Reference Guide provides the cook with a quick access to the "need to know" details of dishes and methodology. It is divided into three sections. The first section of this guide details the critical information concerning the basic cooking techniques. This technique focused section will help the user to review the critical check points of food preparation in order to ensure a properly prepared product. The second section of this reference guide contains formulas and recipes. These recipes and formulas are presented in a matrix format. Details concerning the instruction for use will be detailed on the following page. The third section of the reference guide presents a basic interpretation of over 3000 culinary terms as well as reference charts.

Recipe versus Formula

A recipe can be defined as a framework to work within to ensure a consistent product. A formula, on the other hand, can be defined as an exact ratio that produces a consistent product. Some recipes can be adjusted for similar results. For example, a recipe for stock that uses turkey bones instead of chicken bones will result in a similar finished product. A cook can adjust the ingredients, timing and temperatures to accommodate the primary change in flavor. Formulas on the other hand, if altered, can have an undesired effect. An example of this is pie dough. The correct measure of flour, fat and cold water is the key to successful pie dough. Too much flour and the dough will be tough and dry, too much fat and the dough will taste greasy, too little water and the product will fall apart when baked. It can be difficult to identify some of these potential problems in the preparation of a dough just by looking at it, measurement matters.

φ Mental Mise en Place φ

The recipe charts, which contain the recipes and formulas, have been designed with a recipe reference number to speed the referencing process. Use of the table of contents will primarily aid the user in referencing the categorized recipes through the use of recipe numbers. The numbering system used for these recipes and formulas can be used as a production training tool for managers to plan, organize and control the daily output of preparation.

The spreadsheet recipe format is very different from the standard recipe format found in most books. Let's first look at a traditional recipe so that it can be compared to the spreadsheet format used in this guide. A video of the crêpe making process is available on our YouTube Channel- chefreference.

Crêpe -Recipe Number 10-Yields 20 crêpes

Ingredients

> **2 ounces of clarified butter**
> **1 cup of flour**
> **2 cups of milk**
> **4 each eggs**

Method of Preparation

> **Whisk the flour into the milk and eggs, strain, add butter. Ladle 1 1/2**
>
> **oz of batter for each crêpe and cook until golden brown.**

Now let's look at the spreadsheet format for the same Crêpe recipe.

How to use the Recipe Formula Charts

Column A is the recipe/ formula reference number.
Column B is the recipe /formula name
Column C are the ingredients and the quantity
Column D is a common ingredient amount – refer to the top of the
> **line if no amount is given.**

Column E is a yield or portion
Column F is the method notes or chef notes

A	B	C	D			E	F
	Item		**1**	**2**	**4**	**Yield**	**Method of Preparation**
3	**Crêpe**	2oz Melted Butter	cup Flour	cup Milk	ea. Eggs	20 ea.	Whisk the flour into the milk and eggs, strain, whisk in butter. Ladle 1.5 oz of batter in a 10-inch non-stick pan until golden brown.

This recipe/formula is on the page containing other basic kitchen preparations. This variation of recipe number three is a Crêpe recipe that uses 1 ½ ounces of clarified butter, 1 cup of flour, 2 cups of milk, and 4 each egg. These ingredients will yield 20 crêpes. The process or method of preparation is detailed in the right-hand column. Whisk the flour into the milk and eggs, strain, add butter. Ladle 1.5 oz of batter for each crêpe and cook until golden brown. In many cases the spreadsheet format takes up considerably less space than a traditional recipe format. Each recipe and formula will give the quantity of the ingredient in the individual cell, or box. The numbers across the top of the page are the standard amounts that the recipe will utilize. Recipes and formulas can be quickly recalculated to adjust the desired production amount. This can be accomplished by increasing or decreasing the number or numerator across the top of a spreadsheet. The user can double, halve, and multiply the amount of batter to yield 100 crepes. The conversion is as simple as changing a 1 to 2, a 4 to 8, and so on across the top of the page.

Some recipes, like the crêpe recipe, will have a cell with a certain amount for the ingredient within it. This ingredient has been put in a separate cell because the amount needed for the recipe may differ from the set amounts across the top of the page, like the butter in the recipe example. The consolidated format in these charts allows the user to access up to 20 recipes per page.

The learning style of many Chefs is that of a visual learner. According to psychologist Dr. Linda Silverman of the University of Southern California visual- spatial learners tend to be more successful when information is presented in systematic patterns. Visual learners utilize the right side of their brain more often while reading than learners with other learning style preferences Therefore they are able to process, recall or synthesize information more expeditiously. Dr. Silverman's research also indicated that visual learners also prefer to learn when concepts are presented as a whole first then broken down in parts. The graphic tools detailed in the Culinary Methods section of the book have been developed with this concept in mind: whole then part. The matrix recipe/ formula system in this book helps facilitate these learning processes because the ingredient amounts are separated from the recipe/ formula. By understanding the concept first, the cook is able to begin the process of committing that procedure and ingredients to long term memory. It is this author's belief that through repetitive practice the cook will also begin to form conceptual relationships with the ingredient amounts, therefore gaining a deeper understanding of the recipe/ formula concept.

There are a few things to remember before using the recipe/ formula charts.

A. Acquaint yourself with the cooking methods and culinary terminology sections of the guide. The first key to success is to understand the correct technique for the recipe.
B. When you measure the ingredients for a recipe or formula remember that cups, tablespoons, and teaspoons measure only volume. A recipe or formula that calls for ounces or pounds needs to be weighed with a scale.
C. Use this guide to cross reference recipes, methods and definitions.

Consistency is the most important factor in the preparation of food. Most cooks do not use recipes every time they prepare an item. They rely on memory and repetition. In some situations, this works; however, if continued training and evaluation are not consistent then the final product may deviate from the expected outcome. Consistency of the final product and production efficiency are an advantage that corporate restaurants may have over some independent operators in the same demographic market offering similar fare. Corporations and chain restaurants use recipe cards and pre- prepared components that deliver a known result.

The recipes and formulas in *The Chefs Reference Guide* can be easily referenced for a quality finished product. Quality can be defined as the consistent delivery of a predetermined standard. Successful restaurateurs know that controlling quality will result in repeat customers. Understanding the basic methods and quality points will enable you to prepare countless dishes in an infinite number of combinations which can eventually result in you attaining the certification of Master Chef. To summarize *Mental Mise en Place* is simply the ingredients of knowledge, skill, and repertoire. The road to becoming a Master Chef begins with these foundational concepts, and the consistent execution of preparations is the metric by which all Master Chefs are measured.

Silverman, L. K. (2002). Upside-down brilliance, the visual-spatial learner. DeLeon Publishing, Inc

The symbol ɸ represents the theory of first order logic in math, science, and philosophy

Culinary Methods

Dry Heat Methods

Roasting – *the process of cooking a product while being elevated on a rack in a heated environment, like an oven.* The elevation allows heat to have an effect on all sides of the item for even browning while preventing the rendered fat from having a negative impact on the roasted item. You can use a metal rack and/or mirepoix (chopped vegetables) to elevate the product and add flavor to the roast, jus, gravy, or sauce.

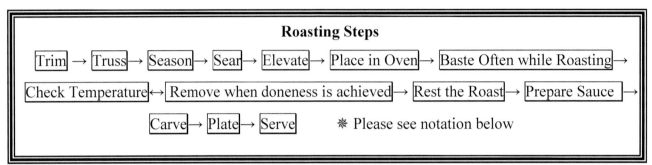

Roasting Steps

Trim → Truss → Season → Sear → Elevate → Place in Oven → Baste Often while Roasting →

Check Temperature ↔ Remove when doneness is achieved → Rest the Roast → Prepare Sauce →

Carve → Plate → Serve   ✳ Please see notation below

✳ *The symbol → is used to show the progression of steps. The symbol ↔ is used when the step of progression might need several check points.*

Mise en Place Needed
 ➢ Item to be roasted
 ➢ Seasonings- salt, pepper, spices (see blends on pages 153-155)
 ➢ Butchers Twine – To Truss poultry and tie some roasts
 ➢ Roasting Pan
 ➢ Large cut mirepoix
 ➢ Metal Rack- for elevation
 ➢ Ladle to baste the roast
 ➢ Liquid to deglaze- wine, stock
 ➢ Wooden Spoon- to scrape the fond and caramelized particles from the pan
 ➢ Sauce Pot
 ➢ Carving Board
 ➢ Carving Knife
 ➢ Carving Fork
 ➢ Calibrated Thermometer- Degree of doneness listed on page 5

Types of meat that may be roasted

 ✧ Large pieces of meat – top round of beef, prime rib, pork loin, leg of lamb, steamship of beef.
 ✧ Un-fabricated pieces of meat – Chicken, Turkey, Duck, Suckling Pig, Whole Roasted Lamb.

The typical temperature range of an oven for roasting is usually between 180° - 475° F

Methods used for roasting

Oven Sear Method –The item is seasoned and then caramelized by direct contact with oven heat. This method should be used for large tender cuts of red meats and large birds. After the product has browned in the oven, the temperature is then reduced to allow for even cooking. A convection oven works very well for this application.

Season Sear Method - The item is rubbed with seasoning then seared over a hot surface pan on all sides. It is then slowly roasted in the oven to the desired degree of doneness. This method can be used for pork loin, beef tenderloin, sirloin, and strip loin of beef. All types of ovens work well for this method.

Rotisserie –The item is seasoned, skewered on metal rods then roasted and rotated over a moderate heat directly in front of the flame. The item self-bastes itself as the fat renders and coats the whole roast. Common items used in the rotisserie process are chickens, ducks, and smaller pieces of lamb leg or pork loin. The item must have some fat on the outside to ensure flavor and color development. There are specialized ovens, called rotisseries that will perform this task on a large scale. In a regular oven this concept can be applied by occasionally rotating the product to expose all sides of the roast to the direct heat.

Low temperature cooking- The item is seasoned and or seared then place in a sealed heated chamber called a slow roasting oven or in a combination oven. The item will roast for an extended period of time depending upon the roast's size and the desired degree of doneness. When using a slow roasting oven, the caramelized flavor development is not as good as traditional ovens; however, it does evenly cook the item. The roast will have very little moisture loss because of the low temperature and sealed environment. Ideally items should be seared first then placed in the cabinet for roasting. This application is commonly used for very large volume production, primarily for larger cuts of beef and other red meats. The low temperature oven was designed to roast 24 prime ribs of beef uniformly. The pitfall of this method is the length of time that the item is in the temperature danger zone, therefore it is not recommended to cook poultry and fish in these types of ovens. Proteins cooked in these ovens must be held at the finished degree of doneness for a defined period of time to ensure that the potentially hazardous foods are served at a safe temperature. Here are the following recommendations from the 2018 National Restaurant Association Guidelines.

130 °F(54°C) for 112 minutes   138 °F(59°C) for 18 minutes
131 °F(55°C) for 89 minutes   140 °F(60°C) for 12 minutes
133 °F(56°C) for 56 minutes   142 °F(61°C) for 8 minutes
135 °F(57°C) for 36 minutes   144 °F(62°C) for 5 minutes
136 °F(58°C) for 28 minutes

Checking the degree of doneness for roasted items

The only method that should be used to check the degree of doneness of a roast is by the insertion of a calibrated thermometer. The thermometer's reading will insure that the proper temperature has been achieved. Always check the temperature in the thickest or widest part of the roast. If the item has a large bone, like a leg of lamb or fresh ham, check the temperature right next to the bone.

Carry-over cooking – Once the roast has been removed from the oven it will continue to cook. This is because most cooking equipment applies heat to the surface of the meat and the heat is retained within the meat. The retained exterior heat in the meat causes the interior of the meat to continue to cook once removed from the heat source. You should always allow the meat to relax so that it will be more tender and juicier when carved. The factors that affect the duration of carry-over cooking include the size of the roast and the temperature of the oven. Simply stated, the larger the roast the greater the degree of carry over cooking. This happens because the greater the mass of roast, the greater the heat retention in the muscle. The higher the oven temperature, the greater carry-over because of the greater amount of specific heat applied to the outer layer of the item. The best way to ensure that the carry over cooking is complete is to use two probes, one in the middle of the roast and one just below the surface. When both temperatures are equal then the roast will no longer continue to cook.

Resting Period – always allow the roasted item to rest in a warm area of the kitchen for at least 4 minutes per pound for items 10 pounds or more and 8 minutes per pound for items that are less than 10 pounds, the longer the rest the better the roast. This will give the meat time for the strands of protein to relax and pressure to equalize so the moisture stays in the product. When the item is carved it will be tender and juicy. This resting time is a factor of the carry over cooking time allowance listed below. Use the two-probe method to ensure that an equilibrium of temperature has been achieved.

Carry-over cooking allowance temperature

The following products will reach their intended finished temperature after the resting period. To allow for carry-over cooking, pull the following roasts from the oven at these recommended temperatures to ensure the desired doneness is achieved. Check the temperature for 15 seconds. Hold roasted meats in an environment that is above 135^0 until service. The cooking temperature of the oven for this chart is 350^0

- Prime Rib- Bone in (12 lb average) – Rare 127 °, Medium Rare 131° , Medium 135°
- Top Round of Beef (10 lb average) – Rare 129°, Medium 135°, Medium Well 142°
- Tenderloin of Beef (4 lb average) – Rare 128°, Medium Rare 132° , Medium 136°
- Pork Loin (4 lb average)– 143°
- Leg of Lamb (7 lb average)– 135° Medium Rare, Medium 142°
- Rack of Lamb (1 lb average) - 125° Rare, 128° Medium Rare, 130° Medium
- Fresh or Smoked Ham (8 lb average) – 150°
- Chicken (3 lb average)– 165°- check in the leg and thigh
- Turkey (12 lb average)– 165°- check in the leg and thigh
- Duckling (5 lb average) – 165°- check in the leg and thigh

Sauces – Always serve au jus, gravy, or sauce with the roasted meat to moisten the slices.

- *Jus* – Add stock to the caramelized particles in the roasting pan, simmer, strain and season.
- *Gravy* – Add flour to the fat and particles in the roasting pan and mix. Add stock or broth, stir and simmer to thicken, then strain the caramelized particles and season to taste.
- *Sauce* – Prepare a sauce recipe for the roasted item that will complement it. For example a mint sauce for lamb or Béarnaise sauce for roasted beef tenderloin.

Precautions

- ✓ When removing items from an oven make sure that you use dry towels or potholders to protect your hands from the heat.
- ✓ Take caution when moving a hot pan because the liquids can splash and burn you or others.

Baking – *is the process of cooking of a product that has been placed on a pan or dish in a heated closed environment.* Very few meat items are actually baked in restaurants; most protein items that are baked are pre-portioned, coated, or even partially cooked convenience foods. The standard baking oven temperature is 350°. When using convection ovens, the common temperature to use is 325°.

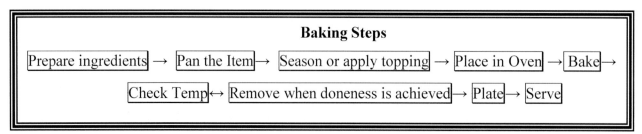

Baking Steps

Prepare ingredients → Pan the Item → Season or apply topping → Place in Oven → Bake → Check Temp ↔ Remove when doneness is achieved → Plate → Serve

Mise en Place Needed

- ➢ Item to be baked
- ➢ Seasonings- salt, pepper, spices (see blends on pages 153-155)
- ➢ Baking Pan or Dish
- ➢ Calibrated Thermometer
- ➢ Utensil to remove item from pan.

Items that may be baked

- Meats, Poultry, and Seafood - Pre-portioned items that are coated with breadcrumbs or encased in dough – refer to manufacturers' specifications.
- Baked Chicken – The chicken is quartered then seasoned with various spices. The quarters are arranged on the baking sheet and cooked to an internal temperature of 165°. The metal pan can cause the chicken to caramelize on the bottom while the direct oven heat evenly cooks the other sides. The pan may be deglazed for gravy.
- Baked Fish – The fish should be sliced into 5 to 6 oz portions. It should be coated with melted butter or olive oil. Seasoning is applied. Citrus juice or wine is drizzled over the fish. The fish is baked until it reaches an internal temperature of 140°.
- Meatloaf – Placed in a loaf pan or directly on a sheet pan to sear in flavor. When brown, the loaf is topped with brown or tomato sauce and cooked to an internal temperature of 165°.
- Bacon Strips – Placed on a parchment lined sheet pans and cooked until brown and crispy. This method allows for even cooking. Reserve the leftover rendered fat for home fries or other applications.
- Pasta – Cooked pasta, filled or combined with a ricotta cheese mixture, topped with tomato sauce and mozzarella cheese. Baked ziti or lasagna should be cooked to 155°.
- Macaroni and Cheese – Elbow macaroni is cooked and combined with cheese sauce then placed in a baking dish or casserole. It is then topped with shredded cheese and the item is baked until golden brown or until the internal temperature reaches 150°.
- Pot Pies, Shepherd's Pie- Stewed preparations that are topped with pie dough are called pot pies. A shepherd's pie uses mashed potatoes over the stewed item; the potatoes are usually piped with a star tip and then baked until golden brown. A pie needs to reach an internal temperature of 165°.
- Breads and Pastries – Baked on parchment lined pans or placed directly on the hearth of stone ovens. Caramelization occurs all around the item.
- Potatoes – Use russet potatoes which have been washed, dried, coated with oil and kosher salt and bake until tender to the touch. An average baked potato will take 1 hour at 350 °
- Vegetables – Winter squash may be sliced then placed in a baking dish and topped with brown sugar or honey and butter with sweet spices such as cinnamon. Eggplant parmesan. Breaded and fried slices of eggplant are layered with parmesan cheese and tomato sauce. The casserole is then topped with shredded mozzarella cheese and baked covered until golden brown. The internal temperature usually reaches 180°.
- Casseroles- Cassoulet, as an example, contains cured duck, beans, and sausage flavored with garlic tomato and herbs. Baked until all items are tender then topped with a crumb mixture and baked again to for a crisp crust, should be cooked to 165°.

Precautions

When removing items from an oven make sure that you use dry towels or potholders and then remove the item from the oven using both protected hands. Use caution when moving a hot pan. Be careful to not splash yourself or others with the contents.

Grilling –*The process used to cook a product on a grated surface to develop a degree of charring on the outside.* A grill has a heat source that comes from below the item. The item should be either seasoned or marinated before the item is grilled to enhance the flavor. Glazes, rubs and BBQ sauces may also be used to complement grilled foods.

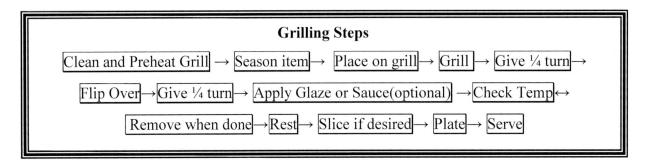

Grilling Steps

Clean and Preheat Grill → Season item→ Place on grill→ Grill → Give ¼ turn→ Flip Over→Give ¼ turn→ Apply Glaze or Sauce(optional) →Check Temp↔ Remove when done→Rest→ Slice if desired→ Plate→ Serve

Mise en Place Needed

➢ Item to be grilled
➢ Seasonings- salt, pepper, spices (see blends on pages 153-155)
➢ Grill Brush
➢ Oil and Rag to Clean and season grill. Cooking spray (use caution to avoid a flame)
➢ Metal Tongs
➢ Glaze, BBQ Sauce (Optional)- apply in the last few minutes of grilling.
➢ Basting Brush (Optional)
➢ Carving Board
➢ Carving Knife
➢ Carving Fork
➢ Calibrated Thermometer
➢ Accompanying sauce, salsa, relish or compound butter.

Common items that may be grilled

✧ Chicken Breast – Boneless
✧ Steaks - New York Strip, Filet Mignon, Porterhouse, Flank, Ribeye, Sirloin
✧ Chops – Pork Chop, Lamb Rib Chop, Veal Chop
✧ Fish – Firm Only – Tuna, Sword, Shark, Salmon
✧ Vegetables – Zucchini, tomatoes, portobello mushrooms, corn
✧ Shellfish – Shrimp Kebobs, Scallop Kebobs
✧ Ribs – Baby Back Ribs

Degree of Doneness – This depends upon the size of the item. The carry over cooking considerations are not as important as it is in the roasting process due to the size of the product. The required resting period is usually 2-5 minutes, basically the time it takes to transfer the product from grill to guest. Use the recommended grilled protein internal temperatures guidelines to ensure accuracy in the degree of doneness.

Complimentary items for grilled proteins.
Traditional sauces such as Béchamel, velouté, and demi-glace generally do not complement grilled food. The following is a list of suggestions to complement grilled items.

- ✿ ***Poultry*** – *fresh salsas, compound butters, fruit sauces*
- ✿ ***Lamb*** – *Mint Jelly, fruit salsa, chutney, savory compound butters*
- ✿ ***Beef*** – *Savory to spicy compound butters, spicy salsas*
- ✿ ***Seafood*** – *Vegetable salsas, herb butters, tropical fruit salsa*
- ✿ ***Pork Chops*** – *Apple chutney, BBQ sauce, fruit sauces, salsa*

Grilled Protein Temperature Chart- Check temp for 15 seconds
- ✧ **6 oz Chicken Breast** – 165°
- ✧ **10 oz New York Strip** – rare 125°, medium rare 130 °, medium 135°, medium well 140°
- ✧ **8 oz Filet Mignon** - rare 125°, medium rare 130 °, medium 136°, medium well 140°
- ✧ **18 oz Porterhouse**- rare 123°, medium rare 127 °, medium 134°, medium well 138°
- ✧ **16 oz Flank**- rare 125°, medium rare 130 °, medium 135°, medium well 140°
- ✧ **8 oz Pork Chop** – 145°
- ✧ **4 oz Lamb Chop**- 128° rare, 132° medium, 140° medium well
- ✧ **6 oz Tuna Fish Steak** – 120° rare, 125° medium, 130° medium well
- ✧ **6 oz Swordfish Steak** – 140°
- ✧ **6 oz Shark Steak** - 145°
- ✧ **6 oz Salmon Steak or Filet** – 134°
- ✧ **6 oz Snapper and Grouper Filet** – 140°
- ✧ **Shrimp and Scallops Kebobs** – until the flesh is firm and opaque all the way through the item

Precautions
- ✓ Always make sure the grill is preheated and clean.
- ✓ Do not grill items that have excess oil or moisture on them.
- ✓ Clean the grill after each use with a metal brush and cloth.
- ✓ To avoid cross contamination and possible allergy related contact surface issues make sure to clean and sanitize the thermometer when checking two different types of protein.

<u>Broiling</u> – *is when a product is placed in an oven proof pan or over an open grate and then cooked with a radiant heat source that is above the product.* Broiler temperatures range from 500⁰ to 1800⁰ therefore it is very easy to overcook foods in a matter of seconds. Broiling allows for a similar flavor to grilling and is used for cooking softer fish, such as flounder and small items like shellfish. The fish or seafood is usually seasoned and flavored with wine and butter or olive oil. Fresh herbs are added last, if desired. When steaks or chops are broiled they are placed directly on the open grates then positioned close to the flame so the product can be seared on both sides. When browning a glaze or cheese over a product it is important to keep the item about 8 inches away from the flame to avoid over caramelization.

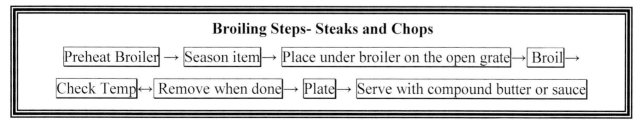

Broiling Steps- Steaks and Chops

Preheat Broiler → Season item → Place under broiler on the open grate → Broil →

Check Temp ↔ Remove when done → Plate → Serve with compound butter or sauce

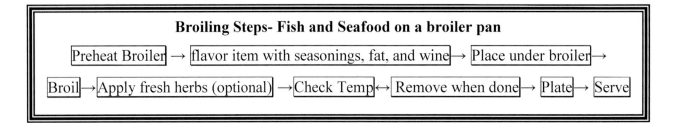

Broiling Steps- Fish and Seafood on a broiler pan

Preheat Broiler → flavor item with seasonings, fat, and wine → Place under broiler → Broil → Apply fresh herbs (optional) → Check Temp ↔ Remove when done → Plate → Serve

Mise en Place Needed

- Item to be broiled
- Seasonings
- Wine or Citrus Juice (if needed for flavor enhancement)
- Oil or Melted Butter

- Spatula
- Calibrated Thermometer
- Accompanying sauce, salsa, and compound butter.

Items that may be broiled

- Fish – Flounder, sole, mackerel, trout, catfish – internal temp of 140°
- Seafood – Bay scallops, shrimp, crab cakes – internal temp of 140°
- Steaks and Chops- Refer to degrees of doneness and suggestions on page 7
- Gratinée – French onion soup, Cheese, cheese sauce, crumb mixture topping– Golden brown.

Precautions

- ✓ The broiler should always be preheated.
- ✓ Avoid too much fat or oil on the product because it may be a fire hazard.
- ✓ To ensure that the item cooks evenly lay them flat on broiler pans that are prepared with fats or flavorings.

Sautéing – *is the cooking of a tender product in a small amount of fat over high heat moving the product with a "jumping" motion in the pan. A sauce is usually prepared in the pan with the product.* Depending upon the item and desired effect, the item may be coated with a drying or breading agent to enhance the flavor and appearance.

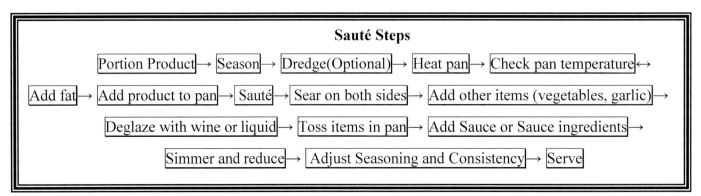

Sauté Steps

Portion Product → Season → Dredge(Optional) → Heat pan → Check pan temperature ↔ Add fat → Add product to pan → Sauté → Sear on both sides → Add other items (vegetables, garlic) → Deglaze with wine or liquid → Toss items in pan → Add Sauce or Sauce ingredients → Simmer and reduce → Adjust Seasoning and Consistency → Serve

Items that may be sautéed

- ✧ Small cuts of meat, poultry breast and seafood- generally no bigger than a half dollar.
- ✧ Portioned items – Boneless and skinless chicken breast, fish, veal scaloppini.
- ✧ Starches – Cut potatoes, pasta dishes
- ✧ Vegetables – Tender vegetables and or blanched harder vegetables for even cooking.

Mise en Place Needed

- ➤ Item to be sautéed
- ➤ Tasting Spoons
- ➤ Seasonings- salt, pepper
- ➤ Dredging Flour
- ➤ Oil or Clarified Butter
- ➤ Other recipe ingredients- Diced, Sliced, Julienne, or Minced
- ➤ Wine or Liquid to Deglaze
- ➤ Thickener- Beurre manié, cornstarch slurry, diced butter to finish the sauce.

- ➤ Sauté Pan
- ➤ Metal Tongs
- ➤ Basting Spoon
- ➤ Sauce Components

Precautions

- ✓ Always cover your hand with a side towel when turning items over, toss items in a circular fashion, and do not use too much fat.
- ✓ Do not overcrowd the pan. Overcrowding does not promote even cooking.
- ✓ Be careful when deglazing with wine or spirit because the alcohol may ignite.
- ✓ Never add wet ingredients or fat to a smoking hot pan.

Methods of sautéing
Small cuts of protein or small pieces of protein

- ❖ Beef Tenderloin Tips – Season first, dredge in flour (optional), brown the tips in a very hot pan, drain the fat, deglaze with wine, add other items, add sauce last, simmer and serve.
- ❖ Veal Emincé (thin strips) – Dredge in seasoned flour, light brown first in hot fat, drain the excess fat, deglaze with wine, add other items, add sauce last, simmer and serve.
- ❖ Chicken Tenderloins - Dredge in seasoned flour, lightly brown first in hot fat, drain the excess fat, deglaze with wine, add other items, add sauce last, simmer and serve.
- ❖ Shrimp and Scallops - Light brown first, drain, deglaze, add other items, add sauce last then simmer.
- ❖ Stir Fry – Brown the thinly sliced protein first in a small amount of fat in the wok, add chopped ginger and garlic, then add julienne vegetables, add liquids or sauce last, and thicken with a cornstarch slurry. The thickening of the sauce allows the sauce to adhere to the vegetables and protein.

Portioned Items – sauce can be served on top or under the item

- ✧ *3 oz Beef Medallions* – Brown the beef in a high heat pan with a small amount of fat. Sear for about 1 ½ minutes per side. Add other items like mushroom and shallots, deglaze the pan with wine or brandy, add sauce last, simmer and serve.
- ✧ *Veal Scaloppini* – Dredge first, lightly brown and drain the excess fat, add other items and toss gently in the pan. Deglaze with wine then add the sauce last, simmer and serve.
- ✧ *4 oz Chicken Breast* — Dredge first, lightly brown and drain the excess fat, add other items and toss gently in the pan. Deglaze with wine then add the sauce last, simmer until the correct internal temperature and desired sauce viscosity is achieved.

- ✧ **5 oz Fish Filet Portion**- Trout, Sole, Cod- dredge first, lightly brown and cook for 2 -3 minutes per side, plate fish, deglaze pan with wine, add herbs and or nuts and finish sauce with whole butter, nappe sauce over the fish.

Sautéed Side Dishes

- ✧ **Potatoes** – Cut and cleaned, partially cooked in salted water, drained. Heat the fat and brown on all sides. Don't overcrowd the pan. Finish with onions, peppers and seasoning.
- ✧ **Pastas** - Sauté protein or garniture items first in olive oil with flavoring agents. Add hot pasta, toss in sauce and cheese, if desired, and adjust the seasoning.
- ✧ **Vegetables** – Heat a small amount of butter or oil first. Add enough vegetables to cover the bottom of the pan, add flavoring agents, toss, add the herbs then season. Always start with firmer vegetables first- (peppers, onions, and mushrooms) then add the softer vegetables, (zucchini and blanched broccoli). Flavoring agents can include minced garlic, pesto, and roasted peppers. It is always advisable to keep a little stock or water near the sauté pan in case the item starts to brown more than you desire. Simply add a little liquid to help form some steam in the pan an slow down the sauté process.

Pan Frying –*is the cooking of a coated product in a moderate amount of fat, ½ way up the side of the product, over medium heat turnover the product until the desired degree of doneness is achieved.* The coating or breading will turn a golden-brown color as it is fried in the fat. The protein used should be tender and should be breaded or coated before cooking. See examples on the following page.

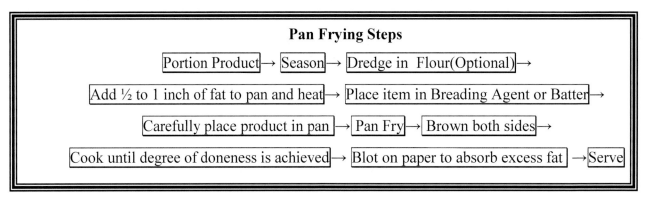

Pan Frying Steps

Portion Product → Season → Dredge in Flour(Optional) →

Add ½ to 1 inch of fat to pan and heat → Place item in Breading Agent or Batter →

Carefully place product in pan → Pan Fry → Brown both sides →

Cook until degree of doneness is achieved → Blot on paper to absorb excess fat → Serve

Mise en Place Needed

- ➢ Item to be pan fried
- ➢ Seasonings- salt, pepper
- ➢ Dredging Flour
- ➢ Breading Agent or Batter
- ➢ Oil or Clarified Butter

- ➢ Straight sided skillet or pan
- ➢ Spatula, tongs
- ➢ Spoon
- ➢ Paper towels to absorb fat.
- ➢ Calibrated Thermometer

Items that may be pan fried

- ✧ Southern fried chicken*
- ✧ Breaded pork chops*
- ✧ Chicken fried steak
- ✧ Breaded Fish Filets
- ✧ Potato Pancakes

- ✧ Breaded or egg battered veal scaloppini or chicken cutlets
- ✧ Breaded or dredged Eggplant, Zucchini etc.
- ✧ French Toast, Monte Cristo Sandwiches

    *Some of these items may need to be finished in a low temperature oven until they reach the proper degree of doneness.

Serve pan-fried items with pan gravy made from caramelized flour particles from the pan with the addition of milk or stock. Veal, chicken, and eggplant may be topped with tomato sauce and cheese, and then broiled to golden brown.

Precautions

- ✓ Always cover your hand with a side towel when turning items over.
- ✓ Use tongs or a spatula, if possible, and <u>turn item away from you</u>.
- ✓ Brown on both sides then remove from the pan.
- ✓ Items should be fried in fat that is 350°.
- ✓ If a battered item is used, be careful not to splash yourself with hot fat.
- ✓ Some fish may require a slotted spatula to be removed from pan depending upon the delicateness of the flesh.
- ✓ Always place the item on a paper towel to absorb excess fat as soon as possible.
- ✓ Use only fat that is clean.

Griddling -*is the cooking of a portioned coated protein or battered product in a light amount of fat on a flat surface that is at a moderate level of heat.*

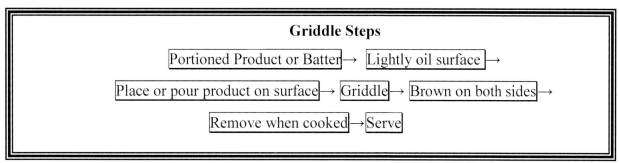

Griddle Steps

Portioned Product or Batter → Lightly oil surface →
Place or pour product on surface → Griddle → Brown on both sides →
Remove when cooked → Serve

Mise en Place Needed

- ➢ Coated Product, Product or Batter
- ➢ Oil or Clarified Butter
- ➢ Preheated griddle
- ➢ Spatula
- ➢ Accompaniment

Example Products – Pancakes, Hash browns, Sausage patties, Bacon, Ham steaks, Eggs, Filled sandwiches, French toast.

Precautions

- ✓ Only use a small amount of fat on a griddle.
- ✓ Keep at a moderate heat level to avoid burning.
- ✓ Always turn the product away from yourself to prevent splashing hot fat on yourself.

Pan Searing – *is cooking of a tender product with very little to no fat on a seasoned pan or on a stick resistant pan over a medium to high heat to achieve a caramelized surface.* Virtually any item that can be grilled can also be pan seared. Pan searing uses a flat conductive cooking surface instead of an open flame, therefore the flavor will be different.

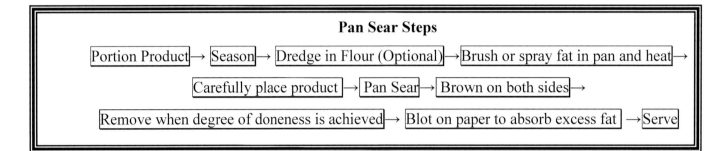

Pan Sear Steps

Portion Product → Season → Dredge in Flour (Optional) → Brush or spray fat in pan and heat →

Carefully place product → Pan Sear → Brown on both sides →

Remove when degree of doneness is achieved → Blot on paper to absorb excess fat → Serve

Mise en Place Needed

- Item to be pan seared
- Seasonings- salt, pepper, the blends are on page 153-155
- Dredging Flour(optional)
- Oil or Clarified Butter
- Seasoned frying pan or non-stick pan
- Spatula
- Paper towels to absorb fat
- Accompaniments
- Calibrated Thermometer

Refer to the grilling internal temperatures on page 7 for pan seared items. Pan sauces accompany pan seared items very well. A pan sauce can be prepared by deglazing the pan and adding other flavoring and thickening components. This method is applied for lower fat versions of sautéed or pan- fried items. Independent sauces like salsas, relishes and coulis may also be served with a pan seared item. Traditional sauces like Hollandaise sauce can be served with a pan seared salmon. Proteins cooked Sous Vide, page 202, can be pan seared to impart flavor, color and texture.

Items that may be Pan Seared
- Chicken – Boneless breast slices that are seasoned and seared in butter or oil
- Beef and Veal – Tenderloin medallions, seasoned and seared in clarified butter or oil.
- Pork – Tenderloin medallions seasoned and seared in clarified butter or oil.
- Lamb – Loin medallions seasoned and seared in plain olive oil.
- Fish – Salmon, Sea Bass, Halibut, Tuna, Turbot- seasoned and seared in butter or oil.
- Scallops – Large sea scallops- seasoned and seared in butter or oil.

Precautions
- If the item is marinated, dry off excess marinade.
- Use only light olive oil or salad oil to season to the pan.
- Extra Virgin Olive oil will burn too quickly and will leave a undesired flavor.
- Generally brown the protein on both sides then finish in an oven. *Over searing can result in a tough product.*

Deep Fat Frying – *is the cooking of a product that is totally submerged in hot fat until golden brown and or cooked until the proper degree of doneness is achieved.* The food product is usually either starch based or coated with a batter or breading. Products that have not been coated with a breading or batter will become tougher when deep fat fried. The term GBD, "Golden Brown Doneness", is used to describe deep fried items and to denote the proper degree of doneness of the coated surface. Some items may need to be cooked longer with dry heat to reach the intended degree of doneness. Generally, the larger the item the less fat absorption.

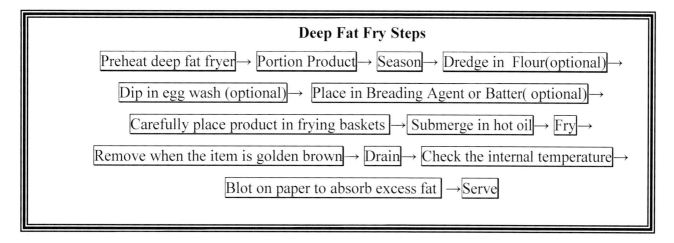

Mise en Place Needed

- ➢ Fryer filled with oil to the designated line
- ➢ Item to be deep fat fried
- ➢ Seasonings- salt, pepper
- ➢ Dredging Flour (optional)
- ➢ Egg Wash (optional)
- ➢ Breading Agent or Batter(optional)
- ➢ Metal Tongs
- ➢ Paper towels to absorb fat.
- ➢ Accompaniments – page 36-47
- ➢ Calibrated Thermometer

Items that may be Deep Fat Fried

- ✧ Portioned and Coated Chicken pieces
- ✧ Portioned and Coated Fish and Seafood
- ✧ Cut Potatoes or Frozen French Fries
- ✧ Cut and Coated Vegetables
- ✧ Portioned Item – egg rolls, doughnuts, appetizers, croquettes.

Proper frying temperatures   300°- 375°

When placing a battered item in the oil make sure that the basket is already submerged. This procedure will prevent the item from sticking to the basket. Breaded items can be added directly to the basket then submerged. Allow the product to fry for at least 30 seconds before shaking the basket, shaking the basket too often may cause the coating to come off the product.

The temperature of the fat depends upon the size of the item, the larger the item the lower the frying temperature. In some cases, you may need to place the fried item on a wire rack in an oven to finish cooking. Always check the internal temperature.

Precautions

✓ Keep the oil at the frying temperatures while you need it.
✓ If the fat remains at high temperature it may catch on fire.
✓ The use and cleaning of a deep fat fryer should only be done after proper training.
✓ Make sure that the oil has cooled to room temperature before draining and cleaning the fryer.

Enemies of the Deep Fat Fryer

☻ **Excess moisture** – Including ice crystals on frozen convenience foods like French fries.
☻ **Excess breading** – Soils the oil and turns it dark brown prematurely
☻ **Light and air** – Fryer oil should be covered when cooled and not in use.
☻ **Salt** – Never season food items over the frying oil.
☻ **High heat** – The oil will break down quicker and catch on fire.
☻ **Negligence** – The fryer must be filtered daily to prolong its life and help food taste fresh.
☻ **Idle** – Turn down the temperature of the fryer down to 200° during those periods of time when it is not immediately needed. Extended heating of the oil will cause it to break down.

Make sure to drain the fried item over the fryer first until the fat stops dripping. Place the fried item in a draining pan and hold fried items under a heat lamp to allow the item to remain crisp and hot.

Moist Heat Methods

Poaching- *is the cooking of a product by submerging it in a liquid that is at a temperature between 125° and 180° until the desired degree of doneness is achieved.*

Poaching liquid – Court bouillon – this can be as simple as vinegar and water for poached eggs. Poached fish is best prepared with wine, stock, fumet, aromatics and shallots as the poaching liquid.

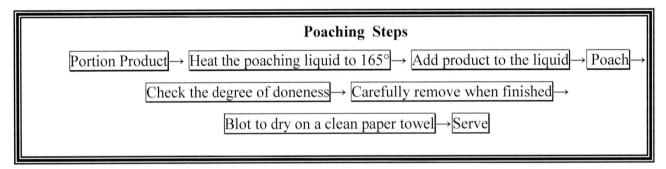

Poaching Steps

Portion Product → Heat the poaching liquid to 165° → Add product to the liquid → Poach →

Check the degree of doneness → Carefully remove when finished →

Blot to dry on a clean paper towel → Serve

Mise en Place Needed

➢ Item to be poached
➢ Poaching Pan
➢ Poaching Liquids – see recipes on page 45.
➢ Slotted or Perforated Spoon
➢ Thickener- Beurre manie, Crème Manie (optional)

➢ Cartouche- to cover the product
➢ Sauce Components
➢ Whole Butter (optional)
➢ Accompaniments
➢ Calibrated Thermometer

Items that may be poached

✧ **Eggs** – in 165° water and vinegar solution for 5 – 7 minutes

✧ **Fish** – in 150° court bouillon or fumet to an internal temperature of 140°

✧ **Shellfish** – in 150° court bouillon until firm

✧ **Chicken Breast**- in 165° stock to an internal temperature of 160°

✧ **Fruits** – Peeled apples and pears cooked in a 180 ° poaching liquid of wine, sugar and whole spices until they are tender.

✧ **Sous Vide**- sealed pouches of product are cooked in a circulating water bath at the finished degree of doneness with or without flavoring utilizing an immersion circulator for a designated period of time to pasteurize, denature, or tenderize to a defined level. Refer to page 202.

Service Applications

✿ **Fish or chicken** – Beurre Blanc, a sauce which is prepared from the reduced poaching liquid, and finished with cream and butter.

✿ **Eggs** may be served plain, with a Hollandaise or Mornay sauce.

✿ **Chicken or fish** may be chilled and used for salad.

Precautions

✓ Always use dry towels when removing or carrying hot pots.

✓ Make sure to warn others when you are holding hot pots and pans.

Simmering – *is the cooking of a product by submerging it in a liquid that is between 185° and 205° until the product is tender and proper flavor and degree of doneness is achieved.* This method is used when you need a high temperature with a limited convection of the liquid.

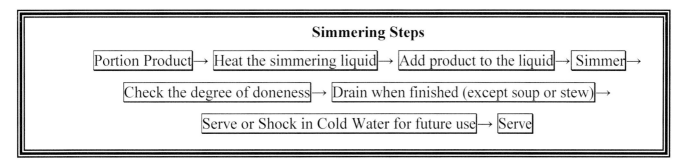

Simmering Steps

Portion Product→ Heat the simmering liquid→ Add product to the liquid→ Simmer→

Check the degree of doneness→ Drain when finished (except soup or stew)→

Serve or Shock in Cold Water for future use→ Serve

Mise en Place Needed

➢ Item to be simmered

➢ Pot with Lid

➢ Liquid- stock or water

➢ Slotted or Perforated Spoon

➢ Colander

➢ Cold Water

➢ Oil for Pasta, to prevent sticking.

➢ Accompaniments

➢ Calibrated Thermometer

Items that may be simmered
- ✧ **Soup** – Prevents excess evaporation, toughening of proteins, overcooking of vegetables
- ✧ **Small or cut potatoes**- Prevents breakage, always start in cold water, never cool off potatoes in cold water, allow them to drain and cool in the refrigerator.
- ✧ **Large cuts of meat, whole birds**- Simmering can prevent the toughening of proteins. Examples include corned beef, fowl, beef brisket, slabs of ribs.
- ✧ **Filled Pasta**- Prevents breakage and leakage of the filling.
- ✧ **Fresh Pasta** – Simmer at 200 ° to prevent potential breakage of thin pasta like angel hair, spaghetti or fettuccine.
- ✧ **Hard Vegetables**- Ensures consistent heat so the item does not break apart, like beets.
- ✧ **Legumes**- Ensures consistent heat so the item does not break apart like lentils.
- ✧ **Delicate Vegetables** – Simmer at 200°- Broccoli spears, cauliflower, asparagus, and snow peas.
- ✧ **Hard Boiled Eggs** – Start in cold water and bring to 200° for 7 minutes

Precautions
- ✓ Always use dry towels when removing or carrying hot pots.
- ✓ Make sure to warn others when you are moving hot pots and pans.
- ✓ Never attempt to lift a pot of water that is too heavy for you to handle, ask for help.

Boiling- *is the cooking of a product that is submerged in water or liquid that is at 212° until the desired degree of doneness is achieved.*

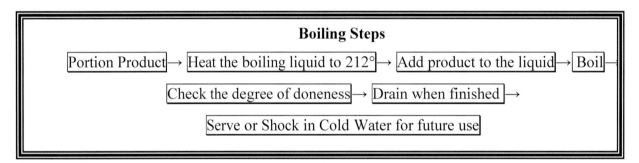

Boiling Steps
Portion Product → Heat the boiling liquid to 212° → Add product to the liquid → Boil → Check the degree of doneness → Drain when finished → Serve or Shock in Cold Water for future use

Mise en Place Needed
- ➤ Item to be boiled
- ➤ Pot with Lid
- ➤ Salt and Seasonings
- ➤ Liquid- stock or water
- ➤ Slotted or Perforated Spoon
- ➤ Colander
- ➤ Cold Water

- ➤ Oil for Pasta
- ➤ Accompaniments
- ➤ Calibrated Thermometer

Items that may be boiled
 ♢ **Large Whole Potatoes** – Always start in cold water, and then bring to boil until tender. Never shock or cool peeled potatoes in water because they tend absorb the cool liquid.
 ♢ **Dry Pasta and Macaroni** – Cook in boiling water with salt and oil until al dente, drain and serve or rinse in cool water and drain for future use. Once the pasta is cool and drained add 1 oz of olive oil per pound of pasta to prevent sticking. Always use a gallon of water for each pound of pasta to ensure that the item cooks evenly without getting too starchy.
 ♢ **Firm Green Vegetables** – Green beans, cabbage, collards, and broccoli flowerets. Add salt to water just before adding the vegetables. Serve immediately or shock in cold water for future service.
 ♢ **Lobster, Crabs, Crawfish** – Court bouillon may be used as a liquid and spices may be added to enhance the flavor. Boil lobsters for 5 minutes, crabs for 4 minutes and crawfish for 3 minutes at a full boil to be served immediately. Blanch 1 ½ lb lobsters for 3 minutes then shock if they are going to be reheated again.
 ♢ **Wild Rice and Hearty Grains** – Cook like pasta so the item does not become too starchy. Use a four to one ratio of water to grains.

Precautions
 ✓ Always use dry towels when removing or carrying hot pots make sure to warn others when you are moving hot pans or pots.
 ✓ When removing product from a range keep your face and hands away from the path of steam and liquid to avoid injury.

Steaming – *Is defined as the cooking of a product that is surrounded by a water vapor in an enclosed cabinet or in a covered steam pot which is between 215° and 250°. The product is finished when it is tender or the desired degree of doneness is achieved.* If the product is placed in a commercial pressure steamer the temperature can increase to 250° which causes the product to cook very quickly.

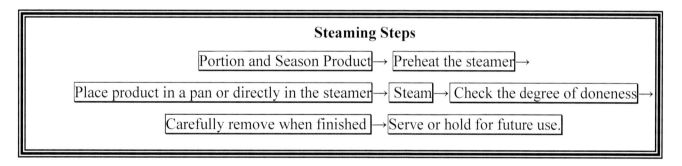

Steaming Steps

Portion and Season Product→ Preheat the steamer→

Place product in a pan or directly in the steamer→ Steam→ Check the degree of doneness→

Carefully remove when finished→ Serve or hold for future use.

Mise en Place Needed
 ➢ Item to be steamed
 ➢ Steamer or pot with lid and steamer basket
 ➢ Liquid- water, wine, beer
 ➢ Slotted or Perforated Spoon

 ➢ Seasonings, Herbs, Butter, Oil to flavor
 ➢ Accompaniments
 ➢ Calibrated Thermometer

Items that may be steamed

- ✧ **Vegetables** – Virtually all vegetables can be steamed. This method is favored over boiling or simmering because the water-soluble vitamins are not leached out as quickly due to the short cooking time and limited exposure to water.
- ✧ **Plain Rice** – Measure the rice. Rinse the 2 cups of rice until the water is clear. Measure 1 ½ parts of water to 1 part of pre-measured rice.
- ✧ **Mock Pilaf** – Sauté onions, add 1-part rice, place in hotel pan with 2 parts stock, bay leaf, steam covered for 18 minutes.
- ✧ **Seafood** – Steamed and served immediately with drawn butter or sauce. Clams, mussels, shrimp, fish may be steamed in a low-pressure steamer pot.
- ✧ **Doughs** – Various dumplings and Asian dim sum buns.
- ✧ **Cous Cous** – Equal parts of stock to cous cous for 4 minutes uncovered
- ✧ **Potatoes** – Place whole red bliss or peeled cut potatoes in steamer for 20 minutes. Toss in herbal butter or use for mashed potatoes.

Precautions

- ✓ Always use dry towels when removing or carrying hot pots make sure to warn others when you are moving hot pans or steamer pots.
- ✓ When removing product from a steamer keep your face and hands away from the path of steam to avoid injury.

Combination Cooking Methods

<u>**Stewing**</u> – *is the cooking of bite size pieces of food that are generally seared or blanched then simmered in a flavorful broth or stock until tender.* You should choose tougher cuts of protein when performing a combination cooking method. A stew is usually served in a bowl and eaten with a spoon.

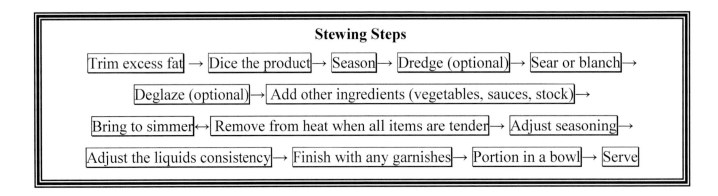

Stewing Steps

Trim excess fat → Dice the product → Season → Dredge (optional) → Sear or blanch →

Deglaze (optional) → Add other ingredients (vegetables, sauces, stock) →

Bring to simmer ← Remove from heat when all items are tender → Adjust seasoning →

Adjust the liquids consistency → Finish with any garnishes → Portion in a bowl → Serve

Mise en Place Needed

- Item to be stewed
- Dredging Flour
- Fat
- Seasonings- salt, pepper, spices see blends on page 153-155
- Stew Pot with Lid
- Other Ingredients (vegetables, potatoes, sauces, stocks)
- Liquid to deglaze- wine, stock
- Wooden Spoon- to scrape the fond
- Fork to check the tenderness of meat.
- Calibrated Thermometer
- Thickener- Beurre Manie, Crème Manie, Cornstarch Slurry, Roux
- Accompaniments
- Ladle

Types of items that may be stewed

- **Beef and Veal** – Including diced chuck, shank, short rib, breast, brisket, knuckle- cook until fork tender
- **Pork** – Diced Shoulder, Diced Boston butt, Ribs – Cooked until fork tender
- **Lamb** – Diced Shoulder, Diced Leg – Cooked until fork tender
- **Poultry Legs and Thigh** – Skin removed then stew until fork tender, about 175^0.
- **Vegetables** – Stew harder vegetables first then add softer vegetables.
- **Seafood** – Stew only until the flesh is firm, don't overcook. Most seafood stews should cook in less than 15 minutes from the time the seafood is added

Traditional Stewing Methods

- *Estouffade* - This is the same as old-fashioned beef stew except all the vegetables are tourneed.
- *Blanquette* – The meat (veal, chicken, or lamb) is blanched in water or stock then placed in pot of stock with aromatics and cooked until tender. Mushrooms and pearl onions are added then simmered until tender. Stew is finished with cream manie or liason, served in a duchess potato or puff pastry shell. Recipe 523
- *Bouillabaisse* – The seafood is simmered in fish stock flavored with fennel, tomatoes, saffron and white mirepoix. Finished with a rouille (red pepper spread). Recipe 499
- *Fricassée* – This is the same as blanquette except for the browning – the meat is dredged and sautéed lightly, then the same steps. Finished with sherry and cream, served over rice pilaf or noodles. Recipe 504
- *Goulash* – Veal, beef, lamb, or chicken is seasoned with Paprika then seared in oil. Brown stock and tomato product is added with onion, garlic and bay leaf. It is simmered until tender. Served with noodles or potatoes. Recipe 512
- *Irish Lamb Stew* – The diced lamb is blanched in stock, removed and rinsed. Then stew the meat in the strained stock, mirepoix and aromatics until tender. Finished with fresh herbs, served with dumplings or potatoes. Recipe 513
- *Ratatouille* – The vegetables are diced then sautéed in olive oil and garlic. Tomato product is added and the vegetables are cooked until they are soft. Served as a side dish. Recipe 518
- *Curries* – Meat, beans and lentils and/or vegetables are sautéed in clarified butter. Ginger, garlic and diced onions are added with mixture of curry spices, then liquid. Simmer until tender; finished with heavy cream, yogurt or coconut milk. Served over rice. Page 102

Types of American Stews

✪ *Old Fashioned Beef Stew* – Chunks of beef are browned in fat. Stock and vegetables are added with aromatics, simmered until tender. Potatoes are added towards the end so that they do not overcook. Recipe 465

✪ *Chili* – Chunks of beef, pork or lamb are seasoned with garlic chili spice mix. The meat is then seared in oil or lard then stock and tomato product is added. Soaked beans, if used, are added with onions, tomato puree and peppers and simmered until the meat and beans are tender. Page 76

✪ *Chicken and Dumplings* – Legs and thighs are blanched in boiling stock, the liquid is reduced in temperature to a simmer and large cut vegetables are added. Simmer until the chicken begins to fall off the bone. Chicken pieces are removed, skin and bones are discarded. Flat or raised dumplings are added and cooked. Recipe 492

✪ *Etouffé* - Chicken, Pork, Shrimp or Alligator pieces are dredged in seasoned flour then pan fried to golden brown. A brown roux is made with some of the pan drippings. A vegetable mixture called "trinity" or Cajun Mirepoix which is equal parts of diced peppers, diced celery, and green onions is added to the roux and drippings and cooked. Spices are added then stock and tomato product. Simmer until tender. Shrimp or crawfish are added at the last moment if used as a main ingredient. The term refers to smothering of the item in sauce. Served with rice. Recipe 476, 477

✪ *Gumbo* – Chicken, rabbit, and seafood are simmered in a dark roux thickened stock that is flavored with vegetables including "trinity" mirepoix, tomatoes, and okra. Served over rice and sometimes accompanied with potato salad. Pages 71, 72

✪ *Brunswick Stew* –Chicken, rabbit, pork are simmered in a tomato and stock based liquid. Vegetables include corn, lima beans, peppers, green beans, mirepoix. Finished with a touch of sugar and black pepper. Recipe 466

✪ *Burgoo* – Ingredients are the same as Brunswick stew. A burgoo also includes lamb, okra, and potatoes. Deglazed with a shot of bourbon after the meat is seared. Recipe 481

✪ *Cioppino* – Similar to bouillabaisse with the addition of white wine, basil, oregano, green peppers, green onions. No rouille is needed with this dish. Served with pasta and crusty bread. Recipe 475

Precautions

✓ Always use dry towels when removing or carrying hot pots
✓   Make sure to warn others when you are moving hot pots and pans.

Braising- *Is defined as a combination cooking method used for larger portions or cuts of tough meat. The item is first seared in fat then vegetables are added and sautéed, deglazed, and liquid is added to ½ the depth of the product. It is covered and baked until the item is fork tender or until it reaches an internal temperature between 165º-185º.*

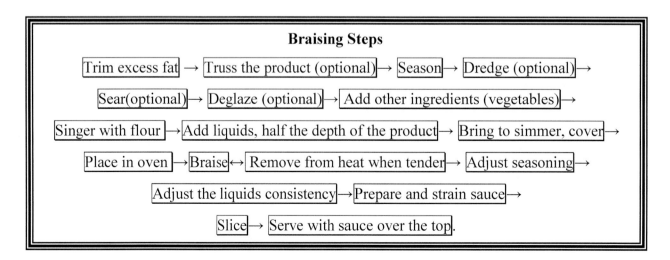

Braising Steps

Trim excess fat → Truss the product (optional)→ Season→ Dredge (optional)→
Sear(optional)→ Deglaze (optional)→ Add other ingredients (vegetables)→
Singer with flour → Add liquids, half the depth of the product→ Bring to simmer, cover→
Place in oven → Braise← Remove from heat when tender→ Adjust seasoning→
Adjust the liquids consistency→ Prepare and strain sauce→
Slice→ Serve with sauce over the top.

Mise en Place Needed

- Item to be braised
- Dredging Flour
- Fat
- Seasonings- salt, pepper.
- Braising pot with lid
- Other Ingredients (vegetables, potatoes, sauces, stocks)
- Liquid to deglaze- wine, stock
- Wooden Spoon- to scrape the fond
- Thickener- Cornstarch Slurry, Roux, Flour
- Accompaniments
- Sauce Pot
- Carving Board
- Carving Knife
- Carving Fork
- Calibrated Thermometer

Items that may be braised

- **Beef and Veal** – Including chuck, shank, short rib, breast brisket, knuckle- cooked until fork tender. Internal temperature is between 170^0 and 185^0.
- **Pork** – Shoulder, Boston butt – cook until fork tender or until 185°.
- **Lamb** – Shoulder – Cook until fork tender or 180°.
- **Poultry Legs and Thigh** – Cook until fork tender or 175°.
- **Game Birds**- Goose, Duck, Pheasant cooked until fork tender or 165°
- **Game Meats**- Venison, Elk, Reindeer, Rabbit until or 165°
- **Vegetables** – Celery, endive, lettuce – Cook until tender.
- **Rice Pilaf** – the rice is sautéed, covered, and simmered until tender.

Basic Applications

- *Pot Roast*- Beef Chuck, brisket, or knuckle are seared then cooked with mirepoix, root vegetables, brown stock and tomato paste. Recipe 494
- *Sauerbraten*- Brisket or knuckle is marinated with red wine vinegar, sugar, mirepoix, aromatics for 7 – 14 days, braised with beef stock, red wine, thickened with crumbled ginger snaps. Recipe 520
- *BBQ Brisket*- Seasoned and seared then braised with a simple BBQ sauce uncovered in a smoker, basted often.
- *Swiss Steak* – Portions of beef chuck steak are tenderized then dredged in flour, seared in fat, then cooked with stock, wine, sometimes beer, and aromatics. Season with Maggi Seasoning ®, a soy based sauce used in European cooking.
- *Carolina Style BBQ Pork*– Smoked and braised with vinegar and pepper based BBQ sauce.
- *Lamb or Veal Roulade*- Boned, portioned, stuffed, rolled and trussed. Seared and braised with an espagnole or brown based sauce.
- *Chicken Cacciatore* – Leg and thigh quarters, seared in olive oil, garlic, oregano, white wine, mushrooms, chopped tomatoes. Serve with pasta.
- *Coq au Vin*- Legs and thighs, dredged, seared in fat, then drained, mirepoix is caramelized, deglaze with wine ,add chicken stock or demi- glace, tomato product, strain when finished, garnish with sautéed mushrooms and pearl onions. Recipe 509
- *Rabbit Stew*- Legs and thighs and front quarters, dredged, seared in fat, then drained, mirepoix is caramelized, deglaze with wine ,add stock or demi- glace, tomato product, dried fruits with aromatics. Recipe 512
- *Rice Pilaf* – Onion is sautéed in butter or oil, rice is sautéed to coat, stock is added and cooked covered in the oven for 17 – 20 minutes. Tender to taste. Recipe 1269

Precautions

- ✓ Always use dry towels when removing or carrying hot pots
- ✓ Make sure to warn others when you are moving hot pots and pans.

Baking Methods

Bread Production

There are ten basic steps in preparing dough for bread baking. These steps help provide consistency to the bread making process.

1. **Scale**- *The measurement of ingredients to ensure consistent quantities and yields*
2. **Mix** – *Combine all ingredients to produce consistent dough. Develop the dough by kneading to allow for consistent fermentation of the dough. The dough should pull away from the sides of the mixing bowl when done. The mixing process usually takes 5 – 7 minutes on second speed in an electric mixer with a dough hook.*
3. **Ferment**- *This step allows the dough to relax and form gases within the dough. This leavens the dough to increase yield and produce the desired tenderness. Long fermentation, overnight, changes the flavor and structure of the dough. Sour doughs are fermented for longer periods of time which affects how gluten affects digestion.*
4. **Divide**- *After the dough doubles in size and has completed the initial proof or leavening, the dough is separated and measured into consistent sized units for uniform baking.*
5. **Round**- *Once the dough is divided into the smaller units they need to be rolled into consistent sized smooth balls of dough.*
6. **Bench Rest**- *This step allows the portioned pieces of dough to relax and prepare for the shaping stage.*
7. **Shape**- *The dough is shaped into the desired form as either a roll or loaf.*
8. **Pan**- *The loaf or roll is then place on a pan, cloth, or peel with equal spacing to allow for the final proof.*
9. **Final Ferment**- *allows the dough to double in size for even rising in the oven. Washes and garnishes should be applied before the next step.*
10. **Baking**- *This stops the fermentation through heat. Baking develops the crust, coagulates proteins and caramelizes the crust for flavor and texture development.*

Generally, the loaf or roll is fully baked when it is golden brown and has a hollow sound when the bottom of the product is tapped with your finger. The internal temperature of the dough should reach a minimum of 200°.

Dough Mixing Methods

❖ **Straight** - Place all dry ingredients *straight* in the mixing bowl; add the wet ingredients on top. Mix on first speed with a dough hook until all of the liquid is absorbed. Knead for 5 – 8 minutes on 2nd speed. This method is used for most types of bread.

❖ **Pre Ferment Sponge** - Combine all of the liquids with yeast, half the sugar, one third of the flour and mix until the dough is combined. Allow the dough to ferment for 30 – 40 minutes. Add the remaining ingredients and follow the straight dough method. This method is used for rich and sweet dough, or when the baker desires a larger yield of bread volume.

❖ **Laminated** - Prepare the dough according to the straight dough method. Prepare the roll-in fat. Incorporate the fat with using a book-fold. Rest and give the dough a three-fold, rest and then roll dough and give a three-fold. Allow the dough to rest again for 15 minutes, repeat for a third and final time. Roll, shape, pan, proof, and bake. When using frozen laminated dough, it is important to allow the dough to defrost overnight before moving on to steps 7 of the 10 steps of bread making process.

Basic Mixing Methods for Batters and Doughs

➤ **Creaming**- Place the sugar and solid fat in the mixer and combine with a paddle on 2nd speed until the mixture is light and fluffy. Add the eggs in three parts. On first speed, add the dry ingredients and liquids alternately, until combined.
Add any garnishes last. **Examples- cookies, buttercream, pound cake.**

➤ **Rubbing**- Place all the dry ingredients in the bowl and rub the fat into the dry ingredients to achieve the desired flakiness, the larger the fat pieces the flakier the dough. Add all of the wet ingredients last and combine until the liquid is just absorbed. Allow the dough to rest for 10 minutes in the refrigerator until it is firms. Roll to the desired shape and size. **Examples: biscuits, pie dough.**

➤ **Blending**- with a paddle on first speed combine all the dry ingredients, in a separate bowl mix the wet ingredients and add to the dry ingredients. Add the **liquid fat** to the batter last to allow for a tender cake like texture. Garnishes, like berries or chips, should be added to each muffin pan or loaf pan to allow for equal distribution. This method is generally used if the fat is in a liquid state. **Examples: Cake Batter, Muffins.**

➤ **Sponge Cake** - Warm eggs and sugar to 100° in the mixing bowl. Whip on third speed until the maximum volume is achieved. Fold in the double-sifted dry ingredients; fold in the melted butter or liquid fat last. **Examples: Genoise, Angel Food Cake, Ladyfingers.**

➤ **Two Stage Cake** - Place all dry ingredients in a mixing bowl. Add the liquid shortening and combine. Add the liquid last on first speed. **Examples: Sheet and High Ratio Cakes**

Basic Dessert Preparations

Anglaise – *This is a milk based sauce used for a dessert sauce, ice cream base, parfait base or even as a component of a mousse.* See formula numbers 843,895,994 .

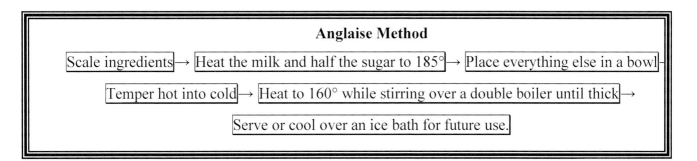

Anglaise Method

Scale ingredients → Heat the milk and half the sugar to 185° → Place everything else in a bowl

Temper hot into cold → Heat to 160° while stirring over a double boiler until thick →

Serve or cool over an ice bath for future use.

Mise en Place Needed

➤ Ingredients
➤ Double Boiler
➤ Whisk

➤ Ice Bath
➤ Rubber Spatula
➤ Calibrated Thermometer

Meringue – *This is a whipped egg and sugar mixture used as a topping, filling, buttercream base or as a component of mousse. See recipes on pages 125,126.*

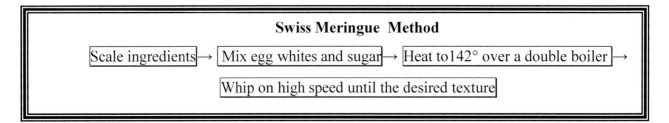

Swiss Meringue Method

Scale ingredients → Mix egg whites and sugar → Heat to 142° over a double boiler →

Whip on high speed until the desired texture

Mise en Place Needed

➢ Ingredients
➢ Mixing Bowl
➢ Double Boiler
➢ Whip
➢ Rubber Spatula
➢ Calibrated Thermometer

Mousse – *This is a light cold dessert composed of whipped egg yolks, egg whites or whole eggs with the pureed or melted main product, and whipped cream. See recipes on page 131.*

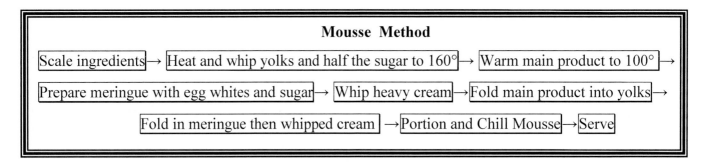

Mousse Method

Scale ingredients → Heat and whip yolks and half the sugar to 160° → Warm main product to 100° →

Prepare meringue with egg whites and sugar → Whip heavy cream → Fold main product into yolks →

Fold in meringue then whipped cream → Portion and Chill Mousse → Serve

Mise en Place Needed

➢ Ingredients
➢ Mixing Bowls
➢ Double Boiler
➢ Whisk, Whip

➢ Rubber Spatula
➢ Calibrated Thermometer
➢ Serving Dish or Glass

Bavarian Cream – *This is a light cold dessert prepared with the same ingredients as a mousse with gelatin added to thicken. See recipes on page 129.*

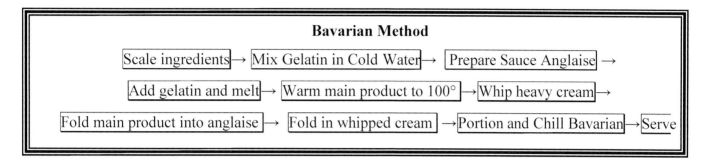

Bavarian Method

Scale ingredients → Mix Gelatin in Cold Water → Prepare Sauce Anglaise →

Add gelatin and melt → Warm main product to 100° → Whip heavy cream →

Fold main product into anglaise → Fold in whipped cream → Portion and Chill Bavarian → Serve

Mise en Place Needed

- Ingredients
- Double Boiler
- Mixing Bowls
- Whisk, Whip

- Rubber Spatula
- Calibrated Thermometer
- Serving Dish or Glass

Custard – *This is a dairy and egg-based preparation for both desserts and savory preparations. Dessert preparations like crème brulee or cheesecake, savory applications like royale or quiche. See recipes on page 125.*

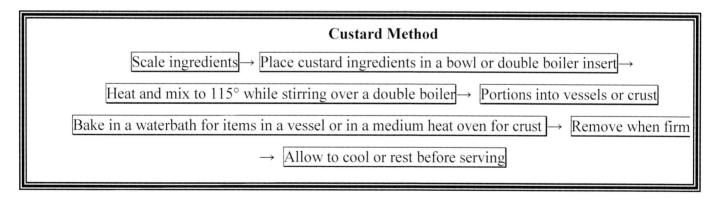

Custard Method

Scale ingredients → Place custard ingredients in a bowl or double boiler insert →

Heat and mix to 115° while stirring over a double boiler → Portions into vessels or crust

Bake in a waterbath for items in a vessel or in a medium heat oven for crust → Remove when firm

→ Allow to cool or rest before serving

Mise en Place Needed

- Ingredients
- Double Boiler
- Whisk
- Vessel or Crust Lined Pan.
- Rubber Spatula
- Calibrated Thermometer

Garde Manger Techniques

Procedures for Food Preservation

Dry Cure- this process uses salt, sugar and aromatics to draw the moisture out of a product to allow it to last longer. The length of cure depends upon the formula or recipe and the thickness of the product.

Examples: Grava Lox, Country Ham. Recipes on page 49.

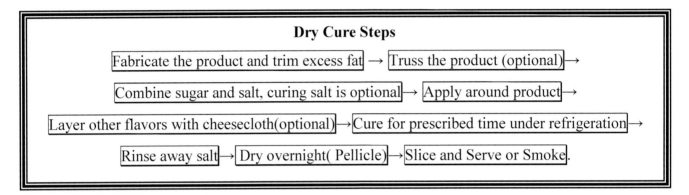

Mise en Place Needed

- Item to be cured
- Butcher Twine (optional)
- Sugar
- Kosher Salt

- Aromatics (herbs, spices, liquors).
- Sealable bag
- Cheesecloth (optional)
- Drying Rack

Marinade- This process uses oil, acid, and aromatics to denature the protein, tenderize and lower the ph level of the product to inhibit bacterial growth. The length of marinade depends upon the formula or recipe and the thickness of the product. Examples: Sauerbraten, Ceviche. Recipes on page 47.

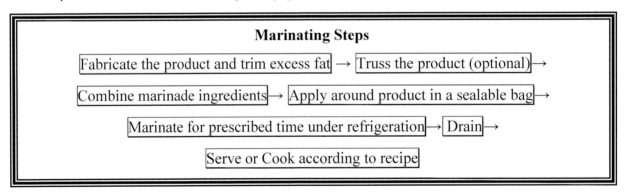

Mise en Place Needed

- Item to be cured
- Butcher Twine (optional)
- Oil

- Acid- Vinegar, Citrus Juice, Wine
- Aromatics (herbs, seasonings).
- Sealable bag

Brine- This process uses salt, sugar, aromatics and liquid to occupy water molecules in the food so that there is very little moisture available for bacterial growth. The length of brining depends upon the formula or recipe and the thickness of the product. Examples of brined foods include hams, corned beef, seafood and fish. This method allows for a variety of flavors to be infused into the product. The function of the salt is to control the bacterial growth and increase moisture retention. The sugar is used to balance the salt flavor.

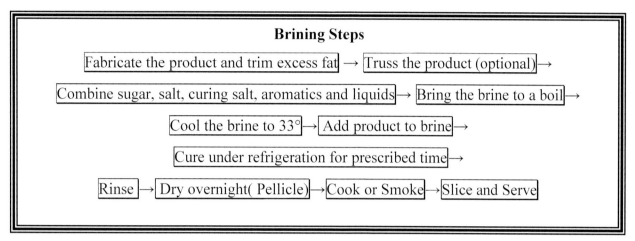

Brining Steps

Fabricate the product and trim excess fat → Truss the product (optional) → Combine sugar, salt, curing salt, aromatics and liquids → Bring the brine to a boil → Cool the brine to 33° → Add product to brine → Cure under refrigeration for prescribed time → Rinse → Dry overnight(Pellicle) → Cook or Smoke → Slice and Serve

Mise en Place Needed

- Item to be brined
- Butcher Twine (optional)
- Sugar
- Liquid
- Kosher Salt
- Aromatics (herbs, spices, liquors).
- Curing Salt
- Sealable bag
- Pot
- Drying Rack

Pickle- This process uses salt, sugar, aromatics, acid and liquid to stabilize the product so that bacteria growth is inhibited by lowering the pH level. The length of brining depends upon the formula or recipe and the item itself. Examples: Pickled Vegetables, Pigs Feet.

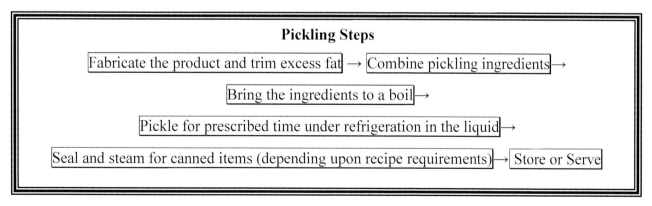

Pickling Steps

Fabricate the product and trim excess fat → Combine pickling ingredients → Bring the ingredients to a boil → Pickle for prescribed time under refrigeration in the liquid → Seal and steam for canned items (depending upon recipe requirements) → Store or Serve

Mise en Place Needed

- Item to be brined
- Ingredients
- Sealable container
- Pot

Smoke- This process dries and coats the product with a layer of tar, alcohol, and formaldehyde to inhibit bacterial growth on the outer layer. The length of smoking and curing depends upon the formula or recipe. Examples: Ham, Bacon.

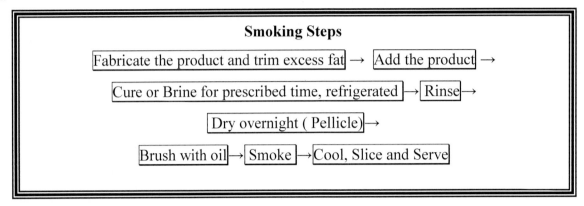

Mise en Place Needed

- Item to be smoked
- Brine or Cure
- Sealable bag
- Pot

- Smoker – Hot or Cold
- Wood Chips
- Drying and Smoking Rack

Confit- This process uses a cured protein with rendered fat that is simmered together. When cool it forms a fat seal across the top which helps prevent oxidation. The length of cure depends upon the formula or recipe. To remove the confit from the fat, use a clean utensil or gloved hands to prevent cross-contamination.

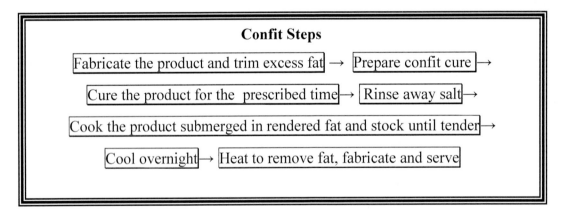

Mise en Place Needed

- Item to be made into confit
- Confit Cure
- Sealable bag
- Braising or Confit Pot

- Rendered Fat
- Stock
- Gloves

Charcuterie Methods

Country Style Method – *The critical attribute of a country style forcemeat is its coarse ground texture. A combination of ground pork, pork liver, and pork fat is preferred for this method.*

Step One – Chill all ingredients to 32°, and chill all grinding attachments to 32° in clean ice water.

Step Two – Grind all proteins utilizing a large size die plate on the grinder. Chill the grinder again in the ice water until needed for sequential grinding or clean and sanitize

Step Three – Season all ground meat with the appropriate seasoning and cures. Place the meat in the freezer until it reaches 35°.

Step Four – Grind the ingredients a second time through a medium sized hole plate in a clean grinder.

Step Five – Place a bowl over a larger bowl containing ice. Place the ground product in a bowl and add anyadditional ingredients, liquids and or garnishes.

Step Six - Cook a small portion of the forcemeat to check the seasoning, flavor, color, and texture.

Step Seven - Utilize for pâtes, terrines, pâte en croûte, and ballottines.

Straight Method – *The critical attribute of a straight forcemeat is its smooth texture. The straight forcemeat is cured, ground, then pureed until smooth.*

Step One – Fabricate the proteins to be used then apply a cure with seasonings and spices.

Step Two - Chill all ingredients to 34° for 4- 6 hours. The use of a vacuum pressure machine will shorten the amount of time needed. Chill all grinding attachments to 32° in clean ice water.

Step Three – Grind all proteins utilizing a large hole plate on the grinder. Chill the grinder again in the ice water until needed or clean and sanitize. Freeze the food processor and blade for 20 minutes. Place the meat in the freezer until it reaches 34°.

Step Four – Grind the ingredients a second time through a medium sized hole plate.

Step Five – Place the ground product in a bowl and add any additional ingredients, including liquids and panadas. Place the bowl over a larger bowl containing ice and chill to 35 °.

Step Six - Puree one half of the forcemeat until smooth. Remove and puree the second half.

Step Seven - Cook a small portion of the forcemeat to check the seasoning, flavor, color, and texture.

Step Eight Utilize for pâtes, terrines, pâte en croûte, and ballottines.

Gratin Method – *The critical attribute of a gratin forcemeat is that a portion of the protein is browned or cooked before being ground. Using this method will reduce the amount of shrinkage.*

Step One – Sear pieces of the main flavor or product to impart flavor.

Step Two – Chill all ingredients to 34°, and chill all grinding attachments to 32° in clean ice water.

Step Three – Grind all proteins utilizing a large hole plate on the grinder. Chill the grinder again in the ice water until needed or clean and sanitize.

Step Four – Season all ground meat with the appropriate seasoning and cures. Place the meat in the freezer until it reaches 34°.

Step Five – Grind the ingredients a second time through a medium sized hole plate. Either leave in a coarse textureor puree until smooth with a panada.

Step Six – Place the ground product in a bowl and add any additional ingredients, liquids and or garnishes. Place the bowl over a larger bowl containing ice.

Step Seven - Cook a small portion of the forcemeat to check the seasoning, flavor, color, and texture.

Step Eight - Utilize for pâtes, terrines, pâte en croûte, and ballottines.

Mousseline Method – *The critical attribute of a mousseline forcemeat is its smooth light texture. The main product is a lean tender poultry or seafood.*

Step One – Chop the proteins to be used and add seasonings and spices.

Step Two - Chill all ingredients to 32° .Chill the grinding attachments to 32° in clean ice water.

Step Three –Place the chopped protein in a food processor and puree until smooth.

Step Four – Add the eggs and puree again.

Step Five – Scrape down the sides and add the very cold heavy cream, puree to emulsify and add air to the product. Keep the mousseline below 35°.

Step Six - Cook a small portion of the forcemeat to check the seasoning, flavor, color, and texture.

Step Seven - Utilize for terrines, quenelles and fish ballottine.

Key points when working with forcemeats and sausages

✓ *Make sure the product and equipment is very cold – keep between $32°$-34°*

✓ *Remove all unwanted membranes and fat before grinding.*

✓ *Season the meat and allow it to cure for at least 20 minutes before grinding.*

✓ *Wear gloves; keep the working area very clean.*

✓ *Don't over mix or over puree the meats –this can result in a grainy texture.*

✓ *Cook convoluted, forcemeat filling to a minimum temperature of $165°$*

Mise en Place Formulas

#	Item			1	2	3	4	8	Yield	Method of Preparation
1	Beurre Manié				oz Flour	oz Soft Butter			5 oz	Knead the flour into the butter, use this paste to thicken small amounts of sauce
2	Bouquet Garni		Thin Slice Celeriac	ea Sprig Thyme	ea Bay Leaf	ea Leaf Leek	ea Parsley Stem		1 ea	Wrap the herbs in celeriac first then in the leek and tie with twine. Use this to flavor stocks.
3	Celestine Crepe	2 oz Melted Butter	tbsp Parsley chopped	cup Flour / pinch Salt	cup Milk		ea Eggs		20 ea	Whisk the flour into the milk and eggs, strain, whisk in butter. Whisk in parsley. Ladle 1.5 oz of batter in a 10 inch non-stick pan until golden brown.
4	Consommé - always serve consommé very hot in a soup cup with very fine cut vegetable and garnitures.	10 ea Egg White (Whipped)	lb. Very Lean Ground Meat	Gallon Cold Stock / ea Sachet	ea. Leftover Chicken Carcass – Roasted Defatted Chopped	cup Mirepoix Thin Julienne	oz. Julienne Leek	oz Tomato Puree	1 gal	Combine all of the ingredients in a tall narrow pot and stir to 120°. Stop stirring, allow the raft to form. Simmer gently until the raft forms at 160°. Make a small hole and baste the raft often, simmering at 190° for 1 ½ hours. Strain just the liquid through coffee filters. Season to taste.
5	Court Bouillon	6 oz Wine	Bouquet Garni	qt Water		oz Vinegar		oz Mirepoix	1 qt	Simmer the ingredients and strain after 30 minutes. Use the liquid for poaching items.
6	Court Bouillon - Simple	ea Bay Leaf		qt Water			oz Vinegar		1 qt	Simmer and use as a poaching liquid
7	Cream Soup	gallon Stock		lb White Mirepoix / pint Cream	lb Vegetable (Main Flavor)	oz Butter	oz Flour		1 gal	Sauté the vegetables and mirepoix in butter. Add in flour then stock. Simmer until tender. Puree until very smooth, strain if needed add hot cream. Season
8	Crème Manie	cup Flour		pint Cream					1 pint	Mix the cream and flour, allow to sit for 20 minutes. Whisk into a gallon of cream soup or sauce to thicken.
9	Duchesse Potatoes	pinch Nutmeg	oz Parmesan Fine	lb Peeled Cooked Potatoes	ea Egg Yolk / oz Melted Butter				10 portion	Pass the hot dry potatoes through food mill. Mix in everything else and season to taste. Pipe and bake or use for croquette.
10	Duxelle - cooked mushroom filling.	4 oz Melted Butter	tbsp Tomato Paste (optional)	oz Shallot	lb White Mushrooms	tsp chopped Parsley	tbsp White Wine		1 lb	Chop mushrooms and press out moisture, sauté shallots and butter, expand with tomato, add in mushroom reduce with wine add parsley and season. Use as filling.
11	Fine Herb Ratio	1 Chervil	Chive	Tarragon	Parsley					Finely chop and mix this ratio.
12	Liaison - temper hot items into cold so it is smooth.	10 oz Heavy Cream		tbsp Sherry			ea Egg Yolk		1.5 cups	Combine the ingredients and use to thicken 1 quart of cream soup or sauce. Temper hot item into the liaison, then heat to 160°. Make sure to serve immediately, this preparation is stable for 10 minutes.
13	Matignon	2 ea Bay Leaves	Sprig Thyme	cup diced Carrot	cups diced Onions	strip Bacon-diced		oz diced Celeriac	3.5 cups	Render bacon, remove, sauté small diced veg, add in herbs, sweat
14	Mirepoix		part Carrot	part Celery	part Onion					Dice and mix this ratio.
15	Mirepoix - White		part Leeks	part Celery	part Onion					Dice and mix this ratio.

Mise en Place Formulas

#	Item	1	1	2	3	4	8	Yield	Method of Preparation
16	Pasta Dough	½ tsp Salt tbsp Olive Oil / tsp Salt	lb Semolina Flour	ea Eggs		oz Water		24 oz	Make well with flour, add eggs oil and salt, mix then add cold water- knead until firm and elastic. This is very dry dough that must be done in mixer on speed 1 for 7 minutes. Allow to rest 30 minutes
17	Pâte à Choux	½ tsp Salt qt Water	pint Eggs / lb. Flour				oz Butter	3.5 lbs	Boil water, salt and butter, add all flour and mix well, cook until it forms a ball, 6 – 7 minutes cool in mixer with paddle to 90°. add in eggs, one at a time. Mix well.
18	Persillade	bunch chopped Parsley	tbsp Herbes De Provençe	cup Panko Bread Crumb	oz Olive oil	ea Garlic Clove	ea Garlic Clove	1 qt	Chop garlic and parsley in a food processor first then add in everything and pulse. Season .
19	Pesto	cup Fresh Basil		tbsp Pine Nuts	oz Olive Oil	ea Garlic Clove		1 cup	Puree all ingredients together until smooth. Refrigerate until needed.
20	Reduction- use for to add flavor.	10 peppercorn cup Wine	Sprig Thyme	oz Shallot	Bay Leaf	oz stem Mushroom	Parsley stems	2 oz	Combine everything and reduce until 3 oz remain, strain.
21	Rouille- use for bouillabaisse.	pinch cayenne / pinch Saffron cup Bread Cubes / tbsp Lemon	ea Roasted Red Pepper	ea Garlic Clove	dash Sea Salt	oz Olive Oil		1.5 cup	Peel pepper remove seeds and puree with everything else. Add a few drops of water if the emulsion begins to break. Refrigerate afterwards.
22	Roux- Blanc	lb All Purpose Flour	lb Clarified Butter					2 lb	Melt Butter, add flour. Stir with wooden spoon over medium heat, 1 minute. Use for béchamel. 3 oz to quart- light consistency 4 oz to quart- medium consistency 6 oz to quart-heavy consistency
23	Roux- Blonde	lb All Purpose Flour	lb Clarified Butter					2 lb	Melt Butter, add flour. Stir with wooden spoon over medium heat, 4 – 5 minutes the roux should have a light nutty scent. Use for veloute. 3 oz to quart- light consistency 4 oz to quart- medium consistency 6 oz to quart-heavy consistency
24	Roux- Brun	lb All Purpose Flour	lb Clarified Butter					30 oz	Melt Butter, add flour. Stir with wooden spoon over medium low heat, 10 -12 minutes. This preparation is very hot. Be careful to slowly stir the roux until it is the color of peanut butter. Use for Espagnole 4 oz to quart- light consistency 5 oz to quart- medium consistency 8oz to quart-heavy consistency
25	Royal	pint Milk			ea Egg Yolk	ea Eggs		24 oz	Combine and strain- use for custard, French Toast Batter.
26	Sachet – herbal spice bag	6 Peppercorn ea Bay Leaf	Sprig Thyme				Parsley Stems	1 ea	Wrap in cheesecloth and tie with twine. Use for stock. Once flavor is achieved, remove.
27	Seasoned Salt	tsp White Pepper		cup Kosher Salt				1 cup	Blend – use to finish seasoning
28	Seasoned Flour	½ tsp White Pepper tbsp Fine Salt					oz Flour	8 oz	Blend – use for dredging.

Mise en Place Formulas

#	Item	1	1	1	2	3	4	8	Yield	Method of Preparation
29	**Jus** (Use beef, lamb, game with veal stock. Use poultry or feathered game with dark chicken stock)	1.5 quart Brown Veal or Chicken Stock	tbsp Olive Oil	lb Lean Meat Scraps	oz Wine			oz small dice Mirepoix	24 oz	In a marmite, heat oil and caramelize the meat scraps. Remove and caramelize the Mirepoix. Deglaze with wine and simmer all ingredients for 30 minutes over low heat, remove scum, strain.
30	**Stock – Beef, White**		ea Sachet	lb White Mirepoix- rough cut	gallon Cold Water		lb Beef Marrow Bones		1 gallon	Rinse the bones. Add all ingredients and gently simmer for 12 hours. Remove any foam or scum that rises to the top of the pot. Remove excess fat. Strain.
31	**Stock – Chicken-** (to prepare a brown chicken stock- brown the Mirepoix and bones before adding water)		gallon Cold Water / ea Sachet	lb White Mirepoix- rough cut			lb Chicken Bone		3.5 quart	Rinse the chicken bones. Heat in water to 140°. Pour off and refill with cold water. Add all ingredients and gently simmer for 4 hours-180°. Remove any foam or scum that rises to the top of the pot. Remove excess fat. Strain.
32	**Stock – Fish-** use lean white fish bones.	1 cup Mushroom Stem	gallon Cold Water	lb White Mirepoix / ea Bouquet Garni		quart Cold Water	lb Fish Bone		3 quart	Use blanched leeks and onions, celery knob for the white mirepoix. Combine everything and simmer for 20 minutes then strain and chill or use immediately.
33	**Stock- Fish Fumet**	1 recipe Fish Stock Ingredients- above	oz Whole Butter / oz Lemon Juice	sprig Thyme	ea Parsley Stem	ea Lemon Slices		oz Nouilly Prat Vermouth	3 quart	Use the above recipes ingredients along with the items on this line. Sweat Mirepoix and fish bones, add lemon and vermouth. Simmer 2 minutes, and then add rest. Simmer 20 minutes, strain and chill.
34	**Stock – Shellfish-** this stock freezes well when you have leftover shells.	1 oz Tomato Paste	quart Water	ea Sachet / cup Mirepoix	oz White Wine	lb Shrimp or Lobsters Shells			1.5 pints	Sauté the shells in a lightly buttered sauce pot then add the mirepoix and tomato paste. Stir and cook for 2 minutes then deglaze with wine, add the water. Simmer for 30 minutes and strain.
35	**Stock – Veal-** veal bones can be purchased from a butcher or meat purveyor.		ea Sachet		gallon Cold Water	lb Mirepoix	oz Tomato Paste	lb Veal Bone	1.5 gal	Roast the veal bones in a 350° oven until golden brown. Brush with tomato paste and roast with the mirepoix. Place in kettle with water to cover. 170° for 12 hours. Remove any scum or foam that rises to the top. Strain and chill.
36	**Stock – Vegetable**	28 oz Chopped Tomato	ea Sachet	cup Mushroom Stems	cup sliced Leek	lb Mirepoix	pint Water		2 qt	Make sure to clean raw vegetables very well. Combine and simmer for 30 minutes.

When using a pressure cooker for the preparation of stock reduce the water by 30% to account for reduced evaporation.

When preparing a fish stock using the sous vide method, reduce the water by 15% to account for reduced evaporation.

Classical Sauces A- C

#	Item		1/2	1	1	2	3	4	8	Yield	Method of Preparation
37	Aurore		cup White Wine	cup Tomato Puree	cup Cream		cup Veloute	oz Whole Butter		1 qt	Simmer tomato puree and wine, reduce, add cream and veloute, simmer then remove from heat, whisk in the whole butter. Season to taste
38	Béarnaise- prepare the béarnaise reduction first. Save leftover reduction for future use.			pint Clarified Butter	tbsp chopped Chervil	tbsp chopped Tarragon	tsp Béarnaise Reduction	ea Egg Yolk		1.25 pint	In a double boiler combine the egg yolk and reduction. Heat and whip until the eggs are 125°. Remove from heat whisk in butter that is at 140°. Add in chopped herbs. Season to taste with salt and Tabasco.
39	Béarnaise-reduction		cup Vinegar	cup Water	cup Fresh Tarragon	ea Shallot Minced	tbsp Fresh Ground Black Pepper		oz White Wine	4 oz	Place all of the ingredients in a pot and slowly reduce until 1/2 cup remains and strain-use liquid, or puree with solids for stronger flavor.
40	Béchamel		ea Onion	qt Milk	ea Bay Leaf	ea Whole Cloves		oz Roux		1 qt	Stud the onion with the clove and bay leaf. Steep the onion cloute in milk for 20 minutes then remove onion. Thicken the sauce will roux and bring to a simmer for 20 minutes. Season to taste.
41	Bercy		cup White Wine	pint of either Veloute or Demi	tbsp Fresh Tarragon	ea Shallot minced		oz Whole Butter		20 oz	Steep the minced shallot in the wine then strain. Add in the demi or veloute. Simmer and add in the chopped tarragon. Whisk in whole butter. Season to taste
42	Beurre Blanc -a beurre rouge can be made by substituting red wine for white wine		ea Lemon juiced	lb Soft Butter	cup Cream	tbsp Shallot minced	tbsp Champagne Vinegar		oz White Wine	3 cup	Combine the wine, vinegar, and shallot in a pot. Reduce over medium heat until ¼ cup remains. Strain into a clean pot. Add in cream and simmer. Remove and whisk in butter.
43	Bordelaise	pinch Fresh Thyme	tsp Cracked Black Pepper	ea Bay Leaf	cup Red Wine	tbsp Shallot minced	oz Glace De Viande	tbsp Whole Butter or Poached Marrow	oz Demi Glace	1 pint	Make a reduction with the thyme, bay leaf, shallot, and red wine. Reduce by half and strain the liquid into a clean pot. Add in the demi and glace de viande and simmer. Whisk in whole butter and season to taste.
44	Chasseur	5 ea julienne Mushroom	oz Cognac	tbsp minced Shallot	tsp Chervil	cup Demi Glace	oz Whole Butter	oz White Wine	oz Tomato Concassé	1 pint	Sauté the shallot and mushroom in ½ butter. Flambé with cognac. Add in the wine and tomato reduce by half. Add in the demi, simmer. Whisk in whole butter, garnish, season to taste .

Classical Sauce C- G

#	Item	1/2	1	1	2	3	4	8	Yield	Method of Preparation
45	Chateaubriand- this sauce is also served with sauce béarnaise for beef tenderloin roast.	ea Bay Leaf	pinch Fresh Thyme			oz Whole Butter	oz Mushroom peeled, sliced	oz White Wine	1 pint	Make a reduction with the thyme, bay leaf, shallot, and red wine. Reduce by half and strain the liquid into a clean pot. Add in the demi and sautéed mushroom. Simmer and whisk in butter season to taste
46	Choron		Recipe of Béarnaise	tbsp Tomato Paste	cup Demi Glace	tbsp Tomato Puree	tsp Glace de Viande		3 cup	In a small hot heat the tomato puree, glace de viande and wine and reduce by half, stir in the tomato paste and blend into the sauce béarnaise.
47	Demi- Glace-make sure to skim the sauce frequently.		recipe Sauce Espagnole	gal Fond de Veau					1 gallon	Combine Fond de Veau and Espagnole. Reduce over low heat until ¾ of a gallon remains.
48	Diable		pinch Cayenne Pepper	oz White Wine Vinegar	tsp Shallot minced		oz White Wine	oz Demi Glace	1 cup	Make a reduction with the cayenne, shallot, vinegar and wine. Reduce by ¾ and strain the liquid into a clean pot. Add in the demi and simmer. Season
49	Dijonnaise	oz Clarified Butter	cup Mushroom sliced	oz Shallot minced	cups Demi Glace		oz Dijon Mustard	oz Heavy Cream	20 oz	Mix the cream and Dijon in a bowl first. Sauté the shallots and mushroom. Add the demi, simmer add Dijon cream. Bring to a simmer for 5 minutes.
50	Duglere- this sauce is goes very well with poached sole, sautéed scallops, or shrimp.	oz Pernod Liquor	lb Tomato Concassé	pint Cream	oz Beurre Manié	tbsp Shallot minced	oz White Wine	oz Strong Fish Stock	3 cup	Reduce the stock, wine, tomato and shallot by half over medium heat. Puree and add the cream and pernod bring to a simmer. Thicken with beurre manie and strain, season.
51	Espagnole		recipe Veal Stock #35	Recipe Roux Brun		oz Tomato Paste	cup Matignon		3 quarts	Produce the Matignon, expand with tomato, and then add the stock. Simmer. Temper stock and roux. Simmer 2 hours. Strain.
52	Estragon – Brown		tbsp Béarnaise Reduction	tbsp Tarragon		oz Whole Butter		oz Demi Glace	12 oz	Simmer the reduction, demi, and tarragon. Whisk in butter, and season to taste
53	Estragon- White	ea Lemon-juiced	tbsp Béarnaise Reduction	tbsp Tarragon		oz Whole Butter		oz Veloute	12 oz	Simmer the reduction, veloute, and tarragon. Whisk in butter, finish with lemon and season.
54	Fond de Veau		Sachet	lb Mirepoix	gallon Veal Stock	lb Veal Bones	oz Tomato Paste		3 qt	Brown the bones, brush with tomato paste. Roast with mirepoix. Place in large pot; add stock and sachet simmer gently for 4-6 hours until 3 qt remain. Strain twice.
55	Foyot		Recipe of Béarnaise		oz Glace de Viande				1.25 pint	Melt the glace de viande and blend into the sauce béarnaise.
56	Glacage Royale		cup Hollandaise	cup Warm Veloute				oz Heavy Cream	3.5 cup	Lightly whip the cream. Fold the hollandaise into the veloute. Fold in the whipped cream. Season. Make sure all ingredients are about the same temp before mixing.

Chefs Note: Make sure to use a rubber spatula to clean the sides of the pot and a skimmer to remove impurities during the simmering process.

Classical Sauces G- P

Item		1/2	1	1	2	3	4	8	Yield	Method of Preparation
57	Grenobloise	pinch Cracked Black Pepper	ea Lemon juiced	pint Sauce Ravigote	tbsp Capers			oz Butter		1.25 pint	Bring the sauce ravigote to a simmer. Add in the capers and lemon juice. Whisk in the butter. Season to taste.
58	Hollandaise		ea Lemon juiced	oz White Wine Vinegar	pint Clarified Butter	oz Water	drops Tabasco®	ea Egg Yolks		1.25 pint	Reduce the vinegar & pepper by ½. In a double boiler combine the egg yolk & reduction. Heat and whip until the eggs are 125°. Remove from heat whisk in butter that is at 140°. Add lemon and water. Season.
59	Hongroise		cup minced Onion	oz Clarified Butter	pinch Cayenne Pepper	tbsp Hungarian Paprika	cups Demi Glace		oz Sour Cream	1 qt	Sauté the onions and paprika. Add the demi and simmer. Temper in the sour cream.
60	Madalainé		oz Clarified Butter	cup Demi Glace	tbsp minced Shallot	tbsp Fresh Tarragon	cups Heavy Cream	oz White Wine	oz Sliced Mushroom	3 cup	Sauté the shallots and mushrooms in the butter. Deglaze with wine and reduce, add in demi and cream, simmer reduce by half. Season.
61	Madére	pinch Fresh Thyme		ea Shallot minced	ea Bay Leaf	cups Demi Glace	oz Whole Butter		oz Madeira Wine	1 pint	Make a reduction with the thyme, bay leaf, shallot, and wine. Reduce by half and strain the liquid into a clean pot. Add in the demi and simmer. Whisk in whole butter and season.
62	Maltaise			recipe of Hollandaise #58	tbsp Triple Sec	ea Blood Orange				1 pint	Juice and zest orange. Simmer and reduce with the triple sec. Add to the Hollandaise sauce.
63	Mornay	pinch Fresh Nutmeg		pint Béchamel		tbsp Parmesan Cheese fine grate	oz Gruyere Cheese grated			1 pint	Heat the béchamel blend in the cheese with immersion blender, season to taste with salt, white pepper. nutmeg. Strain if needed
64	Mousseline			Recipe of Hollandaise					oz Heavy Cream	1.75 pint	Lightly whip the heavy cream and fold it into the hollandaise.
65	Périgueux		oz Cognac	pint Demi Glace	ea Truffle fine julienne		oz Whole Butter	oz Madeira Wine		1 pint	Simmer and reduce the truffle, Madeira and cognac until 1 oz remains. Add in the demi and simmer. Finish with butter.
66	Périgourdine		oz Cognac	cup Demi Glace	ea Truffle fine julienne	oz Soft Butter	oz Foie Gras	oz Madeira	oz Heavy Cream	1 pint	Simmer and reduce the truffle, Madeira until 2 oz remains. Puree the foie gras and cognac. Warm both together until it reaches 130°. Reduce the cream and demi over medium heat until 1.5 cups remains whisk everything together.
67	Piquant			pint Sauce Madere	pinch Cayenne	tsp Vinegar				1 pint	Simmer together several minutes
68	Poivre	1 shot Cognac		cup Demi Glace	tbsp Black Pepper-cracked	tsp Green Peppercorn-rinse off brine			oz Heavy Cream	1 pint	Simmer and flambé the black pepper and green peppercorns. Combine and simmer.

Classical Sauces R-Z

#	Item		1/2	1	1	2	3	4	8	Yield	Method of Preparation
69	**Ravigote**- serve this sauce with poached fish or crab		quart Veloute	ea Shallot minced	oz White Wine Vinegar	tsp Fresh Parsley chopped fine	tsp Fresh Tarragon chopped fine	oz White Wine		1 pint	Make a reduction shallot, vinegar and wine. Reduce by half and strain the liquid into a clean pot. Add in the veloute, simmer. Garnish and season.
70	**Robert**- you can add 2 oz of fine julienne cornichons pickles to make Sauce Charcuterie.		tsp Sugar	cup chopped Onion	tbsp Dijon	oz Whole Butter	cups Demi Glace	oz White Wine		1 pint	Sauté the onions with a tsp of butter and add in the sugar, and wine. Cook until the onions are a medium brown color. Add the demi and Dijon then simmer for 15 minutes. Strain out onions. Finish with butter.
71	**Salmis**- The breasts are pan roasted and the sauce		cup Roasted Duck Juices	lb Roasted Game Bird Bones	pint Demi Glace	oz Butter	oz Mirepoix	oz White Wine	oz Game or Poultry Stock	20 oz	Brown the bones with mirepoix deglaze with wine. Add the demi. Simmer for 45 minutes with dark meat. Strain liquid, dice the meat. Thicken with juices, season.
72	**Soubise**			lb White Onions	pint Thick Béchamel	oz Water	oz Heavy Cream			3 cups	Dice the onions and sweat them with the water in a covered pot. Once cooked add in the béchamel and slowly cook for 20 minutes. Puree and strain. Finish with cream.
73	**Shellfish Cream** Sauce Americaine- Lobster Sauce Nantua –Crawfish Sauce Crevette –Shrimp		1 ea Bay Leaf / 1 Garlic Clove	lb Shellfish Shells / 1 Shallot	pint Fish Stock / 1 Shot Cognac	oz Tomato Paste	oz Mirepoix chopped	oz Whole Butter	oz Heavy Cream	1 pint	Sauté the shells in 1 oz of butter. Add the minced garlic, shallot, tomato paste, and mirepoix. Flambé with cognac. Deglaze with stock and reduce until 1 cup remains. Strain into a pot with cream. Simmer; finish with butter and fines herbes.
74	**Supreme**		1 qt White Stock	pint Cream	qt Veloute		ea Egg Yolks	oz Whole Butter	oz Mushroom Liquid	1.5 qt	Simmer the veloute, mushroom and stock, reduce. Thicken with eggs and cream, butter finish
75	**Tomato- French**	3 tbsp Flour	lb Mirepoix brunoise	tbsp Shallot	tbsp minced Garlic	oz Olive Oil	oz Butter	lb Tomato Concassé	oz Tomato Paste	1 qt	Brown mirepoix in oil, add shallot, garlic, singer with flour. Add tomatoes. Simmer and puree.
76	**Veloute**			qt Stock	cup Cream			oz Roux		1 qt	Thicken stock, simmer 30 minutes , strain. Cream and season
77	**Viennoise**			ea Lemon zested	tsp chopped Caraway	oz chopped Dill Pickle				1 qt	Use 1 recipe of Sauce Hongroise. Add this mixture to the sour cream when tempering it into the sauce.
78	**Zingara**	4 oz White Wine	1 tbsp Black Truffle	oz Dry Sherry	oz Whole Butter	cups Demi Glace	oz Ham fine julienne	oz Mushroom fine julienne	oz French Tomato Sauce	20 oz	Poach the mushroom and fine julienne truffle in wines. Heat sauces, combine everything and finish with butter, season with cayenne and salt

Modern Sauce Preparations

#	Item			1	2	3	4	Yield	Method of Preparation
79	Cauliflower Puree	1 pint Chicken Stock	½ cup Onion diced	head Cauliflower, chopped	cups Cream	tbsp Basmati Rice	tbsp Butter	24 oz	Sweat onions in butter, add all but cream. Simmer over low heat until only ½ cup of liquid remains and rice is falling apart. Add cream, reduce by half. Pour in a Vita prep blender. Puree until very smooth. Season to taste with salt and white pepper.
80	Corn Foam		1/8th tsp Xanthan Gum	oz Butter	sheets Gelatin	oz Cream	ea Corn Cob	12 oz	Soak gelatin sheet in 1 quart of cold water for 1 hour. Cut kernels from corn and milk the cob. Combine all ingredients puree to a liquid using a Vita prep blender. Liquid should be about 130° when done. Pour into a siphon, use 2-3 charges
81	Herb Oil			Tsp Salt	cups Salad Oil	cups Parsley Leaves	cups Herb Leaves	1 pint	Don't pack the herbs when measuring. Boil in salted water for 1 full minute. Strain, shock and squeeze dry. Combine oil, salt and herbs in a Vita prep and blend for 1-2 minutes on high to extract the chlorophyll and flavor. Strain through fine chinoise or linen
82	Hollandaise Foam		1 tsp White Wine Vinegar	cup Melted Butter	tbsp lemon Juice	dash Tabasco	ea Egg Yolks	14 oz	Bring butter to 165°. Place everything else in a blender, cover with foil and poke 12 wholes in foil. Slowly add the hot butter to emulsify and thicken. Season to taste. Pour into a siphon and add 2 charges. The foam yields a quart of hollandaise
83	Mornay Fondue	½ tsp Xanthan Gum	1 ea Shallot	pint Heavy cream	cups grated Gruyere	ea Cloves		28 oz	Stud Shallot with cloves. Steam shallot and cream in stainless steel container, covered with plastic wrap for 10 minutes. Place grated cheese in blender with gum, Strain in hot cream and puree in a Vita prep blender until smooth. Season.
84	Nouvelle Demi		25 lb Veal Bones	Bouquet Garni	cups Tomato Paste	lbs Mirepoix	gallons Veal Stock	1.5 Gal	Roast veal bones until evenly browned. Place bones in a clean roasting pan and brush with tomato paste. Roast again until the tomato paste is dark brown. Sweat vegetables in 1 oz of the veal bone fat until onions begin to caramelize. Add stock, bouquet, bones and simmer covered at 185° for 18 hours. Degrease stock, strain. In a 3 gallon stock pot brown the tomato paste. Add strained stock in thirds; scrape the tomato fond to release from pot. Simmer 2 hours at 200°. Remove any scum that rises to the surface. Sprinkle gum over the demi to thicken. Strain and chill to 40° within 2 hours for future use.
				cup Tomato Paste		tsp Xanthan Gum			
85	Parsnip Puree		1 grate Nutmeg	ea Shallot minced	lbs Peeled Parsnips sliced	cups Cream	tbsp Butter	1 quart	Sweat shallots and butter, add parsnips and cream. Simmer covered until parsnips are very tender, remove parsnips and place in a Vita prep blender. Add seasonings to cream and reduce until it very thick. Scrape liquids into blender, puree until very smooth.
86	Sea Urchin Foam	¼ tsp Xanthan Gum		oz Cognac / Pint Cream	oz Sea Urchin Roe	tbsp minced Shallot	oz Nantue Butter #100	18 oz	Soak gelatin sheet in 1 quart of cold water for 1 hour. Melt 1 oz of Nantue Butter to sweat shallots, flambé with cognac, add cream and simmer. Place Roe in Vita prep blender with remaining butter, gelatin. Strain the hot cream into the blender and puree until smooth. Season. Strain into a siphon, use 2 charges.
87	Sorrel Foam	1½ cup White Wine / ½ tsp Xanthan Gum	1 pint Fish Stock / 1 Sachet	oz Shallot / cup Cream	cups Chiffonade Sorrel	cups Spinach	sheets Gelatin	1 pint	Soak gelatin sheet in 1 quart of cold water for 1 hour. Blanch and shock the spinach, squeeze dry. Reduce the fish stock, wine, sachet and shallots until syrupy. Strain into clean pan and simmer with cream and bloomed gelatin sheets until very thick. Pour liquid, spinach, gum, and Sorrel in Vita prep blender and blend until very smooth. Season, Strain into a siphon, use 2 charges.
88	Sweet Carrot Foam	3 oz Water	½ tsp Xanthan Gum	oz Sugar	ea Cinnamon Sticks	cups Carrots sliced thin	oz Heavy Cream	18 oz	Combine water, sugar, and cinnamon. Microwave covered for 1 minute. Add Carrots, toss, cover and microwave 4 minutes. Discard cinnamon sticks. Puree all ingredients using a Vita prep blender. Strain through a fine chinoise. Season and pour into a siphon, use 2-3 charges.

Compound Butter

#	Item		1	1	2	3	4		Yield	Method of Preparation
89	**Bercy**	8 ea Peppercorn	lb Butter	ea Lemon – juiced	cup White Wine	ea Shallots minced	tsp Tarragon chopped	¼ cup Parsley fine chop	18 oz	Bring wine, peppercorn, and shallots to a boil, reduce until ¼ remains, remove pepper. Cool and work into remaining ingredients. Season with 1 tsp sea salt. Refrigerate 12 hrs.
90	**Café de Paris**	½ tsp Curry Powder ½ tsp Tabasco	lb Butter Clove Garlic minced	tsp Worcestershire ea Lemon-juice and zest	tbsp Dijon tbsp Capers	ea Anchovy Filet-mash tsp Shallot minced	tbsp Fines Herb tbsp Parsley chopped	1 oz Madeira ¼ tsp White Pepper	21 oz	In a small food processor place 2 tsp kosher salt, anchovy, capers, lemon, wine, shallot and garlic. Puree and add rest. Pulse to blend Refrigerate 24 hrs.
91	**Chateaubriand**		tbsp Dijon	Maitre d' Hotel Butter	tbsp Fine Herbes	oz Meat Glace	tsp Tarragon chopped		21 oz	Melt glace, add herbs, mustard- work into soft Maitre d' Hotel butter. Refrigerate 24 hrs.
92	**Colbert**			recipe Maitre d' Hotel Butter	tbsp Tarragon	oz Meat Glace			20 oz	Melt glace, add herbs- work into soft Maitre d' Hotel butter. Refrigerate 24 hrs.
93	**Escargot**	tbsp Shallot minced		recipe Maitre d' Hotel butter	oz Garlic	oz White Wine			20 oz	Reduce shallot and wine until almost dry. Make a paste of garlic; add soft Maitre d' Hotel butter + reduction – Chill 4 hrs.
94	**"Faux" Gras** Use as a substitute for Foie Gras on Steaks or in sauces.	½ tsp Truffle Oil	lb Butter	cup Madeira	ea Shallot – minced	tsp Sea Salt	oz Duck Livers	¼ tsp White Pepper	22 oz	Melt 4 oz of the butter and sweat the shallots, add the liver and wine. Reduce and baste until livers are fully cooked and only 1 cup of liquid remains. Chill 24 hours, puree until smooth, mix in rest, use soft butter. Refrigerate 24 hrs.
95	**Garlic**	tsp Paprika		recipe Maitre d' Hotel butter		tsp Sea Salt	tbsp Garlic Paste		19 oz	Prepared the Maitre d hotel butter with the addition of paprika & garlic – Chill 4 hrs.
96	**Herb**	3 tbsp Basil finely chopped	lb Butter	ea Lemon-juiced	tsp Kosher Salt	tbsp Parsley fine chopped	tbsp Fines Herb	1 tsp Ground Black Pepper	20 oz	Combine all herbs into soften butter. Add seasoning and lemon last. Form and refrigerate 4 hours.
97	**Maitre d' Hotel**		lb Butter	ea Lemon-juiced	tsp Kosher Salt		tbsp Parsley fine chopped	1 tsp Ground Black Pepper	17 oz	Combine all ingredients into soften butter. Form and refrigerate 4 hours.
98	**Marchand de Vin**	10 ea Peppercorn	lb Butter	tbsp Lemon – juiced	ea Shallots minced	cup Red Wine	tbsp Meat Glace	¼ cup Parsley fine chopped	20 oz	Bring wine, peppercorn, and shallots to a boil, reduce until ¼ remains, remove pepper, add glace to melt and cool. Work in remaining ingredients. Season with 2 tsp kosher salt. Refrigerate 12 hrs.
99	**Moutarde**		lb Butter	tbsp Champagne Vinegar	oz Dijon Mustard	oz Pommery Mustard		1 tsp Dry Coleman's Mustard®	21 oz	Combine Coleman's and vinegar; allow to sit for 30 minutes. Add in the rest and mix well. Refrigerate 4 hours.
100	**Nantue**	1 ea Shallot-sliced	ea Bay Leaf	Recipe Maitre d' Hotel butter	oz Cognac	oz Lobster Glace	oz White Wine	¼ cup Tomato Paste	23 oz	Warm wine, add bay leaf and shallot, steep 30 minutes. Add cognac, simmer and reduce by ¾, keep liquid in pot, add tomato, lobster stir and cool. Mix into Maitre d butter- chill 4 hrs.
101	**Verde**	3 tbsp Cilantro chopped	lb Butter	ea Lime juiced	tsp Sea Salt	tbsp Green Onion minced	tbsp Parsley fine chopped	1 tsp Red Pepper Flakes	20 oz	Puree all ingredients first then add into soften butter. Form and refrigerate 4 hours.

Chefs Note: Roll compound butter to form cylinder using wax paper or plastic. The meat glace in several recipes is a highly concentrated stock known as Glace de Viande.

Cold Sauces

#	Item	1	2	3	4	8			Yield	Method of Preparation
102	Aioli	tsp Salt	oz Sherry Vinegar	ea Egg Yolks	tbsp Garlic minced		1 pint Extra Virgin Olive Oil	pinch Cayenne	20 oz	Combine egg yolks, salt, cayenne, garlic in blender. Puree, add vinegar, puree and slowly add the oil on medium speed. If the Aioli becomes too thick add a little water.
103	Chili Sauce	tsp Red Pepper Flake	oz Cider Vinegar	drop Tabasco®	tsp Onion Flakes	oz Ketchup	½ tsp Worcestershire	¼ tsp Allspice	9 oz	Combine vinegar, onion, allspice, pepper. Microwave 45 seconds on high. Stir in rest.
104	Chutney	ea Garlic Clove- minced	oz Red Onion- diced	oz Brown Sugar	oz Vinegar	oz Dried Fruit- diced	2 cup Fruit – Firm Flesh	½ oz Quatre Spice	1.5 lb	Dice fruit, combine with everything and simmer. Reduce by ¾ and chill
105	Cocktail Sauce	recipe Chili Sauce	oz Ketchup	ea Lemon	tbsp Horseradish				1 pint	Juice lemons, add and mix in the rest. Chill overnight
106	Cumberland Sauce	ea Lemon + Orange. zested and juiced	tbsp Shallot- minced	cup Currant Jelly	ea thin slices Fresh Ginger		1 ½ cup Ruby Port Wine	1 tbsp Mustard	1 qt	Combine everything in a pot and bring to a boil for 5 minutes. Season with cayenne pepper and strain- chill.
107	Gribiche Sauce	ea Hard Boiled Egg	oz Vinegar	tsp Fine Herbes	oz Olive oil		tsp Mustard	2 tbsp Capers	8 oz	Chop egg and chop herbs, add to the vinaigrette base and chill
108	Honey Mustard Sauce	Tbsp Cider Vinegar	Tbsp Yellow Mustard	oz Dijon Mustard	oz Honey				8 oz	Combine all and whisk until smooth. Use other mustards for variations.
109	Horseradish Dill	tbsp Lemon Juice	tbsp Fresh Dill - chop						11 oz	Add to the horseradish recipe below.
110	Horseradish Sauce	tsp Worcestershire	oz Horseradish			oz Sour Cream			10 oz	Combine all ingredients and season to taste
111	Marie-Rose	pinch Cayenne		3 tbsp Ketchup		oz Mayo	½ tsp Worcestershire	1 tbsp Brandy	10 oz	Combine all ingredients and season to taste
112	Mustard Sauce		oz Cider Vinegar		oz Dijon Mustard	oz Mayo			14 oz	Combine all ingredients and season to taste.
113	Ravigote Sauce	tbsp Dijon Mustard / ea Shallot minced	ea Hardboiled Eggs- peel and chop fine	tbsp sliced Chive	tbsp Champagne Vinegar	ea Capers minced / oz Oil	¼ cup finely chopped Parsley	4 ea Cornichon minced	9 oz	In a blender combine vinegar, Dijon, and oil. Blend until smooth mix in the rest by hand. Refrigerate 2 hours to serve. Goes well with poached or smoked fish as well as cold roast beef or pork.
114	Red Onion Gastrique	lb Red Onions- Minced	tbsp Lemon Juice	oz Sugar	oz Red Wine Vinegar	oz Red Wine	pinch Fresh Pepper	pinch Salt	1 lb	Marinate all ingredients for 30 minutes. Reduce over heat until liquid is syrupy. Chill before serving.
115	Remoulade Sauce	tbsp chopped Tarragon	ea Cornichon	tsp Caper	tsp Dijon	oz Mayo		1 each Anchovy	10 oz	Chop items very fine then combine with mayonnaise. Season and chill
116	Sauce Vert	cup Mayonnaise	tbsp Tarragon	tsp Caper	oz Sour Cream		1 cup Spinach	1 tbsp Dill	10 oz	Puree herbs, spinach and capers then add the mayo and sour cream. Chill.
117	Tartar Sauce	tbsp Capers chopped		tbsp Fines Herbes		oz Mayo	1 tbsp Dill Pickle- finely minced	½ ea Lemon Juiced	10 oz	For this recipe use fines herbes with equal part parsley, tarragon, chive and dill. Combine with the rest and chill.
118	Virginia Beach Shrimp Sauce		oz Horseradish- grated	oz Lemon Juice	oz Sour Cream	oz Ketchup	½ tsp Tabasco	½ tsp Old Bay Seasoning®	8 oz	Combine all ingredients together and refrigerate overnight. Strain out the horseradish. Serve with fried seafood.

Salsas

#	Recipe			1	1	2	3	4	8	Yield	Method
119	Basic Salsa Recipe	¼ cup Cilantro-minced	¾ cup Red Onion-minced	ea Lime Juice	ea Jalapeño-minced	cup Main Ingredient-minced	ea Serrano Chilies-minced			3 cups	Combine and season to taste. Use fruit or tomato for main ingredient. Pico de Gallo- Use tomato for the main ingredient
120	Black Bean Salsa			cup Black Beans	ea Tomato-diced					3 cups	Add these ingredients to the basic salsa 119
121	Tomato Salsa	½ ea Lime juiced	1 oz Cilantro chopped	ea Jalapeño minced	oz Red Onion minced	ea Tomato diced				12 oz	Combine everything a bowl and season to taste.
122	Tomato Avocado Salsa			ea Avocado-diced						16 oz	Add the diced avocado the tomato salsa recipe 121
123	Tomatillo Papaya Salsa			cup diced Papaya	tbsp Olive Oil				oz diced Tomatillo	24 oz	Add these ingredients to the basic salsa recipe 119 .
124	Mango Salsa	½ cup Red Pepper brunoise	1 ea Jalapeño	ea Mango	oz diced Red Onion	tbsp Cilantro chopped	tbsp Lime Juice			12oz	Dice the mango and finely chop the jalapeno. Mix with everything else. Season.
125	Smoked Tomato Salsa	½ tsp Salt	1 oz Olive Oil	ea Lime juiced	ea Jalapeño-minced	oz diced Red Pepper	ea Chipotle Chilies-pureed	ea Smoked Tomatoes-diced		16 oz	Puree the chipotle with lime juice, oil, and salt. Mix with everything and season to taste.
126	Smoked Pepper Guacamole	¼ cup Lime Juice	¼ cup Cilantro chopped	oz Sour Cream		ea Avocado-ripe	tbsp Red Onion minced		oz diced Smoked Peppers	16 oz	In a bowl mash the avocado, lime, and cilantro. Add everything else and season to taste
127	Salsa Blanca *	1 ea Garlic Clove minced	1 tsp Ground Cumin	cup Mayonnaise*	tbsp Sugar	tsp Jalapeno minced	oz Buttermilk	ea Oregano Leaves-chopped	ea Cilantro Leaves -chopped	1.5 cup	Mix the sugar and water then combine everything in a bowl and season to taste.
128	Salsa Borracha	½ ea Lime Juiced	1 oz Tequila	ea Jalapeño minced	oz Red Onion minced	ea Yellow Tomato diced				12 oz	Combine everything in a bowl and season to taste.
129	Salsa Guacamole			ea Jalapeño seeded-minced	ea Lime juiced	ea Avocado-ripe	tbsp chopped Cilantro	tsp minced Red Onion		1.5 cup	In a bowl mash the chili, avocado, mix in the rest. Season to taste.
130	Salsa Margarita	1 oz Tequila	1 tsp Kosher Salt	ea Orange segmented and diced	ea Jalapeno-minced	ea Limes segmented and diced			oz Jicama shredded	2 cup	Combine everything in a bowl and season to taste.
131	Salsa Roja		oz Cilantro	ea Red Onion	ea Lime-juiced	ea Jalapeño				1.5 cup	Mince everything and combine. Season.
132	Salsa Verde	½ oz Olive Oil	1 tbsp Cilantro chopped	oz Red Onion diced	ea Jalapeño Pepper	tbsp Lime Juice			ea Tomatillos-roast and peeled	16 oz	Puree all of the ingredients until smooth. Season to taste.

*Traditionally this sauce is made from Miracle Whip, this recipe has been adjusted with additional sugar. The original sauce was created at El Torro Mexican restaurant in Virginia Beach in the 1970's.

Condiments

#	Name	1/2	3/4	1	1	2	3	4	Yield	Method of Preparation
133	Mustard	cup Dry Mustard / cup Cider Vinegar	tsp Salt / tsp Tabasco®	tbsp Sugar			tsp Honey	ea Egg Yolks	8 oz	1. Over a double boiler whip the eggs, vinegar, and honey to 120° 2. Whisk in everything else. Pack in sealable container. Refrigerate.
134	Green Peppercorn Mustard			tbsp Green Peppercorns					8 oz	Add the green peppercorns to the mustard recipe #133
135	Horseradish Mustard					tbsp Horseradish			8 oz	Add the horseradish to mustard recipe #133.
136	Tomato Catsup	cup Honey / cup Lemon Juice	cup Sugar	tsp Whole Clove / tbsp Paprika	pint Cider Vinegar	cup chopped Onion / ea Cinnamon Stick	ea clove Garlic- minced	pint Tomato Puree / oz Tomato Paste	28 oz	1. Combine everything in a 1 qt pot and bring to simmer. 2. Simmer for 15 minutes. Strain and chill. Refrigerate.
137	Classic Mayonnaise	tsp Salt	oz Champagne Vinegar	cup Salad Oil / ea Garlic Clove	ea Lemon Juice	ea Egg Yolks	drops Worcestershire Sauce	tsp Dijon Mustard	12 oz	Place mustard, eggs, salt, lemon, vinegar in blender. Puree on high speed for 1 minute. Slowly drizzle in the oil. Adjust the consistency with water. Season Refrigerate.
138	American Mayonnaise	tsp Salt	oz Cider Vinegar	cup Canola Oil	ea Lemon Juice	ea Egg Yolks	drops Tabasco®	tsp Mustard Powder	12 oz	Place mustard, eggs, salt, lemon, vinegar in blender. Puree on high speed for 1 minute. Slowly drizzle in the oil. Adjust the consistency with water. Season with Tabasco® Refrigerate until needed.
139	Chipotle Mayonnaise		tbsp chopped Cilantro	cup Mayo	ea Lime juiced	oz Oil	each Chipotle Chili Pepper		11 oz	In a blender combine chilies, lime, and oil. Puree until smooth. Blend in mayo and herb. Refrigerate
140	Benne Seed Mayonnaise	oz Rice Vinegar		cup Mayo	tbsp Sesame Oil	tbsp Toasted Sesame Seed			9 oz	Mix everything in a bowl until blended. Season to taste. Refrigerate.
141	Spicy Horseradish Mayonnaise			cup Mayo	tbsp Prepared Wasabi		oz Horseradish		10 oz	Mix all ingredients in a bowl until well blended. Refrigerate.
142	Whole Mustard Mayonnaise			cup Mayo			oz Pommery Mustard		10 oz	Mix all ingredients in a bowl until well blended. Refrigerate.
143	Herb Mayonnaise	ea Lemon juiced		cup Mayo		tbsp Fine Herbes minced			10 oz	Mix all ingredients in a bowl until well blended. Refrigerate.
144	Honey Mustard			cup Dijon Mustard		oz Yellow Mustard	oz Honey		13 oz	Mix Well

BBQ Sauces

#	Item	1/2	1	1	2	4	8		Yield	Method of Preparation
145	**Eastern Carolina BBQ**	cup Sugar	tsp Cayenne	qt. Cider Vinegar	oz Molasses	oz Hot Sauce	oz Water	1 tbsp Dry Mustard	6 cups	Mix spices in water. Add rest and whisk. Allow to sit 1 day –covered.
146	**Hawaiian Style BBQ**	cup Hoisin Sauce	oz Soy Sauce	tbsp Fresh Ginger	oz Rice Vinegar	oz Ketchup / oz Honey	oz Pineapple Juice	tsp Black –Pepper	2.5 cups	Combine all ingredients and bring to boil. Serve with roast pig.
147	**Kansas City BBQ**	tsp Allspice	tsp Liquid Smoke	bottle Ketchup (32 oz)	tbsp Dark Chili Powder / tsp Black Pepper	tbsp minced Garlic / oz Molasses	oz Brown Sugar / oz Apple Juice	1 ¼ cup Cider Vinegar	6.5 cups	Simmer spices in apple juice and reduce by half. Add rest and simmer 15 minutes on low heat. Use as a finishing sauce on ribs, or as a dipping sauce.
148	**Kentucky BBQ**	cup Bourbon	tbsp Yellow Mustard	bottle Ketchup (32 oz)	tbsp Worcestershire Sauce	oz Cider Vinegar	oz Brown Sugar	1 tbsp Grilling Spice #1103	6 cups	Combine sugar, bourbon, and spices. Bring to boil and flambé. Add rest simmer for 5 minutes.
149	**Low Country Mustard BBQ**	cup Cider Vinegar	tbsp Red Pepper Flakes	quart Yellow Mustard	tsp Worcestershire	oz Brown Sugar	oz Beer / oz Chili Sauce	2 ½ tsp Garlic Salt	6.5 cups	Mix beer, sugar and spices in a 2 quart pot and simmer for 3 minutes. Add rest and simmer 5 minutes. Use for pulled pork.
150	**Memphis BBQ Dipping Sauce**	oz Hot Sauce / tsp Cayenne	tbsp Chili Powder / oz Yellow Mustard	tsp Thyme / tsp Oregano	tbsp Butter / tbsp Garlic / tbsp Molasses	tsp Worcestershire / oz minced Onion	oz Ketchup / oz Beer	3 oz Vinegar / ¼ cup Brown Sugar	3 cups	In a 1 quart sauce pot sweat the garlic and onion in butter. Add beer and spices, simmer 4 minutes. Add rest and simmer 3 minutes. A thin sauce for dipping dry rub ribs.
151	**Saint Louis Basting BBQ**	oz Tabasco®	#10 can Ketchup (114 oz)	qt Apple Juice / lb Brown Sugar	oz Worcestershire Sauce	oz Molasses	oz Yellow Mustard / cloves Garlic	1 large Onion –chop / 3 cups Cider Vinegar	6 quart	In a blender puree the onion and garlic with 1 cup of the apple juice until smooth. Combine all ingredients and bring to boil, simmer 20 min. Use for grilled pork, chicken, or beef.
152	**Spicy Texas Style BBQ**	cup Chili Powder	tbsp Cumin / tbsp Chipotle Powder	bottle Ketchup (32 oz)	cups Vinegar / oz Worcestershire Sauce	oz Jar Pepper Vinegar / oz Yellow Mustard	clove Garlic / oz Onions minced	1cup Brown Sugar / 1 tbsp Oil	2 quart	Mince garlic and jar of peppers, save juice. Sauté onions, garlic and peppers. Add rest and simmer 20 minutes over very low heat. Use of smoked beef brisket.
153	**Traditional BBQ**	cup Soy Sauce	oz Black Pepper	quart Chili Sauce	tbsp Granulated Garlic	cups Cider Vinegar	oz Brown Sugar	3 cups Ketchup	3 quart	Combine ingredients and bring to a simmer for 5 minutes,
154	**Virginia Beach-BBQ**	oz Tabasco®	cup Yellow Mustard / tbsp Black Pepper	pint Cider Vinegar / tbsp Salt	oz Worcestershire Sauce	tbsp Lemon Juice	oz Honey / oz Ketchup	1 tbsp Red Pepper Flakes	5 cups	Combine – Bring to a boil, allow to stand 30 minutes. Use for pulled pork or a pig picking.
155	**Western Carolina BBQ- Lexington**	cup Chili Sauce	tsp Red Pepper Flakes	cup Ketchup	tsp Salt	oz Sugar / oz Hot sauce	oz Water	3 cups Cider Vinegar	6 cups	Combine all and bring to a boil, simmer for 8-10 minutes. Serve with BBQ pork shoulder slices.
156	**White BBQ Sauce Alabama**	tsp Salt	pint Cider Vinegar	jar Mayo (32 oz)	ea Lemons Juiced	tsp Tabasco		¼ cup Black Pepper	6 cups	Combine and refrigerate overnight. Use to grill chicken or catfish.

Chefs Note: The Carolinas are well known for the various BBQ sauces and methods. Vinegar and spice in the east. Heat and vinegar flavors in the Piedmont. Sweet and tangy in the Blue Ridge and mustard along the Low Country coast of the South Carolina. Whole pig in the East, picnics in the Piedmont and shoulders in the West are smoked until the meat pulls from the bone.

Relishes and Preserves

#	Name			1	1	2	3	4	8	16	Yield	Method
157	Basic Relish Seasoning	½ tsp Salt	1 tsp Cracked Pepper	oz White Wine Vinegar	oz Sugar						2 oz	Combine and bring to a boil to develop the flavor.
158	Corn Relish	½ tsp Dry Mustard	½ tsp Tabasco®	ea Jalapeño-chopped	ea Scallion slice	tbsp Brown Sugar	oz Red Pepper dice	drops Soy Sauce		oz Fresh Corn Kernels	12 oz	Combine everything except for the scallions. Simmer add scallion last.
159	Cranberry Pear Relish	1 tbsp Orange Zest		cup Pears diced	cup Cranberries Sauce						12 oz	Combine the ingredients and add to a single recipe of Basic Relish Seasoning 157.
160	Cranberry Pineapple Relish			cup Fresh Cranberries-crushed		tbsp Sugar			oz Pineapple diced		16 oz	Combine the ingredients and add to a single recipe of Basic Relish Seasoning 157.
161	Green Tomato Relish	¼ cup Kosher Salt	1 ea Onion diced	lb Green Tomato diced	cup Green Cabbage chopped		oz Red Pepper diced	oz Green Pepper diced				Place all of the vegetables in a bowl and toss with the salt. Refrigerate the vegetables overnight.
		½ tsp Turmeric	pint Sugar			tsp Celery Seed	tsp Mustard Seed		oz Water	oz Cider Vinegar	20 oz	Drain the vegetables and rinse very well. Combine veg with the rest of the items and simmer for 15 minutes.
162	Pineapple Vidalia Relish	½ cup Pepper diced		ea Serrano Chili brunoise					oz Vidalia Onion diced	oz Pineapple diced	20 oz	Combine the ingredients and add to a single recipe of Basic Relish Seasoning 157
163	Smoked Corn Chili Relish			lb Smoked Corn Kernels		tbsp Cilantro	ea Serrano Chili brunoise		oz Roast Poblano Chili-dice		20 oz	Combine the ingredients and add to a double recipe of Basic Relish Seasoning 157.
164	Yellow Tomato Relish	1 oz Olive Oil		tbsp Garlic minced	oz White Balsamic	ea Yellow Tomato	tbsp Basil chop	oz Red Onion minced	ea Chives slices		12 oz	Combine all ingredients and season to taste.
165	Chow Chow	2.5 cup Green Bean	1.5 cups Green Tomato	cup Red Pepper diced	head Cauliflower	cup Lima Beans	ea Green Pepper diced	cup Carrot-diced	ea Celery Rib- diced	oz Onion diced	48	Blanch the vegetables separately then add to the mixture below.
		4 cup Sugar	1 tsp Turmeric	quart Roasted Corn Kernels	cup Water			cup White Vinegar		ea Mustard Seed	oz	After all of the items are blanched simmer together for 10 minutes and cool.
166	Jalapeño Jelly	½ cup Pectin		cup Sherry Vinegar	ea Red Pepper	ea Green Pepper		cup Sugar	ea Jalapeño		16 oz	Fine dice all peppers and combine. Simmer for 20 minutes and add the pectin.
167	Basic Fruit Chutney	½ cup Red Onion brunoise	¾ cup Brown Sugar	tsp Garlic	ea Pepper brunoise	lb Fruit-diced	tbsp Ginger grated	oz White Wine Vinegar	oz Dried Fruit- diced		20 oz	Combine and simmer. Season with ground cinnamon, allspice, and coriander to taste.
168	Cranberry Sauce	1 lb Cranberries		ea Cinnamon Stick	ea Orange zested and juiced			ea Cloves	oz Sugar		16 oz	Place the spices in a sachet. Combine and simmer until the cranberries pop.

Chefs Note: Relishes go very nicely with Charcuterie platters of smoked meats and sausages. They are also served with grilled meat to compliment the smoky flavor of pork, steak, fish and seafood over a wood or charcoal fire.

Marinades

#	Recipe	1/2	3/4	1	1	2	3	4	8	16	Amount of product
169	Asian Grilling	cup Peanut Oil	bunch Cilantro	oz Sesame Oil	tbsp Annatto Seeds	oz Soy Sauce	tbsp Ginger Root	Sherry			Heat the oil and annatto, strain. Combine all ingredients in oil. Marinate 3 lbs of chicken, beef, fish, or pork for 30 minutes.
		oz Garlic- minced				tbsp Ground Cumin	tbsp Rice Wine Vinegar	ea Scallions- sliced			
170	Asian Pepper	cup Coconut Milk	oz Ginger- grated	bunch Cilantro	tsp Cracked Black Pepper	ea Garlic cloves- sliced	ea Jalapeño minced	ea Limes	oz Peanut Oil		Combine all ingredients. Marinate 2lb fish or chicken for 30 minutes.
171	Buttermilk		tsp Rosemary	qt Buttermilk	ea Garlic Clove	ea Onion minced	ea Bay Leaf				Combine all ingredients. Marinate 3 lb of white meat for 1 hour.
172	Caribbean Ceviche	cup Red Onion diced	cup Cilantro	cup Tomato diced	cup Mango- diced	ea Jalapeño minced	tbsp Sugar	cup Lime Juice	ea Segment Citrus		Combine all ingredients. Marinate 2.5 lb of seafood for 45 minutes.
173	Catalan Grilling	cup Balsamic	oz Garlic minced	oz Fresh Herbs	tsp Salt	oz Olive Oil	ea Bay Leaves	oz Red Wine	oz Onion sliced		Combine all ingredients. Marinate 3 lb lamb for 2 hours.
174	Chinese BBQ Rib			cup Sherry		oz Rice Wine Vinegar	oz Soy Sauce	oz Garlic Clove	oz Hoisin Sauce		Combine all ingredients. Marinate 2lb of chicken or pork for 1 hour.
175	Classic BBQ	oz Tabasco	oz Crushed Red Pepper	oz Worcestershire	tbsp Cracked Black Pepper	tbsp Brown Sugar	tsp Mustard	ea Garlic Clove	oz Cider Vinegar	oz Chili Sauce	Combine all ingredients. Marinate 3 lb of pork or chicken for 3 hours.
176	Classic Fish	oz Worcestershire	tsp Salt	pinch White Pepper	ea Garlic Clove	oz Lemon Juice		oz Olive Oil			Combine all ingredients. Marinate 2.5 lb of seafood for 20 minutes.
177	Classic French Grill	oz Fresh Thyme	tbsp Fennel Seed	ea Lemon Juice	tbsp Cracked Black Pepper	oz Olive oil	tbsp Shallot	ea Bay Leaves	oz. Burgundy		Combine all ingredients. Marinate 2 lb beef or pork for 2 hours.
178	Fried Chicken	tsp Celery Salt	tsp Thyme	tsp White Pepper	ea Garlic Clove- mashed	tsp Kosher Salt	tsp Black Pepper	tsp Lawry's Seasoning®	drops Tabasco	oz Buttermilk	Combine all ingredients. Marinate 4 lbs of chicken over night. Add 1 egg and mix well coat in flour Fry
179	Game / Braising		tbsp Tarragon			tsp Salt	ea Onions diced	ea Carrot- dice	ea Shallots chop	oz White Wine	Combine all ingredients.
		cup Red Wine Vinegar			tsp Cracked Black Pepper	oz Garlic Clove minced	ea Celery Stalk- slice	ea Bay Leaf			Marinate 5 lbs of game for up to 2 days.
180	Game Fowl Grilling	cup Soy Sauce	tsp Orange Zest	ea Onion minced	tsp Fresh Ginger	ea Garlic Clove	oz Olive Oil	oz Tawny Port Wine		ea Juniper	Combine all ingredients. Marinate 2 lb duck or goose for 2 hours.
181	Game- Steak Grill	tsp Pepper	tsp Marjoram	ea Onion minced	ea Garlic Clove minced	dash Worcestershire				oz Red Wine	Combine all ingredients. Marinate 2lb of venison for 2 hours.

Chefs Note: To save time and reduce waste products can be coated with the marinade then sealed in pouches.

Marinades

#	Recipe	1/2	3/4	1	1	2	3	4	8	16	Amount of product
182	Greek Grilling	bunch Parsley / tsp Fennel Seed		bunch Basil / tsp Oregano	tbsp Thyme / tsp Rosemary	ea Lemon Juice	tbsp Garlic minced	oz Olive Oil			Combine all ingredients. Marinate 2 lb lamb or chicken for 3 hours
183	Havana BBQ	tsp Oregano / tsp Cumin	tsp Allspice / tsp Pepper	packet Goya Sazon® / tsp Salt	oz lime Juice	ea Garlic Clove		oz Lemon Juice	oz Orange Juice		Combine all ingredients. Marinate 2 lb chicken, pork beef or fish steaks for 2 hours
184	London Broil	cup Oil		oz Worcestershire	bunch Thyme	tsp Black Pepper	tsp Old Bay Seasoning	oz Burgundy	ea Garlic Cloves- minced		Combine all ingredients. Marinate 2 lb beef for 2 hours
185	New York Bar & Grill	oz Dry Vermouth	ea Sprig Rosemary	tbsp Cracked Pepper	ea Bay Leaf	ea Garlic Clove	tbsp Dry Gin				Combine all ingredients. Marinate 2 lb venison or lamb for 1 hour in a bag.
186	Sauerbraten	oz Peppercorns		cup Red Wine	tbsp Juniper	ea Onion julienne	ea Bay Leaf	ea Cloves	oz Red Wine	oz Cider Vinegar	Combine all ingredients. Marinate 5 lbs of beef for 72 hours
187	Sautéed Fish	cup White Wine	cup Water	tbsp Worcestershire		ea Lemons Juiced					Combine all ingredients. Marinate 3 lbs of fish for 20 minutes
188	Southwest Lime	oz Cilantro	tsp Black Pepper	tsp Salt	tsp Cumin	dash Tabasco		ea Garlic Cloves	oz Lime Juice		Combine all ingredients. Marinate 2 lbs chicken or fish for 30 minutes
189	Southwest Adobo		tbsp Brown Sugar	oz Chipotle / tsp Cayenne	tbsp Honey	oz Olive Oil / oz Garlic Clove chopped	tbsp Ancho / tbsp Wine Vinegar	tbsp Pasilla Chilies		oz Tomato Puree	Puree all ingredients. Marinate 3 lb pork, chicken for 2 hours
190	Teriyaki Fish	oz Peanut Oil		tbsp Ginger minced	tsp Wasabi	ea Garlic Clove- minced	oz Sake		oz Soy Sauce		Combine all ingredients. Marinate 2lbs fish, shrimp, scallion for 20 minutes
191	Teriyaki Red Meat	bunch Green Onion- sliced		tbsp Ginger minced	oz Honey	oz Brown Sugar	ea Garlic Clove	oz Beer	oz Soy Sauce		Combine all ingredients. Marinate 3lb beef steaks for 2 hours.
192	Teriyaki White Meat			oz Honey	ea Ginger Coins	ea Garlic Clove	oz Sherry	oz Peanut Oil	oz Soy Sauce		Combine all ingredients. Marinate 2 lb chicken, pork for 1 hour
193	Venison Grilling	tbsp Garlic	2 ea Bay Leaf	tsp Juniper	sprig Thyme	oz Red Wine Vinegar	oz Oil	ea Parsley Sprig	oz Shallot - minced	oz Red Wine	Combine all ingredients. Marinate 2 lb of venison for 2 hours
194	Veracruz Grilling	cup Orange juice	cup Chili Powder	ea Lemon Juiced	tsp Cayenne	tsp Salt	tsp Pepper	oz Lime Juice	oz Olive Oil		Combine all ingredients. Marinate 2 lb fish, chicken, or shrimp for 20 minutes.

Chefs Note: When grilling items that have been marinated it is very important to dab dry all of the marinade to avoid the burned oil smoke that can occur. This smoke leaves behind a black soot or carbon that is unhealthy and undesirable.

Garde Manger - Cures, Brines and Seasoning

	Item	1	2	3	4	5	6	7	8	Yield	Method
195	**Basic Cure**	lb Kosher Salt	oz Curing Salt*			16 oz Sugar				1.5 lb	Combine to cure 5 lbs of meat- Rinse, Dry overnight. Can be used for smoked or non-smoked applications
196	**Bourbon Smoked Salmon**	ea Salmon Filet Side		oz Bourbon	tbsp Black Pepper	4 oz Kosher Salt	5 oz Brown Sugar		ea Orange Slices	1 side	Mix the sugar and salt to make cure. Layer in cheesecloth, oranges, cure, salmon, cheesecloth, cure, pepper, cheesecloth, bourbon. Wrap with plastic. Cure for 4 days, flip each day. Rinse, Dry overnight, Cold smoke for 30 minutes.
197	**Fish Brine**	gallon Water	tbsp Pickling Spice	oz Brown Sugar		2 tbsp Honey	6 oz Kosher Salt			1 gal	Boil and cool- use for 5 lb fish brine for 1 hour. Rinse, Dry overnight, Smoke for 30 minutes.
198	**Grava Lox**	ea Salmon Filet Side	tbsp Cracked Black Pepper	oz Pernod	tbsp Dill	6 oz Kosher Salt	5 oz Sugar		ea Lemon Slices	1 side	Mix the sugar and salt to make cure. Layer in cheesecloth, lemon, cure, salmon, cheesecloth, dill, cure, pepper, cheesecloth, pernod. Wrap with plastic. Cure for 4 days, flip each day.
199	**Ham Brine**	Cup Sugar		oz Honey	oz Curing Salt*	1.5 gal Water	1 tbsp Cloves		14 oz Kosher Salt	1.5 gal	Boil and cool- use for 12 lb ham- brine for 7 days. Rinse, Dry overnight- Smoke for 2 hours.
200	**Pickled Meat Brine**	tbsp Curing Salt*	cups Onion julienne	cups Water	oz Pickling Spice	2 Tbsp Salt	1 quart Cider Vinegar		1 cup Sugar	½ gal	Combine- Use to pickle ribs, pork butt, or brisket for 2-5 days, 5-8lbs of meat
201	**Poultry Brine**	gallon Water	Oz Sweet Wine	oz Sugar	½ oz Curing Salt*		6 oz Kosher Salt		oz. Honey	1 gal	Boil and cool- use for 8 lb poultry- brine overnight. Rinse, Dry overnight, Smoke for 30 minutes.
202	**Pastrami Brine**	cup Curing Salt*	Tbsp Black Pepper and Coriander	tbsp Pickling Spice	Quarts Water	1 tsp Cloves and Juniper Berries	2 oz Kosher Salt		Ea Bay Leaf	1 gal	Mix ingredients for brine. Brine 10# of beef for 72 hours, turn daily. Soak in water for 3 days after. Rub with a ½ cup coriander and ¼ cup black pepper, smoke.
203	**Seafood Brine**	gallon Water	tbsp Pickling Spice	tbsp Soy Sauce		5 oz Sugar	6 oz Kosher Salt			1 gal	Boil and cool- use for 6 lb seafood- brine for 30 minutes. Rinse, Dry overnight, Smoke for 30 minutes.
204	**Teriyaki Tuna Cure**	oz Pickled Ginger	oz Soy Sauce	oz Sugar	oz Kosher Salt	2 tbsp Cure Salt*	2 tbsp Black Pepper			10 oz	Combine- use for 2 lbs of tuna. Cure for 5 days, Rinse, Dry overnight, Cold smoke for 30 minutes.
205	**Allemande Spice**	tsp White Pepper	oz minced Onion	tsp Kosher Salt		½ tsp Celery Seed	½ tsp Mace			2.5 oz	Grind the spices and use for ground pork items.
206	**Espagnole Spice**	tsp Black Pepper	tbsp Paprika	tsp Kosher Salt	ea Garlic clove	3 tsp Cr. Red Pepper	1 tsp Oregano			2 oz	Combine and use for ground pork or poultry items.
207	**Italian Spice**	tbsp Fennel Seed	tsp Cr. Red pepper	tsp Paprika	ea clove Garlic	1 tbsp Kosher Salt	1 tbsp Black Pepper			1.75 oz	Combine and use for ground pork or poultry items.
208	**Pâté Spice**	tsp White Pepper tsp Thyme	tsp Dry Ginger tsp Coriander			1 tsp Dry Chervil 1 tsp Nutmeg	1 Bay Leaf 2 tsp Clove			1 oz	Grind to a fine powder Store in sealed container
209	**Quatre Spice**	tsp White Pepper	tsp Ground Ginger			1 tsp Nutmeg	1 tsp Clove			½ oz	Grind to a fine paste

*Use Morton's Tender Quick as the curing salt in these recipes.

Garde Manger Doughs

	Item	1	2	3	4				Yield	Method of Preparation
210	Barquette Dough	cup Semolina Flour	tsp Olive Oil	ea Egg Yolk		1/4 tsp Salt	2 oz Ice Water		12 oz	Combine all ingredients in a food processor and pulse with the dough attachment until smooth. Roll through a pasta machine, cut, and bake at 350° until golden brown.
211	Brioche Dough — Use this dough for canapé toast bases.	lb Bread Flour	oz Fresh Yeast	oz Milk At 110°	oz Sugar	5 ea Eggs	½ oz Salt	11 oz Soft Butter	2 lb	Step 1. Blend the fresh yeast with the warm milk, sugar, and ¼ of the flour for 30 minutes. Knead the remaining flour, eggs, and salt for 7 minutes on medium speed. Cool to 75° Step 2. Mix the soft butter into the cooled dough on low speed with a paddle. Refrigerate dough overnight. Shape, proof at 78° before baking.
212	Cracker Dough	ea Egg	cup Bread Flour	oz Milk	tsp Sugar	3 oz Butter	1 tsp Salt	2 tsp Baking Powder	1 lb	Place the dry ingredient in a food processor with the butter and pulse with dough attachment until it is a coarse texture. Remove, add liquids, and knead consistent dough. Roll in pasta machine.
213	Corn Pâté Dough	lb Bread Flour / tsp White Vinegar	tsp Salt / ea Eggs		oz Cornmeal	2 tbsp Milk Powder	2 tsp Baking Powder	8 oz Butter / 5 oz Milk	3 lb	Follow the same method as recipe # 212. Mix the milk powder into the milk. Butter the mold. Egg wash. Bake at 400° until brown.
214	Pâté Dough	lb Bread Flour / tsp White Vinegar	tsp Salt / ea Egg Yolk		oz Eggs	2 tbsp Milk Powder	2 tsp Baking Powder	8 oz Butter / 4 oz Milk	3 lb	Follow the same method as recipe #212. Mix the milk powder into the milk. Butter the mold. Egg wash. Bake at 400° until brown.
215	Phyllo Dough	ea Egg	oz Extra Virgin Olive Oil		oz Warm Water	1 tsp White Vinegar	pinch Salt	10 oz Bread Flour	1 lb	Place everything in a mixer with a dough hook and knead for 10 minutes. Relax at room temperature for 30 minutes before stretching the dough over a floured pastry/table cloth.
216	Wheat Pâté Dough	tsp White Vinegar	tsp Salt / ea Eggs		oz Yolks	12 oz Whole Wheat / 2 tbsp Milk Powder	2 tsp Baking Powder	8 oz Butter / 4 oz Milk	3 lb	Follow the same method as recipe # 212. Mix the milk powder into the milk. Butter the mold. Egg wash. Bake at 400° until brown.
217	Wisconsin Cheese Crackers	ea Egg	tsp Baking Powder	oz Butter		2 oz Milk	10 oz Flour	9 oz grated Sharp Cheese	1.5 lb	Make paste with cheese and butter. Place the dry ingredient in a food processor with paste and pulse with dough attachment until it is a coarse texture. Add the liquids; knead to form consistent dough. Roll into log. Freeze, slice and bake at 350°.

Garde Manger – Forcemeats and Pâté

	Item	1	2	3	4	5	6	8	Yield	Method
218	Aspic Gelée	cup Mirepoix-julienne	oz Tomato Puree	ea Egg Whites	lb Ground Chicken Carcass- no fat	1 Sachet	1 pint Cold Water	1 gallon Clear Stock 8 oz Gelatin Powder	1 gal	Combining all of the ingredients in this line in a tall narrow stock pot. Place on stove and stir until it reaches 120°. Stop stirring allow the raft to form. Baste the raft over very low heat for 2 hour. Strain the clear liquid through coffee filters. Combine the gelatin and cold water. Add gelatin to the hot consommé and stir with a spoon. Season to taste. Chill to serve.
219	Panada	oz Brandy	ea Eggs	oz Flour	oz Cream				11 oz	Combine all ingredients together until smooth. Use to bind forcemeats
220	Basic Forcemeat	lb Meat- diced				1 tbsp Kosher Salt	8 oz Fat Back	oz Ice	2 lb	Season meat and fat overnight, grind, puree with ice until smooth. Cook to an internal temperature of 165°
221	Chicken Liver Pâté	lb Chicken Liver tbsp Brandy	ea Bay Leaf	tbsp Sherry			1 ea Shallot- sliced	oz Butter	1.5 lb	Simmer butter, shallot and bay covered for 15 minutes. Add Sherry and Poach livers until they reach 165° Discard bay leaf Chill overnight, puree until smooth, season with salt and white pepper add Brandy. Puree until smooth.
222	Contemporary Forcemeat	lb Meat	oz Glace or Flavoring	oz Egg White		1 tsp Curing Salt*		oz Cream	1.5lb	Dice main item. Partially freeze. Grind. Puree in food processor. Add in salt. Flavoring or glace. Puree. Add in egg, puree. Add in cream puree. Season. Cook to an internal temperature of 165°
223	Country Style Forcemeat	1 tbsp kosher salt 1 tbsp Pate Spice	lb Pork Butt ea Garlic Clove		oz Onion	1 tsp Curing Salt* ½ tsp White Pepper	9 oz Panada	oz Liver	3 lb	Dice the pork butt and season with all spices. Large grind with livers Combine with panada and season to taste. Cook to 165°
224	Cured Forcemeat	tbsp Kosher Salt tsp White Pepper	lb Meat tbsp Quatre Spice			1 tsp Curing Salt*		oz Bacon	2.5 lb	Dice the meats and season overnight with all spices. Large grind once Medium grind the second time. Season to taste. Cook to 165°
225	Duck Liver Pâté	lb Ground Duck lb Ground Pork	tsp Flour			1 tsp Curing Salt* ½ tsp White Pepper	1 tbsp Kosher Salt 1 tbsp Pate Spice 1 oz Shallot minced	oz Foie Gras oz Panada	3 lb	Step 1. Season the ground meats with all spices. Dice the foie gras. Cure 30 minutes at 36 °. Step 2. Puree everything with panada until smooth. Season to taste. Cook to an internal temperature of 165°.
226	Foie Gras Mousse	lb Foie Gras- Grade B Or C ea Garlic Clove- minced	tsp Salt	tbsp Sauterne Wine	oz Butter	5 oz Whipped Cream			1 qt	Step 1. Devein the foie gras and dice into 1 inch cubes. Marinate with salt, pepper, shallot, and wine overnight. Step 2. Lightly sear the foie gras in butter then add the shallots, garlic and marinating liquid. Cool and pass through a tamis. Lightly whip cream and fold into the sieved foie gras. Season to taste.

Garde Manger – Forcemeats and Pâté

#	Item	1	2	3	4			8	Yield	Method
227	**Gratin Forcemeat**	oz Butter	oz Shallot					oz Liver		Step 1. Saute the livers and minced shallot in butter until fully cooked. Cool.
		tbsp Kosher Salt	1 lb Ground Pork			1 tsp Curing Salt*		oz Pork Fat Ground	3.5 lb	Step 2. Mix the pork, fat and salts with the cooked liver mixture and grind twice. Keep below 40°.
		tbsp Pate Spice				½ tsp White Pepper	11 oz Panada			Step 3. Puree the forcemeat with the spices and panada until smooth. Season to taste. Cook to 165°
228	**Mousse**- use fruit, cooked vegetables or protein for the base ingredient	oz Gelatin	1 lb Cooked Base Ingredient		oz Liquid-(stock, milk, or juice)		2 cups Cream		3 lb	Mix the gelatin in the 1 cup of cool liquid. Warm to 110° and mix into the base ingredient which is at 80°. Whip the cream and fold into the mixture. Season, portion and chill
229	**Mousseline**- use lean meat, poultry, shellfish, or fish for this method	1 lb Protein				1 ea Egg White	1 tsp Kosher Salt	oz Cream	1.5 lb	Grind the protein chill to 32°. Puree until smooth- DO NOT OVER PROCESS. Puree with egg and seasoning. Keep cold Mix in the Cream, puree until consistent. Season before cooking. Cook to 165° for all items except for seafood. Cook seafood to 145°
230	**Poultry Forcemeat**	1 lb Ground Dark Meat		oz Bacon		5 oz Panada	½ tsp Curing Salt*		21 oz	Bring the protein to 32°. Season and grind. Puree with panada until smooth. Season, shape and cook to 165°
231	**Rabbit Forcemeat**		tbsp Sage / tbsp Italian Parsley		oz Fat Back / oz Panada	24 oz Ground Rabbit	2 tsp Curing Salt* / 2 tsp Allemande Spice #205	oz Bacon	40 oz	Chill all ingredients to 33° Grind meat with spices, bacon and fat. Mix in panada. Use as a component for a rabbit terrine or use for rabbit sausage and serve hot.
232	**Salmon Pate**	1 lb Salmon				11 oz Panada	1 tsp Curing Salt*	oz Smoked Salmon	2 lb	Follow the same process as recipe number 192. Season to taste- Cook to 140°.
233	**Straight Forcemeat**	1 tbsp Kosher Salt	1 lb Pork or Veal			1 tsp Curing Salt*		oz Pork Fat		Step 1. Cure the pork or veal overnight with the salts, then grind
		1 tbsp Pate Spice	Clove Garlic minced			½ tsp White Pepper	11 oz Panada	oz Liver	2 lb	Step 2. Puree the liver, panada and seasoning and mix with the ground cured meat. Puree all until smooth. Cook to an internal temperature of 165°
234	**Torchon of Foie Gras- Salt Cured**	1 lb Foie Gras- Grade A	1 lb Kosher Salt	tsp Ground White Pepper		2 tbsp Curing Salt*			1 lb	Devein foie gras, rub with seasoning. Form into a log using cheesecloth. Roll very tight. Pack with kosher salt, dry cure 24 hours. Remove from salt, rewrap with plastic wrap very tightly into a tube. Seal in vacuum bag sous vide at 60° C for 28 minutes, chill overnight.

*Use Morton's Tender Quick as the curing salt in these recipes.

Classic Charcuterie Preparations

#	Item	1	2	3	4	5	6	7	8	Yield	Method of Preparation
235	Goose Confit	tbsp Quatre Spice	oz Brown Sugar / tsp Thyme	oz Kosher Salt / ea Garlic Clove	ea Juniper Berries / cup Stock	4 lb Goose Legs	4 tsp Cure Salt* / 5 cups Rendered Goose Fat		ea Cracked Peppercorn	3 lb	Step 1. Combine the legs with the seasonings and cure for 7 days. Step 2. Rinse the seasonings off of the legs and place them in tall oven proof dish or pan. Step 3. Pour the stock and rendered fat over the legs and cover. Bake covered in a 300° oven for 3 hours. Cool in fat overnight before using.
236	Campagne Terrine (Country Pork)	1 lb Pork Shoulder large grind / tsp Green Peppercorn	tsp Salt / tsp Quatre Espice	ea Shallot-mince / tbsp Parsley	Clove Garlic-mince	5oz Bacon-large grind / ½ cup Pistachios	2 oz Brandy / 2 oz Wine		oz Liver / oz Panada	2 lb terrine	Combine all, except panada and garnish, marinate for 24 hours. Mix with panada in mixer. Add pepper and herbs, add in pistachios. Line a terrine with sliced fat. Fill with forcemeat and bake in water bath until 160°.
237	Foie Gras Terrine	tbsp Sugar / tsp Curing Salt*	tbsp Kosher Salt		oz Sauterne	1 lb Foie Gras	½ tsp White Pepper			1 lb	Devein the foie gras. Marinate with wine and seasonings for 12 hours at 34° Drain and pack foie gras in a terrine. Place lid on top and Cryovac terrine with probe attachment. Hot water bath until the foie gras reaches an internal temp of 58° C for 68 minutes. Chill overnight.
238	Foie Gras – Conserve	tbsp Salt	lb Foie Gras	oz Armagnac			½ tsp White Pepper			1 quart jar	Devein Foie Gras- Place in 1 quart Mason Jar with salt and Armagnac. Seal. Submerge Jar in circulating water that is 58° C. Ensure internal is 58° C for 68 minutes.
239	Fromage de Tete (Head Cheese)	ea Pigs Head / pint White Wine	ea Pigs Trotters	cup Macedoine Carrot, Leek, and Fennel.	tbsp Chopped Fines Herbes	1 ea Bouquet Garni	1 tbsp Garlic chopped		4ea Shallot minced	1.75 quart terrine	Place pigs head in large pot with water to cover. Add in trotters and bouquet garni and wine. Simmer covered for 3 ½ hours. Remove meat, add garlic, shallot and veg. Simmer and reduce until 1 quart remains. Remove meat, brains, tongue, and eyes- Small dice. Combine with reduction. Add in herbes and season. Pour in terrine and chill.
240	Gibier Terrine (Game)	lb Game Meat-cubed / lb Pork Shoulder – large grind	ea Shallot / tsp Quatre Espice	ea Garlic Clove / tsp Salt	ea Bay Leaf / oz Liver	1 cup Red Wine / 1 tsp Curing Salt	1 tsp Juniper Berry / ½ tsp White Pepper		oz Bacon / oz Panada	2.5 lb	Combine all ingredients on this line, marinate for 24 hours in a sealed container. Drain off red wine and stir into panada. Remove bay leaf, grind the marinated ingredients- Large grind. Combine everything and medium grind. Emulsify in mixer with panada. Form terrine and bake in water bath until internal temp of 160 °.
241	Rillettes Cochon	tsp Pate Spice	lb Pork Shoulder	pint Stock	ea Bay Leaf	1 Bouquet Garni			10 oz Butter	2 lb	Combine everything in a pot and cover with a tight lid. Bake for 3 hours in the oven. Cool overnight. Remove pork and mash. Add leftover butter and seasonings

*Use Morton's Tender Quick as the curing salt in these recipes.

Garde Manger - Miscellaneous

#	Item	1	2	3	4				Yield	Method
242	Bocconicini	recipe of Mozzarella	tbsp Sherry Vinegar	oz Olive Oil		1 tsp Red Pepper Flakes		8 ea Basil Leaves chiffonade	2 lbs	Form mozzarella into small ½ oz balls. Combine remaining ingredients and season to taste. Marinate cheese for 30 minutes.
243	Duck Confit		tbsp Cure Salt*	oz Kosher Salt	oz Brown Sugar	4 lb Duck Legs	ea Thyme Sprig	8 ea Garlic Clove	3 lb	Step 1. Combine the seasonings, rub on duck legs and cure for 24 hours. Step 2. Rinse the seasonings off of the duck legs and place them in tall oven proof dish or pan.
				cup Stock				5 cups Rendered Duck Fat		Step 3. Pour the stock and rendered duck fat over the legs and cover. Bake covered in a 300° oven for 2.5 hours. Cool in fat overnight before using.
244	Gelée Binder	oz Powder Gelatin		cups Liquid					3 oz	Bloom gelatin in cold wine, consommé, or liquid. Warm to melt and use as a binder in cold terrines.
245	Goat Cheese Gelée	cup Cream	oz Goat Cheese		oz Milk	½ oz Powder Gelatin		8 oz Cream Cheese	22 oz	Bloom gelatin in milk. Melt with rest of ingredients and temper to 90° before using as a binder for cold terrines.
246	Lemon Cheese	quart Cream	tsp Kosher Salt	quarts Milk		½ tsp Lemon Zest	10 oz Lemon Juice		2.5 cups	Heat milk and cream to 100°. Add lemon juice. Allow to rest three hours. Skim and hang overnight. Add zest and salt mix well.
247	Mozzarella Cheese	gallon Water at 170°	lbs Fresh Cheese Curd - diced				6 oz Salt		1.75 lb	Add salt to hot water to dissolve. Add cheese curd to hot water and mix until soft. Knead until desired consistency, shape.
248	Panada	oz Brandy	ea Eggs	oz Flour	oz Cream				11 oz	Combine all ingredients together until smooth.
249	Pickle – Garlic Dill Brine	tbsp Pickle Spice	pints Water	oz Fresh Dill		2.5 oz Kosher Salt	1 head Garlic	8oz Vinegar	1 qt	Bring all of the ingredients to a boil for 1 minute. Cool and add 2-3 lbs of vegetables or cucumbers. Allow the pickles to brine for 3 days before using.
250	Pickle- Spicy Ginger	tsp Red Pepper Flake	cups Seasoned Rice Vinegar	slice Fresh Ginger	oz Sugar	1 tbsp Kosher Salt	1 cup Water		3 cups	Heat water, sugar, salt and pepper to a boil. Add ginger and vinegar. Cool overnight. Pickle 3 lbs of vegetable overnight.
251	Pickle – Sweet and Sour Brine	ea Onion	cup Cider Vinegar	tsp Celery Seed	tsp Mustard Seed	1 tsp Turmeric	1 tsp Salt	8 oz Sugar	1 pint	Bring all of the ingredients to a boil for 3 minutes. Cool and add 2 – 3 lbs of vegetables or cucumbers. Allow the pickles to brine for 3 days before using.
252	Red Onion Conserve	lb Red Onions fine julienne	oz Red Wine	oz Red Wine Vinegar	oz Sugar	Pinch Salt			1 lb	Combine onions and vinegar and allow to pickle for 30 minutes. Add the rest. Place all ingredients in sauce pan and reduce over medium heat to cook onions and thicken liquid. Season to taste.
253	Tapenade	tbsp Garlic	ea Anchovy Filets	oz Capers	tsp Lemon	1 oz Olive Oil	1oz Sundried Tomato	¾ cup Niçoise Olives	8 oz	Mince everything very fine and season to taste.
254	Wasabi	oz Wasabi	tbsp Water							Mix well and allow to sit for 20 minutes.

*Use Morton's Tender Quick as the curing salt in these recipes.

Recipes courtesy of Chef Brian Campbell CEC, CCE

Sausages

No.	Item				1	2	3	4	5	8	Yield	Method
255	**Andouille**	2 ¾ tsp. Salt	2 tsp Cayenne	1/3 tsp Cure Salt	Tbsp Cracked Pepper	lb Pork Butt-dice	Garlic Clove		oz. Ice	oz. Fat	2.5 lb	Combine all ingredients and large grind twice. Fill casing, cure 4 days.
				¼ tsp Allspice		tsp Thyme		oz. Water				Smoke until internal temp of 155°
256	**Bangers**	1 tsp Dry Thyme	1 tsp Dry Sage	¼ tsp Ground Cloves	tbsp Kosher Salt	tsp Basic Cure Spice	tsp Chervil	oz. Onion-minced	lb Beef Chuck-dice	oz Ice Water	5.5 lb	Combine the solid ingredients and grind twice. Mix in ice water and stuff into casings. Blanch the bangers and cool. Griddle as needed to 155°.
257	**Basic Cure Spice**	2 tbsp Black Pepper	2 tbsp Mace	2 tbsp Cure Salt	lb Brown Sugar	lb Kosher Salt					3 lb	Combine all ingredients.
			2 tbsp Onion Powder	2 tbsp Allspice		tbsp Gr. Garlic						Place in a sealed container.
258	**Bologna**	1 tsp Celery Seed	1 tbsp Dry Mustard	1 ½ tsp White Pepper	oz Kosher Salt	lb Ground Pork	lb Beef Chuck-dice			oz Milk	6 lb	1. Grind the spices to a powder. Season and cure meat for 24 hours.
	Mortadella is a a variation with small dice of lardo and pistachios mixed in	¼ tsp Nutmeg	½ tsp Caraway	¼ tsp Mace	oz Sugar				gram Pink Salt	oz Panada		2. Keep the cured meat very cold then grind twice. Puree with liquids until smooth. Internal 155°
259	**Bratwurst Spice Blend**	¾ oz White Pepper	1 tbsp Celery Seed	¼ oz Sugar	tbsp Mace					oz Kosher Salt	1 oz	Combine the ingredients and keep in a sealed container.
260	**Bratwurst**				cup Onion-diced	oz Bratwurst Spice		oz Ice	lb Pork Butt-dice		5.5 lb	Season the pork and grind twice. Puree with ice until smooth. Portion, 155°
261	**Breakfast**	1/8 oz White Pepper	2 tbsp Poultry Seasoning	¼ oz Black Pepper	oz Salt	tsp Basic Cure Spice			lb Pork Butt-dice	oz Ice Water	5.5 lb	Season the pork and grind twice. Portion, 155°.
262	**Chorizo** *This is the Central American version*	2.5 lb Pork Jowl Fat	¾ oz Crushed Red Pepper	¼ oz Black Pepper	oz Garlic	oz Paprika	¼ oz Oregano		lb Pork Butt-dice		7.5 lb	Season the pork and grind large grind twice.
		2.5 oz Salt							oz Ice Water			Mix in the ice water then portion, 155°.
263	**Frankfurter** *AKA Wiener Hot Dog*	2 lb Pork Butt-dice	¾ oz Salt	2.5 gram Pink Salt	ea Lemon	oz Onion-diced			oz Ice		2.5 lb	1. Grind the spices to a powder. Season and cure meat for 24 hours.
		1.5 tsp White Pepper	¼ tsp Cumin									2. Keep very cold then grind twice. Puree all ingredients until smooth, fill, cure, smoke to 155°
264	**Greek** *Čevapčići is a similar preparation made with beef, no caul fat, charcoal grilled links*	6 lb Pork Butt-dice	½ tsp Allspice	½ tsp Cayenne	tsp Thyme	tbsp Salt	ea Bay Leaf	oz Stock			7 lb	1. Simmer the onion, bay leaf, and garlic in stock. Cool, remove bay leaf.
		6 oz Ice Water	12 oz Onion-diced	½ tsp Chilli Powder	oz Butter	tbsp Black Pepper	tsp Garlic					2. Combine all ingredients and large grind twice. Portion into patties wrap caul fat, brown until 155°

Cure Salt for these recipes is Mortons Tender Quick which contains .5 % sodium nitrate and .5% sodium nitrite. Pink Salt is Prague Powder #1 which contains 6.25 % sodium nitrite. To ensure that the correct amount always weigh the pink salt in grams.

Sausages

#	Item				1	2	3	4	5	8	Yield	Method
265	Irish	1 ½ tsp Black Pepper	1 ½ tsp Dry Thyme	¼ tsp Allspice	lb Pork Fat-dice	tsp Kosher Salt	lb Pork Butt-dice	oz Onion-diced	clove Garlic-minced		4.5 lb	1. Season the pork and grind large grind twice.
		1 ½ tsp Sage		½ cup Bread Crumbs						oz Milk		2. Blend pork with milk and bread crumbs. Portion into casings, griddle to 155°
266	Italian-Spicy	1.5 oz Salt	¾ oz Cracked Black Pepper	½ oz Fennel Seed	oz Garlic	tbsp Crushed Red Pepper	tbsp Paprika		lb Pork Butt-dice	oz Ice Water	5.5 lb	Season the pork and grind large grind twice. Mix in the ice water with a paddle. Portion into casings cook to 155°
267	Italian-Sweet	1.5 oz Salt	½ oz Cracked Black Pepper	¾ oz Fennel Seed	tbsp Paprika	tbsp minced Garlic			lb Pork Butt-dice	oz Ice Water	5.5 lb	Season the pork and grind large grind twice. Mix in the ice water with a paddle. Portion into casings cook to 155°
268	Kassler Liverwurst	1 cup Onion	15 gram Pink Salt	2 cup Pistachio	dozen Eggs	tsp MSG	oz Salt		lb Pork Butt-dice	oz White Wine	15 lb	1. Cure the items on this line for 12 hours and grind twice.
		2 tsp Pate Spice	2lb Jowl Fat- fine grind	2lb diced Ham	oz Truffle-brunoise	tsp White Pepper	oz Dry Potato	lb Pork Liver –pureed	oz Pistachios	oz Panada		2. Combine the fat, spices, potato, liver and puree until smooth. Bake in a terrine in a waterbath until it reaches 165°
269	Kielbasa	1/3 oz Black Pepper	1.5 oz salt	3.5 gram Pink Salt		tsp Basic Cure Spice			lb Beef chuck-dice		5.5 lb	1. Season the pork or beef and large grind once. Mix the ice water into the meat with a paddle in a mixer.
		1 ¼ tsp Coriander	½ oz Sugar	¾ oz Garlic					oz Cold Water			2. Portion into casings and dry cure for 4 days at 38°. Cold smoke. Cook to 155°
270	Morteau (Lyonnaise – use 1 oz of garlic and coarse grind pork. Add 8 oz of chopped pistacios)	1.5 oz Salt	¼ oz Black Pepper	1/8 tsp Cumin	ea Sachet	oz Shallot-minced		oz White Wine	lb Pork Butt-ground		5.5 lb	1. Simmer everything except for pork and water for 4 minutes. Cool.
		3.5 gram Pink Salt	1/8 tsp Nutmeg	½ oz Garlic	oz Milk Powder			oz Ice Water				2. Remove sachet. Mix everything with a paddle and water. Portion into casing. Dry cure 2 days in cold smoker. Cook to155°.
271	Pepperoni	1 ½ oz Kosher Salt	1 tbsp Crushed Red Pepper	oz Sugar	tbsp Fennel Seed	tsp Coriander Seed	tsp Cure Salt	Clove Garlic	lb Pork Butt-dice	oz. Paprika	5 lb	Large grind all ingredients and portion into casings. Smoke for 48 hours at 45°. Cold dry cure for 30 days. Cook to155°.
272	Weisswurst	2.5 lb Ground Veal	1.5 tbsp White Pepper	¾ tsp Ginger	tbsp Chive	lb Jowl Fat	oz Salt	oz. Onion	tbsp Parsley		7 lb	1. Season meats with all solid items. Grind twice.
		2.5 lb Pork Butt-dice	¾ tsp Mace	½ Lemon Zest	oz Shallot		lb Ice					2. Puree with ice until smooth. Portion in casing cook to 155°

Cure Salt for these recipes is Mortons Tender Quick which contains .5 % sodium nitrate and .5% sodium nitrite. Pink Salt is Prague Powder #1 which contains 6.25 % sodium nitrite. To ensure that the correct amount always weigh the pink salt in grams.

Appetizers

No.	Item		1/2	1	2	3	4		Yield	Method of Preparation
273	Asian Wing Sauce	¼ cup minced Garlic	cup Hoisin Sauce	tbsp Sesame Seeds	tbsp sliced Scallions	oz Teriyaki Sauce		6 oz Honey	20 oz	Combine hoisin, garlic, honey and teriyaki. Fry 2 lbs of breaded wings. Toss in sauce then toss in seeds and scallions.
274	Ahi Poke	1 ea Chili Pepper minced	sheet Nori chopped	lb Raw Ahi-diced	tbsp Shoyu Sauce	Sesame Oil drops	oz Maui Onion		1 lb	Toss like a salad and serve
275	Black Bean Dip Serves 10	1 – 29 oz can Black Beans	cup Cilantro	tbsp Cumin	tbsp chop Jalapeño	oz Cider Vinegar	oz Olive Oil	2 Limes juiced	4.5 cups	Chop cilantro – puree the rest in a blender. Add cilantro to garnish, season to taste
276	Buffalo Wings and Sauce	5lb Raw Chicken Wings	cup Paprika	lb Butter	cups Franks Red Hot®	tsp Garlic Salt		2 tsp Cayenne	100 wings	Season wings with cayenne, paprika and dredge in 1 lb flour. Fry. Warm the rest, whisk butter into the sauce, toss sauce with wings
277	Crab Dip Serves 10	1 tsp Worcestershire Sauce	pint Heavy Cream	lb Backfin Crabmeat	oz Chives sliced	cup diced roast Red Pepper	oz Parmesan Cheese	12 oz Cream Cheese	3 pints	Melt cream and cream cheese over double boiler. Add in cheese, and Worcestershire. Heat crab to check for shells, mix in with rest.
278	Fondue Serve 10	1 large garlic clove	cup Kirsch	tbsp Cornstarch	cups grated Emmethal Cheese	cups White Wine	cups grated Gruyere Cheese	pinch Nutmeg	3.75 pint	Rub the inside of a Caquelon with garlic love. Warm the wine to body temp, add all cheese and heat. Once cheese melts add slurry of kirsch and cornstarch. Mix well , add nutmeg
279	French Onion Dip Serves 10	½ cup White Wine	oz Oil	pint Sour Cream	ea Onions-minced	tbsp Beef Base	Cloves Garlic- chop		22 oz	Sauté onions until tender and brown in oil. Add garlic, bake at 300° 45 minutes. Deglaze with wine, reduce until dry, cool, add rest of ingredients.
280	Hummus Dip Serve 10	1/3 cup Olive Oil	tsp Ground Cumin	lb Cooked Chickpeas	oz Lemon Juice	ea Garlic clove	oz Tahini paste		1.5 lb	Puree the chickpeas and garlic first in a food processor. Add everything else and puree until well blended. Season to taste. Serve chilled .
281	Nacho Cheese Dip Serves 10		lb Cream Cheese	lb Sharp Cheddar	pints Whole Milk	tsp Franks Red Hot®	tbsp Flour		3.5 pint	Whisk flour and milk in a 2 quart pot, simmer, add cheeses, whisk and melt, mix
282	Queso Fundido	1 small can Green Chilies	lb cooked Chorizo	Can Beer	lb grated Jack Cheese	clove Garlic minced	tsp Cornstarch	1 shot Tequila	3.5 pint	Heat beer in a sauce pot, add garlic, then cheese. Whisk to melt. Make slurry of tequila and cornstarch, add to cheese, whisk in rest.
283	Ranch Dip	1 ½ tsp Black Pepper	tsp dried Thyme	tbsp dried Parsley	tbsp dried Onion	tsp Garlic salt	cups Sour Cream	1 tbsp Vinegar	1 qt	Combine vinegar, garlic salt and onion. Whisk in rest. Refrigerate 4 hours.
284	Smoked Salmon Tartar	2 tsp Dijon Mustard / ½ tsp Worcestershire	lb Smoked Salmon-brunoise	tbsp Capers / tbsp chop Parsley	ea Eggs – hard boil and brumoise	tbsp minced Red Onion	tsp Olive Oil / grinds Black Pepper	1 ea lemon juiced	14 oz	Place salmon in bowl first and everything else on top gently toss to season and develop the flavor. Serve with toast points or as the main element on a canapé. Garnish with chives. Makes 20 canapés.
285	Spiced Pecans	2 ea Egg Whites whipped	lb Salted Butter	tbsp Cumin	tsp Dry Mustard	cup Brown Sugar	5 cups Pecan Halves	1 tsp Cayenne	3 lbs	Melt butter and sugar, add spices. Toss pecans in egg whites, toss spice mix with pecans. Spread on pan bake 325° 20 minutes stir twice while baking to break up pieces
286	Spinach Artichoke Dip	1 lb Cream Cheese	cup Heavy Cream	lb Frozen Spinach	tbsp minced Garlic	oz grated Parmesan	tbsp Olive Oil	1 can Artichoke	3.25 pint	Finely chop spinach and artichoke. Sauté garlic in oil, add veg and cream, melt in rest
287	Steak Tartar Serve with rye toast points 10 portions	2 tbsp Worcestershire / 1 tbsp minced Red Onion	ea Shallot minced / tsp Tabasco	1 lb Lean Sirloin / tbsp chop Parsley	tbsp EV Olive Oil / tbsp Capers	tbsp Dijon / grinds Black Pepper	tsp Anchovy Paste / tsp chopped Cornichon	2 each Egg / tsp Salt	22 oz	Use only pasteurized eggs. Separate. Poach the whites, chill and chop fine. Combine everything except finely chopped beef and egg white. Mix well add freshly ground beef to mix with 1 tbsp of the egg white.

Shellfish Preparations

	Item			1	2	3	4		Yield	Method of Preparation
288	Baked Clams	½ lb Bacon diced	ea Medium Onion diced / tsp Black Pepper	tbsp Worcestershire / cup diced Peppers	dozen Cherrystone Clams / tbsp Butter	oz Parsley chopped	tbsp Garlic minced	5 cups Bread diced / Paprika	48 ea	Steam clams, remove meat, chop fine, save juice and shells. Render bacon, sauté veg, add seasoning. Pour over the bread and add the clams and juice. Add Worcestershire and salt as needed. Mix well. Divide mixture into buttered clam shells. Sprinkle with paprika as needed and bake 375°- 20 minutes.
289	BBQ Shrimp — Sauce Base	1 ea Sachet	pint Beer / pint Cream	tbsp Worcestershire / pint White Wine	oz Garlic minced / cup Onion	quarts Shrimp Shells	Bay Leaves / tbsp Oil	1 recipe Cajun Spice 1096	1 qt	In a 1 gallon stock pot heat oil and sweat the diced onions and shrimp shells. Add bay leaf, wine, sachet and enough water to cover. Reduce until 12 of liquid remains. Strain into saute pan; add beer, garlic and spice. Reduce by half. Add Worcestershire and cream, reduce 6 minutes. Refrigerate
290	1 order			oz Butter	tsp Cajun Spice	drops Tabasco®	oz Sauce Base (above)	8 oz Shrimp P+D	13 oz	For 1 order heat butter in pan, season shrimp. Gently sauté and add 4 oz of sauce, Tabasco. Simmer; pour in bowl serve with French bread
291	Clams Casino — Filling	½ lb Bacon minced	ea Red Pepper brunoise	ea Green Pepper brunoise	cups Panko Breadcrumb	ea Shallot minced	tbsp Garlic minced	3 oz Butter	24 oz	Render bacon, save fat and pieces. Pour fat over breadcrumbs and toss. In a sauté pan heat butter and sweat shallots and garlic, add bacon sauté until tender. Add panko.
292	1 order			doz Shucked Littleneck	Wedge Lemon	oz Filling			12 ea	Flavor the clams with a squeeze of fresh lemon. Fill each clam with heaping tsp of filling. Bake in a 450° oven 8 minutes
293	Clams Oreganata	¼ cup chopped Oregano	tsp Red Pepper flakes	tbsp Garlic minced	cup Panko Breadcrumb	tbsp fresh chopped Parsley	oz Extra Virgin Olive Oil	2 tsp Sea Salt	12 oz	Toss all ingredients together. Portion 1 heaping tsp on top of ea shucked Littleneck clam Bake 450° until the crumbs are golden brown, 8- 10 minute. 2 oz of filling per order,
294	Coquille St Jacque		ea Sachet / lb Gruyere	pint Fish Stock / ea finely minced Shallot / ea Lemon Juiced	cup Dry White Wine / cup Cream	3 lbs Sea Scallops 10/20 / cups Mushroom sliced	oz Roux Blanc	Sea salt and white pepper to taste	10 portion	In a 3 quart marmite heat stock, wine, sachet, and shallot to 130°. Add ½ of the scallops and poach, with cartouche to 125°. Place scallops on ice cold plate. Repeat, slice into coins. Remove sachet, Add mushrooms, simmer until liquid is syrupy. Add cream+ roux. Simmer to thicken. Add lemon season. Place 8 scallop pieces in shells, nape with sauce, top with cheese, broil until 135° and golden brown.
295	Crab Imperial	1 ½ cup Panko	tsp Dry Mustard	cup Mayonnaise	lb Lump Crabmeat	oz Butter	oz Sour Cream	2 drop Tabasco®	12 portion	Combine mayo, sour cream, mustard, Tabasco. Melt butter and toss with panko. Add crab to mayo mixture, then fold in bread crumbs. Portion on shells. Bake 350°-30 minutes.
296	Deviled Crab	1 tbsp Lemon Juice	ea Red Pepper brunoise	tsp Worcestershire	ea Scallions sliced / ea Egg Yolk	tsp Prepared Yellow Mustard	drop Tabasco	1 Recipe Crab Imperial	3.5 lb	Add these additional flavorings to the crab imperial recipe. The mixture can be baked, as noted above or form into 2 oz football shaped croquettes, bread and deep fry.
297	Maryland Crab cakes	4 oz Mayo	tbsp Old Bay Seasoning	cup Cracker Crumbs or Panko	lb Lump Crabmeat / tbsp Lemon	ea Egg Yolks	tsp Prepared Mustard	¼ cup Parsley chopped	2.75 lb / 3.5 oz each	Mix egg yolks with lemon, mustard, mayo, Old Bay. Add in the picked crab meat and cracker crumbs or panko, and parsley. Gently toss and form 12 crab cakes Coat with bread crumbs and pan fry in butter

Shellfish Preparations

#	Item			1	2	3	4		Yield	Method of Preparation
298	**Lobster Newburg**	6 ea Egg Yolks	pinch Cayenne grate Nutmeg	oz Sherry tsp Paprika	oz Cognac	cups Light Cream tbsp Flour	ea Live Lobsters	5 oz Butter	8 portion	Blanch lobsters for 3 minutes. Shock. Remove all meat, slice, save liquid. Make a roux from flour and butter add in the spices and cream. Bring to simmer, add cognac, lobster and juice. Gently simmer, remove when cooked, and Temper yolks and sherry into sauce, nape over lobster. Serve in bouchee
299	**Lobster Thermidor**	1 pinch Nutmeg	cup Heavy Cream oz Cognac	cup Fish Stock tsp Paprika	oz Nouilly Prat Vermouth tbsp Flour	tbsp Dijon Mustard oz butter Slices	ea Live Lobsters	½ cup Parmesan grated	4 portions	Blanch and shock lobsters as detailed above. Split lobster in half and remove the tomalley and liver. Blend with Dijon, flour and spices. Bring the vermouth, cognac and stock to a boil, reduce by half until thick, temper in cream and flour mixture. Bring to a simmer, add butter and strain over the lobsters. Top with cheese, bake at 400° for 8 to 10 minutes, golden brown.
300	**Mussels Marinieres**	1 sprig Thyme	ea Shallot minced	lb Mussels- cleaned and beards removed	oz Butter oz Cream	tbsp Parsley chopped	oz White Wine	1 ea Bay Leaf	1 large portion to share	Place bay leaf, thyme, shallot in wine. Simmer then shut off to steep for 10 minutes. Add mussels and bring back to simmer until open. Plate mussels; reduce liquid with butter and cream. Finish with parsley.
301	**Mussels Marseilles**	1 Sprig Thyme	ea Shallot minced tsp Garlic	lb Mussels- cleaned and beards removed	oz Butter oz Tomato Concasse	tbsp Parsley chopped	oz White Wine	1 pinch Saffron	1 large portion to share	Place saffron, thyme, garlic, shallot in wine. Simmer then shut off to steep for 10 minutes. Add mussels and bring back to simmer until open. Plate mussels, reduce liquid mixing in butter, tomatoes, parsley.
302	**Oysters Bienville** Filling	½ cup Red Bell Pepper diced	ea Shallot minced	tbsp Garlic minced cup Mushroom fine dice	oz Butter cup Mornay Sauce (Cheddar)	oz White Wine ea Scallions sliced	oz Panko Breadcrumb	12 oz Shrimp	2.5 lb 12 portion	Melt the butter. Sweat the shallots. Add mushroom, garlic and red pepper. Sauté tender. Deglaze with white wine and poach the shrimp until firm. Remove and cool on an ice-cold plate. Mince shrimp. Add scallions and cold cheddar flavored mornay to mixture with bread crumbs and shrimp. Refrigerate.
303	1 order			tsp Tabasco®		oz Filling		6 Shucked Oysters	6 each	Top each oyster with 1 tbsp of the above filling. Bake 400° for 10 minutes, gratinée
304	**Oysters Rockefeller** Filling	1½ cup Panko	bunch Watercress leaves-	tsp Tabasco® tbsp Garlic minced	tbsp Pernod®	cup Fresh Spinach leaves	ea Scallions sliced	8 oz Butter	8 portions	Finely chop the vegetables in a food processor. Heat butter in sauté pan. Sweat garlic; add veg. then Tabasco and Pernod. Remove from heat and mix in bread crumbs. Season with salt, pepper, and pinch nutmeg. Chill 4 hours.
305	1 order			oz Parmesan shredded		oz Filling		6 Shucked Oysters	6 each	Top each oyster with 1 tbsp of the above filling. Top with cheese and broil to gratinée
306	**Shrimp Creole** 1 order-8 oz shrimp, 1 tbsp butter, 6 oz sauce	¼ lb Butter ½ tsp White Pepper	large Onion diced cup Tomato Sauce	Bay leaf tsp Cayenne tbsp Garlic minced	cups ea Green Pepper and Celery diced tsp Tabasco	cup Shrimp stock tsp Sugar	lb P+D Shrimp sprigs Fresh Thyme	8 ea Roma Tomatoes Concasse	8 portions	In 2 oz of butter sweat and saute the onions, peppers and celery until tender. Add leaves from thyme and stock, reduce by half. Add everything else, except shrimp and butter, simmer 5 minutes. To order heat butter and lightly sauté shrimp add sauce and simmer. Season with salt and black pepper

Composed Salads

	1/2	3/4	1	1	2	3	4	8	16	Yield	Preparation
307 **Artichokes and Hearts of Palm Provençale**	cup Olive Oil		tsp Garlic minced	ea Tomato Concassé	ea Lemons juiced	oz Nicoise Olive -pitted	tbsp chopped Basil	oz Hearts Of Palm sliced	ea Artichoke Hearts	2 lb	Prepare the dressing first then add the other ingredients. Chill.
308 **Antipasto Bean**	cup Olive Oil	lb Salami diced	cup Tomato diced	tbsp Basil chopped	oz Balsamic Vinegar	ea Garlic cloves - minced	oz Red Onion diced	oz Peppers diced	oz Cooked White Beans	2.5 lb	Prepare the dressing first. Add the other items
309 **Black Bean and Corn**	cup Green Chilies diced	tsp Chipotle Chili Powder	tsp Cumin	ea Garlic Clove - minced	oz Red Wine Vinegar	oz Olive Oil	tbsp Cilantro chopped	oz Cooked Corn	oz Cooked Black Beans	2 lb	Prepare the dressing first. Add the other items
310 **Caponata**	cup Red Wine Vinegar	cup Onion diced	tbsp Sugar	tbsp Capers	ea Eggplant- peel and dice, salt and rinse	oz Tomato Paste	oz Olive Oil	oz Celery diced	ea Green Olives	2.5 lb	Sauté the eggplant until light brown. Make a dressing with the rest simmer 5 minutes, cool
311 **Carrot Râpées**	ea Garlic Clove minced	tsp Celery Seed	tbsp Sugar	tbsp Tomato Paste	oz Red Wine Vinegar	oz Olive Oil	tsp Tarragon chopped		oz Carrot fine julienne	1.5 lb	Prepare the dressing first. Add the other items
312 **Cauliflower**	cup Mayonnaise	tsp Curry Powder	large head Cauliflower- cooked	tbsp Cider Vinegar	oz diced Onion	oz diced Celery				1.5 lb	Prepare the dressing first. Add to lightly chopped cauliflower.
313 **Celeriac**	oz sliced Chives	oz Champagne Vinegar	oz Sour Cream	oz Lemon Juice	oz Mayonnaise				oz Celeriac fine julienne	1.5 lb	Prepare the dressing first. Blanch and shock celeriac and combine.
314 **Cole Slaw**	cup Sour Cream	tsp Salt	oz Sugar	tsp Celery Seed	oz Mayonnaise	oz Cider Vinegar	oz Carrot shredded		oz Cabbage-chiffonade	1.5 lb	Marinate the cabbage in the vinegar, salt and sugar for 1 hour. Drain and add rest.
315 **Crab Maryland**	cup Sour Cream	cup Mayonnaise	cup Celery brunoise	tbsp Dill chopped	lb Lump Crabmeat	oz Red Pepper brunoise	tsp Horseradish			2.5 lb	Prepare the dressing first. Add the crab last.
316 **Creamy Chicken**	lb Celery- diced	cup Mayonnaise	tbsp Fresh Tarragon		lb Chicken Breast	tbsp Cider Vinegar	oz Sour Cream			2.5 lb	Poach chicken first, cool, dice. Prepare the dressing first. Add the other items
317 **Cucumber**	ea Red Onion – sliced		tbsp Cracked Black Pepper	oz Honey	oz Dijon Mustard	oz Cider Vinegar	ea European Cucumbers- sliced			3 lb	Prepare the dressing first. Add the other items. Chill 30 minutes
318 **Cucumber - Greek**	ea Red Onion – minced	tbsp Fresh Oregano	tsp Black Pepper	oz Capers	oz Olive Oil	oz Lemon Juice	ea Cucumbers- peel, sliced			2 lb	Prepare the dressing first. Add the other items. Chill 30 minutes
319 **Egg**			cup Mayonnaise	oz Pickle Relish	oz Yellow Mustard	oz Minced Onion	oz Celery minced		ea Hard Boiled Eggs	2.5 lb	Peel and chop the eggs. Add everything else.

Composed Salads

#	Name	1/2	3/4	1	1	2	3	4	8	16	Yield	Preparation
320	Fennel Slaw	ea Red Pepper- fine julienne	cup Shaved Red Onion	tbsp Sugar	tbsp Fresh Dill	oz White Wine Vinegar	oz Olive Oil			oz Shaved Fennel	1.5 lb	Prepare the dressing first. Add the other items. Chill 30 minutes
321	Greek Orzo	cup Green Olives chopped		tbsp Fresh Mint	cup Crumbled Feta	tbsp Fresh Oregano	ea Lemons Juiced	oz Extra Virgin Olive	oz Fresh Spinach chopped	oz Orzo Pasta	2.5 lb	Cook orzo, rinse, and drain - Prepare the dressing first. Add the orzo and chill.
322	Ham			Cup Mayonnaise	oz Sweet Relish	lb Ground Ham	tbsp Dijon				1.5 lb	Combine all ingredients.
323	Israeli Cous Cous	cup Red Onion diced	cup Red Pepper diced	ea Garlic Clove minced	ea Zucchini - diced	oz Lemon Juice	tbsp Parsley chopped	oz Extra Virgin Olive		oz Israeli Cous Cous	2.5 lb	Cook the cous cous in turmeric flavored water. Drain, Rinse and combine with rest.
324	Jicama - Southwest	oz Extra Virgin Olive Oil		tsp Chili Powder	tbsp Orange Zest	oz Orange Juice	ea Scallion sliced			oz Jicama shredded	1.5 lb	Prepare the dressing first and combine.
325	Macaroni	cup Mixed Olives chopped	lb Macaroni	ea Garlic Clove minced	oz Cider Vinegar	oz Onion- minced	oz minced Celery	oz Green Pepper brunoise	oz Mayonnaise		2 lb	Boil the macaroni in salted water. Drain and rinse. Combine season.
326	Mexican Pickled Veg	pint Cider Vinegar	lb Cactus- cleaned, slice	Head Cauliflower	lb Carrots Sliced	cups Corn Oil	ea Cinnamon Sticks	ea Jalapeño	ea Serrano Chili	ea Corn Cobbettes	3 lb	Boil the dressing and seasonings. Blanch the veg and corn in the dressing and chill.
327	Mid East Tabouleh	cup Mixed Olives chopped	cup Diced Peppers	Quart Parsley- chop fine	bunch Mint chopped	ea Lemons juiced	ea Tomato Concassé	oz Olive Oil	ea Scallions sliced	oz Bulgur Wheat Or Cous Cous	2.5 lb	Cook the wheat like pasta, drain and cool- combine with rest, season
328	Potato – American			cup Mayonnaise	tbsp Sugar		lb Cooked, Peeled Potatoes	oz Cider Vinegar	oz Minced Onion		4 lb	Marinate onions, vinegar, and sugar Slice the potatoes, combine and season to taste.
329	Potato - Southern			tsp Celery Seed		oz Yellow Mustard	oz Pickle Relish				4 lb	Add these items to recipe # 328
330	Potato – Cajun	cup Red Wine Vinegar	tsp Tabasco	tbsp Parsley chopped	cup Canola Oil	lb Red Bliss- cooked	oz Red Onions diced	tsp Creole Mustard	oz Smoked Sausage- sliced		2.5 lb	Prepare the dressing first. Add the other items then sliced potato
331	Potato Warm German	cup Cider Vinegar		tsp Salt	lb Bacon diced / tbsp Sugar	tbsp Dijon Mustard	oz Chives sliced thin / oz Salad Oil	lb Cooked Potato- peeled	oz Onion diced	oz Chicken Stock	5 lb	Dice and render the bacon, make warm dressing Slice the potatoes and combine serve warm. Season.
332	Potato - French	*Use Champagne Vinegar*		lb Morteau Sausage sliced					*Use only 4 oz Shallot*	*Do not use stock*		Use recipe 331 – Add cooked sausage.

61

Composed Salads

#	Name	1/2	3/4	1	1	2	3	4	8	16	Yield	Preparation
333	Seafood- lobster, shrimp, or crab	cup Chili Sauce	oz Lemon Juice	cup Mayonnaise	oz Shallot minced	lb Cooked Shellfish	tsp Horseradish	oz Celery minced			2.5 lb	Drain shellfish well. Combine all other ingredients then add seafood.
334	Shepherds Salatsi	cup Red Onion diced	cup Peppers diced	tbsp Dill	tbsp Mint chopped	ea Cucumbers-peeled, seeded and diced	ea Tomatoes diced	tbsp Parsley chopped	ea Pepperocini Peppers-chopped	ea Kalamata Olives	3 lb	Prepare all ingredients in this line and place in a bowl and chill.
		cup Olive Oil		tsp Cracked Black Pepper	ea Garlic Cloves minced	ea Lemons Juiced				oz Feta Cheese		At service combine ingredients, season
335	Smoked Mozzarella Pasta	cup Olive Oil	lb Smoked Mozzarella - diced	tbsp Garlic minced	tbsp Basil chopped	oz Balsamic Vinegar	oz Red Onions julienne	oz Salami julienne	oz Roasted Peppers julienne	oz Tortellini Pasta	2.5 lb	Cook pasta. Cool and drain. Prepare dressing and toss in the rest.
336	Smoked Seafood	cup Mayonnaise	tbsp Horseradish	lb Smoked Seafood	tbsp fresh Dill	tbsp Lemon Juice	tbsp sliced Chives				1.5 lb	Prepare the dressing, combine
337	Swiss Beef	oz Dijon Mustard	lb Swiss Cheese julienne	oz Capers		oz Red Wine Vinegar	tbsp Parsley chopped	oz Salad Oil		oz Roast Beef julienne	2 lb	Prepare the dressing and combine, season.
338	Tomato and Cucumber		cup Red Onion diced	tsp Cracked Black Pepper	tsp Salt	ea Cucumbers-peel, seed and dice	ea Tomatoes diced	tbsp Cider Vinegar	tbsp Salad Oil		2 lb	Prepare the dressing and combine, season to taste.
339	Turkish Chickpea Piyazi	cup Red Onion diced	tsp Cayenne	tbsp Ground Cumin	ea Lemon Juiced	ea Garlic Cloves-minced	oz Extra Virgin Olive Oil	tbsp Parsley chopped	oz Tomato diced	oz Cooked Chick Peas	2 lb	Prepare the dressing, toss in rest and season.
340	Tuna	tsp Worcestershire sauce		cup Mayonnaise	ea Lemon Juice	lb Tuna-cooked	oz Onion minced	oz Celery minced			2.5 lb	Prepare the dressing, flake in tuna and mix.
341	Tuna – Niçoise	oz Red Wine Vinegar	cup Olive Oil	ea Hard Boiled Egg	ea Lemon Juiced	oz Kalamata Olives	tsp Pesto	oz Haricot Vert	oz Tomato Concassé	oz Tuna - Fresh	2 lb	Season and grill tuna. Marinate with everything last minute. Season.
342	Tuna - Palm Beach			can Hearts Of Palm	ea Garlic Clove	ea Lemon Juice	tbsp Parsley	oz Red Pepper brunoise	oz Olive Oil	oz Tuna - Fresh	2 lb	Grill tuna, marinate with everything. Season to taste
343	Virginia Turkey	cup Mayonnaise	bunch Scallions sliced	tbsp Basil chopped		oz Sour Cream	oz Virginia Ham julienne	oz Sharp Cheddar julienne		oz Smoked Turkey julienne	1.5 lb	Prepare dressing and add in meats and cheese.
344	Waldorf		tbsp Sugar	lb Apples diced	ea Lemon Juiced	oz Walnuts chopped - toasted	oz Mayonnaise	tsp Champagne Vinegar	oz Celery diced		1.5 lb	Marinate the apples in vinegar, sugar and lemon, add rest. Season

Make to to cover label and date all cold preparations, use clean utensils when portioning . All cold composed salads should be rotated out after 3 days

Salad Dressings

	Vinaigrettes	1/2	3/4	1	1	2	3	4	8	16	Yield	Preparation
345	Basic	tsp Mustard				tbsp Herbs		oz Extra Virgin Olive Oil	oz Vinegar	oz Salad Oil	28oz	Combine vinegar, herbs and mustard. Add oil season
346	Apple	oz minced Shallot	oz Brown Sugar	ea Green Apple- fine dice	oz Walnut Oil	tbsp Dried Cranberries-chopped		oz Cider Vinegar	oz Salad Oil		16oz	Warm the apples, shallot, cranberries, sugar, and vinegar. Add oil. Season
347	Balsamic			tbsp Basil chopped	tsp Black Pepper	ea Garlic Clove minced			oz Balsamic Vinegar	oz Extra Virgin Olive Oil	24oz	Whisk all together. Season to taste.
348	Greek	tbsp Oregano chopped	tsp Sugar		oz parsley chopped		ea Garlic Clove minced		oz Lemon Juice	oz Extra Virgin Olive Oil	24oz	Whisk all ingredients together. Season
349	Herb	tbsp Sugar	oz Fine Herbes chopped	cup Extra Virgin Olive Oil	Clove Garlic minced	oz Dijon	tbsp Parsley		oz Red Wine Vinegar	oz Salad Oil	32oz	Whisk all ingredients together. Season.
350	Italian	tbsp Oregano chopped	tbsp Garlic chopped	tbsp Basil chopped		oz Extra Virgin Olive Oil	tbsp Red Pepper chopped	oz Red Wine Vinegar	oz Olive Oil		14oz	Whisk all ingredients together. Season
351	Lite Tomato Herb	lb Tomato Concassé	tsp Red Pepper Flakes	ea Garlic Clove minced	tbsp Basil chopped	tbsp Shallot minced		tsp Arrowroot		oz Stock	26oz	Step 1. Mix cold stock and starch, bring to simmer and chill.
					tbsp Parsley	oz Extra Virgin Olive Oil	oz Lemon Juice	oz Red Wine Vinegar				Step 2. Whisk in the vinegar and oil, mix in the rest and season.
352	Raspberry Walnut	oz Shallot minced		oz Raspberry Jam	tbsp Parsley chopped	oz Walnut Oil		oz Raspberry Vinegar	oz Salad Oil		16oz	Whisk all ingredients together. Season
353	Southern Herbal	oz sliced Chives and chopped Cilantro		tsp Cracked Black Pepper	ea Garlic Clove minced	oz Brown Sugar	tbsp Red Pepper brunoise		oz Malt Vinegar	oz Peanut Oil	24oz	Whisk all together adding the herbs in last. Season
354	Sundried Tomato		tbsp Garlic chopped	tbsp Basil chopped		oz Sundried Tomato chopped		cup Balsamic Vinegar	oz Extra Virgin Olive Oil		12oz	Whisk all ingredients together. Season
355	Warm Bacon		cup Salad Oil	tsp Cracked Black Pepper	oz Shallots minced	ea Garlic Clove minced	oz Raspberry Vinegar	oz Brown Sugar	oz Bacon diced		14oz	Render the bacon in oil. Rough chop. Warm the shallots and garlic in fat. Add the rest, simmer, and season.
356	Warm Sherry Tomato	oz Sherry	tsp Cracked Black Pepper	tbsp Parsley chopped	tbsp Shallot minced	oz Sherry Wine Vinegar	oz Tomato Concassé	oz Extra Virgin Olive Oil			10oz	Warm the shallot in the sherry and bring to a simmer for 30 seconds. Add rest & season

Salad Dressings

#	Dressings	1/2	3/4	1	1	2	3	4	8	16	Yield	Preparation
357	**Blue Cheese**		tbsp Worcestershire	pint Mayonnaise	tbsp Lemon Juice	tsp Garlic minced		oz Buttermilk	oz Sour Cream	oz Blue Cheese-crumbled	32oz	Whisk together except for cheese. Add cheese and season
358	**California Caesar**	tbsp Worcestershire	oz Dijon Mustard	tsp Cracked Black Pepper	oz Lemon Juice	ea Egg Yolks	ea Anchovy Filet	ea Garlic Clove minced	oz Red Wine Vinegar	oz Olive Oil	28oz	Blend and puree until smooth.
359	**Catalina**	cup Cider Vinegar	cup Olive Oil	ea Garlic Clove	tbsp Paprika	oz Dijon Mustard	oz Ketchup	oz Brown Sugar	oz Salad Oil		30oz	Warm the paprika in the olive oil. Blend all chill. Dash allspice
360	**Cracked Pepper Parmesan**	tsp White Pepper		pint Mayonnaise	tbsp Cracked Pepper	ea Garlic Clove minced	oz Red Wine Vinegar	oz Parmesan Cheese	oz Sour Cream		28oz	Blend all ingredients Season.
361	**Creamy Italian**	pint Mayonnaise	tbsp Sugar	tbsp Fresh Oregano	Red Pepper brunoise	ea Garlic Clove minced	tbsp Fresh Basil	oz Red Wine Vinegar	oz Extra Virgin Olive Oil		28oz	Mix mayonnaise with oil and vinegar. Add the rest and season.
362	**Creamy Mustard**	tbsp Worcestershire	tbsp Sugar	ea Lemon Juiced	tbsp Dijon	oz Pommeray Mustard		ea Egg Yolk	oz White Wine Vinegar	oz Salad Oil	25oz	Blend all ingredients on low speed. Season.
363	**Cucumber**		cup Mayonnaise	tbsp Sugar	oz Dill chopped	ea Cucumbers- peel, seed	oz Lemon Juice		oz Sour Cream		24oz	Chop the cucumbers in a food processor. Whisk, season.
364	**French**	tsp Salt	tsp Dry Mustard	tsp Celery Seed		tsp Garlic minced	oz Sugar	oz Wine Vinegar	oz Ketchup	oz Salad Oil	28oz	Blend all on low speed. Season.
365	**Green Goddess**	tsp Salt	oz Lemon Juice	ea Garlic Clove	tbsp Parsley	oz Spinach Leaves			oz Mayonnaise		16oz	Step 1. Puree until smooth.
			tbsp Chives	tbsp Dijon	tbsp Tarragon				oz Sour Cream			Step 2. Add the rest. Season
366	**Honey Mustard**			tsp Mustard Seed		tsp Poppy Seed	oz Honey	oz Cider Vinegar	oz Dijon Mustard	oz Salad Oil	32oz	Blend all ingredients, Season.
367	**Japanese**	tbsp Ketchup	tbsp Ginger grated	ea Scallion		oz Celery chopped	tsp Soy Sauce	oz Onions	oz Mayonnaise		12oz	Blend until smooth. Season
368	**Ranch**	oz Worcestershire		tbsp Garlic		oz Red Wine Vinegar			oz Sour Cream	oz Mayonnaise	32oz	Blend all together until smooth.
		tsp Celery Seed	ea Shallot	tbsp Parsley	tbsp Chives	tbsp Dijon			oz Buttermilk			Season to taste.
369	**Raspberry Rose Petal**	tbsp Shallot minced	tbsp Sugar	tbsp Rose Water		oz Frozen Raspberry	oz Salad Oil	oz Raspberry Vinegar	oz Sour Cream	ea Rose Petal	20oz	Blend all ingredients Season to taste.
370	**Russian**	tbsp Worcestershire	ea Shallot minced	pint Mayonnaise	cup Chili Sauce	tbsp Horseradish					24oz	Blend everything. Strain next day
371	**Thousand Island**	cup Pickle Relish		pint Mayonnaise	ea Chopped Boiled eggs						28oz	Add the items to the Recipe 370
372	**Turkish Yogurt**	tbsp Oregano	tbsp Cracked Black Pepper	ea Cucumber-		oz Red Onion minced				oz Yogurt	22oz	Peel, seed, and chop the cucumber. Blend.

Basic Soup Recipes

#	Name	1/2	3/4	1	2	3	4	8	Yield	Method
373	**Bean**			gallon Stock	each Sachet / lb Onion diced	ea Ham Hock	cup Beans	oz Bacon diced	oz Celery and Carrots brunoise	3 quart	Soak beans overnight and rinse them. Place the beans in a pot with the stock, sachet and ham hock. In a separate pan render the bacon and sauté the vegetables. When tender add to the soup and simmer covered until the beans are tender. Season.
374	**Bisque**	tsp Tabasco®	cup Shallot minced	tbsp Garlic minced	tbsp Paprika	lb Seafood Shells	tbsp Butter	oz Rice		3 quarts	In a marmite melt the butter and sauté the shells until they turn red add the paprika and rice. Add the tomato paste, deglaze with brandy add stock; simmer until the rice is tender. Strain & puree the solids. Combine everything. Strain through a fine chinois and finish with sherry reheat to 145°, season.
			tsp Worcestershire	oz Brandy	quart Cream	oz Sherry	quart Stock	oz Tomato Paste			
375	**Cheese**	cup Pepper diced		lb Cheese grated / lb Mirepoix diced	can Beer or / cup White Wine	quart Veloute			oz Cream	5 pints	Simmer the mirepoix and pepper in the beer until tender. Add the veloute and bring to a simmer. Remove from heat and whisk in cheese. Add the cream and reheat to 135°. Season with salt &cayenne
376	**Consommé**	tsp Black Peppercorns	pint Egg Whites	gallon Stock	cups Mirepoix julienne	lb Lean Ground Meat	ea Bay Leaf	ea Parsley Stem	oz Tomato Puree	3 quarts	Combine everything cold. Place in tall narrow pot. Stir and heat to 120° Stop stirring and heat the mixture at 180°. Baste the raft after it forms for 2 hours Pass the liquid through coffee filters. Season to taste.
377	**Cream of Mushroom**		qt Stock	oz Madeira	oz Clarified Butter	each Thyme sprig	lb Mushroom-sliced	oz Celery diced	oz White Leek diced	1 gallon	In a marmite heat the butter and sauté mushrooms until brown, sweat veg. Add the thyme, wine and stock. Cook covered until tender. Puree until smooth. Combine the puree with the veloute and lemon juice. Simmer. Temper in cream. Season to taste, strain through a chinois.
				tbsp Lemon Juice	quart Cream	quart Veloute					
378	**Cream of Vegetable** *use for Broccoli, Asparagus, Celery Soup*	cup Flour	gallon Stock	cup White Leek-chopped	ea Sachet	lb Vegetable – chopped	oz Celery diced	oz Onion diced	1 gallon	In a marmite heat the butter and sauté the vegetables until the onions are translucent. Singer with flour and add in the stock. Cook covered until tender with sachet. Strain and puree the solids until smooth. Place in a clean pot. Bring the cream, liquid and puree to simmer. Strain, season- garnish with small dice or pieces of the main vegetable used to flavor.
				pint Cream	cup Vegetable for garnish						

65

Basic Soup Recipes

#	Recipe	1/2	3/4	1	2	3	4	8	Yield	Method
379	Potage of Root Vegetables or Winter Squash		gallon Stock	cup White Leek - chopped; ea Sachet for savory **or** ea Cinnamon Stick for sweet; cup Veg for garnish	oz Butter	lb diced and peeled Root Vegetable or Squash; pint Cream	oz Celery diced	oz Onion diced	3.25 quarts	In a marmite heat the butter and sauté the vegetables until the onions are translucent. Singer with flour and add in the stock. Cook covered until tender with sachet or cinnamon. Strain the liquids from the solids and reserve. Remove sachet or cinnamon. Puree the solids until smooth. Place in a clean pot. Bring the cream, liquid and puree to simmer. Strain through a fine strainer and season to taste. Garnish the top of the potage with diced cooked main vegetable.
380	Potato	bunch Chives sliced	Gallon Chicken Stock; lb Potato cooked diced for garnish	bunch Leeks- dice clean	quart Cream	oz Melted Butter	lb Potato diced	rib Celery chopped	1 gallon	Sweat the onions, celery and leeks in the butter until translucent. Add the stock and potatoes. Simmer until the leeks are very tender. Strain and puree until smooth, strain. Add the heavy cream and season to taste. Garnish with potato and chive.
381	Split Pea	gallon Chicken Stock; tsp Salt	Bay Leaf	lb Split Green Peas; lb White Mirepoix diced; tsp Garlic minced; pint Light Cream	ea Smoked Ham Hocks; oz Clarified Butter	oz Carrots brunoise - cooked	oz Bacon diced; slices Bread	oz Potato diced	3 quarts	Render the bacon and sauté the mirepoix. Add the rest of the items on this line. Simmer until the potatoes fall apart. Puree the soup. Strain the soup and finish with cream and seasoning. Add the carrot for garnish. Dice the bread and make croutons with the garlic and butter on the toasted bread. Season to taste.
382	Tomato	qt Crushed Tomato; cup Flour	cup Onion diced; gallon Strong Chicken Stock	oz Olive Oil; tbsp Flour; tbsp Oregano	ea White Leek sliced; tbsp Basil	ea Shallots - diced; ea Bay Leaf; cups Cream	ea Garlic cloves-chop; lbs Tomato diced	oz Bacon diced; oz Tomato Paste	1 ¼ gallon	Render the bacon in oil. Add the garlic clean vegetables. Add the tomatoes and simmer for 10 minutes. Singer with flour. Add the tomato paste, herbs and stock. Simmer for 45 minutes. Strain solids and puree - smooth. Combine the liquids, puree. Mix flour and cream. Temper into soup. Bring to a simmer. Strain and season to taste.
383	Veloute		cup Flour	quart Cream		quart Stock	oz Melted Butter		1 gallon	Make a roux with the flour and butter. Add in the cold stock and bring to a simmer for 30 minutes. Temper in the cream. Season to taste.

American Regional Soups

#	Name	1/2	3/4	1	1	2	3	4	8	16	Yield	Method
384	Farmers Vegetable	lb Onions diced	oz Garlic minced	gallon Chicken Stock	ea Sachet	lb diced Beef	oz Clarified Butter	oz Leeks-diced		oz Mirepoix-diced	1 gallon	In a soup pot heat the butter and sear the beef until brown. Add the vegetables on this line and sauté until tender. Add the stock and sachet and bring to a simmer for 30 minutes
		lb diced Cabbage		cup Turnip diced	cup Tomato diced			oz Lima Beans	oz Corn	oz Potato diced		Add the items on this line and continue to simmer for 20 minutes. Season to taste.
385	Amish Chicken and Corn		tsp Turmeric	gallon Chicken Stock	ea Sachet	lb Chicken Thigh		oz Leeks		oz Mirepoix small dice	1 gallon	Bring the stock to a boil and add the items on this line. Simmer until the chicken is tender. Remove skin, dice meat.
					oz Parsley chopped		oz Ham diced	oz Hominy	oz Fresh Corn	oz Spatzlé recipe # 702		Add the ham, hominy and corn to the soup and simmer for 15 minutes. Add the chicken back to the soup with the cooked Spatzlé. Season to taste. Garnish with parsley.
386	Wisconsin		lb White Mirepoix – small dice	cup Flour	ea Sachet	ea Garlic clove minced	quarts Chicken Stock	oz Butter		oz Beer	1 gallon	In a soup pot heat the butter and sauté the mirepoix until translucent. Singer with flour and add in the beer and garlic. Add the stock and bring to a simmer for 30 minutes.
	Cheddar	ea Red Pepper – roasted and diced	oz sliced Chives	pint Heavy Cream	ea. Green Pepper roasted and diced	lb Cheddar – medium to sharp flavor-grated						Strain the mirepoix and garlic. Return to a simmer with the cream. Remove from heat and gradually add in the cheese. Add the peppers and season to taste. Chive garnish
387	Minnesota	ea Sachet	lb Leeks fine dice	gallon Chicken Stock	cup Flour			oz Butter	oz Wild Rice	oz Mirepoix – fine dice	1 gallon	In a soup pot heat the butter and sauté the mirepoix until translucent. Singer with flour. Add the stock, sachet and rice and simmer for 45 minutes or until tender. Season
	Wild Rice		cup Poultry-cooked diced	pint Cream	oz Chives		oz Sherry Wine					Temper in the cream and sherry and bring back to a simmer. Add poultry and chives to garnish.
388	Senate Bean	ea Sachet	tbsp Garlic	gallon Chicken Stock	lb Navy Bean					oz Mirepoix small dice	1 gallon	Soak beans overnight in water. Drain the beans and bring them to a simmer with the items on this line.
			oz Chives sliced	lb Potato diced					oz Cream			Add the potatoes and cream and bring back to simmer. Season to taste. Chives last.

American Regional Soups

#		1/2	3/4	1	1	2	3	4	8	16	Yield	Method
389	**Philadelphia Pepper Pot**	oz Butter	lb Large Mirepoix	lb Tripe - cleaned	gallon Veal Stock	ea Veal Shank	ea Bay Leaf				1 gallon	In a soup pot heat the butter and sear the veal shank until brown. Add the other line items and simmer covered for 3 hours.
			lb Potato diced	cup Tricolor Peppers small diced	ea Sachet	cup Mirepoix small diced	Cups Spatzlé recipe # 702					Strain the liquid and save. Discard mirepoix, bay leaf. Dice the meats. Bring back to simmer with sachet and potatoes and veg. Cook until tender. Season to taste with salt and cracked pepper. Add Spatzlé last.
390	**Suffolk Peanut**	cup Roasted Peanut Oil		oz Bourbon	cup Onions fine dice	qt Chicken Stock	oz Flour	oz Celery brunoise			1 gallon	Heat the oil in a soup pot and sauté the vegetables until tender. Singer with flour and deglaze with bourbon. Stir in the chicken stock and simmer for 20 minutes.
		cup Country Ham brunoise		dash Tabasco	qt Light Cream	oz Green Peppers brunoise				oz Peanut Butter		Add the ham and simmer. Temper in the peanut butter and cream. Garnish with peppers and season to taste.
391	**Ham and Collard Greens**	cup Bacon chopped	cup Flour	Sachet		lb Collards – fine chiffonade	qt Chicken Stock	oz Celery diced	oz Onion diced	oz Ham Hock	1 gallon	Render the bacon in a soup pot. Sauté the vegetables until the onions are translucent. Singer with flour and add the stock, ham hock. Bring to a simmer. Add the collards and sachet and simmer until the collards are tender.
				tsp Cracked Black Pepper	cup Potato diced				oz Heavy Cream			Add in the dice potato and continue to simmer until the potatoes are tender. Season and temper in cream. Remove any meat from the ham hock and add it to the soup.
392	**She Crab**	gallon Crab Stock	tsp Paprika	ea clove Garlic- minced	cup Flour	quarts Half and Half Cream	oz Crab Roe (optional)	oz Dry Sherry	oz Whole Butter	oz Onion minced	1 gallon	Heat the butter in a soup pot and sauté the onions until translucent. Add the garlic, roe, and paprika. Singer with flour. Deglaze with sherry and add in the stock and cream. Simmer for 20 minutes
		pinch Mace	tsp Old Bay Season	oz Parsley chopped	lb Crab Meat							Add the spice and simmer for 5 minutes. Pick and heat the crab to check for shells. Add to the soup. Parsley garnish. Offer additional sherry for each guest to add to their soup.

American Regional Soups

	1/2	3/4	1	1	2	3	4	8	16	Yield	Method
Tortilla Soup 393	oz Olive Oil	lb Onion dice	tbsp Toasted Cumin	gallon Chicken Stock	lb Chicken Thighs	ea Bay Leaf	ea Garlic Clove minced	oz Hominy Kernels cooked		1 gallon	In a soup pot heat the oil and sauté the onions and garlic until translucent. Add the chilies and cumin. Add the stock and chicken thighs and bring to a simmer for 45 minutes.
	cup Cilantro Leaves	lb Jack Cheese	pint of Corn Oil (to fry tortillas)	tbsp Ancho Chili	tbsp Pasilla Chilies chopped	ea Tomato chopped		ea Corn Tortilla-chiffonade			Add the hominy ad remove the chicken thighs. Cool the thighs slightly. Remove the meat from the bone. Shred and reserve. Fry the tortilla strips in corn oil that has reached 325° until light golden brown. Serve the broth with all of the garnitures on the side. Cilantro, Cheese, Chicken, Tomatoes and tortillas.
Harvest Pumpkin 394	ea Bay Leaf	ea Cinnamon Stick	oz Clarified Butter	gallon Chicken Stock	ea Ham Hock	oz Apple Brandy	lb Raw Pumpkin – peeled and diced		oz Mirepoix diced	1 gallon	In a soup pot heat the butter and sauté the mirepoix until translucent. Flambé with brandy. Add the pumpkin, ham hock, stock and spices. Bring to simmer for 1 hour.
	pinch Nutmeg		oz Parsley-chopped (garnish)		ea Apples-peeled and fine diced	cup Cream					When the pumpkin is very tender strain the solids and puree. Add the apples and nutmeg, bring back to simmer. Temper in the heavy cream. Adjust seasoning and garnish.
Thanksgiving Turkey 395			gallon Turkey Stock	tbsp Cracked Pepper	lb Mirepoix-medium dice	lb Turkey-leftovers				1 gallon	In a soup pot simmer the broth and add the leftover turkey with the mirepoix and seasonings. Simmer until the meat is very tender.
		cup Corn	tsp Thyme	tbsp Salt	ea Bay Leaves			oz Green Bean	oz Egg Noodle		Discard bay leaf. Simmer the beans and corn with the noodles until they are tender. Season to taste.
Santé Fe Black Bean 396	tsp Ground Cumin	tbsp Garlic	lb Black Beans	gallon Chicken Stock	ea Jalapeños minced			oz Chorizo Sausage-	oz small dice White Mirepoix	1 gallon	Soak beans overnight in water. Render the chorizo and sauté the veg until tender. Drain the beans and bring them to a simmer with stock
		oz Cilantro Leaves	cup Fresh Pico de Gallo					oz Sour Cream			When the beans are beginning to fall apart season to taste. Garnish to order with the items in this line.

Chowders and Gumbos

No.	Recipe	1/2	3/4	1	1	2	3	4	8	16	Yield	Method
397	New England Clam Chowder	tsp White Pepper	cup Flour / Cup Celery diced	qt Water		qt Half And Half Cream	ea Sprig Thyme	oz Salt Pork- diced small	oz Onion diced	ea. Quahog Clams	1 Gallon	Wash and purge clams, steam in pot with water until they open. Strain the liquid through a coffee filter and chop the clams. Render the salt pork in a clean pot. Sauté the onions and celery. Singer with flour. Add in the liquids and simmer with the bay leaf .
		tsp Tabasco®	tsp Worcestershire	ea Bay Leaf	pint Cream	tsp Salt	ea Potato diced					Once the chowder has simmered for 5 minutes add in the diced potatoes and continue to simmer until they are tender- about 20 minutes. Finish with cream and clams .Season.
398	Manhattan Clam Chowder	tsp White Pepper	tsp Oregano	qt Water		qt Clam Stock	cup Tomato Juice	oz diced Leeks	oz diced Onion	ea. Quahog Clams	3.25 quart	Wash clams, steam in pot with water until they open. Strain the liquid through a coffee filter and chop the clams.
		tsp Tabasco®			ea Sprig Thyme	cups Potato diced	oz Bacon diced	oz Carrot diced	oz Celery diced	oz Tomatoes diced		Render the bacon in a clean pot. Sauté the onions and leeks. Add all of the remaining ingredients
		tsp Worcestershire	tsp Old Bay Seasoning®	ea Bay Leaf	tsp Salt			oz Green Pepper diced				Simmer for 30 -40 minutes. Season to taste. Add the clams last.
399	Outer Banks Oyster Chowder	gallon Clam Stock	cup Flour	qt Half And Half Cream	ea Sprig Thyme	ea Bay Leaf	oz Bacon diced	oz Celery diced	oz diced Onion		serves 12 / 12 oz portion	Render the bacon in a clean pot. Sauté the onions and celery. Add the stock and cream with seasonings and simmer.
			oz Clarified Butter	qt Shucked Oysters	tsp Salt	tsp Garlic minced			oz White Wine	oz Spinach julienne		Poach the oysters in the soup for 5 minutes. Sauté the spinach in the garlic and butter. Add the wine and add to the soup. Season to taste.
				qt Mashed Potato						oz Fried Leeks		Present -scoop potatoes on a soup plate. Pour the soup around. Place oysters. Garnish with fried leeks
400	Virginia Corn Chowder	tsp White Pepper	cup Flour	ea Bay Leaf	tsp Salt	qt chicken stock	oz Virginia Ham diced	oz Salt Pork- small dice	oz Onion diced		3 quart	Render the salt pork. Sauté all of the veg in fat and singer. Add stock and ham. Simmer for 20 minutes.
		tsp Tabasco®	tsp Worcestershire	qt Half And Half Cream	lb Corn Kernels	lb Potato diced	oz Red Pepper diced	oz Green Pepper diced	oz Celery diced			Add the cream, potatoes and seasoning. Simmer the potatoes until tender.

Chowders and Gumbos

	1/2	3/4	1	1	2	3	4	8	16		Method
401 Fish Chowder	cup Flour	quart Cold Water	tsp Cracked Black Pepper	ea Bay Leaf	qt Fish Stock	oz Salt Cod	oz Salt Pork		oz Mirepoix		Soak salt cod in cold water for 24 hours. Rinse. Render the salt pork in a clean pot. Sauté the onions and celery. Singer with flour. Add in the liquids and simmer with the bay leaf. Add the salt cod and simmer for 35 minutes.
	tbsp Fresh Thyme Leaves		lb Potatoes diced	qt Half And Half Cream	tbsp Parsley chopped				oz Fresh Cod or Pollack	3.5 quart	Add the potatoes, thyme, and temper in the cream. Simmer for 15 minutes and add the cod. Simmer 5 minutes. Season. Garnish.
402 Blue Crab Chowder	tsp White Pepper	cup Flour	ea Bay Leaf	tsp Salt	qt Crab Stock	oz Celery diced	oz Salt Pork	oz Onion diced	oz Potato diced		Render the salt pork in a clean pot. Sauté the onions and celery. Singer with flour. Add in the liquids and simmer with the bay leaf. Add the salt cod and simmer for 35 minutes. Add potatoes
	tsp Tabasco®	tsp Old Bay Seasoning®	qt Half And Half Cream	lb Corn Kernels		oz Red Pepper diced	oz Green Pepper diced		oz Crabmeat	3.25 quart	Temper in the cream and add the peppers and corn. Simmer until the potatoes are tender. Season and add the picked crab last.
403 Hearty Seafood Gumbo		tsp Salt	tbsp Cajun Spice	lb White Mirepoix	lb Shrimp – peel and devein	ea Tomatoes diced	quarts Water				Prepare a stock from the shrimp shells and the other items on this line. Simmer for 30 minutes. Remove the shells. Reserve the rest.
	tsp Cayenne	cup Clarified Butter	cup Flour	tsp Thyme	cups Trinity small diced	ea Bay Leaf		oz Bacon diced			In a clean pot render the bacon and add the butter. Make a brown roux. Sauté the trinity in the roux with the seasonings. Add the stock. Simmer for 30 minutes.
	qt Okra sliced	tsp Oregano	tsp Basil		tbsp Garlic minced			oz Tomato Puree	oz Crayfish Tail Meat		Add the okra and seasonings, tomato puree and simmer for 20 minutes.
			Tbsp File Gumbo Powder				oz Oysters	ea Green Onions	oz Crabmeat	1 gallon	Add the shrimp, crayfish oysters, and file. Simmer for 5 minutes and add the crabmeat. Add in the green onions. Discard the bay leaf. Season to taste Serve over steamed rice.

Trinity is equal parts of Green Pepper, Celery and Onion

71

Chowders and Gumbos

	1/2	3/4	1	1	2	3	4	8	16		Method
404 Chicken and Shrimp Gumbo *Trinity is equal parts of Green Pepper, Celery and Onion*	oz Garlic minced	cup Clarified Butter	ea Jalapeño minced	cup Toasted Flour	ea Bay Leaves		qt Chicken Stock	ea Chicken Thigh - diced	oz Shrimp – peel and devein		In a large pot simmer the chicken, shrimp shells, bay, jalapeno, and garlic for 30 minutes. Remove the chicken and cool. Strain everything else out and save the liquid. In a clean pot prepare a brown roux.
	tsp Cayenne	lb Trinity diced	tsp Oregano	lb Andouille diced	cup Tomato diced		oz Green Pepper diced	oz Okra sliced		3.5 quart	Saute the trinity and peppers in the roux. Add in the stock and simmer with the okra, sausage and tomatoes for 30 minutes. Add all of the seasonings and file powder.
	tsp Cracked Black Pepper		tsp Thyme	tbsp File Powder				oz Green Onion sliced			Dice the chicken. Add the shrimp to the soup and simmer for 5 minutes. Add the cooked chicken Serve over steamed rice. Garnish with scallions.
405 Big Easy Ya Ya	lb Lard	tbsp Black Pepper	tbsp Cajun Spice	lb Onion diced	cup Flour	lb Andouille- sliced	lb Chicken Thighs- debone and split into quarters				Heat the lard in a large braising pan. Season and dredge the chicken in flour. Fry the chicken in the lard until golden brown. Remove chicken when done. Make a brown roux. Sauté onions.
	tsp Cayenne	tsp Thyme	lb White Rice	cup Celery diced	tbsp Garlic minced	ea Red Pepper diced	ea Green Pepper diced	quarts Chicken Stock	ea Green Onion - sliced	1.25 gallon	Add the stock, peppers, garlic and celery. Simmer for 30 minutes with rice then add chicken and sausage. Simmer 15 minutes. Add green onions and season to taste.
406 Low Country Crab Gumbo *Trinity is equal parts of Green Pepper, Celery and Onion*		gallon Crab Stock	tsp Thyme	lb Smoked Sausage- diced	qt Beef Stock	Bay Leaf	oz Brown Roux	ea Tomato diced	oz Trinity small dice	1 gallon	Saute trinity in roux. Simmer with stock and tomato. Add the herbs and sausage.
		tsp File Powder	tsp Cracked Black Pepper	lb Okra sliced	lb Crabmeat			ea Green Onion- sliced			Simmer for 20 minutes and add the okra. Simmer for 20 minutes. Thicken the soup with the file powder. Season and add the crabmeat. Garnish with the green onions

International Soups

#	Recipe	1/2	3/4	1	1	2	3	4	8	16	Yield	Method
407	Avgolémono	cup Fresh Lemon Juice		ea Whole Chicken		cups Rice	tbsp Parsley chopped	quart Chicken Stock	ea Eggs		1 gallon	Simmer stock and chicken for 1 hour. Add rice and simmer for 25 minutes. Remove chicken, debone, dice meat. Remove fat, whisk eggs then lemon. Slowly add liquid. Heat to 145°. Season add chicken
408	Borscht	oz Brown Sugar	gallon Beef Stock	oz Red Wine Vinegar	cup Carrot diced	ea Bay Leaves	lbs Beets diced	cups Cabbage diced	oz Onion diced	oz Beef Chuck	3.5 quart	Bring the stock to a boil. Add the beef and simmer for 20 minutes. Add the remaining ingredients on this line and simmer until the beef is very tender. Season to taste.
									oz Sour Cream		3.5 quart	Spoon a dollop of sour cream on top.
409	Caldo Verde	oz Garlic minced	qt Kale chopped	lb Ham Hock	ea Bay Leaf	oz Olive Oil	quart Chicken Stock	oz Chorizo Sausage	ea Small Potato – peeled and diced	oz White Mirepoix	3 quart	Heat the oil in a soup pot and render the chorizo. Sauté the vegetables, ham hock and stock simmer for 30 minutes. Add the potatoes and simmer until tender. Remove the bay leaves. Season to taste .
	Cock a Leekie		lb Barley	gallon Chicken Stock	Sachet	ea Onion-small dice	rib Celery small dice	lb Chicken leg quarters	ea Leeks clean & slice		1 gallon	Place stock in 2 gallon pot Add everything except barley. Bring to a boil, remove scum, reduce to a simmer for 1 hour, add barley and simmer for 1 hour. Season and dice chicken meat, garnish.
411	Egg Drop	cup Cornstarch	cup Water	tbsp Peanut oil	tbsp Ginger-grated	oz Scallion sliced	quart Chicken Stock	drop Yellow Food Color	ea Eggs		3.25 quart	Bring the stock to a boil. Add the oil and ginger. Make cornstarch slurry. Thicken the stock with slurry. Add the yellow color. Whisk the eggs in a bowl and pour the eggs through a colander over the simmering soup. Season. Serve with the sliced scallions.
	French Onion	gallon Beef Stock	oz Clarified Butter	sprig Thyme	ea Sachet	qt Chicken Stock	oz Sherry	lb Onion julienne			10-12 serving	In a marmite heat butter and onions and sweat covered until very tender. Sauté uncovered until well caramelized while stirring. Singer with a Tbsp of flour. Deglaze the marmite with sherry, add the stocks and herbs. Simmer for 30 minutes. Season to taste
412		lb Provolone Cheese Sliced		lb Gruyere Cheese-sliced	loaf French Bread slice ½ inch thick		oz Clarified Butter					Toast the French bread slices. Brush the bread with butter, toast again. At service portion into crocks. Place the crouton on top and layer the top with the Gruyère cheese then provolone. Place under a broiler, gratinee.

International Soups

#	Name	1/2	3/4	1	1	2	3	4	8	16	Yield	Method
413	Harira			ea Lamb Head	cup Chick Peas	oz Ginger	lb Mirepoix		quart Water		1 gal	Simmer lamb head for 3 hours at 170°. Strain stock into a clean pot; Add veg, chick peas simmer 1 hour.
		cup Parsley chopped	tsp Coriander	cup Lentils	tbsp Turmeric	tsp Cinnamon	oz Rice	lb Tomato diced				Add all but parsley, simmer 1 hour. Remove meat from lamb and dice. Puree soup, season, add lamb and parsley
414	Hot and Sour	cup Cornstarch	tsp Black Pepper	tbsp Ginger grated	tsp White Pepper	tbsp Peanut Oil	quart Chicken Stock	oz Bamboo Shoot julienne	oz Roast Pork julienne	oz Black Mushroom		Bring the stock to a simmer. Add the oil, ginger, pepper, and mushroom. Simmer for 5 minutes. Make cornstarch slurry and thicken the soup. Bring to a boil and add the pork
		cup Eggs		lb Tofu-diced	tbsp Sesame Oil	oz sliced Scallion	oz White Vinegar	tbsp Soy Sauce			3.5 quarts	Add the vinegar and soy. Whisk the eggs and pass them though a colander over the soup. Add the tofu. Season to taste. Garnish.
415	Minestrone	tsp Cracked Black Pepper	quart Ripe Tomato diced	lb Onion diced	gallon Chicken Stock	oz Pancetta brunoise	ea Garlic Cloves	tsp Olive Oil	oz Celery diced	oz Cabbage julienne		Render the pancetta in the olive oil. Sauté the veg in the oil until the onions are translucent. Add the tomatoes, stock and pepper. Simmer until all veg is tender.
		cup Parmesan Cheese	cup Pepper diced	tbsp Pesto	pint Cooked Beans	cups Ditalini Pasta			oz Carrots diced		1 gallon	Flavor the soup with pesto and add the beans and pasta. Simmer until pasta is cooked. Season, Garnish with cheese.
416	Mulligatawny	tsp Ground Clove	tsp Salt	tsp Black Pepper	tsp Cumin	tbsp Coriander	ea Garlic Cloves	tsp Turmeric	ea Green Chilies			Place all of the items in this line in a food processor and grind to a fine paste.
			lb Chicken Thigh Meat – diced	oz Clarified Butter	pinch Nutmeg	tbsp Ginger – grated	quart Stock		oz Lentils	oz Onion diced	1 gal	In the soup pot heat the butter and sauté the onion until tender. Add the spice blend from above. Add the chicken lentils and spices. Simmer until the chicken is cooked and the lentils are tender. Season
									oz Heavy Cream	oz Basmati Rice cooked		Finish the soup with a cream liaison. Garnish with the rice.
417	Scotch Broth			ea Bay Leaf	lb Mirepoix brunoise	lb Lamb-small dice	oz Leek brunoise	quart Stock	oz Barley			Blanch the lamb in boiling salted water and remove. Bring the stock to a boil and add the lamb, barley, bay leaf, leek and mirepoix. Simmer for 20 minutes
		cup Parsley chopped					oz. Swedes brunoise	oz Turnip brunoise	oz. Cabbage diced		1 gal	Add the Swedes (rutabaga), turnip and cabbage and simmer until all of the items are very tender. Finish the soup with chopped parsley.

Chilled Soups

	Item	1/2	1	1	2	3	4		Yield	Method of Preparation
418	Avocado	cup chopped Arugula	tsp Cumin / tbsp Cilantro	oz Lime Juice / tsp Salt	cups Sour Cream	cups Chicken Stock	ea Haas Avocado / oz Chablis	1 tsp Tabasco	2 quarts	Puree everything in a blender until smooth. Check seasoning. Garnish with Pico de Gallo or Crabmeat with Fresh Cilantro. Good for shooters.
419	Cherry Fruit (Fructsuppe)	cup Sugar	bottle Dornfelder Red Wine / pint Blackberries	ea Pear-diced / ea small diced Plums	cups Cherries- / ea small diced Peaches	oz Lemon Juice		1 stick Cinnamon / 1 cup Apple Juice	Serves 8 / 8 oz portion	Simmer the pear, cherries, wine, sugar and cinnamon for 20 minutes; covered. Strain and pass through a food mill. Chill and then finish with the remaining ingredients. Serve with Vanilla ice cream.
420	Consommé Madrilène — Pour into cups while warm and allow to set, top with sour cream and chives	1 Sachet	1 Red Pepper – pureed	quart Fresh Tomato Juice strained	cups cleaned Sliced Leeks	Qt. Clear Chicken Stock	ea Egg Whites	4 tbsp Gelatin	3 quarts	Combine the stock and juice in a tall stock pot. Whisk egg whites and whisk into stock with leeks and pepper. Add sachet, Sprinkle gelatin on top, cover and steam for 1 hour. Add seasoning and Carefully strain out liquid through coffee filters. Chill.
421	Cucumber Dill		cup Leeks sliced thin and cleaned	cup Yogurt / cup Heavy Cream	cups Chicken Stock	tbsp Butter / tbsp Flour	ea Cucumbers peeled, seeded	2 tbsp chopped Dill	1 ½ quarts	In a 2 quart sauce pot heat butter, sweat the leeks. Singer with flour add stock. Simmer for 10 minutes. Chill. Add cucumbers puree until smooth. Mix in cream, yogurt. Season add dill.
422	Curry Vegetable	ea Large Onion diced	ea Eggplant- roast- peel	pint Cream / lb Potato diced	quarts Chicken Stock	tbsp Garlic / oz Melted Butter	oz Green Peas	1 tbsp Curry Powder / 1 tsp Saffron	3 quarts	In a 6 quart sauce pot sauté onion, garlic in butter. Add potatoes and spice. Add stock and simmer until onions are soft. Chill. Puree the roasted eggplant with the soup. Season, chill, garnish with peas
423	English Pea	oz Butter	cup Fresh Spinach	quart Chicken Stock	cup Onion diced	cups English Peas-		2 cups Heavy Cream	2.5 quarts	In a 4 quart stock pot sauté the onions in butter. Add stock. boil, add peas. Cook until tender, quickly chill, puree all, season
424	Gazpacho	cup Fresh Bread Crumbled / cup Cucumber brunoise	oz Garlic minced / oz Red Wine Vinegar	lb Cucumber peeled seeded / cup Crouton	oz Olive Oil	lb Ripe, Peeled Tomato / oz Red Pepper brunoise	oz Red Pepper diced / oz Green Pepper brunoise	8oz Red Onion / ½ cup Sliced Olives	2 / quarts	Roughly chop all items on this line and puree until smooth. Refrigerate 4 hours and strain through fine mesh. / Season the soup with salt and cayenne. Add in the vinegar and veg. Use the croutons and olive to garnish
425	Melon	tsp Salt	ea Lime Juiced	cup Yogurt	cups Orange Juice	oz Sugar	cups Melon diced		1.5 quarts	Puree all until smooth. Strain through a fine mesh strainer. Use apple juice for Honeydew and OJ for cantaloupe.
426	Peach	ea Lemon Juiced	cup Orange Juice	cup Pineapple Juice	cups Sour Cream	lbs Frozen Peaches with Juice	oz Peach Brandy		2.5 quarts	Puree peaches and juice in a blender; add other juices and brandy, puree. Add sour cream last, puree. By Hermann Rusch.

Chili and Beans

Item	1/2	1	2	3	4		Yield	Method of Preparation
428 Black Bean Chili	cup Tomato Paste	cup Anaheim Chilies roasted and diced or 2 small cans diced green chilies / cup diced Onion / quart diced Tomato	lbs Ground Chuck (90% lean) / cups Beef Stock	tbsp Dark Chili Powder	cups Cooked Black Beans or (3 ea 15 oz cans)	2 ½ tsp Ground Cumin / 2 tsp Salt	10 port	Brown the ground beef over medium heat, add the onions and sweat. Add chili powder, cumin, and tomato paste. Stir and add stock, simmer and add rest. Simmer over low heat for 30 minutes. Adjust seasoning to taste with additional salt and prepared hot sauce.
429 Boston Baked Beans	cup Molasses / tsp Ground Cloves	tsp Baking Soda / tsp Black Pepper / lb Smoked Bacon-diced	lbs Navy Beans / oz Tomato Paste	tsp Dry Mustard / cups minced Onion	oz Brown Sugar	7 cups Water	3 qt	Soak beans overnight. Heat 2 quarts of water and add beans with the baking soda. Boil for 8 minutes. Drain. In a 1 gallon casserole render the bacon until half done. Add onions and sweat. Add remaining ingredients including blanched beans and the 7 cups of water. Bring to simmer, tightly cover and place in a 325° oven for 6 hours.
430 Carolina BBQ Beans	lb Apple Smoked Bacon-diced / cup Pinto Beans / bottle Beer	cup Navy Beans / tsp Pepper	cup Kidney Beans / cup BBQ Sauce	tbsp Garlic chopped / oz Molasses	oz Dark Brown Sugar	2 cups Onion fine dice / 2 tsp Salt	3 qt	Soak beans overnight In a 1 gallon heavy casserole/pot slowly simmer beans in 1 ½ quarts of water covered for 1 ½ hours. Once beans are tender, in a separate pan render bacon until almost crisp, add onions and sweat. Combine all ingredients in pot with beans. Bake in oven for 1 hour.
431 Chuck Wagon Beans	lb Slab Bacon / tsp Cayenne	gallon Water / tbsp Cumin	lb diced Onion / tbsp Salt / lb Pinto Beans / oz Molasses	tbsp Granulated Garlic	cups Crushed Tomato	¼ cup Dark Chili Powder	3 qt	Soak beans overnight, drain off water. In a 2 gallon heavy bottom pot add everything. Bring to a boil and reduce to a simmer for 2 ½ hours or until the beans are tender and liquid is thickened. Avoid stirring beans.
432 Frijoles Charros	lb Smoked Bacon-diced	can Pinto Beans w liquid (40 oz) / tbsp Garlic	lb Ground Chorizo / cup diced Onion	ea Jalapeños diced / oz Tomato Paste	oz canned Chipotle in Adobo-minced	4.5 oz can Green Chilies	10 port	Render the bacon until almost crisp, add chorizo and cook until fully cooked. Add onions and garlic, cook until tender. Add the rest and bring to a simmer for 20 minutes. Adjust seasoning
433 Frijoles Negros	lb Smoked Ham Hock / tsp Pepper	lb Dried Black Beans / tbsp Salt / tbsp Red Wine Vinegar	tsp Paprika / ea Bay Leaf	clove Garlic-sliced	tbsp Olive Oil	1 ea Red Cubanelle Pepper-diced	8 port	Bring 3 quarts of water and the dried beans to a boil for 2 minutes. Turn off and allow to sit for 1 hour. Add the remaining items, except vinegar and seasoning, and simmer for 2 hours. Add vinegar and seasoning last.
434 Frijoles Rancheros	cup roasted, seeded Jalapeño	lb Bacon-diced / tbsp Salt	lb Pinto Beans	ea Onions-diced	tbsp Garlic chopped	3 quarts Water	3 qt	Soak beans overnight. In a 6 quart Dutch oven render the bacon, saute the onions. Add the rest. Bring to boil and reduce to a simmer for 1 ½ - 2 hours. Adjust the seasoning to your taste
435 Frijoles Refritos	cup Oil or Lard	cup Onion diced / lb Dry Pinto Beans	tbsp Garlic		ea Arbol Chilies	1 tbsp Salt	8 port	Follow same method as frijoles negro to cook the beans. Sauté onions, chilies, garlic in oil add to beans and simmer 2 hours. Remove chilies and puree. Season
436 Hot Dog Chili	tsp Cayenne / tsp Cumin	pint Beef Bouillon / cup minced Onion	lbs Ground Beef (80% lean) / tsp Paprika	tbsp Chili Powder / tbsp Flour	oz Ketchup / tbsp Yellow Mustard	tbsp Sugar	24 port	Brown the ground beef in a 1 gallon heavy bottomed pot. Add the onions and spices, stir to sweat onions. Add the flour to absorb fat. Add remaining ingredients and bring to a simmer for 30 minutes. Adjust salt to the type of hot dog. 2oz per portion

Chili and Beans

Item	1/2	1	1	2	3	4		Yield	Method of Preparation
437 Old Fashion Chili	cup diced Green Chilies / oz Oil	can Dark Kidney Beans (40 oz) / tbsp Salt	can Pinto Beans (40 oz) / tbsp Cumin	ea Onion diced / oz Tomato Paste	lbs Ground Chuck (90% lean) / cup Water	tbsp Dark Chili Powder / tbsp Flour	3 can diced Tomato (15 oz can)	1.25 gal	Coat the inside of a 2 gallon pot with oil. Brown the beef, add the onions, spices, flour. Stir and add paste, tomatoes, water, salt, chilies. Simmer 10 minutes add canned bean with liquids. Simmer 2 hours. Add black pepper to taste.
438 Pork Chili Verde	cup Garlic chopped / tsp Ground Coriander	tbsp Cumin / cup Cilantro Leaves	lb Anaheim Chilies roasted and diced / tbsp Salt	ea Poblano Chilies- roasted and diced	ea Onions diced / ea Serrano Chilies	lbs Pork Shoulder- diced 2" / ea Tomatillo diced	¾ cup Masa Harina	3 qt	Place pork shoulder in a slow cooker with enough water to just cover. Layer chilies, onions, tomatillo, seasoning and garlic on top. Cover with a lid and turn on high for 3 hours. Carefully drain off liquid into a pot. Bring to a boil and thicken with masa. Stir in cilantro Season to taste. Serve with lime and fresh corn tortillas.
439 Sloppy Joe	cup Brown Sugar / tsp Clove	cup minced Onion / tbsp Worcestershire	cup fine dice Green Pepper / can Beer	cup Ketchup / tbsp Salt	oz Water / tsp Garlic Powder	lb Ground Beef (90% lean)	1 tsp Coleman's Mustard	16 port	Brown the beef in a 2 gallon pot. Add the onions and peppers and cook until soft. Combine mustard, water, and salt – save for last. Add everything else to the pot and simmer for 30 minutes over low heat. Add mustard mix last. 5 oz portion
440 Texas Chili	cup Masa Harina / cup Water	tbsp Dried Oregano / qt Tomato Puree	cup Dark Chili Powder / tbsp Pepper	tbsp Ground Cumin / cup Onion diced	tbsp Garlic minced / tbsp Salt	oz Rendered Beef Fat / pint Beef Stock	5 lbs Chuck- ½"dice	1.25 gal	Season beef with chili powder, salt and pepper. In a heavy pot heat beef fat and slowly brown the beef, add the onion and garlic, then remaining ingredients, except masa. Simmer for 2 hours. Mix masa and water then temper in to the sauce to thicken. Simmer 5 minutes.
441 Turkey Chili-Oaxaca Mole	tsp Cinnamon / tsp Coriander	ea Onion diced / ea Poblano Chili diced	pack Ground Turkey (20 oz) / tbsp Cumin	oz Crumbed Mexican Chocolate / tsp Salt	oz Ground Almonds / Clove Garlic	Tomatoes diced / tbsp Dark Chili Powder	1 tbsp Peanut oil / 14oz can Black Bean	6 port	Make a paste from the almond, garlic, chocolate, chili, spices with a mortar and pestle. In a 4 quart pot heat the oil and brown the turkey. Add the onions and poblanos, cook until tender. Add the tomatoes, simmer covered 10 minutes. Add the spice paste and drained beans; bring back to a simmer for 5 minutes.
442 Vegetable Chili	cup Jalapeño seeded, minced / oz Oil	cup Dry Dark Kidney Beans / tbsp Ground Cumin / tsp pepper	cup Dry Pinto Beans / cup Frozen Edamame	ea Onions diced / cup Corn / tsp Salt	cups Tomato diced / tbsp Garlic minced	oz Tomato Paste / tbsp Ancho Chili Powder	1 ea Red and Green Pepper diced	10 port	Soak beans overnight In a 1 gallon pot bring beans and 3 quarts of water to a boil. Reduce to a simmer for 1 hr. In a sauté pan heat oil and sauté onions, peppers, garlic and chilies. Add spices and tomato. Add to beans and simmer for 1 hr. Add rest of the ingredients, simmer, season to taste.
443 Venison Chili	each Jalapeño minced	ea Poblano diced / ea Onion diced	lb Ground Venison / cup Merlot	ea Grilled Corn Cob	tbsp Olive Oil	ea Tomato diced	1 recipe Chili Spice 1095	4 port	Heat the olive oil in a large skillet. Add the venison and brown; add the chilies, tomatoes onions and chili spice, stir. Add the red wine and simmer 20 minutes. Remove kernels from the corn and stir into chili. Serve with jack cheese.
444 West Virginia Pinto Beans	tsp Black Pepper	cup Onion fine diced	lb Dry Pinto Beans	tsp Salt	ea Bay Leaf	oz Bacon Fat	3 ea. Ham Hock	10 port	Soak beans overnight, drain. In a 1 gallon pot heat bacon fat, sauté onions, add 2 quarts water, bay, beans, hock, simmer 2 ½ hrs, season salt and black pepper.

Chefs Note: The Brown Beans, recipe 444 was one of the favorite dishes served at the Greenbrier Chefs Table. It was served with warm cornbread, a ham steak and diced raw onions. The Chefs Table was our family meal time as apprentices. The Greenbrier has created a great number of Certified Master Chefs thanks to leadership of The Executive Chefs Hermann Rusch, Rod Stoner, Hartmut Handke CMC, Walter Scheib, Robert Wong Peter Timmins CMC, Rich Rosendale CMC and Bryan Skelding CEC.

Casseroles

	Item	1/2	1	1	2	3	4	8	Yield	Method of Preparation
445	**Breakfast**	cup Sour Cream	lb Cooked Sausage	cup Salsa	tbsp Chives sliced	cup Cheese shredded	oz Onion sautéed	ea Eggs	Serves 8	Blend the eggs and sour cream. Pour into a greased pan, bake in water bath for 30 minutes at 325°, until eggs begin to set. Top with layers of salsa, sausage, and cheese. Bake for 15 minutes garnish with chives. By Greenbrier Executive Chef Hermann Rusch "Eggs Fantastic".
446	**Chicken Pot Pie**	quart Heavy Cream	quart Frozen Mixed Vegetable	pint chicken Stock	recipe Pie Dough #945	oz Flour / oz Butter	ea Chicken Breast (8 oz ea)	oz Mirepoix	Serves 8	Melt butter in a 2 quart sauce pan, sweat mirepoix, add flour then stock and simmer. Poach chicken in same pot. Once chicken is 165° remove and cool. Add cream simmer for 10 minutes Add frozen veg to cool. Dice breasts add to filling. Roll out dough 2 times the size of pan. Grease, place bottom layer, fill with chicken filling, top with dough. Bake at 350° 1 hour
447	**Chili Rellano Casserole**	cup Cream	cup Sour Cream	cup Queso Blanco	cups grated Jalapeño Jack Cheese	tsp Masa Harina	ea Eggs	ea Poblano Chilies roasted	Serves 8	Blend the, eggs. Cream and sour cream. Combine 1 cup of Jack with Queso Blanco and masa. Fill the chilies and lay in greased pan. Pour egg mixture over the chilies and bake covered in a 300° oven for 30 minutes. Top with remaining jack cheese and bake until firm and brown.
448	**Grits Soufflé**	dozen Eggs	stick Butter (4oz)	cup Sharp Cheddar	cups Milk	oz Parmesan Cheese	cups Water	oz Grits	Serves 8	In a 2 quart pot bring water to a boil, add 1 tsp salt. Simmer grits 10 minutes, add milk simmer 5 minutes. Melt in butter and cool. Mix in cheese and egg yolks. Once room temp, whip egg whites, fold in, pour in pan, bake at 375° for 45 minutes. Serve immediately.
449	**Huevos Charros** Serve with fresh tortillas and pico de gallo	cup Sour Cream	lb Cooked Chorizo Sausage	cup Onions dice sauté	cups Refried Beans	cup Jack Cheese	oz Can Diced Green Chilies	ea Eggs	Serves 6	Blend 2 eggs, 1 cup of cheese, and sour cream. Layer beans on bottom, make 6 wells for eggs. Crack eggs into wells. Top with chorizo, onions, chilies, pour cream mixture over the top then cheese. Bake in a 325° oven for 20 minutes, until eggs begin to set.
450	**Macaroni and Cheese**	lb Sharp Cheddar Cheese	tsp Mustard	ea Egg / cup Cheese Crackers	oz Roux Blanc / tbsp Melted Butter	cups Half And Half Cream / oz Cream Cheese	oz Extra Sharp Cheddar Cheese	oz Macaroni	Serves 6	Simmer the cream and thicken with roux. Boil macaroni until al dente. Blend Dijon and egg. Once sauce has simmered for 10 minutes, remove from heat and whisk in cheeses and the egg mixture until sauce is smooth. Drain macaroni once done and mix with sauce. Grind cheese crackers and toss with butter. Top the mac and cheese Bake in a 350° oven for 15 minutes.
451	**Oatmeal Brunch**	cup Brown Sugar	tbsp Ground Cinnamon	pint milk	cups Apple Cider	cups Steel Cut Oats	cups Green Apple diced	oz Walnuts chopped	Serves 8	Combine all together and place in greased pan. Bake at 325° for 1 hour. Cut into 8 squares; serve with dried and fresh fruits, yogurt on the side. Easy breakfast for a crowd or as a healthy item on a brunch buffet.
452	**Tamale Pie**	ea Onion minced	pint Warm Water	cup Lard	tsp Salt	cup Masa Harina	tbsp Jalapeño minced			Break up the lard in the masa harina , add the remaining ingredients on this line and mix Refrigerate for 2 hours
		lb Onion diced	recipe Chili Spice 1095	can Refried Beans (15 oz)	lb Ground Beef	oz Tomato Paste	oz Peppers diced	oz Water as needed	Serves 8	Brown the ground beef, add the onions and peppers, add the rest, except beans and simmer 20 minutes. Add beans and mix in. Roll out 1/3 of the dough into pan Fill with beef mixture Roll out a layer of the remaining masa, place on top of filling, bake 350° 45 minutes
453	**Sweet Potato Casserole**	recipe Streusel 792	tsp Cinnamon	cup Brown Sugar	ea Eggs	lbs Sweet Potato	oz Melted Butter	oz Pecans chopped	Serves 8	Bake sweet potatoes until tender. Peel and mash, add sugar, cinnamon, eggs, and butter. Mix and pour in pan. Top with pecans and streusel. Bake 350° 30 minutes

All recipes are for a standard half hotel pan or a 9" by 13" casserole

Ground Meat Preparations

	Item	1/2	1	1	1	2	4		Yield	Method of Preparation
454	**Albondigas**	cup Onion minced	tsp Paprika	cup Milk / pinch Nutmeg	lb Ground Beef / tsp Black Pepper	lbs Ground Pork / tsp Sea Salt	slices Stale Bread / ea Eggs	¼ cup Parsley chopped	6 doz	Soak the bread in milk for 5 minutes. Break apart into fine crumbs. Add the meats and mix in. add rest of ingredients and mix well. Chill for 30 minutes .Form into 1 oz meatballs. Fry in olive oil, serve with spicy tomato sauce at internal temp of 165°.
455	**Frikadeller** — To prepare a **Veal Pojarski** use only ground veal. shape, standard bread and pan fry in butter	tsp Ground Allspice	pint Cold Heavy Cream	cup Onion minced	lb Ground Pork / pinch White Pepper	lbs Ground Beef	ea Eggs	1 ½ cups Flour	3 doz	Mix flour, spice and seasoning with cream together. All to stand for 5 minutes. Add everything else to the mixture and mix well. Form into 2 oz flat balls and fry in butter until they reach 165°
456	**Italian Meatballs** — Aunt Yolanda's Recipe	cup Onion minced / cup Milk	lb Ground Pork / tbsp Onion Salt	lb Ground Beef / tsp Black Pepper	lb Ground Veal / tsp Crushed Red Pepper	Cloves Garlic minced	ea eggs / oz Grated Parmesan Cheese	1 ½ cups Italian Bread Crumbs	2 doz	Mix meat, add seasoning, mix. Add rest. Adjust seasoning. Form 3 oz meatballs. Brown in light olive oil. Top with tomato sauce and bake in 350° oven until they reach 165°.
457	**Meatloaf- NY Style** — Grandpa Joe's Recipe			pint Onion diced	dozen Stale Burger Buns- crumbled	quarts Tomato Sauce	ea Eggs	6 lbs ground chuck	Serves 18	Mix 1 quart of the tomato sauce into the remaining ingredients. Form 3 loaves. Bake on sheet pan for 20 minutes at 350°. Pour 1 qt sauce over the loaves. Bake to 155°.
458	**Meatloaf- Southern**	lb Onion minced / lb Bacon	cup Green Peppers diced	lb Country Sausage	cup Bread Crumbs / tsp Worcestershire Sauce	lbs Ground Beef / tsp Salt	oz Ketchup / oz Milk	2 ea Eggs	Serves 8	Microwave the peppers and onions in a covered container for 1 minute. Line 9" loaf pan with bacon. Place ingredients in mixing bowl and knead with a paddle for 1 minute. Portion into loaf pan. Bake in a 350° for 1 hour. Bake until 165°. Serve with brown gravy.
459	**Salisbury Steak** — Dad's Recipe	cup Bread Crumbs	cup Minced Onion	oz Dijon / tsp Salt	oz Worcestershire / tsp Pepper	lbs Ground Beef	tbsp Parsley chopped	2 ea Eggs	Serves 10	Combine all ingredients in a mixing bowl with paddle. Mix until well blended. Portion 10 oval patties. Brown patties in butter, add brown gravy to simmer covered until 155°
460	**Spicy Turkey Burger**	cup Onion minced	tsp Chipotle Chili Sauce	tbsp Garlic chopped	ea Jalapeño minced	lbs Ground Turkey	oz Salsa	1 tsp Salt	Serves 8	Combine and mix well. Refrigerate for 2 hours. Form 8 patties. Grill to an internal temp of 165°
461	**Stuffed Cabbage Filling**- Mom's Recipe		1 ½ cup Onion minced	lb Sauerkraut (chopped)	lb Ground Pork	lbs Ground Chuck	oz Egg / tbsp Brown Mustard	3 cup Cooked Rice	24 rolls	Combine together, season with salt and pepper. Roll into 2 heads blanched cabbage leaves. To with crushed tomatoes and bacon. Bake covered at 325° until they reach 165°
462	**Swedish Meatballs** — Sauce – 2:1 beef stock to cream, simmer. S+P	cup Cream	lb Ground Chuck	lb Ground Pork	cup Milk	ea Eggs	tbsp Shallot minced	3 cup Bread Crumb	4 doz	Prepare a seasoning blend with ¼ tsp allspice, ¼ tsp fresh nutmeg. ¼ tsp white pepper, 1 tbsp salt. Mix with meats, add rest. Portion 1 tbsp each-form balls. Bake 400° 15 minutes. Bake until they reach 165°
463	**Sweet and Sour Meatballs** — Mom's Recipe	cup Bread Crumbs / tsp Pepper	tsp Salt / cup Grape Jelly	lb Ground Beef	tsp Worcestershire Sauce / ea Egg	oz Onion minced / oz Milk		1 jar Chili Sauce (12 oz)	2 doz	Prepare meatballs by combining everything but the jelly and chili sauce. Form 1 oz meatballs, brown in oil. Place in casserole or chafing dish. In a separate pan heat jelly and chili sauce to a boil. Pour sauce over meat balls and heat until they reach 155°

New World One Pot Dishes

Page	Dish	1	1/2	1	2	3	4	8		Serves	Method of Preparation
464	**BBQ Beef**	1 cup Vinegar	tbsp Soy Sauce	tbsp Chili Powder	cup Ketchup	tbsp Oil	lb Beef Chuck- dice	oz Onion diced	12oz Beer	serves 10	Sear the beef in heavy bottomed pot over high heat with the oil. Add the onions and sauté until tender. Deglaze, add remaining
		1 cup Brown Sugar	tsp Ground Clove	tsp Tabasco	oz Molasses					7 oz portion	Bring to a simmer and cover. Place the pot in a 350° oven for 2 hours. Shred the beef with a large fork.
465	**Beef Stew**	1 Sachet	cup Tomato Paste	cup Flour	lb Diced Mirepoix	ea Parsnips Sliced	lb Beef Chuck- 1" cubes	oz Red Wine	2 lb White Potato diced	serves 10	Season and sear the beef in heavy bottomed pot over high heat with oil. Expand with tomato paste. Add the mirepoix and caramelize. Singer. Deglaze with wine and stock, add sachet and parsnips. Bring to boil. Reduce to a simmer, stew over low heat tender. Add potatoes, simmer till tender.
		2 qt Beef Stock		— oz Oil						10 oz portion	
466	**Brunswick Stew**	qt Chicken Stock / 1 lb Pork Shoulder diced	gallon Tomatoes diced	cup Seasoned Flour	cup Onion- diced	oz Bacon- diced	lb Chicken Thigh- boneless and quartered	oz Celery diced	2 oz Clarified Butter	serves 12	Render the bacon and butter until crisp. Dredge chicken in flour and fry until golden brown. Remove chicken and repeat the process with diced pork. Remove the pork and saute the celery and onions in the fat. Singer with flour. Add the tomatoes and stock. Bring to a simmer with meat.
		oz Sugar / 1 tsp Black Pepper	tbsp Thyme	lb Corn	tsp Salt	cup Lima Bean	ea Potato diced	oz Carrot diced		10 oz portion	After 40 minutes add the rest of the ingredients and continue to simmer until tender. Season.
467	**Carne Adovada**	cup Crushed Dried Anaheim Chilies	oz Oil	tbsp Masa Harina	ea Onion diced	lb Pork Butt- diced	oz Tomato Paste	cups Water	5 Clove Garlic- sliced	serves 6	In a heavy bottomed pot sear the pork in oil until brown. Remove and add onion, garlic and masa, stir 2 minutes, add tomato paste, and stir. Bring all ingredients to a simmer and braise for 2 hours at 325°, covered. Remove pork, puree sauce. Pour over pork.
		1 tbsp each Dried Oregano and Cumin Powder								7 oz portion	
468	**Carne Picado** *use for burrito*	quart Beef Stock	bulb Garlic- chopped	oz Oil	ea Onion diced	cups Tomato diced	lb Bottom Sirloin – 1" cube	ea Jalapeño sliced	3-5 ea Serrano Chilies	serves 8	In heavy bottomed pot, sear beef in oil, add onion and brown. Add rest. Braise for 1 ½ hours covered.
469	**Carnita - Mexican Pork-** (Serve with toasted corn tortillas and salsa roja.)	qt Oil	lb Jalapeno Chilies	can Cola	tsp Clove	lb Pork Butt- diced	ea Cinnamon Stick		2 Onions quartered	serves 6	In a 4 qt oven proof pot heat the oil with everything except for the pork. Once the oil reaches 170° add the pork. Cover and place in a 275° for 3 hours. Once tender carefully remove the pork, chilies and onion. Reheat fat – fry the pork crisp.
		2 ea Oranges								7 oz portion	

New World One Pot Dishes

#	Dish		1/2	1	1	2	3	4	8		Yield	Method of Preparation
470	**Carapulcra** *Peruvian Pork and Potatoes*	2 oz Achiote Oil	lb Peanuts chopped	recipe Matignon / tbsp Cumin	ea Onion-julienne / qt. Stock	ea Ancho Chilies / tbsp Garlic	lbs Pork Shoulder 1" cube	oz Sherry	ea Purple Potatoes diced	5 each Yellow Wax Chilies-diced	serves 6 / 10 oz portion	In a heavy casserole, season and sear pork in oil, add onions, spice, chilies, liquids, vegetables Simmer and braise 2 hours, add potatoes simmer 30 min, add nuts last.
471	**Carolina Pork BBQ**	1 tbsp Salt	tsp White pepper	tbsp Black Pepper	pint Water	cup Chili Sauce					serves 12	Marinate all ingredients together for 3 days. Smoke pork for 1 hour.
471			cp Sugar		cup Brown Sugar	cup Cider Vinegar	tbsp Crushed Red Pepper		lb Pork Picnic or Shoulder		6 oz of pork per portion	Place the pork in a coverable braising pan. Add the liquid and cover with lid. Braise in a 300° oven for 5 hours, slice, pull or chop. Simmer liquid until thick.
472	**Colorado Lamb Stew**	2 tbsp Lard or Oil	lb Carrots sliced	cup Red Pepper diced	cup White Wine	ea Onion diced	lbs Lamb Shoulder-1" cube	Clove Garlic - sliced	ea Small Potato quartered	5 cups Lamb Stock	serves 6 / 12 oz portion	In a cast iron Dutch oven, heat lard, season and brown lamb, add vegetables and stock. Simmer and braise for 1 hour covered. Add potatoes simmer 20 minutes. Season
473		½ cup Flour	tsp White Pepper	tbsp Salt	tsp Paprika			oz Oil	ea Large Chicken Breasts		serves 8	Season the chicken with salt, pepper and paprika. Dredge in flour. Brown the chicken over medium heat a skillet with the hot oil.
473	**Chicken ala King**	¼ tsp Nutmeg	tsp Curry Powder	cup Onion	cup Celery	cup Mushroom		cups Stock		ea Lemon	10 oz per portion	Remove chicken and excess fat. Sauté the vegetables lightly and singer with flour. Stir in the stock and seasonings. Bring to a simmer, add chicken. Gently simmer until the chicken reaches 165°. Add the juice of a lemon to the sauce, season
474	**Chipotle Beef Barbacoa**	2 tsp Salt	cup Chili Powder	lb Anaheim Chilies sliced	quart Tomato Puree	ea Onion-diced	lb Chuck diced	ea Chipotle Chilies		oz Oil	serves 6 / 6 oz per portion	Sear the beef in heavy bottomed pot over high heat with the oil. Add the onions and chilies, sauté until they are tender. Add everything else and braise for 2 hours at 350°. Season.
475	**Cioppino** *Serve with Crisp Sour Dough Bread*	¼ cup Extra Virgin Olive Oil	lb Shrimp / cup Shallot minced	ea Red Jalapeño-minced	lb Dungeness Crab Legs and Claws	Clove Garlic minced	ea Tomatoes-peeled and diced	oz White Wine	ea Mussels and Clams	1 cup Clam Juice	serves 2	In a large coverable sautoir, heat shallot and garlic in oil, add chile tomato, seafood Cover and simmer 1 minute, add liquids. Stir and Simmer 6 minutes.
476	**Etouffé-Chicken**	1 pint Stock	cup Celery-small dice	cup Scallion sliced	cup Green Pepper-small dice	cup Tomato diced	tsp Cajun Spice	lb Chicken Thigh	oz Flour	4 oz Oil	serves 8 / 10 oz portion	Dredge the chicken in flour. Brown the chicken over medium heat with oil in a rondeau. Remove chicken and make a brown roux. Sauté the veg in the roux and add spices and stock. Braise for 1 hour in oven at 325°.

New World One Pot Dishes

#	Dish		1/2	1	1	2	3	4	8		Yield	Method of Preparation
477	Etouffé- Crawfish	1 pint Stock	cup Celery- small dice	cup Scallion sliced	cup Green Pepper- small dice	oz Flour	tsp Cajun Spice	ea Tomato- diced		2 oz Butter	serves 6	Make a brown roux. Sauté the veg in the roux and add spices and stock. Simmer for 30 minutes.
			Sprig Thyme			lb Crawfish Tail meat					8 oz portion	Add the thyme, crawfish or shrimp last and simmer until tender. Season to taste
478	Feijoada	2 ea Onion diced	cup Garlic chopped	lb Pork Butt, large dice	lb Black Beans	oz Olive Oil	cups Tomato diced	oz Tasso Ham	oz Fresh Chorizo or Linguica	1 lb Smoked Beef Sausage	Serves 12	Bring 1 gallon of water to a boil, pour over the beans to soak for 1 hour. In a heavy pot sear the pork in oil, add onions and garlic. Add beef, ham, bay, beans and water. Simmer for 2 hours, add the rest simmer for 30 min. Add tomatoes and serve.
						lb Beef Tongue Cooked Peeled	ea Bay Leaves				10 oz portion	
479	Frijoles Charros	5 ea Jalapeño- sliced	gallon Stock	lb Pinto Bean	quart Crushed Tomato	lb Chorizo Sausage	cup Onion diced	cup Pepper diced	oz Bacon- diced	2 oz Chili Powder	serves 10	Soak beans overnight. Render the bacon and add the stock and beans. Simmer until beans are tender. Reduce stock until 1 pint remains. Add the remaining ingredients simmer 45 minutes. Season to taste
	Garnish	8 oz Jack Cheese- shredded	cup Scallions- sliced								12 oz portion	Place either in individual serving dishes or large tureen and garnish with cheese, scallion.
480	Jambalaya		cup Celery diced	ea Green Pepper diced	ea Onion diced	oz Oil	sprig Thyme	ea Garlic Clove chopped	oz Tasso Ham diced	12 oz Smoked Sausage sliced	serves 6	In a 4 quart marmite sauté the onion, pepper and celery in oil. Add ham, sausage, lightly brown, add thyme garlic
		1 tsp Cayenne Pepper	tsp Tabasco	lb Tomato diced	ea Bay Leaf	cup Rice	ea Green Onions sliced thin	cup Shrimp stock		18 ea U-10 Shrimp		Add rice, tomato, stock and bay. Simmer for 5 minutes Place covered in oven for 10 minutes. Add shrimp, seasoning, and onion, cover and bake 8 min.
481	Kentucky Burgoo	1 ½ cups Celery diced	qt Beef Stock	gallon Tomatoes diced	cup Seasoned Flour	cup Onion- diced	lbs Diced Stew Meat-use a blend of pork, beef, chicken	oz Bourbon	oz Smoked Bacon- diced	2 oz Clarified Butter	serves 8	Render the bacon in butter until crisp. Dredge stew meat in the seasoned flour. Brown in fat. Remove the meat. Sauté the celery and onions in the fat. Singer with flour. Add the tomatoes and stock. Add meat and simmer.
		1 tbsp Cracked Black Pepper	tbsp Thyme	oz Sugar	lb White Corn	tsp Salt	cup Butter Beans	ea Potato diced	oz Carrot diced	1 lb Okra	12 oz portion	After 30 minutes add the remaining ingredients and continue to simmer until everything os tender. Season.
482	Kilauea Short Ribs	1 oz Garlic	cup Honey	cup Terriyaki sauce	oz Ginger Root - grated	cup Pineapple Juice	oz Rum	lbs Beef Short Rib	ea Green Onions sliced		serves 8	Combine everything Place in a braising pan and cover. Braise in an oven at 300° for 3 hours. Remove excess fat add onions.

New World One Pot Dishes

#	Dish		1/2	1	1	2	3	4	8		Serves	Method of Preparation
483	**Machaca** – Shredded Beef for tacos or to be added to scrambled eggs	5 oz Light Soy Sauce	gallon Beef Stock		head Garlic-chopped	ea Onion-diced	ea Anaheim Chilies – sliced	lb Beef Chuck-sliced thin	ea Jalapeños-remove stem		serves 8 7 oz portion	Season beef with soy, place on racks and dry in refrigerator overnight. Place all ingredients in a braising pan and bake covered for 5 hours at 225°, or use Crockpot. Remove beef and shred. Reduce the liquid, puree with veg and pour over the beef.
484	**Moqueca de Peixa** *Brazilian Fish Stew*	2 Clove Garlic minced	lb Tomato diced	ea Red Onion julienne	oz Palm Oil / cup Peppers julienne	lbs Fresh Saltwater Fish Steaks	ea Serrano Chile Pepper minced	tbsp Lime Juice	ea Large Rock Shrimp	1 can Coconut Milk	serves 4	Sweat the onions and garlic in oil. Add the peppers and tomato, simmer 5 minutes. Top with fish shrimp. Pour lime juice and coconut over. Cover with cartouche and simmer for 5 minutes, garnish with cilantro.
485	**New Bedford Fish Stew**	1 ea Sachet	cup Roux Blanc	quart Clam or Fish Broth	pint Cream	lbs Haddock diced	cups Mirepoix small dice	strip Smoked Bacon diced	oz Fresh Corn Kernels	3 ½ cup Potato small dice	Serves 4	Render bacon until crispy, Melt roux, sauté mirepoix, add stock sachet and simmer 5minute. Add potatoes and corn simmer for 10 minute, add fish simmer and turn off
486	**Nova Scotia Finnan Haddie** (Salted and Smoked Haddock)	1 ea Bay Leaf	cup Flour	lb Finnan Haddie	pint Half and Half Cream	cups Milk	cups Leeks cleaned julienne	ea Eggs	oz Butter	1 quart Yellow Potatoes diced cooked	Serves 8	Soak Finnan Haddie in milk and bay leaf for 1 hour. Warm in oven for 20 minutes covered. In a heavy casserole heat butter and sweat leeks, add flour to make a roux. Add milk from fish, cream, and potato, flake the haddock and stir. Bake in oven at 350° for 20 minutes
487	**Penn Dutch Ribs and Kraut**	6 ea Green Apples- peel and sliced	lb Smoked Bacon diced rendered	tbsp Caraway Seeds	recipe Pickled Meat Brine # 200	ea Onion julienne	lbs Fresh Sauerkraut-rinsed	ea Bay Leaf	oz Amish Brown Beer	5 lbs Pork Country Style Ribs	Serves 10	Pickle ribs for 5 days in the brine, remove and place ribs in a 2 gallon marmite, cover with water and bring to a boil, simmer for 30 minutes. Remove ribs save 3 cups of liquid add everything but the apples. Bring to a simmer, layer with apples then cover, braise for 2 hours at 325°.
488	**Pork Posole**	8 ea Jalapeno	gallon Tomato Puree	oz Garlic minced	lb Onion diced	oz Oil	ea Poblano Chilies- sliced	lb Pork Shoulder-diced	ea Ancho Chilies-crushed		serves 10	Make a paste from the jalapeños, ancho, and garlic. Rub the mixture on the pork. Sear the pork hot oil in a rondeau. Add the onions and sauté. Stir in the tomato.
			gallon Stock	ea Red Pepper diced	tbsp Ground Cumin	cups Cooked Black Beans	ea Avocado-diced	tbsp Lime Juice		3 cups Cooked Hominy	10 oz portion	Add the stock, pepper, and spice and bring to a simmer for 1 hour. Add the hominy and beans and return to a simmer for 30 min. Serve with avocado flavored with lime and salt

New World One Pot Dishes

No.	Dish		1/2	1	1	2	3	4	8		Serves	Method of Preparation
489	Ropa Vieja	12 oz Tomato Puree	bunch Cilantro chopped	tbsp Cumin / ea Onion julienne	pint Beef Stock	tbsp Garlic minced	ea Cubanelle Peppers – julienne	lb Skirt Steak	oz Tomato Paste	1 oz Red Wine Vinegar	serves 6	Season beef with salt, cumin, and pepper sear in a lightly oiled heavy casserole. Remove beef and add onions, garlic, peppers, and tomato, add simmer, add meat. Simmer, cover, place in a 275° oven for 3 hours.
490	Shrimp Purloo	1 ½ cups Carolina Long Grain Rice	lb diced Tomato	Clove Garlic	cup Onion diced	tsp Salt	Dash Worcestershire	slices Bacon diced	oz Peppers diced	20 ea U-10 Shrimp P&D	serves 4	In a large sautoir render bacon until crisp. Add the onions and peppers. Add rice and coat with fat. Add all except shrimp. Simmer covered 5 minutes. Bake covered 10. Add shrimp stir, cover, bake at 350° - 8 min.
491	South Carolina Frogmore Stew	3 lbs Red Bliss Potato halved	1 each sachet	bottle Beer	tbsp Old Bay Seasoning	qts Water	lb Shrimp	ea small Onion quartered	ea Corn on Cob, halved	2 lbs Smoked Sausage	Serves 8	Place everything in a pot except for shrimp. Simmer 15 min or until the potatoes are tender. Add shrimp, simmer 5 minutes. Slice sausage.
492	Southern Chicken and Dumplings	2 tsp Thyme	gallon Chicken Stock	oz Chicken Base		lb Mirepoix – small dice	ea Bay Leaf		ea Chicken Legs and Thighs		serves 6	Place all of the items in this line in a large pot and bring to a simmer. Simmer the chicken until tender about 1 hour Depouille. Once tender remove and cool the chicken. Season. Pick the chicken meat; discard skin, bones.
492	Southern Chicken and Dumplings	cup Lima Beans	pint Green Peas	cup Green Beans	recipe Southern Dumplings #768	cup Corn			oz Cream		12 oz per portion	Add the vegetables and cream to the stock, simmer. Add the dumplings and simmer for 5-8 minutes. Add chicken, season
493	Winnipeg Venison Stew	1 cup Currant Jelly	cup Tomato Paste	pint Pearl Onions	recipe Game Braise Marinade #179	cups Brown Sauce or Demi Glace	oz Oil	lb Venison Stew Meat large dice	Ea Juniper Berries- wrapped in a sachet		serves 10 / 8 oz portion	Marinate the venison for 24 hours. Drain and reserve the marinade. Heat a rondeau and sear the Venison. Deglaze with the marinade liquid. Add the remaining ingredients braise in the oven at 300° for 2 hours.
494	Yankee Pot Roast	1 Sachet	cup Flour	qt Beef Stock	lb Parsnip-sliced	lb Mirepoix-large dice	oz Tomato Paste	lb Beef Chuck	oz Red Wine	2 oz Clarified Butter	serves 8	Season and sear the beef in a rondeau. Remove the beef and caramelize the mirepoix. Add the tomato paste and brown. Deglaze with wine and add the rest. Bring to simmer and braise beef 350° for 2 hrs.
494	Yankee Pot Roast	Seasoning to Taste		oz Apple Butter (optional)					ea Potatoes- peeled quartered		10 oz portion	Add the potatoes and braise until tender and the beef is fork tender. Slice the beef. Sweeten the gravy with apple butter.

European One Pot Meals

#	Recipe		1/2	1	2	3	4	8		Serves	Method of Preparation
495	**Basque Style Chicken** — Fabricate -remove the legs, thighs, and wings at the first joint. Leave breast on the carcass. French the legs. See the Poulet Saute Demo on our YouTube Channel-Chefreference	½ each Lemon-juiced	1 each Roasted Red Pepper- peel and dice	1 ea Whole Chicken	oz Serrano Ham diced	ea Tomatoes Concasse / oz Olive Oil	tsp Parsley chopped	oz Demi Glace / oz White Wine	1 each Sachet / 2 each Garlic Clove minced	Serves 4	Season then sear the chicken in oil. Once brown remove and brown the onions and ham. Deglaze with wine, add demi, tomatoes, and sachet. Place chicken breast section back in pot, arrange other pieces around. Cover with cartouche and simmer on range until 165°. Combine rest and add to sauce, Simmer 1 minute. Serve each guest 1 piece of dark meat and a ¼ of the breast, sauce on top.
496	**Beef Stroganoff**	1 qt Brown Beef Stock	cup Clarified Butter	large Onion – fine julienne / cup White Wine	tbsp Dijon Mustard	cups Mushroom sliced	lb Beef Chuck 1 inch cubes	oz Sour Cream	ea Sachet	serves 8 / 10oz portion	Season and sear the beef in heavy bottomed pot over high heat with the butter. Remove and sauté mushrooms until brown, remove and sauté onions until brown. Deglaze with wine. Add mushrooms and beef back with stock with sachet. Simmer covered for 1 hour. Whisk sour cream and mustard into sauce.
497	**Belgium Beer Braised Short Ribs**	3 ea Sweet Onions julienne	cup Crumbed Bread	ea Bay Leaf / Pint Chimay Beer or Dark Beer	pint Beef Stock	oz Smoked Bacon-diced	lbs Beef Short rib trimmed	oz Apple Cider	2 oz Tomato Paste	serves 8 / 10 oz portion	Render bacon and remove. Season beef and sear in fat. Remove and lightly brown the onions. Expand with tomato paste, deglaze with beer, juice and stock and simmer. Add bay leaf, bacon, and bread, simmer. Arrange ribs back in pot and cover. Braise for 4 hours at 275°. Until fork tender. Season.
498	**Bœuf Bourguignon**	1 qt Brown Veal Stock	cup Clarified Butter	cup minced Shallot / cup Flour / ea Sachet	pints Burgundy	cups Quartered Mushroom	lb Beef Chuck 2 inch cubes	oz Carrot julienne	1 pint Pearl Onions- peeled	serves 10 / 10 oz portion	Season and sear the beef in heavy bottomed pot over high heat with the butter. Singer with flour. Add the pearl onions, and mushroom and sauté until brown. Deglaze with wine. Add in the remaining ingredients and bring to boil. Reduce to a simmer on low heat until the beef is tender.
499	**Bouillabaisse**	1 bulb Fennel-julienne	bulb Garlic minced	qt Freshly Chopped Tomatoes / ea Leek-sliced	quart Fish Stock	tsp Saffron	tbsp Olive oil	Small Potatoes peeled quartered	2 oz Pernod	serves 6	Sweat the julienne vegetables and garlic in oil. Add the puree, stock and saffron simmer 30 minutes. Finish with Pernod and season to taste.
	(Remove gills from fish before using)	Whole Haddock 2Lb	lb Langoustine	lb Monkfish Filet	dozen Mussel	ea Whole Mullet		oz White Wine (Sancerre)	1 recipe Rouille recipe # 21	16 oz portion	Arrange the fish and seafood in e large marmite. Pour the broth and vegetables and wine over the fish. Cover and poach in the oven until fish is 135°. Serve with rouille and crusty bread

European One Pot Meals

#	Recipe	Ingredient	1/2	1	2	3	4	8		Serves	Method of Preparation
500	Cassoulet	2 ea Smoked Ham Hocks	cup Tomato Paste / cup Garlic chopped	oz Olive Oil / lb Onions diced	sprigs Thyme	cups White Beans	ea Bay Leaf	strips Apple Smoked Bacon, fine dice	1 ½ qts Duck or Chicken Stock	serves 8	Soak the beans overnight. Place in and pot with stock, ham hocks, and herbs. Simmer until the beans are tender. Strain and save stock. Render the bacon in oil then sauté the garlic and onions; add the tomato paste and leftover stock. Reduce until the liquid is thick. Remove the meat from the ham hock, combine with beans and liquid. Season to taste.
				cup White Bread Crumbs	lb Morteau Sausage recipe # 270			ea Duck Leg Confit recipe #243		12 oz per portion	Arrange the duck legs, ½ cup of duck fat, sausage in the casserole. Cover and bake in a 350° for 45 minutes. Remove cover and sprinkle crumbs over beans to absorb fat. Brown topping in oven
501	Chicken Chasseur	12 oz Mirepoix (small dice)	cup Seasoned Flour	lb Italian Sausage / cup diced Pepper	cup Tomato Concasse	ea Bay Leaf	ea Garlic clove minced	ea Chicken Legs and Thighs	3 oz Olive Oil	serves 4	Season and dredge the chicken in seasoned flour and brown in a skillet with olive oil over medium heat. Remove chicken and excess fat. Brown the sausage and remove. Caramelize the mushroom and mirepoix. Deglaze with wine. Add remaining items in a marmite simmer cover. Place in a 350° for 1 hour. Season to taste
		8 oz Mushroom quartered		tsp Thyme / cup White Wine	cups Demi				1 each Sachet	12 oz per portion	
502	Cottage Pie *Grandma Sheena's Recipe*	1 Carrot (small dice)	1 ½ cup English Peas	cup Onion diced / oz HP Sauce	lb Ground Beef Sirloin 90/10	tbsp Flour	tsp L&P Sauce	oz Beef Stock	5 cups Mashed Potatoes	serves 6	Brown the beef until fully cooked. Remove meat, leave the fat. Brown the onions, add the flour and carrots, stir. Add liquids and simmer. Add beef and veg. stir. Season to taste. Top with layer of mashed potatoes and bake in a 350° oven for 1 hour
503	Chicken Paprikash	¼ cup Oil	1 tbsp Freshly Ground Black Pepper	tbsp chopped Garlic / cup Flour	tbsp Hungarian Hot Paprika	ea Tomatoes peeled and small diced	ea Hungarian Wax Peppers or Banana Peppers chopped	each Chicken Legs or Thighs	2 each minced Onions	serves 4	Season the chicken with salt, black pepper and hot paprika. Dredge in flour. Heat oil in braising pot, brown the chicken. Remove and fry the pepper, onion, and garlic.
			3 cups Chicken Stock	tbsp Hungarian Sweet Paprika	ea Bay Leaf	tbsp Parsley finely chopped		oz Sour Cream	2 tbsp Tomato Paste	10 oz portion	Add any leftover flour to the pan, Expand with tomato paste, sweet paprika, and stir in the stock. Add the chicken back to the pot and add bay leaf. Gently Simmer covered 1 hour. Finish with sour cream and parsley, season to taste.

86

European One Pot Meals

#	Recipe		1/2	1	2	3	4	8		Yield	Method of Preparation
504	Chicken Fricassee	½ cup Flour	tsp White Pepper	tbsp Salt tsp Paprika			oz Oil	ea Large Chicken Breasts		serves 8	Season the chicken with salt, pepper and paprika. Dredge in flour. Brown the chicken over medium heat in a skillet with the hot oil.
		¼ tsp Nutmeg	tsp Curry	cup diced Onion cup Celery diced	cup Mushroom sliced		cups Stock		ea Lemon	10 oz per portion	Remove chicken and excess fat. Sauté the vegetables lightly and singer with flour. Stir in the stock and add the chicken. Bring to a simmer and add the seasonings. Gently simmer until the chicken reaches 165°. Add the juice of a lemon to the sauce and season.
505	Choucroute Step 1 *Sauerkraut - use this recipe or purchase fresh kraut.*			gallon Water	oz White Vinegar	oz Kosher Salt			8 lb Cabbage sliced very thin	this yields 4 lbs of kraut	Dissolve the salts and vinegar. Place the cabbage in a sealable clean plastic container. Pour the liquid on top and weigh it down with a stainless steel lid. Store covered in refrigerator for 1 week. Remove any scum. Seal the lid and refrigerate for 3 weeks.
506	Step 2 Cured Pork			qt Ham Brine recipe #199	Lbs Pork Ribs	Lb Pork Belly cut into 10 pieces					Combine and allow the pork to brine for 1 week. Rinse when you are ready to cook the Choucroute.
507	Step 3		lb sliced Onions	liter Riesling	tbsp Caraway Seed	ea Bay Leaves		ea Juniper Berries		serves 15	Render the bacon and sauté the onions until tender. Combine everything on this line with the pork and sauerkraut. Braise in a 300° oven for 1 hour.
		2 # Kielbasa recipe #269		Lb Knack Wurst	lb Potatoes diced				2 lb Bratwurst recipe #260	14 oz per portion	Add the sausages and potatoes to the Choucroute and continue to braise for 45 minutes. Season.
508	Cochon d'Auvergne (Pork)	12 oz White Wine	2 lb of Small Potatoes	large head Savoy Cabbage (8 wedge)	lb White Mirepoix	lb Cured Pork Shoulder Or Butt	ea Smoked Pork Sausage (1 ½ lb total)	oz Smoked Bacon- dice into 8 pieces	16 ea Baby Carrot And Baby Turnip	serves 8	Add enough water to cover pork butt and bacon, add mirepoix and sachet. Simmer for 1 hour on low heat. Add rest simmer covered for 45 minutes.
509	Coq au Vin	8 oz Bacon Lardon	cup Olive Oil	cup Seasoned Flour cup Pearl Onions	cup Cepe Mushroom	Clove Garlic Sliced	cup Burgundy or 1 Liter	ea Chicken Leg And Thigh Quarters	16 pieces tourne Carrots And Celeriac	serves 8	Marinate chicken 24 hrs. Drain wine and save. Render bacon in olive oil and save. Dredge and brown the chicken over medium heat with oil in a rondeau. Remove and caramelize the mirepoix. Drain fat sauté the mushrooms until brown. Add the shallots and garlic deglaze the pan with wine and combine all the ingredients. Braise in a 350° oven for 1 hour or until tender.
				pint Demi Glace	cup Tomato Puree	oz Shallot - minced			8 Prunes	10 oz per portion	

European One Pot Meals

#	Recipe		1/2	1	2	3	4	8		Yield	Method of Preparation
510	Dutch Chicken and Dumplings	2 tsp Thyme	gallon Stock	oz Chicken Base / ea Sachet	lb Mirepoix – small dice			ea Chicken Legs And Thighs		serves 6	Place all of the items in this line in a large pot and bring to a simmer. Simmer the chicken until tender about 1 hour. Remove any scum that rises to the top of the pot. Once tender remove and cool the chicken. Season. Pick the chicken meat; discard skin, bones, and bay.
				cup Green Peas	cup Green Beans-sliced			oz Cream	4 oz Flour	12 oz per portion	Add the vegetable and simmer. Combine the cream and flour. Temper some of the stock into the cream. Use this mixture to thicken the liquid. Add the chicken to the mixture and serve with steamed dumplings recipe # 765.
511	Fricassee de Lapin Alsace (Rabbit)	8 each Pearl Onions halved	cup Seasoned Flour	ea Sachet / ea Rabbit	oz Clarified Butter	cups chicken stock	strips Smoked Bacon	oz quartered Mushroom	6 oz Riesling	serves 4	Remove loins from rabbit, wrap with bacon and render with butter. Reserve loins for later. Dredge the rabbit legs, brown in the fat, sauté mushrooms and onions, add remaining flour to make roux. Deglaze with wine and stock. Add sachet and legs, Braise 40 minutes, add loins, and braise 15 minutes. Serve each person a slice of loin and 1 leg.
512	Hungarian Goulash	1/2 cup Oil	cup Tomato Paste	qt Brown Veal Stock	ea Bay Leaf	ea Onions-diced	lb Veal Shoulder		12 oz Red Wine	serves 10	Season and sear the veal in a heavy bottomed pot over high heat with the oil. Add the onions, sauté until they are tender. Add tomato paste, and bay leaf. Stir until it lightly browns. Deglaze with wine and add stock. Bring to a simmer.
				cup Hungarian Hot Paprika	oz chopped Garlic	ea Red Peppers-diced	ea Green Peppers diced			10 oz portion	Simmer the stew for 30 minutes then add the garlic and peppers and paprika. Cover and place in a 350° oven for 45 minutes or until the veal is tender.
513	Irish Lamb Stew	2 ea Bay Leaves	cup chopped Parsley	gallon Chicken Stock / sprig Rosemary	sprig Thyme	cups Mirepoix- large dice	lb Lamb Shoulder- large dice	ea Small Potatoes- peeled and quartered	5 ea Garlic cloves- crushed	serves 10 / 12 oz portion	Blanch the diced lamb in salted water for 2 minutes Drain the liquid Add the stock. Make a sachet from the rosemary, parsley stem, thyme, garlic and bay leaf. Simmer the lamb for 30 minutes and add the mirepoix. Simmer for 30 minutes, add the potatoes. Simmer until the potatoes are done. Add the parsley and season.

European One Pot Meals

#	Dish		1/2	1	2	3	4	8		Serves	Method of Preparation
514	Navarin de Agneau (Lamb)	12 oz Heavy Cream	lb Onion diced	cup White Wine / oz Clarified Butter	tbsp Flour	lbs Lamb Shoulder 2" cubes	cup Chicken Stock	oz Leeks sliced	16 ea Baby Carrot	serves 8	Season and brown the lamb in a hot rondeau with butter, add leeks and onions to sweat, singer with flour and add wine and stock
515	Pot au Feau	1 ea Bouquet Garni	oz Oil	ea Oxtail sliced / Onion Pique	Large Turnips diced		cups diced Cabbage	ea small Carrots sliced	2 ea Parsnips sliced	serves 6	Brown the tail in oil, add onion, bouquet and enough water to cover. Simmer covered, skim scum regularly for 1 ½ hour. Add rest and simmer1 hour. Serve with boiled potatoes and parsley.
516	Poulet au Pot	1 ea Bouquet Garni	lb Leek Whites sliced	Onion Pique	cups Turnips diced	lb Stewing Hen	ea Carrots sliced		1 small Celery Knob diced	serves 6	Blanch hen for 6minutes drain and rinse. Place everything else around the hen and cover with water. Simmer for 1 ¾ hours over low heat. Serve with Fleur de sel.
517	Osso Bucco	½ cup Olive Oil	gallon Veal Stock	oz chopped Garlic / cup Tomato Paste	ea Bay Leaf	cup Mirepoix	oz Seasoned Flour	ea Veal Shanks- 6 oz each	12 oz White Wine	serves 8	Dredge the shanks in seasoned flour. Sear in a rondeau with the olive oil. Sauté the mirepoix in the same pan. Add the garlic and tomato paste and lightly brown. Singer with flour. Deglaze with wine and add in the stock and bay leaf. Cover.
				ea Lemon zested	tbsp Parsley chopped	ea Garlic cloves minced				10 oz portion	Braise the osso bucco in a 325° for 2½ hours. Remove shanks. Strain sauce and add the gremolata items in this line. Season to taste. Nappe the sauce over the shanks.
518	Ratatouille - Veg Stew	3 cups Tomato Sauce / 1 cup Yellow Squash-diced	cup Red Pepper-diced	cup Green Pepper-diced	cup Eggplant-peeled and diced	oz Olive Oil	tbsp Garlic minced	ea Tomatoes-diced	1 cup Onion-diced	serves 12	Salt the eggplant and rinse. In a rondeau heat the oil and sauté the garlic and onions until translucent. Sauté the eggplant and peppers. Add the tomato sauce and tomatoes. Braise for 20 minutes.
			oz Basil fresh chopped	cup Zucchini-diced	cup Green Beans – dice and blanch					6 oz portion	Remove rondeau from oven and add the items on this line. Place on the range and simmer until the squash is tender. Season to taste
519	Ragout de Agneau Bretonne	3 cups Veal Stock	lb Carrots sliced	Bouquet Garni / quart Fresh Diced Tomato	cups Dried White Beans (Soak overnight)	lb Lamb Shoulder-defatted – 1 " dice	large Cloves Garlic – rough chop	oz Smoked Bacon-diced	1 sprig Rosemary	serves 8	Render the bacon and remove. Season and brown the lamb in a heavy pot with lid. Add everything to the pot and bring to a simmer. Braise in 350° oven for 2 ½ hours or until the beans are tender. Season to taste

European One Pot Meals

		1/2	1	2	3	4	8		Serves	Method of Preparation
520 **Sauerbraten**	1lb Parsnips-sliced	pint Demi Glace	recipe Marinade #186		pint Veal Stock		oz Ginger Snaps-crushed	5 lb Beef Brisket	serves 10 / 10 oz portion	Marinate the beef for 72 hours. Drain and reserve the marinade. Heat a rondeau, sear the beef. Deglaze with the marinade and add the demi, stock and parsnips. Braise for 3 hours at 325°. Remove beef thicken the sauce with ginger snaps. Strain and puree the vegetables add back to the sauce. Slice beef, nappe.
521 **Schweinhaxe** *Eisbein mit Gruenkohl Pinkel* (Ham Hocks with Kale and Sausage)		1lb Smoked Bacon	large Onion cut into 8 wedges	ea Eisbein (Large Salted Pig Hocks)	lbs Kale Chopped	ea Juniper Berries in a sachet	ea Sausage Pinkel Brägenwurst or Knackwurst		Serves 8	Render bacon lightly in a heavy bottomed, place hocks, kale and onions on top with sachet, cover with water and simmer 1 ½ hours over low heat. Add sausages and simmer 10 minutes covered. Shred hock meat into kale. Season to taste. Serve with Bratkartoffeln or Home Fries
522 **Shepherd's Pie**	1 cup Carrot small Dice / tbsp Garlic chopped	1 cup Green Peas tsp Thyme	cup Leek Whites diced / tbsp Tomato Paste	lb Ground Lamb / tsp Rosemary Leaves	tbsp Flour	oz Guinness		5 cups Mashed Potatoes with Chives	serves 6	Brown the lamb until fully cooked. Remove meat, leave the fat. Sweat the leeks, add the flour and carrots, herbs, stir Add liquids and simmer. Add meat and veg, stir. Season. Top with layer of mashed potatoes and bake in a 350° oven for 1 hour
523 **Veal Blanquette**	1 Bouquet Garni	cup Flour	qt Stock lb White Mirepoix	lb Veal Shoulder diced	oz Sherry			12 oz Cream	serves 6 7 oz portion	Simmer the veal and mirepoix covered until the veal is tender. Discard bouquet. Thicken the blanquette liquid with a mixture of cream, flour and sherry. Simmer 10 minutes Season to taste.
524 **Viennese Goulash**	¼ cup Oil / 2 each Lemon zested	cup Tomato Paste	qt Brown Veal Stock / oz Garlic chopped / cup Hungarian Sweet paprika	ea Bay Leaf / tsp Thyme	ea Onions-diced / tsp Caraway Seed-chopped	lb Beef Shoulder large dice / tbsp Vinegar	oz Sour Cream	6 oz Red Wine (Zweigelt) / 4 oz Dill Pickles finely minced	serves 10 / 10 oz portion	Season and sear the beef in a heavy bottomed pot over high heat with the oil. Add the onions, sauté until they are tender. Add tomato paste, and bay leaf. Stir until it lightly browns. Deglaze with wine and add stock. Bring to a simmer. Simmer the stew for 30 minutes then add the garlic, vinegar paprika. Cover and place in a 350° for 45 minutes or until the beef is tender. Combine zest, caraway, pickle and sour cream. And add to stew at service. Serve over Spatzlé

European Ala Carte Entrees- 1 portion yield

#		1/2	1	1	2	2	3	4	8	Method of Preparation
525	**Beef Tips Bourguignonne**	oz Shallot-minced	oz Whole Butter		oz Demi Glace	oz Burgundy Wine	oz Mushroom sliced	oz Beef Tenderloin Tips- sliced		Heat a skillet over high heat. Season beef with salt and pepper. Add butter to pan and sear beef. Add in shallot and mushroom. Sauté. Deglaze with wine. Simmer with Demi 20 seconds.
526	**Entrecôte Bercy**		oz Butter	tsp Tarragon chopped	oz White Wine	tsp Shallot minced			oz Trimmed Ribeye Steak	Season steak well with salt and pepper. Sear over high heat until well caramelized in a seasoned pan until the desired degree of doneness. Remove steak from pan, remove excess fat. Sauté the shallot, deglaze with wine. Add tarragon and whisk in butter.
527	**Entrecôte Bordelaise**		oz Butter	ea Mushroom fluted	oz. Bordelaise Sauce recipe #43	oz Bordeaux Wine			oz Trimmed Ribeye Steak	Season steak well with salt and pepper. Sear over high heat until well caramelized in a seasoned pan until the desired degree of doneness. Remove steak from pan, remove excess fat. Sauté mushroom until brown, remove. Deglaze pan with wine. Simmer with sauce. Nappe.
528	**Steak Au Poivre (Contre- Filet)**	oz Cognac	oz Butter		tsp Cracked Pepper	oz Poivre Sauce recipe # 68			oz Strip Steak	Season steak well with salt and a lot of cracked black pepper. Sear over high heat until well caramelized in butter until the desired degree of doneness. Flambé steak with cognac, add sauce to pan. Nappe sauce.
529	**Steak Diane**	tsp Lea and Perrins	ea Filet Mignon 6 oz	oz Cognac	oz Butter	each Mushroom sliced	oz Dijonnaise sauce recipe # 49			Season steak well with salt and a lot of cracked black pepper. Sear over high heat until well caramelized in butter with mushrooms. Flambé steak with cognac to deglaze. Add sauce to pan with Worcestershire. Nappe sauce over steak.
530	**Tournedos Chasseur**		pair Mushrooms fluted	oz Butter	ea 3 oz Beef Tenderloin – Petite Filets	tbsp White Wine / ea Round Buttered Croutons	oz Chasseur Sauce recipe # 44			Season steak well with salt and pepper. Sear over high heat until well caramelized in butter until the desired degree of doneness. Remove steak from pan, place on croutons. Sauté mushrooms until brown, remove. Deglaze pan with wine. Simmer with sauce. Nappe sauce.

91

European Ala Carte Entrees- 1 portion yield

		1/2	1	2	1	2	3	4	8	Method of Preparation
531	Tournedos Choron			ea 3 oz Beef Tenderloin – Petite Filets	oz Butter	ea Round Buttered Croutons	oz Choron sauce recipe # 46	ea Asparagus Spears-steamed, seasoned and buttered		Season steak well with salt and pepper. Sear over high heat until well caramelized in a clarified butter until the desired degree of doneness. Remove steak from pan, remove excess fat. Place steaks over croutons. Garnish with asparagus. Nappe the Choron sauce over asparagus.
532	Tournedos Niçoise	ea Garlic clove, minced	tsp Tarragon-chopped	ea 3 oz Beef Tenderloin – Petite Filets	oz Olive Oil	oz Tomato Concassé	ea Chateau Potatoes-cooked and seasoned		ea Haricot Vert blanched	Season steak well with salt and pepper. Sear over high heat until well caramelized in oil until the desired doneness. Remove steak from pan. Sauté garlic, tomatoes, and beans in pan. Finish with tarragon. Serve steaks over beans. Glaze steaks with leftover liquid. Place potatoes around the steak
533	Tournedos Rossini	oz Clarified Butter	oz Foie Gras- 2 slices	ea 3 oz Beef Tenderloin – Petite Filets	oz Madeira Wine	ea Round Buttered Croutons	oz Sauce Périgueux recipe # 65			Season steak well with salt and pepper. Sear over high heat until well caramelized in a clarified butter until the desired degree of doneness. Remove steak from pan, remove excess fat. Place steaks over croutons. Sear the foie gras and place on steaks. Deglaze pan with wine, add in sauce and simmer. Nappe sauce over steaks.
534	Chicken Piccata	ea Garlic Clove-minced	oz Olive Oil	tsp Parsley	ea Lemon-juiced	oz Heavy Cream		oz Boneless Skinless Breast-Cutlet	ea Capers	Flatten chicken breast with mallet. Season. Dredge in seasoned flour. Fry chicken in olive oil until golden brown and fully cooked. Add in garlic, lemon juice, capers and reduce. Remove breast and plate. Whisk cream into sauce; finish with parsley. Nappe over chicken.
535	Chicken Française	tbsp. Parsley chopped	oz Olive Oil	tbsp Parmesan Cheese	ea Egg	oz Tomato Concassé	oz Bercy Sauce recipe # 41	oz Boneless Skinless Breast-Cutlet		Prepare a batter with the egg, oil, Parmesan and parsley. Flatten chicken breast with mallet. Season. Dredge in seasoned flour. Dip in batter. Fry chicken in a small amount olive oil until golden brown and fully cooked. Remove from pan. Degrease pan. Simmer the bercy with tomato. Nappe over chicken.

European Ala Carte Entrees- 1 portion yield

#		1/2	1	1	2	2	3	4	8	Method of Preparation
536	**Pork Chop Normande**		oz Demi Glace	oz Cream				oz Apple Cider		Prepare sauce by reducing cider to 1 oz., add demi, cream reduce
		oz Calvados	Tbsp Butter					ea Apple Slices	oz Pork Chop	Season the pork chop and sear on both sides in butter. Remove when brown and finish in oven. Sauté the apples, flambé with calvados. Add in cream sauce. Arrange over pork with sauce.
537	**Pork Chops Robert**	oz Clarified Butter			ea 4 oz Pork Chops	oz White Wine	oz Sauce Robert Recipe #70			Season the pork chops and sear on both sides in butter. Remove when brown and finish in oven. Deglaze, add the sauce to the pan and simmer.
538	**Lamb Noisette Niçoise**	cup diced cooked New Potatoes	oz Olive Oil clove Garlic sliced tsp Fresh Rosemary	ea Artichoke Bottom-cooked	oz Tomato Concassé	oz Demi Glace	ea 2 oz Lamb Loin Noisettes	ea Pitted Olives	ea Haricot Vert - blanched	Season the lamb well with salt and pepper. Heat a skillet over high heat. Rub a little olive oil on the lamb and sear on both sides, add garlic and herb. Remove lamb. Sauté the potatoes in olive oil, add the olives, artichoke, tomato concassé and beans. Sauté. Then add in the demi. Return lamb to pan. Stack lamb over the artichokes and ragout.
539	**Veal Cordon Bleu**		oz Gruyere Cheese-sliced thin	oz Clarified Butter	Paper Thin Slices Prosciutto Ham	oz Oil	oz Sauce Chateaubriand recipe #45	oz Veal Scaloppini		Tenderize and flatten the veal until very thin. Roll the ham and cheese together. Roll the veal around the ham and cheese. Standard Breading Procedure. Pan Fry the veal in oil and butter until golden brown on all side. Cook until it reaches 130° in oven. Serve with sauce chateaubriand. Slice in half.
540	**Veal Emince ala Suisse**	oz Clarified Butter	oz Demi Glace	oz Cream	tsp Shallot minced	oz White Wine	ea Mushroom peeled, stemmed, sliced	oz Veal Cutlet cut into very thin strips		Season and dredge the veal. Remove excess flour. Heat a skillet over high heat. Add the butter and sauté the veal until light brown. Add in the shallots, sweat, then mushrooms. Deglaze with wine. Reduce. Add in cream, demi Reduce., season.
541	**Veal Marsala**	ea Garlic Clove-minced		oz Clarified Butter	oz Marsala Wine	oz Demi Glace	ea Mushroom sliced	oz Veal Scaloppini		Tenderize and flatten the veal until very thin. Dredge the veal and brown in butter until golden brown. Add in garlic and mushrooms and sauté. Deglaze with wine, reduce add demi.

European Ala Carte Entrees- 1 portion yield

		1/2	1	1	2	2	3	4	8	Method of Preparation
542	**Veal Saltimbocca**	oz Olive Oil	oz Asiago Cheese shaved	ea Sage Leaf- split in half	ea 2.5 oz Veal Scaloppini	oz Marsala Wine	oz Demi Glace	ea Thin Slices Prosciutto		Tenderize and flatten the veal until very thin. Place a sage leaf and 2 prosciutto slices one side of the veal. Dredge the veal and brown in oil until golden brown. Deglaze with wine, reduce add demi – Nappe with sauce, top with cheese, gratinee.
543	**Sweetbreads Grenobloise**	oz Lemon Juice		tbsp Capers	tsp Parsley chopped	oz Butter	tbsp White Wine	ea Poached Sweetbread Medallions – 1 oz each		Slice the veal into medallions. Dredge in flour. Fry the veal in butter until brown. Add in the capers and lemon juice. Deglaze with wine and reduce. Finish with parsley .
544	**Sweetbreads Polignac**	oz Ham julienne	ea Mushroom julienne	slice Truffle - fine julienne	oz Sherry	oz Heavy Cream	oz Sauce Supreme recipe # 74	ea Poached Sweetbread Medallions – 1 oz each	oz Veal Stock	Warm the sweetbreads in veal stock. Remove and the sweetbreads warm. Reduce the stock with cream, add in the sauce supreme. Poach the truffle, ham and mushroom in the sherry. Add the liquid to the sauce. Nappe the sauce over the veal, Garnish with rest.
545	**Scallops Duglere**		oz Butter	tbsp Capers	tsp Parsley chopped		oz Sauce Duglere recipe # 50		ea Sea Scallops	Dredge the scallops in seasoned flour. Pan fry the scallops in butter until brown. Remove and plate. Degrease pan. Simmer sauce with capers and parsley. Serve around the scallops.
546	**Scampi**		tbsp Basil-chopped	ea Sundried Tomato-julienne	oz Butter	ea Garlic Clove-chopped	oz White Wine		ea. Large Shrimp	Season the shrimp. Sauté the garlic and shrimp together. Add in the tomatoes and wine. Remove shrimp and plate. Reduce- nappe sauce.
547	**Shrimp Boursin**	tbsp Parsley chopped	oz Clarified Butter	oz Panko Bread Crumbs	oz Boursin Cheese	tsp Garlic chopped			ea Large Shrimp	Combine the butter with crumbs garlic and parsley. Butterfly the shrimp. Place on a well buttered broiler pan. Spoon ¼ oz of Boursin on each shrimp. Top with the bread crumb mixture. Bake in a 400° oven until the crumbs are brown, shrimp are cooked

Make sure to review the station mise en place equipment list on page 10. All of these entrées work very well in a 10" stainless steel sauté pan that has an aluminum core. Check out our Youtube Channel - chefreference for sauté demonstrations.

94

European Side Dishes

Item			1	1	2	3	4	8	Yield	Method of Preparation
548	Artichokes Barigoule	2 ea Lemon halved.	pint Chicken Stock	oz Basil Leaves	ea Bay Leaves	ea Garlic Clove	ea Artichokes-trimmed	oz Olive Oil	4 portion	Bring everything else to a boil. Simmer the trimmed artichokes, bottom side up in the liquid until tender. Season
549	Broccoli Polonaise	2 ea Garlic clove- minced	oz Parsley-chopped	lb Broccoli Flowerets-blanched and shocked	Slices Bread-press, cut brunoise	oz Clarified Butter	ea Eggs-hard boiled and chopped		6 portion	Toast diced bread in the oven. Heat the butter, sauté the garlic. Sauté the toasted bread until brown. Add in the eggs and parsley. Season. Use on top of broccoli.
550	Carrots Vichy			lb Carrots-peeled and bias cut	tbsp Sugar	tbsp Butter			6 portion	Place the carrots in a small pot. Add enough water to just cover. Add sugar and simmer until tender. Reduce liquid finish with butter.
551	Chou-fleur Puree		head Cauliflower-chopped-		oz Parmesan	oz Butter			3 cup	Boil the cauliflower until tender. Remove and drain. Puree in food processor. Mix in rest, season.
552	Creamed Spinach	2 oz Whole Butter	pinch Nutmeg / clove Garlic-minced	lb Spinach-blanched and chopped	oz Parmesan-grated	tbsp Shallots chopped	oz Heavy Cream		2 cup	In a sauté pan heat the butter, sauté the shallots and garlic. Add in the spinach stir. Add rest, stir and reduce until cream is thickened. Season.
553	Endive Bourgeoisie		sprig Thyme	ea Shallot		ea Strips Bacon	ea Head Endive	oz Veal Stock	4 portion	Slice the endive in half lengthwise. Render bacon in pan, add everything else. Braise in oven for 30 minutes.
554	Peas Bonne Femme	½ cup Onion small diced		oz Butter	cups Peas shelled or frozen		oz Bacon-small dice		2 cup	Heat the butter in a sauté pan and render the bacon until crisp. Remove bacon, save. Sauté the onions until tender. Add the peas and bacon. Bake in oven covered until tender.
555	Polenta Piémontaise		qt Stock		oz Butter	ea Egg Yolk	oz Parmesan	oz Fine Corn Meal	1 qt	Bring the stock and butter to a boil. Sprinkle the cornmeal over the stock and whisk until blended. Simmer for 30 minutes over low heat. Remove and temper in rest. Season.
556	Pomme Dauphinoise	¼ cup Parmesan		pint Cream		lb cooked Potatoes-sliced thin	ea Garlic clove-minced	oz Gruyere-grated	12 portion	Shingle potatoes in a buttered pan. Bring cream and garlic to a boil and season, pour on top. Top with cheese and bake covered until brown. Season to taste.
557	Pomme Duchesse	1 ½ lb Cooked Riced Potatoes (Russets or Yukon Gold)	pinch Nutmeg		oz Parmesan Cheese	oz Melted Butter	ea Egg Yolk		8 portion	Combine and use for borders, pancakes or piped into rosettes and baked. This preparation can be used for pomme marquise, pomme Macaire, pomme Galette, and as a border, or as a croquette.

European Side Dishes

#	Item			1	2	3	4	8	Yield	Method of Preparation
558	**Pomme Gratin Savoy**		cup Grated Cheddar Cheese	pint Sauce Béchamel		lb Cooked Potatoes-sliced	oz Heavy Cream	oz Sharp Cheddar Cheese grated	10 portion	Add the sharp cheddar to the hot béchamel. Thin with the heavy cream. Combine with potatoes. Place in baking dish. Top with cheese and bake 30 minute.
559	**Pomme Macaire**	1 tbsp sliced Chive	lb Cooked Riced Potatoes		ea Egg Yolk	oz Cheese grated			8 portion	Combine all ingredients. Make 8 patties, fry in butter until brown.
560	**Pomme Mousseline**		lb Cooked Riced Potatoes		oz Butter	oz Cream			6 portion	Add melted butter and hot cream to potatoes, season to taste.
561	**Potato Pancakes**	¼ cup Flour	lb Potatoes-peeled and grated	pinch Nutmeg	ea Eggs	oz Onion minced			10 ea	Combine all ingredients in a bowl. Portion into 2 oz patties over a buttered griddle. Fry on both sides until golden brown. Season.
562	**Potato Rösti**	Clarified Butter as needed			lb Potatoes-peeled Cooked and grated		oz Onion minced		6 ea	Combine potato and onion in a bowl. Portion into 6 oz patties over a buttered griddle. Fry on both sides until golden brown. Season.
563	**Red Cabbage (Braised)**	2 ea Lemon-juiced	head Red Cabbage-chiffonade	ea Apple peel and grate	oz Bacon Fat	oz Red Wine Vinegar	oz Sugar	oz Onion-minced	8 portion	Combine cabbage, juice, vinegar, sugar. Stand for 30 minutes. Braise in pan with sautéed onions until tender. Season. Simmer with apple to thicken.
564	**Risotto Milanaise**	2 oz White Wine	cup Risotto	pinch Saffron	oz Butter	cups Chicken Stock	oz Parmesan		3 cup	Heat butter. Sauté rice, add saffron. Add ½ of stock, wine and simmer 2 minutes. Cover and hold 30 minutes. Slowly add stock until tender and creamy. Add additional butter if desired, cheese, season.
565	**Salsifis a la Crème**	1 tbsp Parsley-chopped	cup Cream	lb Salsify-peel, slice	tbsp Shallot-minced	grates Nutmeg			2 cup	Blanch salsify. Combine and simmer with rest until tender. Season to taste.
566	**Sauerkraut**	1 oz Cider Vinegar	lb Sauerkraut-rinsed	tsp Caraway / cup diced Onion	ea Bay Leaves	oz Potato – grated	oz Bacon Fat	oz Veal Stock	3 cup	Sauté the onions in fat. Add in everything except potato. Braise 30 minutes add potato. Braise 20 min.
567	**Savoy Cabbage**		lb Cabbage-chiffonade		oz Butter	oz diced Onion	Strips Bacon-chopped	oz Cream	3 cup	Sauté the onion in rendered bacon. Add rest and simmer until tender.
568	**Serviette Knödel**	1/2 tsp Thyme / 1/4 cup Stock	tsp Sage	ea Shallot minced	ea Eggs	slices Bacon-chopped and cooked	oz Cream	ea Stale Rolls	2 lb	Dice rolls. Sauté the shallot in bacon fat. Combine rest add stock if to dry. Shape into a cylinder with cheesecloth. Steam 30 minute. Slice

Chinese Cuisine

	Item			1	1	2	3	4		Yield	Method
569	Bao	½ cup Cool Water	¼ cup Warm Water	oz Lard	tbsp Sugar	tsp Fresh Yeast	cup Flour	drops Sesame Oil	1 tsp Baking Powder	22 oz	Mix the yeast with the warm water and sugar. In a mixer combine the flour, lard, baking powder and oil. Add the yeast and cool water. Knead until elastic. Use for stuffed dumplings that are steamed.
570	Black Bean Sauce	1 oz Blended Sesame Oil	2 tbsp Soy Sauce	oz Rice Wine	tbsp Ginger minced	tbsp Black Bean Paste	Clove Garlic minced	oz Water	1.5 tsp Sugar	8 oz	In wok heat sauté the garlic and ginger in the oil. Add the rest of the wet ingredients and simmer.
571	Cornstarch Slurry	½ cup Cornstarch	½ cup Water							1 cup	Combine the ingredients with a whisk. Use to thicken sauces.
572	Dim Sum Sauce		1 tbsp Sugar	cup Soy Sauce	cup Rice Vinegar	tsp Sesame Oil	tbsp Scallion minced	tsp Sesame Seeds		2 cup	Mix all ingredients together. Allow to sit for 20 minutes. Add scallions last to garnish.
573	Dragon Juice			cup Sesame Oil	cup Peanut oil		oz Chilies crushed			1 pint	Combine all ingredients and heat to 150°, cool to 100° then strain.
574	Garlic Sauce			tbsp Ginger minced	oz Garlic chopped	tbsp Soy Sauce	tsp Blended Sesame oil	oz Oyster Sauce		6 oz	In wok heat sauté the garlic and ginger in the oil. Add the rest of the wet ingredients and simmer.
575	Ginger Sauce		½ tsp Sugar	oz Ginger grated	tbsp Rice Vinegar		tbsp Soy Sauce			3 oz	Combine everything and allow it to stand overnight. Strain.
576	General Tso Sauce	½ cup Black Rice Vinegar	½ cup Rice Wine	cup Sugar	cup Soy Sauce	tsp Garlic	tsp Ginger	tbsp Chili Sauce	2 cup Chicken Broth	3.5 cups	In a wok caramelize the sugar rice wine and vinegar. Add in the ginger and garlic and simmer with broth. Add the chili and soy sauces. Thicken with slurry.
577	Kung Pao Marinade	2 tbsp Cornstarch		oz Soy	oz Peanut Oil				2 Eggs	5 oz	Whisk these items together. Marinate 2 lbs of the diced protein for 15 minutes.
578	Kung Pao Sauce	2 tbsp Water	2 tbsp Black Vinegar	tbsp Ginger- grated		oz Rice Wine	tsp Sesame Oil	tbsp Sugar	6 ea Thai Chilies	5 oz	Heat the oil over low heat and fry the chilies. Caramelize the sugar with the wine and water. Add the black vinegar with ginger.
579	Kung Pao Stir Fry	1 ea Red Pepper diced	1 ea Green Pepper diced	cup Peanuts- toasted	bunch Scallion - sliced	ea Celery Ribs - diced		tsp Peanut Oil		10 portions	In a wok heat the oil. Sauté protein first until fully cooked. Add the vegetables and stir fry. Toss the stir fry with the sauce add the peanuts and scallions last.
580	Lemon Chicken	½ cup Cornstarch	½ tsp Salt			oz Water		ea Chicken Breast- cut into strips	4 ea Eggs	24 oz	Prepare a batter first with the items on this line. Batter the chicken and place each piece directly in a fryer. Deep fry until golden brown. Hold in oven.
	Orange Chicken- substitute orange juice for water	1½ cup Water	½ cup Lemon Juice	bunch Green Onion	oz Honey	tsp Ginger	tbsp Cornstarch	tbsp Sugar	2 cups Snow Peas cleaned	10 portions	In a wok combine the honey, water and sugar and bring to boil. Combine the cornstarch and lemon juice. Use this to thicken the water. Add in the scallions last. Toss the sauce with chicken, snow peas.

Chinese Cuisine

				1	1	2	3	4		Yield	Method
581	Liang Ban Dressing	2 oz Sesame Seed toasted		oz Dragon Juice	tsp Sugar	tbsp Palm Vinegar	tbsp Soy Sauce	oz Peanut Butter	3 tbsp Chili Garlic Sauce	10 oz	Blend all ingredients in a blender until well combined.
582	Liang Ban Salad	1 Carrot – fine julienne		lb Lo Mein Noodles	lb Cooked Chicken Breast - julienne	bunch Scallion sliced				10 portions	Boil the noodles and cool under running water. Drain. Toss the chicken, noodles, dressing, carrots and scallions. Season to taste
583	Mongolian Marinade	1 tbsp Oyster Sauce	1 tbsp Hot Bean Paste	tbsp Sugar	tbsp Sesame Oil	tbsp Rice Wine	tbsp Soy Sauce	ea Clove Garlic-minced	pinch Baking Soda	5 oz	Combine all ingredients and use for thinly sliced meats on a Mongolian flat BBQ range.
584	Pork Filling	1 tbsp Soy Sauce	½ tsp White Pepper	lb Ground Pork	tsp Salt	tbsp Ginger	clove Garlic minced	oz Water Chestnut- fine dice	1 tsp Black Vinegar	1.25 lb	Refrigerate all items and combine them over a bowl of ice. Use for dumplings or pearl balls.
585	Pot Sticker Dough	¾ cup Hot Water	tsp Sesame Oil	tsp Sesame Oil		cup All Purpose Flour				18 oz	Place the flour in a mixer with a paddle and the oil. Boil the water and add to the flour. Mix until well kneaded. Cool before rolling the dough out over a cornstarch dusted workspace.
586	Shanghai Fish Batter	12 oz Ice Water	tsp Salt	cup Cornstarch	cup Flour	tbsp Peanut Oil		ea Eggs		24 oz	Prepare a batter by combining all of the ingredients. This batter is used for whole fried fish with garlic sauce.
587	Shrimp in	1 tsp Ginger grated	pinch Black Pepper	lb Shrimp	tsp Cornstarch	tsp Rice Wine	tbsp Black Soy Beans- chopped	tsp Garlic		8 portions	Peel and devein the shrimp. Marinate the items in this line. Heat a wok and stir fry the shrimp mixture for 30 seconds.
	Lobster Sauce	1 cup Scallions sliced	2 oz Water	cup Onion diced	cup Green Pepper diced	tsp Cornstarch	tsp Oyster Sauce	oz Chicken Stock	ea Egg Whites		Combine the water and cornstarch. Add the stock, onions and peppers to the shrimp. Thicken with slurry add the oyster sauce. Whisk in egg and cook for 1 minute. Garnish with scallions
588	Sweet and Sour Sauce	1 cup Pineapple Juice	2 oz Guava Jelly	tbsp Sugar	tbsp Black Vinegar	tbsp Cornstarch	tbsp Brown Sugar	tbsp Rice Vinegar	½ tsp Ginger	14 oz	Combine all ingredients cold with a whisk and bring to a boil in a pot. Whisk constantly until thickened.
589	Szechwan Sauce	1 tbsp Sweet Bean Paste	1 tbsp Hot Bean Paste	tsp Sugar	tsp Ginger	tbsp Rice Wine	tbsp Soy Sauce	ea Clove Garlic-minced		5 oz	Combine all ingredients and use flavor 1 lb of roasted meat for a stir fry with vegetables.
590	Tangerine Sauce	3 oz Hoisin	6 ea Thai Chilies	tbsp Ginger grated	cup Black Vinegar	cup Sugar	clove Garlic minced	ea Tangerine- coin cuts for the zest. Reserve the juice.	2 tsp Peanut Oil	27 oz	Heat the oil in a wok. Slowly brown the orange zest and ginger. Add in the garlic and ginger. Add the sugar and caramelize. Add the vinegar and juice. Thicken with the hoisin sauce.

Japanese Preparations

#	Item				1	2	3	4	Yield	Method
591	Dashi					qt Water	oz Bonito Flake	oz Konbu Seaweed	2 qts	Bring all ingredients to a boil for 5 minutes. Stand for 10 minutes, strain
592	Ginger Sauce	tbsp Sugar			cup Rice Vinegar	cup Shoyu	slices Ginger	oz Minced Onion	3 cup	Puree until smooth. Use as dip for teppan yaki and hibachi grilled meats
593	Kara - age Chicken	2 cloves Garlic	oz Ginger-grated		lb Chicken Breast-large dice		tbsp Soy	½ tsp Salt	6	Marinate for the items on this line for 30 minutes
		½ cup Cornstarch	½ cup Flour	oz Chive sliced	tbsp Black Pepper	ea Eggs		oz Water		Prepare a batter with the items on this line. Mix the wet ingredients into the dry. Dip the chicken pieces into the batter, deep fry golden brown.
594	Miso	½ cup Miso Paste	oz Wakame-Seaweed-julienne		qt Dashi #591	pint Water	ea Scallion sliced	1 lb Tofu diced	3 quarts	Combine the miso paste, seaweed dashi and water. Bring to a boil. Portion into cups and garnish with the tofu and scallion.
595	Ponzu	½ cup Rice Vinegar	1 ea Scallion sliced	cup Shoyu	cup Lime Juice		tbsp Mirin		2.5 cups	Combine all ingredients and use for steamed dumplings or gyzo.
596	Rice Cracker	1 cup Rice	dash Salt			cup Cold Water	tbsp Black Sesame Seeds			Boil rice in water until overdone, make paste, spread thin on sheet, with black sesame seeds and dehydrate. Fry until puffed.
597	Seafood Sauce	1 tsp Sirachi Sauce	1 tbsp Shoyu Sauce	tbsp Ginger minced	Clove Garlic	cup Mayo	oz Mirin	oz Ketchup	2.25 cup	Blend mirin, garlic, ketchup, shoyu and sirachi and ginger until smooth. Mix in mayo. Use for teppan yaki seafood and chicken.
598	Sushi Rice	¼ cup Sugar	quart Water		tbsp Sea Salt	oz Rice Vinegar		cup Short Grain Rice	1.75 quart	Wash rice twice. Mix sugar, salt and vinegar together. Place rice in rice cooker with water and. Cook. When rice is done place in bowl to cool. Season with vinegar. Gently mix
599	Tempura Batter	pinch salt	1ea Egg Yolk	cup Cold Club Soda	cup Cake Flour				12 oz	Whisk egg with soda, whisk in flour and salt. Season item. dredge in additional flour, dip, fry until crisp.
600	Tempura Sauce					oz Mirin	oz Dashi #591	oz Shoyu - Soy Sauce	9 oz	Combine ingredients and use for tempura fried items.
601	Teriyaki Marinade	¼ cup Soy Sauce	½ tsp Ginger	tbsp Sugar		oz Mirin	tbsp Sake		3 oz	Combine ingredients and use for 1 lb of seafood and chicken
602	Tonkatsu Sauce	1 tbsp Pickled Ginger	½ cup Soy Sauce	oz Mirin	cup Ketchup				13 oz	Combine and bring to a boil. Serve with breaded and fried pork cutlets.
603	Yakisoba Sauce		6oz Oyster Sauce	tsp Sesame Oil	tbsp Sugar	oz Mirin	oz Sake	oz Soy Sauce	1 pint	Combine and use for Yakisoba, noodles, vegetables, and meats.
604	Yakitori Marinade	1 tbsp Ginger	1 Garlic Clove minced		cup Soy Sauce	oz Brown Sugar	oz Mirin	8 oz Plum Wine	19 oz	Combine the ingredients and use for grilled 2.5 lbs of chicken skewers.

Korean Preparations

#	Item				1	2	3	4		Yield	Method
605	**Bibim Sauce** *Use for cold noodles*	2 tbsp Rice Vinegar	1 tbsp Honey	tbsp Soy Sauce	oz Red Pepper Paste (Gochujang)	tsp Brown Sugar	tsp Sesame Oil	tsp Toasted Sesame Seed		Serves 4	Whisk all ingredients together. Use as dressing over 1 lb of cooked soba noodles. Garnish with carrots, sprouts, lettuce, and Kim Chi.
606	**Bulgogi**	¼ cup Sesame Seed	2/3 cup Soy	bunch Green Onion - sliced thin	oz Water	lb Sirloin-thinly sliced	oz Sugar	ea Clove Garlic-minced	2 tbsp Sesame Oil	8 portions	Marinate the beef with everything. Griddle on a hot surface to order.
607	**Ddukbokki** *Rice / Fish Cake Stew*	8 oz Dried Fishcake	cup Fish Stock Green Onion sliced	lb Rice Cake (Garaeddeok) tbsp Red Pepper Paste (Gochujang)		tsp Honey	oz Zucchini julienne	oz Carrot julienne	1 tbsp Sugar	Serves 4	In small pot add fish stock or water, bring to boil. Reduce to a simmer; add red pepper paste and stir. Add sugar, honey and carrot simmer 1 - 2 minutes. Add zucchini and rice cake and simmer 7-8 minutes. Add fish cake and green onion, simmer 2 min.
608	**Kalbi** *(BBQ Short Rib)*	½ cup Water	½ cup Soy Sauce	tsp Ginger minced	tbsp Garlic minced	tbsp Sesame Oil	ea small Green Onion minced	lb Beef Short Ribs	½ cup Sugar	Serves 4	Combine soy sauce, sugar, water, sesame oil, and garlic, ginger and green onion. Stir until sugar is dissolved. Place short ribs in baking dish and pour marinade over ribs. Cover and refrigerate for a minimum of 2 hrs. Grill ribs on preheated grill over low heat until tender.
609	**Kimchi-Cabbage**				cup Kosher Salt		lbs Napa Cabbage		6 cup Cold Water	2.5 lbs	Combine the salt and water. Brine the halved heads of cabbage for 2 hours and rinse.
		1 tbsp Fish Sauce	1.5 tbsp Sugar	bunch Green Onion sliced thin	head Garlic-minced	tbsp Ginger		tbsp Korean Red Chili Pepper			Combine the items in this line and toss with the cabbage. Store cold in a sealed container for 7 days.
610	**Kimchi - Radish**	1 tbsp Korean Chili Powder	1 tbsp Brown Sugar	tsp Salt	tbsp Anchovy Sauce	lb Daikon shredded	ea Garlic Clove minced			2 lbs	Combine everything except daikon. Add Daikon and mix well.
611	**Mandoo** *Korean Dumplings*	1 tbsp Sesame Oil	1 tsp Ginger minced 1 packet Mandoo Wrapper	1 lb Ground Beef 1 ea Egg	cup Cabbage shredded	ea Green Onion sliced	ea Garlic Clove minced	oz Tofu diced	2 tbsp Soy Sauce	36 each	In a bowl combine all mandoo filling ingredients. Fill mandoo wrapper with 1 tablespoon of filling. Brush edges of wrapper with water and pinch edges together to create a fold. Can be fried, simmered, steamed or pan fried.
612	**Pajeon** *Scallion Pancake*	½ tsp Salt	1 bunch Scallion thin slice	cup All Purpose Flour	ea Egg	tbsp Kim Chi Liquid	tbsp Oil	oz Water		24 each	Mix liquids and egg, whisk in flour and salt. Mix in scallions. Portion 2 tbsp size pancakes on oiled griddle.
613	**Spicy Cucumber**	3 tsp Chili Powder	2 oz Rice Vinegar	bunch Green Onion sliced thin	oz Garlic	oz Soy		ea Cucumbers-thinly sliced	dash Sesame Oil	1.75 lbs	Combine the marinade items and marinate the cucumber for 30 minutes before serving.

Recipes courtesy of Chef James O'Hara PCEC

South East Asian Cuisine

#	Item		1	1	1	2	3	4		Yield	Method
614	Green Curry Paste	2 ea minced Shallot	1 tsp Cumin	tsp Fish Sauce	bunch Cilantro-chopped	tbsp Thai Chilies-minced	ea Kaffir Lime Leaves	ea Clove Garlic-minced	3 ea Lemon Grass-bruised	12 oz	Place all ingredients in a blender or food processor and blend until smooth. Use with coconut milk based stir fry .
615	Nam Chili Sauce	4 oz Tomato Paste	8 ea Clove Garlic minced	cup chopped Jalapeño	tbsp Anchovy-minced			oz Water	1 oz Fish Sauce	10 oz	Combine all items on this line and bring to a simmer for 5 minutes.
					Scallions-thinly sliced	tbsp Cilantro					Cool the sauce and add the scallions and cilantro to garnish
616	Nasi Goreng	16 oz Rice	tbsp Sesame Oil	tsp Chili Paste	tbsp minced Garlic	cups Water			½ tsp Turmeric	5 lb	Soak the rice and rinse. Cook the rice, water, and turmeric in a steamer. Stir in oil, garlic and chili.
		1 lb Chicken Breast	1 lb Shrimp	tbsp Soy Sauce	bunch Scallions sliced	cups diced Onion	oz Blended Oil	ea Eggs-made into omelet			Stir fry the chicken and shrimp with the eggs. Remove the meat stir fry the onions and rice. Slice the eggs. Toss with protein, add rest of items
617	Peanut Sambal	1 cup Toasted Peanuts	1 pint Chicken Stock	tbsp Tamarind	oz Oil	ea Garlic Cloves minced		tbsp Brown Sugar	12 ea Red Chilies-chopped	12 oz	Place everything in a pot and simmer for 15 minutes. Puree until smooth.
618	Pad Thai Sauce	1 oz Fish Sauce	½ cup Soy Sauce	cup Ketchup	oz Garlic minced	bunch Scallion sliced	ea Limes-juice	oz Chili Garlic Sauce		1 pint	Bring the fish sauce, chili sauce, ketchup, soy sauce to a simmer. Cool and add the rest.
619	Red Curry Paste	1 ea Lemon Grass-bruised	3 ea Kaffir Leaves	tbsp Galangal	oz Garlic-Minced	tsp Anise Seed			12 oz Water	7 oz	Wrap the lemongrass, kaffir, and galanga in cheesecloth. Simmer with garlic, anise and water.
		5 ea Shallots minced	1 tsp Salt	tsp Black Pepper	tbsp Oil	tbsp Cilantro	tbsp Tomato Paste	16 ea Red Chilies-chopped			Sauté the chilies and shallots in oil. Add the rest and the reduction. Reduce until thickened
620	Rendang	tsp Sugar	tsp Cayenne	tbsp Turmeric	ea Sliced Onion	oz Garlic minced	lb Meat	6 ea Red Chilies-chopped			Slice the meat. Prepare a rub from the items in this line. Rub the meat and marinate for 30 minutes.
		1 oz Blended Oil	5 ea Kaffir Leaves	tbsp Galangal	oz Ginger		cup Coconut Milk	5 ea Lemon Grass-		1 qt	Sear the meat and add the remaining ingredients simmer for 1 hour. Remove the lemon grass, season.
621	Sate Marinade	1 oz Lime Juice	1 oz Sugar	cup Soy Sauce	oz Oil Sesame	oz Rice Vinegar	clove Garlic minced			12 oz	Combine and use for 1 lb skewered meat , and poultry
623	Spicy Pepper Sambal	1 tsp Fish Sauce	2 oz Tomato Paste	oz Red Chilies	oz Peanut Oil	oz minced Onion	tsp Brown Sugar	ea Cloves Garlic minced		4 oz	Sauté the onions, garlic and chilies in oil. Add the rest and reduce. Puree. Season to taste.
624	Sweet Sambal	1/2 cup Peanuts	4 Clove Garlic	cup Sugar	cup Rice Vinegar	cup Water	tbsp minced Ginger		3 oz Chili Garlic Sauce	2.5 cups	Bring all items to a simmer except for peanuts and reduce. Chill and add chop peanuts when serving.
625	Som Tam Dressing	1 tbsp Palm Sugar	1 tbsp Fish Sauce	Clove Garlic	ea Chile	tbsp Cilantro	oz chopped Peanut	oz Red Onion	1 tbsp Lime Juice	¾ cup	Mix all in mortar and pestle. Mix with 2 cup grated green papaya. Season
626	Tamarind Sambal	12 ea Red Chilies	1 pinch Salt	tbsp Tamarind	cup Water	tsp Sugar				1 cup	Bring all items to a simmer, puree, and then strain.

Indian Cuisine

No.	Item	1	1	1	2	3	4	Yield	Method
627	**Chapati Dough**	3 cup Water	tsp Salt	1 lb Whole Wheat Flour				3.5 lb	Knead the ingredients. Portion 2 oz ball. Flatten, griddle
628	**Coriander Chutney**	¾ tsp Salt	½ tsp Cumin	ea Lemon Juiced	ea Clove Garlic-minced	cup Cilantro	oz Chilies-minced	¾ cup	Puree all ingredients and keep cold
629	**Keema Mattar**	½ cup Vegetable Oil	2 tbsp Tomato Paste	lb Ground Lamb	ea Tomato	ea Onions diced	1 tbsp Cumin	24 oz	1. Brown the lamb in oil, add the onions, then tomato. Simmer with all spices covered for 10 minutes.
		2 tsp Ginger-minced	2 tsp Salt	tbsp Garlic minced / tbsp Paprika	ea Potato diced / ea Chilies-minced	1 bunch Cilantro	1.5 tsp Turmeric / 1 cup Peas / 1 tsp Cardamom / 1 Cinnamon Stick		2. Add the potatoes and cook until tender. Finish with peas and cilantro- season to taste
630	**Kheerni – rice pudding**	1/8 tsp Cardamom / ½ cup Sugar	pint Milk	cup Basmati	oz Coconut	oz Raisins	Thread Saffron / 3 oz Almonds / ½ cup Heavy Cream	1 qt	Bring the milk, spice, sugar and basmati to a boil. Simmer for 10 minutes. Add rest and chill
631	**Kofte – meatballs**	1 oz chopped Garlic / 2 tsp Ginger	cup diced Onion	ea Jalapeño-minced	1 lb Ground Lamb		oz Bread Crumb / 1 tbsp Garam Masala #1107	2.5 lb	Place all items in a food processor and blend well. Season to taste, Portion into 1 oz balls and bake.
632	**Naan – onion**	½ tsp Baking Powder / ½ tsp Salt	tbsp Sugar	lb Bread Flour	oz Ghee	oz Onion minced	oz Bread Crumb / 1 oz Fresh Yeast / 5 oz Warm Milk / oz Yogurt	4 loaf	Combine the yeast, milk and sugar. Add the rest and knead until elastic Portion 8 oz loaf. Flatten and bake at 450°
632	**Patna**	1 tsp Turmeric / 1 tsp Black Pepper	cup Onion minced	cup Yogurt	tbsp Cumin	oz Ghee	ea Eggplant-diced / oz Tomato Puree / 1 ea Potato / 2 ea Potato	2 quart	1. Sauté onions and eggplant together first. Add the rest on the items on this line.
632	**Korma**	1 tsp Cayenne / 1.5 tsp Garam Masala #1107	tbsp chopped Garlic	cup Cream	tbsp Coriander		tbsp minced Ginger / 1 head Cauliflower / 12 oz Green Beans		2. Bring to a simmer and add the items on this line. Simmer until the potatoes are cooked.
633	**Poori Bread**	½ tsp Baking Soda	9 oz Water	1 tsp Kosher Salt	tsp Sesame Oil	cup Flour	tbsp Oil	12 loaf	Mix the wet ingredients into the dry. Portion into 2 oz balls. Flatten and deep fat fry.
634	**Raita**	cup Yogurt	cup Yogurt	bunch Scallions sliced	oz Red Onion minced		oz mince Cucumber / ¼ cup Cilantro	2 cup	Combine all ingredients and season to taste.
635	**Samosa Dough**	½ tsp Salt / ¼ cup Oil			cup All Purpose Flour		oz Water	17 oz	Rub the flour and oil. Add the salt and water. Mix well.
636	**Tandoori**	1.5 cup Yogurt / ¼ cup Ghee / ½ tsp Beet Powder / 1.5 tbsp Coriander	Lemon Juiced	tsp Saffron	ea Chicken (skinned)	tsp Salt	tbsp Paprika / Tbsp Garam Masala #1107 / 1 tbsp Cumin / oz Water	16 pieces	Cut each chicken into 8 pieces. Make a marinade with the rest and marinate for 48 hour. Bake at 500° oven until chicken reaches 165°
637	**Zucchini Pakora**	¾ cup Flour / 2 tbsp Ginger minced		oz Garlic minced / tsp Garlic	cup Zucchini grated		Oil To Fry	20 pieces	Mix all ingredients then form into 2 oz patties. Adjust consistency with flour if wet.
		Salt to taste / 1 tbsp Madras Curry		tsp Black Pepper	cups Pureed Cooked Chick Peas		Flour To Dry		Dredge the patties in flour and deep fat fry until crispy.

Eastern Mediterranean Dishes

No.	Item	1	2	3	4	8	Yield	Method of Preparation
638	**Baba Ganoush** (Eggplant Dip)	ea Large Eggplant / ½ tsp Garlic	Tbsp Olive Oil	Tbsp Lemon Juice	tbsp Tahini		3 cup	Prick eggplant with fork. Roast in oven for 20 minutes at 350°. When tender allow to cool. Peel skin and puree with remaining ingredients. Garnish with 1 tsp chopped chili, 2 tbsp chopped parsley and ½ cup diced tomato.
639	**Baklava** (Honey Nut Pastry)	box Phyllo / stick Cinnamon / 2 ½ cup Pistachios ground	oz Lemon Juice	oz Water	oz Honey / oz Sugar	oz Butter / ea Clove	48 Pieces	Melt butter. Butter and layer 2 sheets phyllo. Sprinkle with nuts. Roll into a log. Place on half sheet pan. Repeat until all phyllo and nuts are used. Slice logs on bias 1 inch. Bake 30 min 350°. Bring rest to boil for 2 minutes. Cool 30 minutes. Drizzle over.
640	**Barbunya Fasülye Piyaz** (Bean Salad)	lb Roman Beans / ¼ cup chopped Parsley	cups Onion / tbsp Tomato Paste	ea Carrot- / tbsp Lemon	oz Olive Oil / clove Garlic	oz Potato	Serves 12	Soak beans overnight. Simmer in fresh water for 1 ¼ hours, until tender. Drain reserve 1 pint of liquid. Mince garlic, dice carrot, onion, pepper, and potato. Heat olive oil, sweat garlic and onions, add pepper and tomato paste until tender. Add carrots, potatoes and half of the liquid simmer until tender. Add beans and simmer 10 minutes. Finish with lemon and parsley.
641	**Dolma** (Stuffed Grape Leaves)	cup Rice / stick Cinnamon / lb Ground Lamb / 50 Grape Leaves / Salt and Black Pepper to taste	ea Bay Leaf / oz Pine Nut / cup Chicken Stock	oz Dried Currant / Tbsp Chopped Dill	tbsp Parsley chopped / oz Olive Oil	ea Scallions sliced / ea Lemon slices	50 Pieces	Use 1 tbsp of olive oil to sweat the onions. Add the rice, cinnamon, bay and stock. Simmer covered for 15 minutes. Add the scallions and currants. Allow to stand uncovered for 15 minutes. Remove bay and stick. Mix in the ground lamb. Season. Blanch grape leaves. Fill each grape leaf with 2 tbsp filling, roll tight. Place in a 4"half hotel pan, layer with lemons and olive oil. Repeat. Cover with foil. Steam 45 minutes or until middle layer reaches 165°.
642	**Dönar Kebap** (Skewered Beef)	pint Olive Oil / tsp Cinnamon / 6 oz Red Wine	cups Red Wine Vinegar / oz Garlic	tbsp Black Pepper / tbsp Salt	oz Lemon Juice / ea Cardamom Pods	lbs Beef Sirloin / ea Allspice Berries	Serves 20	Heat red wine, spices, garlic, seasoning to a boil. Allow to cool for 3 hours. Add vinegar, olive oil, lemon. Slice beef into very thin steaks ½ "thick by 8" diameter. Marinate beef overnight. On a vertical spit layer the slices of beef on top of each other. Roast on a rotisserie to the desired degree of doneness, Slice portions of beef to order or the beef can be threaded on skewers for Kebabs.
643	**Falafel** (Chickpea Fritter)	lb Chickpeas / tsp Coriander / ¾ cup Parsley chopped / tsp ground Cumin	ea Onion diced / tsp Cumin	oz Bread Flour	Clove Garlic		48 Pieces	Soak peas overnight. Rinse. Bring to a boil in 2 quarts of water and simmer on very low heat for 1 hour. Drain and dry in oven for 5 minutes. Pulse peas in food processor with onions and garlic. Mix in remaining ingredients. Dough should be firm. Season with salt and pepper. Portion 1 oz balls. Fry at 350°
644	**Gyro** (Ground Grilled Lamb)	lb Onion minced / tbsp Oregano / ¼ cup Parsley / 1 ½ tsp Pepper	lb Ground Lamb / tsp Cumin	Tbsp chop mint / tsp Kosher Salt	clove Garlic-minced / tbsp Flour	oz Cold Milk	3.5 lb	Microwave onions for 30 seconds then cool. Whisk flour and milk, refrigerate 30 minutes. Place all ingredients in a food processor and blend together until smooth. Freezer in a loaf pan until the mixture reaches 15°. Slice very thin on meat slicer on to wax paper. Keep frozen until needed. Griddle to order.
645	**Hummus** (Chickpea Dip)	cup Tahini / 1 tsp ground Cumin	cups Chick Peas	ea Lemons / oz Olive Oil	clove Garlic	oz Water	6 cups	Soak Chickpeas over night. Boil until tender and drain. Puree all ingredients together until smooth. Season with salt to taste.
646	**Iç Pilavi** (Liver Pilaf)	ea Onion minced / Tbsp Honey / 5 cups Chicken Stock	oz Butter / tsp Cinnamon	cups Long Grain Rice / oz Parsley	oz Currants / oz. Pine nuts	oz Calves Liver-diced	Serves 8	Soak currant in hot water for 30 minutes. In a 3 quart marmite heat butter and sweat onions. Add pine nuts and toast 2 minutes. Add liver and rice stir 1 minute. Add stock, spice, currant, honey. Simmer and place in 350° oven 20 minutes. Season. Add parsley.
647	**Irmika Helvasi** (Semolina Dessert)	quart Milk / Tbsp Cinnamon / 1 ½ cups Sugar	cup Semolina / tsp Vanilla	oz Walnut-chopped	oz Butter	oz Water	Serves 8	Heat butter and toast semolina until light brown. Add hot milk and water. Cover and allow to steep 10 minutes. Stir in sugar and vanilla, transfer to a wet, round bowl. Cover and cool 2 hours. Top with nuts and cinnamon. Recipe by Melahat Kantar
648	**Kibbeh -Dough**	lb Lean Ground Beef / ½ tsp Allspice / ¾ tsp Salt	lb Fine Bulgur Wheat		oz Ice Water	oz Onion minced	4.5 lbs	Soak wheat in cold water for 15 minutes. Rinse well. Grind in food processor to a paste with seasoning and onions. Cool 2 hours. Blend meat, wheat paste and ice water until smooth. Lamb can be substituted for the beef in both the dough and filling. Traditionally lamb in this preparation is called Kibbi-next.

Eastern Mediterranean Dishes

	Item	1	2	3	4	8	Yield	Method of Preparation
649	**Kibbeh -Filling** (Arabic meatballs)	oz Oil tsp Sumac ½ tsp Cinnamon	cups Minced Onion	grinds Black Pepper	oz Toasted Pine Nuts	oz Minced Beef	36 pieces	Sweat onions in oil. Add beef and brown. Add seasonings, salt to taste. Mix in nuts. Form 2 oz balls of the Kibbeh Dough, make a pocket and fill with ½ oz of filling. Shape into a football, use wet hands to shape. Fry at 325° until brown.
650	**Köfte** (Meatball)	tsp Cumin tsp Oregano large Red Onion minced ½ tsp ground Chili 1 tbsp Salt	tsp Paprika lb Ground Lamb oz Pine nut	tbsp Tomato Paste tsp Cinnamon	cups Bread Crumbs ea Eggs	oz Water Clove Garlic	30 Pieces	In a blender combine seasoning, spices, water, tomato paste and garlic. Blend until smooth and refrigerate 3 hours. In a bowl add the remaining ingredients and mix well. Add the seasoned liquid and mix well until forcemeat is sticky. Portion 2 oz meatballs. Bake, fry or grill the meatballs on a skewer. Make sure meatballs reach an internal temp of 165°. Serve with lemon wedges or in a tomato based sauce.
651	**Moussaka** (Eggplant and Lamb Casserole)	oz Olive Oil ½ tsp Cinnamon 4 Russet Potato-Baked 3 cup Béchamel recipe #40	lb Ground Lamb tsp Dried Oregano	lb Eggplant-Peel oz Tomato Paste	ea Onions - diced Clove Garlic minced ea Egg Yolk	oz Red Wine ea Roma Tomato oz Feta	Serves 10	Slice eggplant ¼ inch thick, soak in salted water for 30 minutes. Dredge eggplant and pan fry in olive oil. Drain well. In a large sautoir heat olive oil, sweat onions and cook the ground lamb. Once lamb is full cooked add spices, paste, wine, garlic and cook 5 minutes. Slice tomatoes, peel and slice potatoes. Layer eggplant with meat filling, tomatoes and potatoes. Repeat. For top layer blend béchamel, yolks, and feta. Spread evenly over the casserole. Bake 45 minutes at 350°
652	**Poğaça** (Baked Cheese Pastry) *A Kantar family recipe*	tsp Baking Powder ½ cup Dill 6 oz Oil	ea Egg	cups Bread Flour	oz Feta	oz Yogurt	36 Pieces	Prepare dough with 6 oz yogurt, oil, flour, baking powder. Rest dough 20 minutes. Roll thin, cut 3 "disks. Prepare filling with feta, dill, 2 oz yogurt, and 1 egg white. Brush dough with other egg white, fill and fold in half Brush outside with egg yolk. Place on trays in cold oven then turn on. Bake in 325°oven–10 minute
653	**Salata Horiatiki** (Country Salad)	ea Cucumber tsp Oregano ¼ cup Parsley chopped	ea Tomato tsp Capers	oz Feta Cheese tsp Dill chopped	oz minced Red Onion oz Lemon Juice	oz diced Pepper oz Olive Oil	Serves 6	Peel, seed and dice cucumbers. Crumble feta. Dice tomatoes. Rub a wooden bowl with garlic. Add olive oil and lemon juice. Toss remaining ingredients. Serve over a bed of romaine lettuce. Garnish with kalamata olives, pepperocini peppers, and shaved red onion. The marinated salad can be held refrigerated.
654	**Shawarma** (Lebanese grilled Chicken)	tsp Oregano tbsp Paprika 1 oz Oil 1 tbsp Vinegar	lbs Chicken Breast tsp Curry Powder	tsp Tomato Paste	oz Lemon Juice oz Yogurt	Clove Garlic	2.25 lb	Place all ingredients, except chicken in a food processor and blend until smooth. Either marinated chicken breasts whole or cut into strips for a kebab. Allow the chicken to marinate from 24-48 hours. Grill until the chicken reaches an internal temp of 165°. Serve on pita or over a salad
655	**Souvlaki** (Greek meat marinade)	tbsp Fresh Oregano 1 ½ tsp Sea Salt	tsp Fresh Rosemary	oz Olive Oil clove Garlic	oz Lemon Juice	oz Wine	1 Pint	Combine all ingredients together and marinate meat for 24 hours. White wine for chicken and pork, red wine for meat.
656	**Spanikopita** (Feta Cheese Pastry)	cup minced Onion 1 box Phyllo 1 tbsp lemon	tbsp Olive Oil cup Feta	tbsp chopped Dill	cups Chopped Spinach	oz Butter-Melted	36 Pieces	Sweat onions in olive oil. Add spinach and slowly cook. Remove from heat and cool. Add feta cheese and dill. Season with salt, pepper. Mix butter and lemon. Brush 2 layers of dough with butter, slice into 4 long strips. Fill and fold like a flag or Chinese football. Brush butter on outside. Bake 375° until golden brown.
657	**Taratur Sauce**	pint Yogurt tsp Cumin ¼ cup chopped Parsley	oz Tahini Paste	tbsp Lemon	tsp Olive Oil	Slices Garlic	20 oz	Blend tahini, lemon, garlic and oil until smooth. Mix in yogurt with whisk. Add cumin, season to taste with salt pepper and additional lemon if desired. Finish with parsley.
658	**Tzatziki** (Cucumber Yogurt Sauce)	ea Cucumber ¼ tsp white pepper	Clove Garlic	sprig Dill	tsp Lemon Juice	oz Greek Yogurt	12 oz	Peel and seed cucumbers slice. Salt cucumbers for 30 minutes with a little kosher salt, rinse, drain. Chop dill, garlic and cucumber in food processor. Blend in yogurt and juice by hand
659	**Zeytinyağli pirasa**	cup Onion minced cup Stock ½ cup Rice	lbs Leek White- sliced tsp Sugar	ea Small Carrot slice	oz Olive Oil	slices Lemon	5 cups	Thinly slice the white of leeks. Clean to remove dirt. In a 2 quart marmites heat oil and sweat onions. Add carrot, leek, and lemon, sauté until leeks are tender. Add rice, chicken stock and sugar. Simmer and place in a 350° oven for 20 minutes- Recipe by Dr. Mine Cinar .

Italian Appetizers and Soups

#	Item			1	2	3	4	8	Yield	Method of Preparation
660	Baccala	¼ cup Parsley chopped	1 tbsp Lemon Juice	lb Salt Cod Fillets	oz Olive Oil	oz Flour	oz Water		1 ½ lbs	Soak salt cod in water in refrigerator for 2 days. Change water daily. Shred fish and mix in the remaining ingredients. Season to taste. Form into patties or balls and fry until crisp and golden brown.
661	Bagna Cauda	pinch Red Chili Flakes	4 oz Butter Sliced	tbsp Parsley chopped	tbsp Olive Oil	clove Garlic minced	ea Anchovy minced		5 oz	Sauté garlic, chili and anchovy in oil, do not brown garlic. Whisk in the slices of butter off the heat, and then add in the parsley. Use as dip.
662	Caponata	2 tsp minced Capers	8 oz jar Sundried Tomatoes minced	cup Celery fine dice / tbsp Sugar	lb Eggplant / tbsp Pesto	oz Green Olives chopped	oz Virgin Olive Oil / tbsp Wine Vinegar	oz Shallots minced	1 ½ lbs	Peel and slice eggplant lengthwise ¼ inch thick. Salt and allow to drain for 1 hour. Rinse and dice. Heat half the oil and sauté the eggplant first. Remove and add in shallots, celery and oil. Sweat until tender. Add the rest simmer 8 minutes.
663	Fonduta		1 ½ tsp Wondra® Flour	lb Fontina Cheese diced	cups Light Cream	drop Truffle Oil	ea Egg Yolks		3 cups	Place cheese and cream in double boiler bowl and allow to temper for 30 minutes. Combine yolks, flour and oil, mix until smooth. Heat cheese mixture in double boiler. When melted whisk into egg base. Heat and whisk to 160°
664	Melanzana Scapece	¼ cup Parsley chopped	2 tsp Chili Paste	ea Anchovy filet	ea Eggplant - Peel and slice	tbsp Wine Vinegar	ea Garlic cloves	oz Olive Oil	Serves 12	Salt eggplant and allow to stand for 1 hour. Rinse and brush with olive oil. Grill the eggplant and place on large tray. Combine remaining oil with the rest and drizzle over the eggplant to marinate.
665	Peperonata	¼ cup Parsley chopped	1 tbsp Red Wine Vinegar	cup Tomato diced	ea Garlic Cloves- minced	oz Virgin Olive Oil	ea Bell Peppers - julienne	oz Onions julienne	1 ½ lbs	Heat olive oil and sweat the garlic and onions, add in multi colored julienne peppers with vinegar and tomato. Reduce and season to taste
666	Stracciatella		½ cup Parsley chopped	dozen Eggs	oz Olive Oil	tbsp Flour	quarts Chicken Broth	oz Parmesan Cheese	1 gallon	Finely grate the cheese. Whisk eggs with oil, flour, and half of the cheese. Bring broth to a boil. Stir quickly to form a vortex. Pour egg mixture through a colander into the liquid. Simmer and stir. Garnish -cheese and parsley.
667	Supli di Riso			lb Leftover Risotto Blanco	lb Eggplant – peeled	oz Prosciutto-Brunoise	oz Fontina Cheese	oz Olive Oil	24 Portion	Slice the eggplant lengthwise very thin. Dip in salted water. Brush with olive oil and broil for 1 minute to soften. Mix cheese and prosciutto into risotto. Portion into 1 oz balls. Wrap the balls with eggplant, fold like a paper football. Pan fry/
668	Zuppa di Pesce	½ cup Parsley	3 pints Fish stock	lb Cod- small dice / oz Olive Oil	cups Mirepoix- small dice	ea Garlic Clove minced	ea Tomatoes – fine dice	oz Squid– Rings / oz Wine	6 portion	Sweat the mirepoix in olive oil with garlic. Add the wine, stock, tomatoes. Simmer covered 10 minutes. Add the fish and squid, remove from heat allow to stand covered for 5 minutes. Season , garnish
669	Zuppa di Vongole	1 oz Virgin Olive Oil	1 tsp Red Pepper Flakes	quart Clam Broth	dozen Baby Clams	clove Garlic minced	ea Tomato peeled diced	oz White Wine	4 portion	Scrub and purge clams. Heat sautoir. Add in olive oil pepper, and garlic with clams. Add wine and cover. Simmer 1 minute. Add rest and simmer 4 minutes.
670	Zuppa Toscana	1 ea Bouquet Garni	1 gallon Chicken Stock	lb Dried Cannellini Beans / pint Tomato diced	lbs Mirepoix- small dice	lbs Savoy Cabbage small diced	oz Pancetta-brunoise / oz Olive oil	oz Leeks- Cleaned fine dice	1 Gallon	Soak beans over night. Simmer beans in stock with bouquet garni for 1 ½ hours, keep covered. Render pancetta with olive oil in separate pot. Sweat the mirepoix, leeks, tomato and add to beans. Simmer for 20 minutes. Add in the cabbage and simmer 15minutes. Season to taste. Garnish fresh basil chiffonade.

Pasta Sauces

#	Sauce	1/2	3/4	1	1	2	3	4	8	16	Yield	Method of Preparation
671	Alfredo			quart Heavy Cream	cup Parmesan Cheese		oz Butter	Clove Garlic-minced			1 quart	Sweat garlic in butter. Add cream and simmer. Whisk in cheese. Season to taste
672	A La Greque	cup Parsley-chopped			oz Oregano-chopped		ea Garlic-chopped	ea Lemons Juiced	oz Olive Oil		1 pint	In a 1 quart sauce pot heat the oil. Lightly sauté the garlic. Add the herbs and lemon. Season
673	Bolognese — Use for lasagna filling or with hearty pasta.		cup Red Wine	oz Butter	ea Onion diced	tbsp Pancetta		tbsp Olive Oil		oz Ground Meat	1 quart	In a 2 quart sauce pot render the pancetta in oil. Brown the ground meat. Add the onion wine and butter. Simmer.
673		1 ea Bay Leaf	Pinch Thyme	Stalk Celery	ea Carrot	ea Garlic-minced		oz Milk	oz Tomato Puree	oz Crushed Tomato		After 10 minutes add the garlic, celery, carrot with herbs. Add the tomatoes and simmer for 1 hour. Add the milk and simmer for 30 minutes- season to taste.
674	Carbonara — Use fettuccine or tagliatelle with this sauce	lb Parmesan	qt Cream	lb Pancetta	cup Green Peas	oz Olive Oil	ea Garlic Clove-minced		oz Egg Yolks		1 quart	In a 2 quart sauté pan heat the oil and render the pancetta. Lightly sauté the garlic and add the cream. Simmer and add the peas and cheese. Simmer and temper in the egg yolks. Season, toss with pasta.
675	Gorgonzola Cream — use for gnocchi			qt Heavy Cream	tbsp Thyme	oz Olive Oil	ea Garlic Clove-minced	oz Parmesan		oz Gorgonzola	40 oz	In a 2 quart sauce pot heat the oil and sauté the garlic. Add the cream thyme and parmesan. Simmer for 5 minutes and add the gorgonzola.
676	Marinara		tbsp Oregano	oz Garlic minced	lb Tomato Puree	tbsp Basil	tbsp Olive Oil	lb Ripe Tomato-diced	oz Onion minced		3 pint	In a 3 quart sauce pot heat the olive oil and sauté the garlic and onions. Add the tomatoes and herbs. Simmer for 45 minutes.
677	Marinara Spicy	lb Onions diced	tbsp Oregano	oz Minced Garlic	cup Carrot-diced	tbsp Crushed Red Pepper	tbsp Olive Oil	lb Ripe Tomato-diced	oz Tomato Paste	lb Tomato Puree	3 pint	In a 3 quart sauce pot heat the olive oil and sauté the garlic, carrots and onions. Add the tomatoes and herbs. Simmer for 45 minutes. Puree until smooth and season to taste.
678	Marsala Herb Cream — use for meat tortelloni		oz Butter	Sprig Rosemary	Sprig Sage	ea Garlic Clove-minced		oz Brown Sauce	oz Marsala Wine	oz Heavy Cream	20 oz	In a 2 quart sauce pot heat the butter and sauté the garlic and herbs. Add the brown sauce and wine. Simmer and temper in the cream. Reduce over medium heat. Season to taste
679	New York Gravy — use for hearty pastas	head Garlic minced	lb Onion-chopped	lb Pork Shoulder-diced	lb Meatballs	lb Sausage	oz Olive Oil	lb Tomatoes-chopped		oz Tomato Puree	2.5 quart	Heat the oil in a 4 quart sauce pot. Sear the pork until well caramelized. Remove and brown the sausages and meatballs. Once they are brown remove. Sauté the garlic and onions. Add the tomatoes and meats. Simmer over very low heat for 2 hours then add items on this line. Simmer for 30 minutes. Season to taste.
679		bunch Basil		tbsp Oregano			tsp Sugar	oz Tomato Paste				

Chefs Note: Traditionally some pasta dishes are not prepared with a previously prepared sauce. This includes Alfredo which is simply prepared with the cooked pasta, pasta water. Cacio e Pepe only has three ingredients pasta and some its water, freshly toasted ground pepper , and grated Romano cheese. Carbonara is the same but uses rendered pancetta with a liaison on egg yolks with Romano cheese. The pasta water and fat (butter, cheese, cream , olive oil) become an emulsion through this process. Aglio et Olio or garlic and olive oil is tossed with pasta and the pasta water to make an creamy sauce.

Pasta Sauces

		1/2	3/4	1	1	2	3	4	8	16	Y	Method of Preparation
680	**Parma Cream**		cup Parmesan				ea Garlic Cloves - minced	oz Prosciutto Ham julienne	tbsp Butter	oz Heavy Cream	20 oz	Heat the butter in a 2 quart sauce pot and sauté the garlic and ham. Add the cream and bring to a simmer. Add the cheese and simmer. Season to taste.
681	**Pesto**	cup Pine nuts	cup Olive Oil	cup Parmesan	tsp Black Pepper	cup Basil	oz Romano Cheese		ea Garlic Clove-minced		1 pint	Place all ingredients in a food processor and puree until smooth. Refrigerate or freeze until needed.
682	**Portofino** Toss the mussels and sauce with thin pasta	bunch Parsley	pinch Saffron	oz Minced Garlic	cup White Wine	oz Olive Oil	lb Mussels			oz Chopped Tomato	20 oz	Scrub and clean the mussels. Remove the beard. In a 2- gallon pot heat the oil and sauté the garlic lightly. Add the Mussels and wine. Simmer and add the tomatoes. Cover and simmer until the mussels open. Remove the mussels from their shell and reserve. Add the saffron and parsley to the sauce and simmer for 5 minutes. Add the mussels.
683	**Puttanesca** Use spaghetti for this sauce	tbsp Crushed Red Pepper	oz Anchovy	tbsp Capers	Bunch Parsley	oz Sundried Tomato	oz Olive Oil	ea Garlic Clove-minced		oz Crushed Tomato	1 pint	In a 1 quart sauté pan heat the oil and sauté the garlic and chilies. Add parsley, anchovy and capers and sauté lightly. Add the tomatoes and simmer for 15 minutes. Season to taste.
684	**Ragu Piedmont** Use Gnocchi for this sauce	lb Ham julienne	pint Heavy Cream	cup Onion-small dice			oz Butter	oz Prosciutto julienne	oz Porcini Mushrooms sliced	oz Chopped Tomato	3 cups	Sauté the mushrooms and onions in the butter. Add the hams and tomato, simmer for 5 minutes. Add the cream and reduce over low heat. Season to taste.
685	**Red Clam** Use linguine for this sauce	cup White Wine		lb Cooked Clams-chopped		oz Olive Oil	ea Garlic Clove	tbsp Parsley		oz Crushed Tomato	20 oz	In a 1 quart sauce pot sauté the garlic in olive oil. Add the wine and clams and simmer. Add the tomato and herbs. Simmer for 15 minutes.
686	**Rustica**		lb Italian Sausage	lb Broccoli Rappini	tsp Crushed Red Pepper		ea Garlic Clove	oz Olive Oil		oz Orechiette Pasta	3 cups	Brown the sausage in the olive oil. Finish cooking the sausage in the oven. When fully cooked slice. In a 2 quart sauté pan heat the leftover oil and sauté the garlic, red chilies and sausage. Boil the Rappini in the last two minutes of boiling the pasta. Then saute all together

Pasta Sauces

#		1/2	3/4	1	1	2	3	4	8	Yield	Method of Preparation
687	Salsa Cruda			cup Tomato Puree		lbs Ripe Tomato diced	Clove Garlic	oz Extra Virgin Olive Oil	ea Basil Leaves		Puree tomato, garlic, olive oil in blender for 2 minutes on high. Add chopped basil and season with salt and black pepper.
688	Salsa di Pomodoro		cup Onion diced	tbsp Basil	ea Garlic Clove-minced	lb – Crushed Tomatoes	tbsp Olive Oil			1 pint	In a 1 quart pot heat the olive oil and sauté the onions and garlic. Add the basil and tomato simmer for 20 minutes. Season to taste.
689	Salsa Romesco	cup Almonds	tsp Chili	head Garlic peel chop	Bread Slice	ea Roasted Red Pepper	ea Tomato-diced	cup Wine Vinegar	oz Extra Virgin Olive Oil	1 pint	Peel peppers. Puree all ingredients until smooth. Adjust with water. Season to taste with salt.
690	Salsa Verde — use thin pasta	cup Parsley-chopped	tsp Salt	ea Bread Slice	tbsp Basil			ea Garlic Clove-minced	oz Olive Oil	1 pint	Puree all of the items on this line.
		cup Lemon Juice	tsp Sugar	ea Green Pepper-brunoise		tbsp Capers			ea Green Olives-chopped		Bring the puree to a simmer and add the items on this line. Simmer for 10 minutes. Season.
691	Tetrazzinni	tsp Pepper	oz Butter	qt Heavy Cream	lb sliced Mushroom	lb Cooked Poultry-diced	oz Sherry		oz Parmesan	40 oz	In a 2 quart sauce pot heat the butter and sauté the mushrooms. Add the pepper and cream. Simmer and add the sherry. Simmer for 5 minutes and add the Parmesan. Toss in the cooked poultry with desired pasta in casserole, top with cheese Bake for 30 min 350° in casserole.
692	Tomato Arrabbiata				tsp Red Pepper Flakes		ea Garlic Clove – minced			1 quart	Add to the recipe detailed below. Season to taste.
693	Tomato Classico	Bunch Basil-chopped	ea Onion diced			oz Olive Oil	ea Garlic Clove – minced	cups Tomato-diced		1 quart	In a 2 quart sauce pot with lid heat the oil and sauté the onions and garlic. Cover and swet for 20 minutes. Add the herb and tomato. Simmer uncovered.
694	Tomato Romano		oz Bacon Fat	ea Garlic Clove-minced	oz Parsley-chopped	lb Tomatoes-diced	tbsp Olive Oil	tbsp Butter	oz Mirepoix minced	1 quart	In a 2 quart sauce pot heat the oil and bacon fat. Sauté the garlic and mirepoix. Add the tomatoes and simmer for 30 minutes. Puree the tomato sauce and whisk in the butter and parsley. Season.
695	Tomato Vegetable	tbsp Oregano-chopped	tbsp Basil-chopped	lb Mirepoix		oz Olive Oil	lb Tomato-diced	ea Garlic Clove-minced		1 quart	In a 2 quart sauce pot with lid heat the oil and sauté the mirepoix and garlic. Cover and swet for 20 minutes. Add tomato. Simmer uncovered for 30 minutes. Puree. Add herbs, simmer for 5 minutes. Season.
696	Walnut Sauce — Use this sauce for filled pasta	cup Bread Crumb	qt Cream	oz Walnut Oil	oz Olive Oil	cup Walnuts	oz Butter	ea Garlic Clove-minced	oz Parmesan	1 quart	In a 2 quart sauce pot sauté the garlic in oils Add the nuts and lightly sauté. Add the cream and simmer. Thicken with bread crumbs and Parmesan. Strain the solids and chop in a food processor. Add back to the cream and Season to taste.

Pastas and Fillings

		1/2	3/4	1	1	2	3	4	8	Yield	Method of Preparation
697	Egg Pasta	Gallon Durum Flour		Dozen Eggs	Pint Yolk					5 lb	Place flour in 20 quart mixer, make a well. Add eggs In the middle. Mix on first speed for 7 minutes. Portion into 8 oz balls. Freezes well.
698	Potato Gnocchi			tsp Salt	ea Egg		lb Potatoes Cooked		oz Durum Flour	22 oz	Dry the cooked potatoes in a warm oven until they are very dry. Place the potatoes in a mixer and cool with a paddle. Add the remaining ingredients and mix until well blended
699	Polenta To bake or grill this polenta temper in 4 oz of egg yolk after cool.	lb Cheese (Parmesan, Romano, or Asiago)			lb fine Cornmeal		oz Butter		cup Liquid (Milk or Stock)	3.5 lb	Bring the liquid and butter to a simmer. Slowly add the cornmeal with a whisk. Once the cornmeal is added use a wooden spoon to stir the polenta over low heat for 15 minutes. Remove and slowly add the cheese. Season to taste.
700	Ricotta Cavatelli	tsp Salt	lb Ricotta	lb Bread Flour 00	ea Eggs	oz Parmesan grated			oz Durum Flour	2 lb	Combine the cheeses and eggs. Add the dry ingredients and knead well in a mixer. Allow to rest. Roll the dough into ¼ inch logs and slice the cavatelli on the bias 1 inch long. Press with a fork into a shell shape.
701	Semolina Dough			tbsp Salt	pint Cold Water	oz Olive Oil		lb Semolina Flour	ea Eggs	6 lb	Pour flour in 20 qt mixer bowl. Pour everything else on top. Mix and knead on first speed for 7 minutes. Portion 8 oz balls- cover, rest 30 minutes.
702	Spatzlé	pinch Nutmeg	pint Milk	tsp Salt	lb Bread Flour		ea Eggs			2 lb	Add the liquids to the dry ingredients and beat well until it is very elastic. Allow the batter to rest for 15 minutes before pressing through a colander, ricer or Spatzlé press into boiling salted water.
703	Gorgonzola Filling	lb Gorgonzola		lb Ricotta	tbsp Basil	tbsp Parsley	ea Eggs	oz Parmesan		3 cups	Combine all ingredients in a bowl and season to taste. Use for ravioli or Tortelloni.
704	Meat Filling	tsp Fennel Seed		lb Ground Meat	ea Garlic Clove	tbsp Parsley	oz Onions minced	oz Parmesan		1 pint	In a large sauté the onions and garlic in the oil. Add the meat and cook with the fennel until well brown. Remove from the stove and cool. Add the parsley and cheese and season.
705	Ricotta Filling	lb Mozzarella grated		lb Ricotta	tbsp Basil	tbsp Parsley	ea Eggs	oz Parmesan		3 cups	Combine all ingredients together. Season to taste. Use for Cannelloni, stuffed shells, manicotti, lasagna or Calzone.
706	Veal and Spinach Filling		oz Olive Oil	lb Ground Veal	pinch Nutmeg	Ea Garlic Clove minced	cups Fresh Spinach chopped fine	oz Shallot minced		1.5 quart	In a large sauté pan sauté the garlic and shallots in the oil. Add the veal and cook until brown. Add the spinach and nutmeg. Cook until the spinach is wilted. Cool the mixture and add to the cheese filling – recipe #705

Chefs Note: When ever you cook fresh pasta always use a gallon of salted water for each pound of pasta. When cooked to the desired degree of doneness drain well and toss with the hot pasta sauce, season to taste. Filled pasta like tortelloni and ravioli should be simmered in salted water, carefully removed and served with the appropriate sauce. 00 is a fine bread flour of 8.5% protein and excellent for filled pastas. Durum flour and semolina flours are used to produce firmer doughs for long thin pasta like spaghetti and fettuccine.

Italian Preparations

#	Item		1	2	3	4	8	Yield	Method of Preparation
707	Cannelloni Piedmont	2 lbs Pasta Dough	Recipe Veal Filling	Recipes Pomodoro Sauce #688	oz Butter			16 pieces	Prepare associated recipes. Roll pasta dough very thin. Cut into 5"x5" pieces. Blanch 1 minute. Fill with 3 oz of filling. Arrange in buttered dish. Top with sauce and bake 45 minutes covered
708	Crespelle Florentine	¼ cup Melted Butter	recipe Celestine Crepes #3	cups Chopped Spinach	oz Shallot minced	oz Parmesan Cheese grated	oz Ricotta Cheese	24 ea	Prepare crepes. In a large sauté pan sweat shallots in butter. Add spinach and lower heat. Season to taste. Cool. Add cheeses. Portion 1 oz of filling per crepe, bake 350°- 10 min.
709	Lasagna Napolitano	½ recipe Semolina Dough #701	Recipe Meat Filling #704	Recipes Ricotta Filling # 705 / qt Tomato Sauce	cups Grated Mozzarella	ea Sweet Italian Sausage	ea Meatballs # 456 / oz Parmesan grated	12 portions	Prepare fillings and pasta sheets, cook meats. Grease a 4 inch full hotel pan. Pour 1 cup of sauce in pan to coat. Alternate layers of pasta sheets with ricotta fillings, sliced sausage, sliced meatballs, sauce and meat filling. This recipe will yield 7 layers with a final layer of pasta sheet, tomato sauce and grated cheeses. Bake 2 hours at 325°. Allow to rest for 20 minutes. Cut 3"x5"
710	Melanzana Rollatini	Olive Oil as needed	Recipe Ricotta Filling #705	ea peeled Eggplant	cups Bread Crumb	ea Eggs / cup Tomato Sauce	oz Flour	24 pieces	Slice eggplant lengthwise ¼" thick. Sprinkle with salt, drain for 30 minutes, rinse. Standard bread eggplant. Fry in olive oil to golden brown. Portion 1 oz of filling on each slice and roll into a 3" log. Place in baking dish top with sauce and bake covered 350° -45 min.
711	Polenta - Basic	1 cup Parmesan (Opt)	cup Milk	tsp Salt	cups Polenta Cornmeal	oz Butter	cups Water or Stock.	10 portions	Bring salt, butter and water or stock to a simmer in a 1 gallon pot. Slowly whisk in fine cornmeal. Reduce heat, stir over low heat for 20 min. Finish with milk. Season.
712	Polenta Fontina	1 ½ tsp salt	pint Milk	cups Polenta Cornmeal	cups diced Fontina	cups Water	oz Heavy Cream	6 portions	Bring salt, milk and water to a simmer in a 1 gallon pot. Slowly whisk in fine cornmeal. Reduce heat, stir over low heat for 25 min. Mix in cream and cheese. Season.
713	Risi e Bisi	20 oz Chicken Stock	ea Onion brunoise	oz Olive Oil	cups Green Peas	oz Pancetta fine dice / oz Parmesan	oz Long Grain Rice Carnaroli	6 portions	Sauté pancetta and onions in olive oil until translucent. Add rice and sauté to coat. Add stock and simmer over low heat for 20 minutes or use a rice cooker. Add peas to heat. Finish with grated cheese and seasoning
714	Risotto Blanco		ea Onion brunoise	cups Arborio Rice	oz Parmesan Cheese grated	oz Butter	cups Chicken Stock	8 portions	Sauté onions in butter until translucent. Add rice and mix to coat with fat. Add ½ of the stock bring to a simmer, turn off an cover for 30 minutes. Add stock slowly and stir until al dente. Finish with parmesan and season to taste.
715	Risotto Fruiti di Mare	2 tbsp Olive Oil / 5 cups Fish Stock	cup Bay Scallops	cups Arborio Rice	oz Parmesan Cheese grated	oz Butter / tbsp Shallot	oz White Wine / oz Shrimp	6 portions	Sauté minced shallot in oil until translucent. Add rice and mix to coat with fat. Add ½ of the stock bring to a simmer, turn off an cover for 30 minutes. Add 2 cup stock slowly and stir until al dente. Add seafood and ½ cup of stock and stir. Finish with parmesan , season.
716	Timpano	½ recipe Meatballs #456	recipe Pasta Dough #701	cups Diced Soppressata / recipe # 673 Bolognese	oz oil / cups Grated Provolone	lbs Cavatelli-blanched #700	ea Hard Boiled Eggs-Peel and Quarter	12 portions	Prepare meatballs, pasta dough, cavatelli and sauce Bolognese. Grease a 12 inch round casserole with oil. Roll out dough to a 20 inch circle. Line dough in casserole. Place half of the cavetelli in mold; add half meats, cheese, eggs, sauce. Repeat. Cover with dough, wrap with foil, and place in a 325° for 3 hours. Rest 30 minutes. Slice, serve with tomato sauce

Italian Entrees

Item	1	2	3	4	8	Yield	Method of Preparation
717 **Brasato Bartolotti** (Beef Stew)	1 sprig Rosemary / 2 tbsp Garlic Minced / bottle Barolo Wine	lbs Mirepoix / tbsp Olive Oil	lbs Beef Chuck Diced 2"	tbsp Flour	oz Pancetta-Diced	Yields 6 / 9 oz Portion	Place Pancetta and Oil in a braising pot render and remove pieces. Season beef with salt and pepper. Brown in hot fat, remove and soak in wine. Caramelize the mirepoix singer with flour, add all of the ingredients back to the pot and simmer over low heat until the beef is very tender. 2 hours.
718 **Braciole di Maiale Calabrese** (Slow Roasted Pork)	1 large Onion sliced / ea Pork Shoulder 4.5 lb / 1 pint White Wine	ea Red Pepper-roasted		oz Tomato Paste	ea Garlic cloves-sliced	Yields 8 / 8 oz Portion	Peel and dice peppers, chop rosemary and add to the garlic. Season with salt and black pepper. Make deep incisions in the pork shoulder and stuff the pepper mixture in the cuts. Season the outside of the pork with salt and pepper Place over sliced onions in roasting pan. Roast covered for 4 hours at 250°. Remove roast, deglaze pan with wine, add tomato paste and simmer until thickened, season. Slice roast.
719 **Brodetto d' San Marino** (Fish and Seafood Stew)	¼ cup Parsley fine chop / 2 Bay leaf / lb Monkfish / ea Sweet Chile Pepper	dozen Mussels / cup dice Onion	clove Garlic-Minced / oz Wine	ea large Tomato-chopped / oz EVOO	ea Large Scampi or Shrimp P+D	Yields 4 / 12 oz Portion	Dice monkfish, season and dredge in flour. Heat Oil and fry the fish until brown, remove. Add onions and sweat, add chili, garlic, bay, wine and tomato. Simmer 5 minutes. Season. Arrange mussels, fish and shrimp in sauce. Cover and bake for 10 minutes at 350°. Sprinkle with parsley.
720 **Capra d' Abruzzo** (Braised Goat)	3 cups Abruzzo Wine / tsp Red Pepper Flakes	ea Bay Leaf and Sage Leaf	lb Goat-leg / tbsp Olive Oil	ea Large tomato-chopped	oz Onion diced / oz Water	Yields 6 / 10 oz Portion	Marinate goat in wine, herbs, pepper for 24 hrs. Remove and reserve the marinade. Heat oil in a large braising pan and sear the goat on all sides. Add onions and caramelize. Add all ingredients and braise for 3 hours at 325° until tender. Season, slice, and serve over polenta with sauce on top.
721 **Osso Bucco Milanese**	2 quart Veal Stock / 1 ea Lemon Zest, Juice / lb Matignon / sprig Rosemary	Tbsp Chopped Parsley / cup Wine	oz Tomato Paste / tsp Garlic	ea Tomatoes Concasse / oz Olive Oil	ea Veal Shank / oz Flour	Yields 8 / 6 oz Portion	Season veal with salt and pepper. Dredge in flour. Heat oil in large braising pan. Sear the veal on both sides and remove, flavor with juice. Brown matignon in pan,add juice. Expand with tomato paste. Add tomatoes, 2 tsp garlic, and rosemary, liquids and simmer. Add veal back to pan. Cover and braise until tender 325° for 2 ½ hours. Season. Combine parsley, zest, 1 tsp garlic Use as a gremolate garnish on the marrow.
722 **Petti di Pollo Parma**	1 slice Prosciutto julienne / cup wine / tsp Garlic	ea Split Chicken Breast-	oz Roasted Peppers	oz Tomato diced	oz Veal Stock	Serves 2	Season chicken breast, slowly brown in a small amount of oil. Add ham and tomato, sauté. Deglaze with wine, pour stock over skin on breast. Cover and bake until chicken reaches 165° Add diced peppers and garlic. Simmer. Salt and pepper to taste
723 **Petti di Pollo Marsala**	2 tbsp Butter / Breast Chicken	oz Demi Glace	oz Mushroom	oz Marsala		Serves 1	Season chicken, dredge in seasoned flour. Brown in butter, add mushroom, sauté. Deglaze, Serve chicken at 165°
724 **Pollo alla Cacciatore**	1 pint White Wine / tbsp Fresh Oregano	cup Peperonata #665	tbsp Olive Oil	large Mushroom sliced	ea Chicken Leg Quarter	Serves 8	Season chicken legs and thighs. Brown in oil. Sauté mushrooms. Deglaze, add rest. Braise 45 minutes. Season to taste Serve chicken at 180° with sauce on top
725 **Spezzatino di Vitello e Pepe** (Veal and Peppers)	2 can Whole Tomatoes (28 oz ea) / lb dice Onion / cup Flour	tbsp Oregano oz / Garlic	cups Bell Peppers diced	lbs Veal Shoulder-cubed	oz Olive Oil / oz Wine	Yields 8 / 12 oz Portion	Mince garlic. Heat large braising pan, add half of the oil. Season veal, sear half of the veal. Remove veal and repeat. Heat remaining fond. Sauté veg and herbs. Singer with flour. Add tomato, veal , wine- simmer 1 hour
726 **Stufato D' Agnello Giardiniera** (Lamb Stew with Vegetables)	1 Sprig Rosemary / pint Tomato Puree / recipe Peperonata #665	cups Matignon	lbs Lamb Shoulder 1" dice	cups Eggplant-peel, dice	oz Red Wine / oz EVOO	Yields 8 / 10 oz Portion	Salt eggplant, stand for 30 minutes. Rinse. Prepare matignon in braising pan, remove, prepare peperonata, and remove. Heat ¼ oil, season and sear lamb. Remove. Heat pan and fry eggplant. Add all and simmer for 1 hour until all ingredients are very tender.

Italian Desserts

#	Item			1	2	4	8	Yield	Method of Preparation
727	Baba au Rum		¼ recipe # Babka 1021	cup Currants	cups Sugar	cups Water	oz Dark Rum	24 ea	Prepare dough and mix in currants. Portion 24 ea 2 oz ball from babka dough. Proof in greased tins. Bake 375° for 20-25 minutes. Combine sugar and water in copper pot bring to a boil, cook to 225°. Cool to 120° Stir in rum. Dip cooled babas in syrup, rest 1 hour
728	Cremolata Fragole		9 oz Sugar	pint Strawberry Sauce Rec #1005	oz Lemon Juice	ea Oranges Juiced	oz Fresh Strawberry Crushed	1 Quart	Dissolve sugar in juices. Add the strawberry sauce. Spin in a ice cream maker until the blade starts to clean the bowl. Add crushed strawberries and spin another 10 minutes. Store at 15°
729	Granita Choccolato	½ cup Cocoa Powder		quart Water	cups Chocolate Syrup	cups Sugar		1 ¾ quart	Bring ½ of water a boil, whisk in sugar and cocoa powder to melt. Mix in remaining water and syrup. Chill to 35°. Spin in a ice cream machine to produce this "Italian Ice"
730	Panforte di Siena	1 tsp Cinnamon / 1/8 tsp Cloves	1 cup Flour / 2 tbsp Cocoa Powder	cup Dried Figs / cup Honey	oz Almonds / oz Rum	oz Sugar / oz Filbert	oz Raisin / ea Prunes minced	1 torte	Grease a spring form pan and dust with cocoa powder. Mix the spices, measured cocoa powder, flour in a bowl with nuts. In a copper pan bring to a boil the sugar, honey, rum. Cook to 240°. Add the fruits and add to nut mixture. Mix well and pour into pan. Bake at 310° 45 minutes. Cool overnight. Wrap Age for 1 month
731	Panna Cotta	1 Vanilla Bean	6 ea Gelatin Sheet	quart Cream	cups Half and Half	cups Cold Water	oz Sugar	1 ½ Quarts	Combine creams and sugar. Bring to 150°. Add vanilla bean and steep for 30 minutes. Soak gelatin sheets in water for 30 minutes. Drain and squeeze sheets, add sheets to cream and heat to melt. Scrape bean into mixture. Portion in cups chill 6 hours.
732	Semifreddo di Palermo	1 drop Green Color	½ tsp Almond Extract	doz Egg Whites	cups Sugar	cups Heavy Cream	oz Green Pistachio	2 Quarts	Make sure pistachios are peeled. In a small food processor puree half of the pistachios with half the sugar, extract and color to a paste. Warm the other half of sugar and egg whites to 115° and whip to medium peak. Whip cream to soft peaks, combine with paste. Fold together add nuts and pour into molds or loaf pan. Freeze 24 hours.
733	Torrone	10 ea Egg Whites	6 oz Honey / 2 ½ tsp Almond Ext.	cup Sugar / tbsp Vanilla	oz Candied Orange Peel	cups Toasted Hazelnuts	oz Water	40 oz	Combine sugar and water in a copper candy pot and simmer until it reaches 290°. Stir in honey. Place egg white in small mixer and whip, gradually add in all of the syrup. Add extracts, nuts and peel. Pour into butter a 9" x 5" loaf pan. Cover with wax paper, let stand 24hrs.
734	Torta di Ricotta	1 tbsp Orange Zest	¾ cup Sugar	lb Cream Cheese	cups Ricotta Cheese	cups Heavy Cream	oz Eggs	Serves 12	Drain ricotta overnight. Cream the cheeses with sugar until smooth. Add rest and mix for 2 minute on low. Pour into prepped spring form pan. Bake 340° 70 min.
735	Torta di Mele	¾ cup Honey / ¼ cup OJ	3 cup Flour / 1 tbsp Baking Powder	tbsp Cinnamon / tsp Salt	cups Sugar / tsp Vanilla	ea Granny Smith Apples / ea Eggs	oz Oil / oz Walnut	1 Cake	Peel and slice apples very thin. Toss with cinnamon and honey. Place all dry ingredients in a bowl. Whisk all liquids in separate bowl. Combine dry and wet to form smooth batter. Layer batter, apples, batter, apples in greased Bundt pan. Bake 1 ½ hours at 350°
736	Tortoni	1 tsp Vanilla and Almond Extract	1 cup Light Cream	quart Heavy Cream	cup Powdered Sugar	ea Egg Whites	oz Macaroon Crumbs	15 Portions	In a mixer whip the creams to medium peaks. Mix in sugar and extracts. In a separate bowl whip the egg whites to a stiff peak. Fold into cream with crumbs. Portion with a 3 oz scoop into paper lined tins and freeze 3 hours. Garnish with almond slices, cherry.
737	Zabaglione		½ cup Sugar	oz Grappa		oz Marsala Wine	ea Egg Yolks	Serves 8	Combine Grappa, egg yolks, egg sugar in a copper sabayon pan. Warm to 100° while whipping. Add wine and whip until foam form a ribbon - 145° Serve over fresh berries
738	Zuccoto Florentine		1 recipe Ganache # 1044	ea 10" Sponge Cake	pint Praline Semifreddo #927	oz Sliced Toasted Almonds	oz Florentine #853	Serves 16	Slice sponge into 2 disks. Line a 10" cake pan with plastic wrap. Place cake slice on wrap. Prepare semifreddo, fold in nuts, and pour on cake, top with sponge. Freeze overnight. Cover with ganache. Chill and slice 16 portions. Keep frozen, garnish with ½ oz Florentine Cookies.

Italian Pastries

#	Item			1	2	4	8	Yield	Method of Preparation
739	Cannoli Filling	½ tsp Vanilla	¼ tsp Almond Extract		lb Strained Ricotta	oz Candied Rind or Choc Chip	oz 10X Sugar	2.75 lb	Cream cheese and sugar until smooth, add extracts and mix. Add Garnish of choice. Fill each Cannoli shell using piping bag. Dust with additional powdered sugar and serve.
740	Cannoli Shell	1 ea egg white	1 ¼ cup Marsala	lb Flour	oz Salted Butter	tsp Sugar		2 doz	Pulse dry ingredients with butter in food processor. Remove and add the wine. Mix by hand. Roll 1/8" thick; cut 4 " squares. Wrap on greased Cannoli tubes, Seal ends with egg white Fry at 325°. Cool
741	Cartellate	¾ tsp Salt	2 tsp Cinnamon	pint Water	oz Olive Oil	cups Flour	oz Honey	4 doz	Place dry ingredients in mixing bowl, water on top. Mix two minutes until ball forms. Allow to rest 30 minutes. Roll out in pasta machine, cut into Fettuccine by hand. Fry spiral in 360° fat. Drizzle warm honey.
742	Chiacchiere		1 ½ tsp Vanilla	oz Wine	oz Sugar	cups Flour	oz Eggs	3 doz	Place dry ingredients in mixing bowl, water on top. Mix two minutes until ball forms. Allow to rest 30 minutes. Roll out in pasta machine, cut ½ "by 3 ". Fry in 350° fat. Dust with powdered sugar.
743	Pannettone	14 ½ oz Flour ¾ tsp Salt	½ ea Orange and Lemon - Zest	tbsp Dry Yeast tbsp Sugar	oz Buttermilk oz Sugar	oz Salted Butter oz Raisins	oz Eggs tbsp Candied Peel	1 ea	Warm milk to 105°. Mix in yeast and tbsp sugar. Cream remaining sugar, zest and butter, add in eggs slowly, cream again. Add yeast mixture and flour, mix on low speed scraping sides often. Knead 3 minutes add rest and knead in 2 minutes. Portion into wax paper lined tin. Proof 1 hour, bake 350°for 45 minutes.
744	Pastaciotti	¼ cup Flour ½ cup Almond Slices.	1 recipe Pate Sucree #864	tsp Almond Extract	ea Egg Yolk	oz Sugar oz Mascarpone	oz Milk	15 ea	Combine milk, flour, sugar in sauce pot. Whisk and bring to a boil. Cool while whisking. Whisk in extract, egg and cheese. Mix well. Rolls out Pate Sucree to ¼ thick. Brush 15 ea 2 ¼ tins with butter and line dough in tins. Portion filling equally. Garnish with almonds. Brush with egg wash. Bake in a 425° oven for 10-13 minutes.
745	Pizelle	½ tsp Extract	1 ½ tsp Baking Powder	cup Sugar	cups Flour	ea Eggs oz Salted Butter		2 doz	Mix eggs and sugar until smooth. Add in melted butter and extract of choice to taste. Sift rest and add to batter. Portion onto Pizelle griddle and follow manufactures directions.
746	Sfogliatelle	¼ tsp Salt 1 ¼ cup Melted Butter ¼ cup Sugar		cup Cold Water	cup Semolina	cups Flour	oz Butter Cubed	3 doz	Rub the cubed butter in the dry ingredients in a small mixer bowl. Pour water on top and mix until dough forms. Chill 2 hours. Roll dough on pasta machine. 1/16". Seal 3 sheets of dough together, like siding. Brush with melted butter. Roll like jellyroll. Cut 1½"pieces. Shape into sea shell, Fill with 1 ½ - 2 tbsp filling. Bake 420° -18 minute- Powder Sugar Dust
747	Sfogliatelle-Filling	4 ¼ oz Sugar	ea Orange - Zest	pint Ricotta	ea Eggs	tbsp Semolina	oz Milk	2 lb	Bring sugar and milk to bowl, thicken with semolina. Cool 3 hours. Mix the rest in until smooth. Add cinnamon or vanilla to taste.
748	Strufoli	Warm Honey as needed	1 ½ tsp Vanilla	cup Sugar	tsp Baking Powder	cups Flour oz Butter	oz Eggs	6 doz	Place dry ingredient in bowl. Break up butter into dry ingredients to a coarse texture. Add eggs and vanilla. Knead to soft dough. Refrigerate 2 hours. Roll dough to a ½ inch thick rectangle. Cut strips ½". Portion ½" thick slices and round. Fry at 350°. Drizzle honey, garnish with candy sprinkles and nuts.
749	Zeppole	1 tbsp Orange Zest	1 tsp Baking Powder	pint Milk	cups Bread Flour	oz Butter	ea Eggs	4 doz	Bring milk, zest and butter to a simmer. Add flour all at one time. Cook on stove and mix with wooden spoon until ball forms. Transfer to mixing bowl and cool with paddle. Add eggs in one at a time. Mix in baking powder last. Portion 1 oz Quenelles on top greased parchment and fry to order at 350°. Dust with powdered sugar.

American Quickbreads and Batters

#	Name			1	1	1	2	3	Yield	Method of Preparation
750	Beer Batter	1 ½ tsp Salt	10 oz Flour	bottle Beer	ea Egg		tsp Baking Powder	drop Tabasco®	1 pint	Sift dry ingredient, blend egg and beer, and add to dry. Season to taste.
751	Berry Cobbler	6 Eggs	1 ½ tbsp Baking Powder	ea Lemon zested	tbsp Vanilla	pinch Nutmeg	cups Milk	cup Sugar / cups All Purpose Flour	10 serving	Combine the eggs, sugar, nutmeg and vanilla. Whip on high speed until light. Fold in the milk and remaining ingredients. Spread over 3 cups of sweet berries. Bake at 350° for 30 minutes.
752	Boston Brown Bread	1 cup Raisins	2/3 cup Molasses	cup Corn Meal / cup Coarse Whole Wheat Flour	cup Rye Flour	tsp Salt	cup Buttermilk / tsp Baking Soda		2.5 lb	Blend all the ingredients on this line together and refrigerate overnight. Mix in the items on this line and portion into round loaf pans. Place in a steamer pan and steam covered for 90 minutes. Cool 1 hour.
753	Buttermilk Honey Short Bread	1/3 cup Sugar	4 oz Butter	½ cup Buttermilk	ea Egg	tbsp Baking Powder	cup All Purpose Flour / tbsp Honey		24 oz	Cut the butter into the dry ingredients and rub until the butter is pea size. Combine the items on this line and add to the dry. Portion and bake at 350° for 20 minute, glaze with additional honey.
754	Buttermilk Biscuits	6 oz Buttermilk	¼ tsp Baking Soda	oz Butter sliced thin	oz Shortening		cup Self Rising Flour		20 oz	Combine the dry ingredients. Rub the fats into the dry until the fat is pea size pieces. Add the buttermilk last. Knead until the dough comes together. Drop the biscuits on to a buttered pan with a portion scoop. Egg wash if desired for color. Bake at 350°.
755	Clam Fritter (Corn Oyster- substitute corn for clams)	½ cup Milk / ½ tsp Black Pepper	½ cup minced Onions / ½ tsp Sea Salt	cup Flour	tbsp Sugar	tsp Baking Powder / ea Eggs	cups Minced Clam		1 qt	Combine dry ingredients. Mix milk egg and ¼ cup of clam juice or water. Add to the dry ingredients and stir. Add in clams and onions. Drop 1 tbsp portions into fryer.
756	Corn Bread	10 oz Corn meal / 12 oz Corn Oil	20 oz Water	20 oz Sugar	1 ½ lb Bread Flour	9 ea Eggs	oz Milk Powder / oz Baking Powder		3.25 / quart	Place all ingredients in a mixer with a paddle. Mix until smooth. Spread on a greased pan and bake at 375° until golden brown. This batter can also be used for muffins.
757	Fish Batter	1 tbsp Onion Salt	2 cup Flour	tbsp Sugar	tsp Baking Powder		cup Club Soda	ea Egg White	24 oz	Mix flour, salt, baking powder. Whip egg white and sugar. Mix soda into dry ingredient, fold in meringue.
758	French Toast	½ tsp Vanilla	¼ tsp Cinnamon	oz Bourbon	pint Milk	cup Milk	tbsp Sugar	ea Eggs	1 pint	Mix well – use for 8 slices of bread
759	Fruit Fritter	6 ea Eggs	1 tsp Vanilla Extract	1 tbsp Orange Juice / 1 lb All Purpose Flour	cup Coconut Flakes / pint Milk	tsp Salt	tbsp Baking Powder	oz Sugar	1 / quart	Combine all ingredients and allow it to rest under refrigeration for 1 hour. Dredge slices of banana or apples in flour then dip in the batter. Deep fat fry in 340° oil until golden brown.
760	Fry Bread		½ tsp Salt	quart Flour	pint Buttermilk		tbsp Baking Powder		3.5 lb	Sift all dry ingredients. Add the buttermilk and knead into dough. Roll out ¼" thick. Cut into 3x3 squares and fry to golden brown.
761	Funnel Cakes	2/3 cup Milk	¼ tsp Salt / ¾ tsp Baking Powder	1 1/3cup Flour			tbsp Sugar		10 each	Combine the wet ingredients first. Mix the wet into the dry ingredients. Portion through a funnel into 340° oil. Turnover with a wooden dowel or spoon. Finish with powdered sugar.

American Quickbreads and Batters

No.	Name	Ingredients	Yield	Method of Preparation
762	**Hush Puppies**	1 cup Milk; 1 ½ tsp Salt; cup Corn Meal; dash Tabasco®; tbsp Onion minced; tsp Sugar; 1 ea Egg; ¼ cup Scallion-sliced; cup All Purpose Flour; tbsp Baking Powder	3 dozen	Mix the dry ingredient then add the rest. Mix until blended. Portion with a scoop, spoon, or pipe the mixture with a pastry bag directly into 350° oil. Fry until golden brown and remove.
763	**Johnny Cakes**	½ tsp Salt; ¾ cup Milk; cup White Cornmeal; cup Boiling Water; 1 oz Sugar; 1 tsp Baking Powder	18 each	Add the hot water to the cornmeal stir and allow it to stand for 30 minutes. Add the remaining ingredients and stir. Portion on to a buttered griddle like pancakes. Brown on both sides.
764	**Pancakes**	2 ea Eggs; 4 tsp Baking Powder; oz Butter; cups Flour; 2 cups Milk; ½ tsp Salt; tbsp Sugar	2 dozen	Sift all the dry ingredients together. Combine the eggs and milk. Mix the wet ingredients into the dry, blend. Melt the butter and stir into the batter portion on to a buttered surface. Brown on both sides over medium heat.
765	**Penn Dutch Dumplings**	½ tsp Salt; 4 tsp Baking Powder; oz Butter; cups Flour; ½ cup Milk; ea Egg	20 ea	Mix the dry ingredients together. Add in the butter and rub into the flour. Add in the eggs and milk and mix well. Shape the round dumplings and simmer for 20 minutes in stock.
766	**Popovers** (portion 2 tbsp of fat into each popover tin)	¼ tsp Salt; cup Milk; tbsp Butter; ea Eggs; 8 oz of Fat for the popover tin; cup Flour	9 each	Preheat oven to 450°, grease 9 tins with 1 oz. of liquid fat in each tin. Place in oven when batter is ready. Combine the milk and eggs. Add the flour and salt. Whisk in melted butter. Portion the batter into the preheated greased tins. Be careful of the hot fat. Place back in the oven for 12 minutes until crispy and brown.
767	**Spoon bread**	1 ¼ cup Cornmeal; tsp Salt; tbsp Baking Powder; tbsp Butter; tbsp Sugar; cups Milk; ea Eggs	1 quart	Bring the milk and butter to a simmer with the salt and sprinkle in the cornmeal. Simmer for 5 minutes. Cool to 40°. Separate the eggs. Whisk the yolks into the cool mixture. Whip the egg whites with sugar to form a soft meringue. Portion into a round dish and bake at 350° for 25 minutes.
768	**Southern Dumpling**	¼ cup Rendered Chicken Fat; 2 ea Eggs; tsp Salt; tsp Baking Powder; cup Flour; oz Milk	3 doz pieces	Combine dry, add in fat, mix eggs and milk. Mix until firm, roll out, cut 1 inch wide dumplings. Simmer in chicken stew.
769	**Tamale**	4 tsp Baking Powder; 10 oz Lard; quart Cool Stock; pint Cold Water; tbsp Kosher Salt; lbs Masa Harina	6 lb	Mix the dry ingredients. Break up the lard into the masa harina. Add liquids and mix.
770	**Tortilla - Corn**	pint Warm Water; tbsp Corn Oil; tsp Salt; cups Masa Harina	18 ea	Mix masa with salt and oil. Add warm water and knead well. Portion 1 ¼ oz, roll and press between 2 sheets of plastic. Griddle.
771	**Tortilla- Flour**	10 oz Warm Water; 5 tbsp Lard; tsp Salt; tsp Baking Powder; cups Flour	16 ea	Mix dry ingredients, rub in lard. Knead in warm water. Portion 1 ½ balls. Roll out and griddle.
772	**Waffle**	¼ cup Cornstarch; 4 tsp Baking Powder; ½ tsp Salt; oz Oil; cup Milk; cup Buttermilk; cups Flour; tbsp Sugar; ea Eggs	12 ea	Sift all the dry ingredients together. Combine the eggs and milks. Mix the wet ingredients into the dry, blend. Stir oil into the batter. Portion on to a greased waffle iron. Follow manufactures directions.

Quick Breads

773 — Banana Bread (Yield: 11 lb)

Ingredients:
- 22 oz Butter
- 7 ea Eggs
- 1 lb Chopped Walnuts
- 1 lb Sugar
- 1 lb Ripe Banana Pureed
- tsp Vanilla Extract
- oz Honey
- oz Whole Wheat Flour
- 4 tsp Baking Powder

Method of Preparation: Cream together the fat and sugar. Add vanilla honey. Cream well. Add the banana. Mix for 1 min on 1st speed. Add the eggs slowly and mix with paddle for 2 min. Add the remaining ingredients and mix. Portion 1lb units bake at 350°.

---

774 — Biscuits (Yield: 3 lb)

Ingredients:
- 5 cup All Purpose Flour
- 2 tsp Salt
- Tbsp Sugar
- cup Buttermilk
- Tbsp Baking Powder
- oz Sliced Butter

Method of Preparation: Rub the fat into the dry ingredients until the fat pieces are the size of peas. Add the buttermilk and mix until all the liquid is absorbed. Roll out 1 inch thick bake at 425° Brush with additional butter if desired

---

775 — Blueberry Muffins (Yield: 10 lb)

Ingredients:
- 8 oz Shortening
- ½ oz Salt
- 1 ¼ Baking Powder
- 2 ½ cup Milk
- pint Eggs
- 1 lb Sugar
- 1 lb Blueberry
- oz Butter
- 2 ½ lb Cake Flour

Method of Preparation: Cream the sugar and fats until light. Slowly add the eggs and mix in. Combine the flour and baking powder. Add it to the above mixture and mix until smooth. Add the blueberries last. Portion. Bake at 350°

---

776 — Bran Muffins (Yield: 8 lb)

Ingredients:
- ½ oz Salt
- 1 ½ lb Bread Flour
- 1 ½ pint Milk
- 1 lb Eggs
- 1 lb Raisin
- oz Honey
- oz Molasses
- oz Shortening
- oz Bran
- 1 ½ oz Baking Powder

Method of Preparation: Cream the sugar, honey and fat until light. Slowly add the eggs and mix in. Then add the salt. Combine the dry items. Add to the above mixture. Add the molasses and milk and mix until the flour is absorbed. Add raisins last. Portion. Bake 340°

---

777 — Corn Muffin (Yield: 5 lb)

Ingredients:
- ½ oz Salt
- 1 ½ oz Baking Powder
- 1 lb Cornmeal
- 1 lb Sugar
- cup Milk
- ea Eggs
- oz Shortening
- 1 ½ lb Pastry Flour

Method of Preparation: Cream the sugar and fat until light. Slowly add the eggs and mix in. Then add the dry ingredients. Mix and add the milk in last. Portion. Bake 350°

---

778 — Crumpets (Yield: 8 lb)

Ingredients:
- ½ oz Sugar
- ¾ tsp Baking Soda
- oz Salt
- oz Yeast
- lb Warm Water
- lb Bread Flour
- oz Cold Water
- 16 oz Milk

Method of Preparation: Mix the warm water, sugar and yeast. Add the dry ingredients and milk. Mix well. Allow the mixture to ferment for 20 minutes. Portion on to a griddle in crumpet rings. Turn when the bottom is brown. Allow the crumpets to brown on the griddle and serve immediately.

---

779 — Date Nut Bread (Yield: 9 lb)

Ingredients:
- ¾ oz Baking Soda
- ½ oz Salt
- 1 ¼ lb Brown Sugar
- lb Shortening
- oz Baking Powder
- qt Water
- lb Dates
- ea Eggs
- oz Nuts
- 2 ½ lb Pastry Flour

Method of Preparation: Cream the dates, sugar and fat until light. Slowly add the eggs and mix in. Add the dry ingredients. Mix and add the water and nuts last. Portion 1 lb. Bake at 350°

Quick Breads

	Item		1	1	1	2	3	4	8		Y	Method of Preparation
780	English Muffins	1 oz Yeast	1 oz Shortening	oz Salt	oz Sugar	oz Dry Milk	lb Water	lb Bread Flour			7 lb	Follow the same method as the crumpet dough. Portion into ring pans, proof. Bake at 375°
781	Irish Soda Bread	2 ½ lb Pastry Flour	4 tsp Baking Soda	tbsp Salt	oz Caraway	oz Baking Powder	oz Sugar	oz Butter	oz Currants	36 oz Buttermilk	5 lb	Follow the same method as the biscuit dough. Portion into 12 oz units. Egg wash. Bake at 340°
782	Pumpkin Muffins	2½ cup Pumpkin Puree	4 tsp Baking Powder	tsp Nutmeg		cup Sugar	tsp Cinnamon	ea Eggs	oz Butter	½ tsp Vanilla	3 lb	Cream the sugar and fat until light. Slowly add the eggs and mix in. Add the other line items and mix.
		½ tsp Salt	4 cup Flour	cup Pecans	pint Milk				oz Currant			Add the salt, flour and milk and mix to incorporate. Add the nuts & currants last. Bake at 350°
783	Scones	10 oz Pastry Flour		lb Bread Flour	tsp Salt	Tbsp Baking Powder		oz Sugar			3.5 lb	Sift the ingredients on the first line. Mix the cream, honey, and sour cream. Add currant and zest. Mix the flour in by hand until smooth. Portion. Bake 400°
					ea Orange Zested		cups Heavy Cream	oz Sour Cream	oz Currants	4 oz Honey		
784	Sour Cream Coffee Cake	2 lb Butter	2 lb Sugar	tbsp Salt	tbsp Baking Soda	pint Eggs	1 lb Cake Flour	oz Walnut	oz Light Brown Sugar		15 lb	Cream the butter and sugar. Add in the eggs and dry items. Mix
		3 ½ tsp Vanilla	3 tbsp Baking Powder			pint Sour Cream	oz Pecans					Add the sour cream last and mix until smooth. Portion into 6 10" ring pans or 3 ½ sheet pans
						cups Shredded Coconut						Combine the topping items and sprinkle over the batter. Bake at 350°. Cool and slice.
785	Sweet Potato Biscuits	14 oz Cooked Sweet Potato	pinch Nutmeg	cup All Purpose Flour	cup Shortening	cup Self Rising Flour	oz Brown Sugar		oz Milk	2 tbsp Baking Powder	2 lb	Prepare the dough the same as biscuit dough. Add the potatoes with the flour, milk and mix. Floured surface, knead, cut, brush with egg wash, sugar on top- 350°
786	Zucchini Bread	3½ lb Zucchini	3½ lb Sugar	tsp Nutmeg		tbsp Salt			ea Eggs		12 lb	Mix the eggs, sugar and shredded zucchini. Add other line items.
		½ oz Baking Soda	2 tsp Ground Clove			tsp Cinnamon				12 oz Chopped Pecan		Add all of the dry ingredients and mix with a paddle for 3 minutes on 2nd speed.
		2 ¼ lb Bread Flour	6 oz Pastry Flour							18 oz Oil		Add the oil and mix for 2 minutes on 2nd speed. Add the nuts last. Portion. Bake at 350°

Breakfast Doughs and Batters

No.	Item		1	1	2	3	4	8		Yield	Method of Preparation
787	Danish Dough	10 oz Shortening / oz Salt	tbsp Mace	1b Sugar	1b Cold Milk	1b Butter	oz Fresh Yeast / 1b Bread Flour	oz Cake Flour		10 lb	Dissolve the yeast and sugar in the milk. Add the mace / Add the dry ingredients to form the dough. Add the fats and mix for 3 min on 2nd speed. Chill 2 hours before rolling and portion. Egg wash, proof, and bake at 350°.
788	Sweet Dough		qt Milk / pint Eggs	1b Sugar / pint Yolks	1b Bread Flour / 1b Butter	tbsp Salt	oz Honey / 1b High Gluten Flour	oz Fresh Yeast		13 lb	Combine the yeast, sugar, honey and milk. Add the bread flour. / Add the salt, high gluten flour and eggs and knead for 5 – 7 minutes. Add the butter in last. Ferment. Portion. Proof. Wash. Bake 350°
789	Cinnamon Smear	5 lb Sugar / 5 lb Brown Sugar	oz Salt	1b Honey	1b Butter	oz Apple Juice	tbsp Cinnamon	oz Orange Juice	2.5lb Shortening	15 lb	Cream the sugars and fat. Add the remaining ingredients.
790	Cheese Filling	5 oz Sugar / tsp Vanilla	1b Bakers Cheese	ea Lemon Zest	oz Milk	oz Eggs	oz Butter		2 oz Cake flour	2 lb	Cream the sugar and butter. Add the eggs and cheese. Blend in the rest in until consistent.
791	Almond Filling	8 oz Sugar		ea Egg	oz Pastry Flour		oz Butter	oz Almond Paste		1 lb	Cream the almond paste and sugar first. Then add the butter and cream. Add the eggs and flour. Mix
792	Streusel	8 oz Sugar	1b Pastry Flour	tbsp Cinnamon	1b Butter			oz Butter		2 lb	Rub the butter into the other ingredients.
793	Doughnuts Yeast	2.5 lb Bread Flour / 1.5lb Shortening	oz Salt		1b Water 90° / oz Baking Powder	oz Fresh Yeast		oz Milk Powder / oz Sugar	8 oz Eggs	9 lb	Combine the yeast, water and milk powder. / Add the remaining ingredients and knead until smooth. Ferment. Portion. Proof. Fry at 340°.
794	Doughnuts Cake	3lb 6 oz Sugar / 7 lb Cake Flour	oz Mace / 4.5 Pint Water	1.25lb Yolks	1b Bread Flour	oz Salt		oz Shortening	8 oz Dry Milk / 4.5 oz Baking Powder	18 lb	Cream all of the items on this line together until smooth. / Add the dry ingredients and the water. Mix on low speed until blended. Portion and fry at 345°
795	Rice Waffle Batter	1 oz Sugar	½ tsp Salt	tsp Vanilla	oz Rice Flour	ea Eggs	oz Melted Butter	oz Pastry Flour	14 oz Milk	1 qt	Separate the eggs. Combine the yolks, milk and sugar. Mix in the dry ingredients. Whip the egg whites and fold in. Fold in the butter last. Preheat the waffle iron. Portion on to a greased waffle iron and set the timer.

118

Doughnuts

#	Name			1	2	3	4	8		Yield	Method of Preparation
796	**Beignets** *top with sifted 10x sugar*	2 each Eggs	½ cup Sugar	tsp Salt / pint Warm Water	tbsp Active Yeast		tbsp Butter	oz Evaporated Milk	2lbs 6 oz All Purpose Flour	3 doz	Cream salt, sugar and butter, blend in eggs and milk. Dissolve yeast in water, add in with flour. Mix until firm. Refrigerate overnight. Roll out ½ inch thick on floured surface, cut 4 inch squares, Fry 355° 1 minute each side.
797	**Berliner**	10 oz Water / 3.75 oz Sugar	½ oz Yeast / 6 oz Egg Yolk	lb Pastry Flour / lb Pastry Flour / pinch Nutmeg	tsp Salt	oz Milk	oz Butter		3½ oz Fresh Yeast	3.75 lbs	Dissolve the yeast and water. Whisk in the flour into the mixture to form a sponge. Add the rest and knead for 7 minutes on second speed. Portion into 1.5 oz balls and proof on a cloth. Carefully transfer to a preheated 325° fryer and fry on both sides until golden brown. Remove and cool for 10 minutes. Fill with raspberry jam, dust with sugar.
798	**Cake**	3 ½ oz Sugar / 6 ¾ lb Cake Flour	1 ¼ lb Yolks / 4 ½ pint Whole Milk	tbsp Mace / oz Vanilla	tsp Nutmeg / lb Bread Flour	oz Salt		oz Shortening	4 ½ oz Baking Powder	18 lb	Cream all of the items on this line together until smooth. Add the dry ingredients and the water. Mix on low speed until blended. Portion and fry at 345°
799	**Chocolate**	¼ oz Salt	½ oz Vanilla / 1 oz Baking Powder	tbsp Baking Soda / lb Cake Flour / lb Bread Flour	oz Milk Powder / lb Water	oz Cocoa	oz Shortening	oz Sugar	6 each Eggs	4.5 lb	Cream shortening, sugar, salt, vanilla, milk powder. Add eggs in 2 stages. Combine water and soda, add in. Sift dry items, add to liquid then mix until smooth. Rest 15 minutes. Scoop ½ oz balls and fry 45seconds each side in 375° fat.
800	**Cider**	½ cup Butter	½ cup Apple Butter / ½ tsp Nutmeg	cup Buttermilk / tsp Cinnamon / tsp Salt	cups Sugar / tsp Baking Soda		ea Eggs		7 cups All Purpose Flour	3 doz	Cream together sugar and butter; blend in eggs, buttermilk, and apple butter. Sift all dry together, add to batter and mix until smooth. Roll out ½ inch thick on floured surface. Dry 375° for 2 minutes per side.
801	**French Cruller**	12 each Eggs	2 tsp Salt	cup Sugar	pints Water	tsp Vanilla Extract			1 quart Bread Flour	5 lb	Bring water, shortening, sugar, and salt to a boil. Remove from heat and add the flour all at once – Stir 2 minutes over heat. Blend in mixer; add the eggs in one at a time. Add extract last. Pipe on to oiled paper with star tip. Fry 375° 2 minutes per side, glaze.
802	**Glaze-Buttermilk**	½ cup Buttermilk		tsp Vanilla Extract	cups Powdered Sugar					12 oz	Heat buttermilk and vanilla to 120°. Add all of the sugar and whisk until smooth. Keep warm to glaze.
803	**Glaze-Chocolate**			tsp Vanilla Extract	oz Milk	tsp Honey	oz Salted Butter	oz Sifted Powdered Sugar	4 ¼ oz Chocolate Chips	14 oz	Heat butter, milk, honey, and vanilla until 125°. Add in the chocolate and stir to melt. Add all of the sugar at one time. Whisk until smooth. Apply to the outside of room temperature dough nuts by dipping one side.

119

Doughnuts

#	Name / Notes			1	2	3	4		8	Yield	Method of Preparation
804	Glaze - Honey		½ tsp Salt	tsp Vanilla Extract	tbsp Water	oz Honey	oz Powdered Sugar			8 oz	Combine until smooth, Heat in the microwave for 30 seconds and stir. Keep warm to glaze.
805	Glaze-Krispy		½ tsp Salt	½ tsp Vanilla Extract		cups Powdered Sugar	oz Cola			16 oz	Heat Cola to a boil and add in vanilla, salt and half the sugar. Bring back to a boil and add in the rest of the sugar Stir well and keep warm to glaze
806	Pączki — Based upon the Selega Family Recipe	4 ¼ cups Flour	½ tsp Nutmeg	stick Butter (4oz); oz Plum Brandy	tsp Vanilla Extract	tsp Dry Yeast	oz Sugar	4 ea Eggs	oz Warm Buttermilk	2 dozen	Combine yeast, sugar, and milk. Melt butter. In mixing bowl place flour and nutmeg, pour everything on top with dough hook. Knead 6 minutes. Rise 1 hour, roll on floured table, portion into 3 inch circles and fry 330°. Fill with plum jelly. Toss in sugar.
807	Southern Glazed	1/3 cup Sugar	½ tsp Salt	pinch Nutmeg; Tbsp Instant Yeast	oz Butter	cups Bread Flour	oz Flour For Dusting	2 each Eggs	oz Milk	2 dozen	Heat Milk, salt, sugar, nutmeg, and butter. To 160°. Cool to 105°. Whisk in yeast, then eggs and bread flour. Knead for 5 minutes. Add additional flour at the end to pull the dough away from the bowl. Allow to rise covered for 1 ½ hours. Roll out to ¼ inch thick, cut and place on floured cloth. Rise 35 minutes. Drop into 360° oil for 2 minutes per side, Drain then glaze with recipe # 805.
808	Sour Cream	11 oz Sugar; 2 lb Bread Flour	½ oz Salt; 1 lb Cake Flour	pint Sour Cream; tbsp Vanilla Extract	tsp Lemon Extract	oz Powdered Milk	oz Shortening	3 cups Water; 2 ½ oz Baking Powder	oz Eggs	7 lb	Cream together sugar, salt, powdered milk, shortening. Add eggs in 2 stages. Blend in sour cream and liquids
809	World's Fair	2 oz Sugar	½ oz Baking Powder	tsp Nutmeg; tbsp Vanilla Extract	oz Milk Powder		oz Eggs	6 oz Shortening	oz Water		Blend shortening, vanilla, sugar, salt, milk powder, spice. Add eggs in 2 parts, stir and blend in water
809	World's Fair	12 oz Cake Flour		oz Dry Active Yeast				1 lb 4 oz Bread Flour	oz water (warm)	4 doz	Mix yeast and warm water, stir into batter. Sift rest and mix until smooth. Proof 30 minute. Roll out ¼ inch on floured surface, portion. Fry 380° for 1 min each side. Glaze finish.
810	Yeast	2 ¼ lb Bread Flour	1 ¼ lb Cake Flour		lb Water 90°	oz Fresh Yeast		8 oz Eggs	oz Milk Powder	9 lb	Combine the yeast, water and milk powder.
810	Yeast	1 ½ lb Butter	¾ oz Salt	tsp Nutmeg	oz Baking Powder				oz Sugar		Add the remaining ingredients and knead until smooth. Ferment. Portion. Proof. Fry at 340°.

Bread Doughs

No.	Name	Ing. A	Ing. B	1	2	3	4	8	Yield	Method of Preparation
811	Brioche Dough	11 oz Fresh Yeast	6 lb Bread Flour; 30 ea Eggs	cup Milk		oz Salt	1 lb Butter	1½ lb Sugar	14 lb	Warm the milk and dissolve the yeast. Add ½ lb of sugar and allow a sponge to form. Add the flour, eggs, salt and the rest of the sugar. Mix the dough for 6 minutes on second speed with a paddle. Slowly add the butter on first speed. Once incorporated refrigerate it overnight before portioning, proofing and baking. Eggwash. Bake at 340°
812	Challah	1½ oz Salt	5 lb High Gluten Flour	lb Egg Yolks / qt Water	oz. Honey	oz Sugar	oz Fresh Yeast	oz Oil	9 lb	Place the dry ingredient the mixing bowl. Combine the yeast with ¼ of the water warm. Place the remaining ingredients with the yeast mixture on top of the dry ingredients. Knead the dough on 2nd speed for 8 minutes. Ferment, portion, braid. Proof egg wash. Bake 360°
813	Croissant Dough	5 oz Fresh Yeast; 1½ oz Salt	1½ qt Cold Milk; 4lb 10oz Bread Flour			oz Bread Flour	oz Butter	4½ oz Sugar; 10 oz Pastry Flour; 3 ¾ lb Butter	12 lb	Combine the yeast milk and sugar. Place the dry ingredients in the mixing bowl. Pour the yeast mixture and butter on top. Knead for 6 minutes on second speed. Roll on to a sheet pan and chill. Combine these two ingredients and cream. Roll the dough out to the size of a sheet pan. Portion the butter over ½ the dough and seal. Chill the dough for 30 minutes. Roll out to a sheet pan size. Fold the dough with a 3 fold. Repeat 2 times. Refrigerate overnight. Portion.
814	Dill Rolls	6 oz Eggs; 5 oz Fresh Yeast	¼ oz Baking Soda; 12 oz Water	oz Salt / tbsp Horseradish; oz Fresh Dill chop	oz Diced Onion; lb High Gluten Flour	lb Cottage Cheese; lb Bread Flour	oz Sugar; oz Soft Butter	1 lb Bread Flour	10 lb	Place the items in this line in a mixing bowl and combine with a paddle. Dissolve the yeast in water add to the bowl with the other ingredient. Knead for 7 minutes on second speed. Ferment and portion. Proof and Eggwash. Bake at 375°. Butter and salt.
815	French Bread	½ oz Malt	2 oz Salt		oz Shortening	oz Fresh Yeast	pint Water	2 oz Sugar	12 lb	Dissolve the yeast, sugar and water. Place all ingredients in mixer. Knead for 7 minutes on second speed. Ferment and portion. Bake 450°.
816	Hard Rolls	3 pint Water	2 oz Salt		oz Shortening; lb High Gluten Flour	oz Fresh Yeast	lb Bread Flour; oz Egg White	2 oz Sugar	10 lb	Dissolve the yeast, sugar and water. Place all ingredients in mixer. Knead for 7 minutes on second speed. Ferment and portion. Steam 1 min. Bake 400°
817	Olive Focaccia	2 oz Chopped Garlic		oz Fresh Yeast / oz Salt	lb Olives	oz Olive Oil	pint Water	1 lb Bread Flour	14 lb	Dissolve the yeast, sugar and water. Place all ingredients in mixer except for the olives. Knead for 5 minutes. Add olives and knead for 2 more minutes. Ferment. Roll on a sheet pan. Proof, drizzle with oil. Bake at 340°

121

Bread Doughs

#	Name			1	1	2	3	4	8	Yield	Method
818	Pretzel	½ oz Fresh Yeast	18 oz Water			tbsp Sugar			oz Bread Flour	4 lb	Combine all ingredients and allow them to form a sponge. Add these items to the sponge and knead for 6 minutes. Combine these ingredients. Portion the pretzels into 2 oz balls. Rest. Roll and shape. Dip into the baking soda water. Garnish with salt if desired.
					lb Bread Flour	2 tsp Salt			oz Pastry Flour		
				oz Baking Soda					oz Warm Water		
819	Pita	½ oz Salt	1 oz Sugar	oz Fresh Yeast	1 lb Bread Flour	cup Water	oz Yogurt	tsp Olive Oil	oz Whole Wheat	3 lb	Dissolve the yeast, sugar and water. Place all ingredients in mixer. Knead for 7 minutes 2nd speed. Ferment Portion into 2½ oz balls. Proof and bake at 350°
820	Pizza Dough	1 oz Olive Oil	5 lb High Gluten Flour	oz Salt	oz Fresh Yeast	oz Sugar	lb Bread Flour	pint Water		12 lb	Dissolve the yeast, sugar and water. Place all ingredients in mixer. Knead for 8 minutes. Portion 12 – 16 oz balls. Retard 12 hours. Roll out, top, bake at 475° until dark brown
821	Pumpernickel	7.25 lb High Gluten Flour	5.75 pint Water / 5 oz Salt	2 oz Caramel Color		oz Caraway	lb Rye Meal	oz Fresh Yeast	lb Sour Culture- recipe #826	24 lb	Dissolve the yeast, sugar and water. Place all ingredients in mixer. Knead for 8 minutes on second speed. Ferment. Portion. Proof. Steam 1 minute. Bake at 400°
822	Raisin Bread	14½ oz Sugar	5½ lb Raisin	pint Rum Syrup		qt Milk			oz Fresh Yeast	20 lb	Soak raisins in warm rum flavored simple syrup. Make a sponge with yeast, milk and sugar. Place all of these items in a bowl and add the sponge on top. Knead on 2nd speed for 6 minutes. Add the raisins and knead on 1st speed for 2 minutes. Ferment. Portion. Proof. Bake at 350°.
		6½ lb Bread Flour	2½ oz Salt / ½ oz Cinnamon	1¼ lb Shortening					oz Eggs		
823	Rye - Cheddar	6 lb Bread Flour	8 oz Fresh Yeast	lb Sugar	lb Shortening	oz Salt		pint Water	oz Milk Powder	14 lb	Dissolve the yeast, sugar and water. Place all ingredients on this line in mixer. Knead. Add these items to the dough and knead on 1st speed two minutes. Ferment. Portion. Proof.
			12 oz Dark Rye		oz Onions	oz Caraway			oz Sharp Cheddar Cheese		
824	Rye - Jewish	5 lb High Gluten Flour	2 oz Molasses	oz Caraway		oz Sugar	oz Fresh Yeast	cup water	oz Rye Flour	10 lb	Dissolve the sugars into the water with yeast. Add the rest of the items on this line in mixer. Knead for 6 minutes. Ferment. Portion. Proof. Spray with water, garnish with additional seeds. Stipple. Steam 1 minute. Bake at 425°.
		5 lb High Gluten Flour	2 oz Shortening		lb Rye Flour	oz Salt					

Bread Doughs

Item			1	2	3	4	8	Yield	Method
825 Rye - Onion	1½ lb Rye Flour		qt Water	oz Malt syrup	oz Onions	oz Fresh Yeast		6 lb	Dissolve the yeast and cool water. Add the malt, flour and onions. Mix well. Ferment for 2 hour at room temp.
	2 lb High Gluten	2 oz Shortening		oz Salt	oz Caraway	oz Eggs			Add the items on this line to the sponge and knead on 2nd speed for 8 minutes. Ferment. Portion. Proof. Steam 1 minute. Bake at 400°.
826 Rye - Sour Culture	2½ pint Water		oz Fresh Yeast	ea Onion	lb Bread Flour	lb Rye Flour		7 lb	Dissolve the yeast and cool water. Add the flour and onions. Mix well. Allow the mixture to ferment 24 hours.
827 Soft Rolls	6 oz Fresh Yeast			oz Salt		oz Shortening	oz Eggs	8 lb	Dissolve the yeast, sugar and water. Place ingredients in mixer.
	10 oz Sugar	7 oz Butter		lb High Gluten Flour					Knead the dough for 7 minutes on 2nd speed. Ferment. Portion. Eggwash and garnish. Proof. Bake at 370°.
828 Sour Dough	3 cup Water			lb High Gluten Flour	oz Fresh Yeast			13 lb	Dissolve the yeast and water. Mix in the flour. Cover and ferment the mixture for 24 hours.
	3 cup Water			lb High Gluten Flour					Mix in the water and flour on this line with the fermented sour and refrigerate overnight.
	2½ oz Salt	4½ lb High Gluten Flour	oz Shortening / oz Butter	pint Water	oz Sugar / oz Malt	oz Fresh Yeast			Add the items on this line to the sour mixture and knead for 8 minutes on 2nd speed. Ferment. Portion. Proof. Bake at 350° until golden brown.
829 Stollen	1½ lb Sugar	3 oz Rum	qt Milk / pint Eggs	lb Bread Flour		lb High Gluten Flour	oz Fresh Yeast	15 lb	Combine the rum, 1 cup of the sugar, and the raisins. Warm the mixture. Dissolve the yeast, sugar and water. Place all dry ingredients in mixer.
	1½ oz Salt	1½ lb Raisin or Dried Fruits- diced	pint Yolks / lb Candied Citrus	lb Soft Butter					Pour the liquid ingredients on top and blend with a paddle on 2nd speed. Once the dough is elastic add in the fruits and combine. Add the butter last on first speed. Portion, fill with almond filling recipe #543. Pan and proof. Bake at 350°. Brush the loaves with simple syrup and dust with additional sugar.
830 Whole Wheat Bread	3 oz Fresh Yeast	4 oz Sugar		lb High Gluten Flour	lb Wheat Flour	pint Water		12 lb	Combine the dry milk with sugar, yeast and water. Add the remaining ingredients.
		4 oz Dry Milk		oz Salt	oz Shortening				Knead the dough on 2nd speed for 7 minutes. Ferment. Portion. Eggwash and garnish. Proof. Bake at 350°

European Style Bread

No.	Item	Ingredients	Yield	Method of Preparation
831	**Baguette**	2.268 kg Poolish recipe # 838; 2.325 kg Bread Flour; 70.5 gr. Salt; 1.247 kg. Water / 10 gr. Instant Yeast; 5 gr. Malt	6 kg	Mix flour, water and poolish for 2 minutes and allow to rest for 20-25 minutes. Add salt and yeast and mix for 1 minute on first speed and 1 ½ minute on second speed. Check for gluten development. Rest for 1 ½ hour with 1 stretch and fold after 45 minutes. Divide, shape, proof for 1 hour. Bake 480° for 22 minutes.
832	**Bavarian Pretzel**	20 oz Bread Flour; 10 oz Milk-Room Temp; 1.5 oz Butter / 30 gr. Baking Soda; ¾ oz Salt; ¼ oz Instant Yeast; 17 ¼ oz Biga recipe # 833; 1 liter Water	4 ¾ lb	Prepare dough by mixing flour, milk, butter, salt, yeast and Biga. Mix on 2$_{nd}$ speed for 6-8 minutes. Cover and rest 30 min. Divide into 4 oz pieces, roll into cylinders and rest 15 minutes. Shape into pretzels, flour pan cover and rest 45 min. Chill for 10 minutes. Bring water + baking soda to a boil. Blanch each pretzel for 45 seconds. Drain. Place on sheet pan. Sprinkle coarse salt on top. Bake 425° for 15 – 20 min.
833	**Biga**	12 oz Whole Wheat Flour; 9 oz water; 3 gram Instant Yeast	21 oz	Mix yeast and water. Mix in flour. Dough Temp 74° 12 hour ferment
834	**Ciabatta**	1.9 kg. Poolish recipe #838; 1.55 kg. Bread Flour; 50 gr. Salt; 951 gr. Water / 4 gr. Instant Yeast; 50 gr. Olive Oil	4.5 kg	Mix all ingredients. Then knead for 3 minutes on first speed and 2 minutes second speed. Should be sticky. Rest for 2 ½ hours with 2 – 3 folds. Divide. Shape, Proof. Bake at 450° for 25- 30 minutes.
835	**Country Bread (Fruit and Nut)**	2 ½ lb Bread Flour; 4 oz Rye Flour; 1 ½ lb Levain recipe #836; 1 lb 5 oz Biga recipe #833; 3 ½ oz Honey; 1 ½ oz Salt; ½ oz Yeast; 1lb 12 oz Water; 1lb 1 oz Pecan; 1lb 12 oz Raisin; 4 oz Cranberry	11 lb	Mix all except fruit and nut. Then mix in fruit and nut. Rest 1 hour 45 minutes. On stretch after 50 minutes. Scale 24 oz. Final Proof 1 hour 10 min. Bake 475° for 23-25 minutes
836	**Levain**	12 oz Rye Flour; 12 oz water; 1 ½ oz Culture	25.5 oz	Mix well. Dough Temp 74° 12 hour ferment
837	**Multigrain Bread**	10.5 oz Bread Flour; ⅔ oz Salt; 14 oz Whole Wheat Flour; ⅛ oz Instant Yeast; 13.5 oz Levain recipe #836; 8 oz Mixed Seeds; 3 oz Honey; 18 oz Water	3 loaves	Toast seed then soak in 4 oz of water for 2 hours. Mix water and yeast together, add rest and mix 3 minutes on low and 4 minutes on medium speed. Rest 2 hours. Stretch and fold, retard overnight. Temper 1 hour. Divide in three loaves. Round, rest 30, shape/mold rest 90 minutes. Bake 450°.
838	**Poolish**	950 gr. Bread Flour; 950 gr. Water; 1 gr. Instant Yeast	1.9 kg	Mix all ingredients. Dough Temp 70° for 12 – 15 hours.
839	**Pre-ferment Levain**	7.5 oz Bread Flour; 5 oz Water; 1 oz Sourdough Culture	13.5 oz	Mix the dough into a smooth mixture. Rest the preferment overnight (covered) at room temperature.
840	**Pumpernickel Black Bread**	2 lb 3 oz Pumpernickel Flour; 10 ½ oz Sunflower Seed; 5 lb 4 oz Soaker recipe #842; 8 oz Whole Wheat Flour; 6 oz Honey; 7.5 lb Water	20 lb	Mix all ingredients on low speed for 15 minutes. Bulk fermentation for 30 minutes. Divide into 2 lb loaves roll in pumpernickel flour and place in Pullman loaf pan. Proof 1 hour. Bake at 450° for 15 minutes and 400° for 55 minutes. Cool 24 hours before slicing
841	**Rye Preferment**	2.75 lb Water 65°; 3 lb Pumpernickel Flour; 4oz Levain seed	6 lb	12 hours before the final mix, combine all ingredients together until smooth consistency. Cover and rest for 12-14 hours at 73°-76°F
842	**Soaker**	2 ½ lb Cracked Wheat; 2 ½ lb Water 185°; 3 oz Salt	5 lb 3 oz	Soak the cracked wheat and salt with hot water at least 12 hour prior to the final mix.

Formulas courtesy of Chef Harry Peemoeller GMB

Pastry Mise en Place Formulas

#	Item	1/2	1	2	3	4	8	Yield	Method of Preparation
843	Anglaise	6 ea Egg Yolk	pint Cream	cup Heavy Cream		oz Sugar		5 cup	Temper the hot milk into everything else. Whisk over a double boiler until it is 160°.
844	Chocolate Dough	1 tsp Vanilla	lb Bread Flour	lb Butter	tbsp Cocoa Powder	oz Egg	oz Sugar	2.5 lb	Cream butter, vanilla, and sugar. Add in eggs, mix well. Mix in rest to form ball. Chill 1 hr.
845	Cinnamon Sugar	1 ¼ oz Cinnamon	lb Sugar					1 lb	Combine and mix well.
846	Crème Chantilly	tsp Vanilla	pint Heavy Cream	tbsp Sugar				3 cup	Make sure cream is very cold. Freeze bow and whip. Mix and whip until desired peak.
847	Crème Parisian	5 oz 54-60% Cocoa, Dark Chocolate	pint Heavy Cream		oz Whole Milk	tbsp Sugar		3.5 cup	Use a 6 prong ice shaver to chop chocolate very fine. Bring the rest to a simmer and pour over chocolate in a bowl. Mix well. Chill over night. Whip until desired texture.
848	Crêpe	2.5 oz Melted Butter	cup Flour	cup Milk	tbsp Sugar	ea Eggs		20 ea	Whisk the flour into the milk, sugar, and eggs, strain, whisk in butter. Ladle 2 oz of butter in a 10 inch non-stick pan until golden brown
849	Custard	lb Sugar	qt Milk or Light Cream				ea Eggs	1.25 qt	Combine, warm to 115°, strain. Portion, water bath bake 275° until firm
850	Egg Wash	½ tsp Salt				tbsp Milk	ea Egg Yolk	2 oz	Mix well and strain.
851	Feuilletine	14 oz Egg White	lb Powdered Sugar	cup Melted Butter			oz Pastry Flour	2.75 lb	Combine the sugar and egg white. Whip until soft peak. Fold in pastry flour. Add melted butter and fold in. Spread 1 tbsp per cookie on a silicon mat and bake at 350° until golden brown. Roll into cigarettes
852	Floating Island	¼ tsp Tartaric Acid	cup Egg Whites	lb Sugar	tsp Gelatin			1.5 lb	Heat the ingredients to 140°. Prepare a Swiss meringue to soft peaks. Shape into quenelles and poach in simple syrup. Serve chilled with sauce Anglaise.
853	Florentine	½ cup Sugar	cup Chopped Hazelnuts	tbsp Honey	tbsp Heavy Cream	oz Salted Butter	cup Sliced Almonds	1 lb	Bring cream, butter, sugar, and honey to a boil. Add in rest and simmer for 1 minute. Portion 1 oz each and bake in a 375° oven on silpat.
854	Frangipane	5 ea Eggs	lb Almond Paste	oz Bread Flour	oz Sugar	cup Butter diced		2.25 lb	Cream almond paste and sugar, add butter and cream again. Add eggs slowly then add flour last. Mix until smooth
855	Hippen Paste	lb 10x Sugar	lb Flour			tsp Almond Extract	ea Eggs	3 lb	Blend all ingredients in food processor until smooth. Spread on a silicon mat and bake at 350° until golden brown. Carefully remove and shape
856	Lemon Curd	6 ea Egg Yolk	cup Sugar	tbsp Lemon Zest	oz Lemon Juice	oz Butter- sliced thin		14 oz	Combine sugar and yolks in double boiler bowl, mix well. Add zest and juice. Whisk until it reaches 145°. When ribbons form mix in butter and cool
857	Meringue- Basic	½ tsp Lemon Juice	cup Sugar	cup Egg Whites				2.5 quart	Whip egg whites and lemon juice for 2 minutes in copper bowl. Slowly add sugar while whipping an additional 3 minutes

Pastry Mise en Place Formulas

#	Item		1/2	1	2	3	4	8	Yield	Method of Preparation
858	Meringue- Italian	¾ cup Corn Syrup		cup Egg Whites		cup Sugar		oz Water	2.5 quart	Combine water, syrup, and sugar in copper pot, bring to 230°. Begin whipping eggs. Continue heating sugar to 238°. Slowly pour syrup into whipping egg whites. When meringue reaches max volume turn off.
859	Meringue- Swiss			cup Egg Whites	cup Sugar				2 quart	Combine eggs and sugar. Whisk and heat to 142° over a double boiler. Whip on high speed until desired texture is achieved.
860	Pastry Cream- Prepare and cool quickly. Discard after 3 days if not used.	1 quart Milk	cup Sugar	tsp Vanilla	ea Eggs	oz Butter	oz Cornstarch	ea Egg Yolks	1.25 qt	Mix half of the sugar with the cornstarch and milk. Heat to 180°. Mix other half of sugar with eggs. Temper hot into cold and whisk over double boiler until 165°. Add in the butter and vanilla.
861	Pâte Brisée	½ tsp Kosher Salt		tbsp Sugar		cup Pastry Flour	oz Ice Water	oz Unsalted Butter- cold	1.75 lbs	Slice butter into flour and rub until coarse, add sugar, salt. Add in ice water, mix until it forms a ball. Add water if needed. Chill 1 hour before using.
862	Pâte Choux- use for éclairs, cream puffs, profiteroles.	pint Eggs		lb Flour	pint Water or Milk			oz Butter	3.5 lbs	Boil liquid and butter, add all flour and mix well, cook until it forms a ball, 6 – 7 minutes cool in mixer with paddle to 90°, add in eggs, one at a time. Mix well. Bake 375°
863	Pâte Sablee	¾ cup Powdered Sugar	tsp Salt	tbsp Vanilla Extract	tbsp Lemon Zest- fine	cup All Purpose Flour		oz Butter	1 lb	Cream butter and sugar, add in salt, extract and zest. Mix well. Add flour and mix slowly until consistent. Chill 1 hour.
864	Pâte Sucree	¼ tsp Sea Salt	cup Sugar	tbsp Apple Juice	ea Egg Yolks	cup All Purpose Flour		oz Unsalted Butter	2 lbs	Slice butter into flour and rub until coarse, add sugar, salt. Combine egg and juice and knead in. Wrap and Chill 2 hours before using.
865	Savory Custard	¼ tsp Nutmeg	tsp Salt	cup ½ +½	cups Heavy Cream		ea Eggs		40 oz	Mix all ingredients together. Season to taste to white pepper. Warm to 90°. Strain
866	Sabayon- a warm dessert sauce	cup Wine		cup Egg Yolks			oz Sugar		1 qt	Combine the items and whip over double boiler until light and foamy until about 120°.
867	Short Dough	1 tsp Extract	lb Bread Flour	lb Butter		oz Egg		oz Sugar	2.5 lb	Cream butter, vanilla, and sugar. Add in eggs, mix well. Mix in flour to form ball. Chill 1 hr.
868	Simple Syrup	qt Water		lb Sugar	Oranges	Lemons			1 qt	Slice the citrus, add rest. Then simmer for 15 minutes. Cool.
869	Tuiles	14 oz Eggs	lb Ground Almonds	lb Ground Hazelnuts	lb Sugar			oz Pastry Flour	5.5 lb	Combine all ingredients with a spoon and allow resting for 30 minutes. Portion with a tbsp and bake at 350° until light brown. Shape and cool.
870	Vanilla Extract	Bottle Vodka 750ML						Vanilla Beans	750 ml	Split beans in half. Soak beans in Vodka for at least 1 month.
871	Water Icing			lb 10x Sugar	tbsp Corn Syrup	oz Water			19 oz	Heat water, add syrup, mix into sifted sugar

Puddings

#	Item	1	2	3	4	8	Yield	Method of Preparation
872	Bread Pudding	1 ½ tsp Cinnamon lb Stale Bread	6 oz Sugar oz Butter	qt Milk oz Raisins	tsp Vanilla grates Nutmeg	ea Yolk ea Eggs	Serves 12	Preheat to 325°. Combine the items on this line to make custard. Dice the bread. Melt the butter and drizzle over the bread. Toast in the oven. Place the bread in a deep ½ pan and pour the custard over. Allow the bread to soak up liquid Cover with foil and bake in a water bath for 1 hour. Serve warm.
873	Chocolate Pudding	¾ cup Sugar 1/3 cup Dutch Cocoa	Pinch Salt cup Cream	tsp Vanilla cup Milk	tbsp Cornstarch ea Egg Yolks	oz Semisweet Chocolate	Serves 8	Blend cornstarch, ½ of sugar, salt, and yolks. Warm remaining sugar, cocoa, cream and milk to 170°. Slowly whisk the wet into the dry. Place in a sauce pot and heat to a boil. Strain into chocolate, mix and add vanilla. Cool 4 hours, Top with whipped cream. Garnish chocolate
874	Christmas Plum Pudding	5 oz Guinness ½ tsp Allspice ¼ tsp Cinnamon 1 Orange	¼ tsp Nutmeg cup Raisins oz Candy Peel ea Apple 1 Lemon	oz Self Rising Flour ea Eggs oz Rum	oz Dried Cherries tbsp Almond-chopped oz Suet oz Bread Crumbs	oz Dark Brown Sugar oz Currants	Serves 10	Mix bread crumbs, flour, suet, spices and sugar. Add in dried fruits and nuts. Mix. Peel and finely chop apple grate citrus rind and add to dough. Whisk eggs with rum and beer. Tradition dictates that each child "Makes a wish" while stirring. Mix into dough until sticky. Wrap in cheesecloth lined pudding bowl. Tie and allow to set overnight. Steam for 8 hours. Prepare 4 weeks in advance. Steam 2 hours flambé with rum
875	Figgy Pudding	¼ tsp Ginger ½ tsp Cinnamon	cup Milk Tbsp Honey	oz Prunes oz Raisins	oz Brandy oz Dates oz Suet ea Apricot	oz Flour oz Figs	Serves 8	Pit all fruits and quarter them. Soak Raisins in brandy. Soak all other fruits in 2 cups hot water. Allow fruits to soak overnight. Sift flour in a bowl, rub in suet, and then add milk, Knead for a few minutes. Line a buttered 8 inch pudding mold with dough. Melt honey and spices and mix in all fruits. Cover fruits with dough, seal edges. Steam for 2 hours. Serve with Sauce Anglaise recipe # 994.
876	Indian Pudding	½ tsp Cinnamon ¼ tsp Ginger	qt Milk pinch Nutmeg ea Eggs	oz Butter	oz Sugar oz Molasses	oz Cornmeal	Serves 10	In a 2 quart pot bring the milk and butter to a boil add the cornmeal. Simmer for 2 minutes. Allow the mixture to cool to about 100°. Add the remaining ingredients and blend well. Spread the mixture evenly in a casserole. Bake at 325° for 2 hour in water bath. Serve with Vanilla Ice Cream.
877	Lemon Posset	3 cups Cream		ea Lemon Juiced		oz Sugar	3 cup	Boil heavy cream and sugar together for 3 minutes. Mix in lemon. Cool for 10 min. Portion into glasses, refrigerate 3 hrs
878	Rice Pudding	¼ tsp Cinnamon pint Milk	1 tsp Vanilla oz Sugar	oz Rice	tbsp Raisin		3 cup	Bring milk and rice to simmer. Reduce to very low heat. Simmer 20 minutes. Add rest, chill overnight
879	Spotted Dick	10 oz Self Rising Flour cup Currants	5 oz Suet tbsp Lemon Zest	oz Sugar	oz Milk		1 ea	Shred suet, combine with rest. Butter a 10"x8" sheet of cheesecloth. Prepare a Torchon, steam 2 hours. Slice.
880	Sticky Toffee Pudding	1 cup Water cup Dark Brown Sugar	1 cup Flour tsp Baking Powder	oz Butter	ea Eggs	oz chopped Dates	Serves 10	Boil dates and water for 5 minutes. Cool and puree. Add butter and sugar, puree. Sift flour and baking powder. Mix flour into batter by hand. Portion into ramekins. Bake in a 350° in a water bath for 12 minutes. Unmold Serve with Toffee sauce # 1007
881	Tapioca	½ cup Sugar pinch Salt	1 tsp Vanilla ea Egg Yolk	cups Milk	oz Tapioca		3 cup	Simmer tapioca in salted milk for 6 minutes. Mix sugar and yolks, temper into pudding. Simmer 2 minute. Add vanilla.
882	Vanilla Pudding	¼ cup Cornstarch cup Sugar cup Cream	¼ cup Sugar oz Butter	tsp Vanilla	ea Egg Yolks	oz Milk	Serves 8	Blend cornstarch, ½ of sugar, salt, and yolks. Warm remaining sugar, cream and milk to 170°. Slowly whisk the wet into the dry. Strain into bowl and add vanilla and butter. Cool 4 hours, Top with whipped cream. Garnish
883	Hasty Pudding	1 cup Cornmeal cup Brown Sugar	1 qt Light Cream cup Raisins	cup Cream tsp Salt	tsp Cinnamon tsp Ginger oz Butter ea Egg Yolk	oz Molasses	Serves 12	Bring the liquids to a boil, add in cornmeal and simmer for 10 minutes over medium heat. Add the rest of the ingredients and mix well. Pour into a buttered casserole and bake at 325° for 2 hours. Allow to set and serve with ice cream.

Basic Dessert Creams

No.	Name			1	1	2	3	4	8	Yield	Method of Preparation
884	Bavarian Cream			qt Vanilla Sauce	oz Gelatin	pints Whipping Cream			oz Cold Water	3 qt	Bloom the gelatin in water, dissolve in warm vanilla sauce. Cool the mixture to 90°. Whip the cream to a soft peak. Fold together. Portion into molds or between slices cake and refrigerate until set. 2 hrs.
885	Chocolate Pot au Crème	2 ½ cup Heavy Cream	¾ cup Sugar	oz Kirsch		ea Eggs	oz Shaved Bittersweet Chocolate	oz Yolk		24 oz	Warm the cream add the chocolate, sugar, and kirsch, melt. Cool to 100° and blend in eggs. Portion and bake in a water bath at 300° until set
886	Crème Brûlée	½ ea Vanilla Bean	10 oz Egg Yolks	qt Heavy Cream	cup Half And Half				oz Sugar	48 oz	Bring half of the sugar, all the creams and vanilla to a boil. Temper in eggs. Portion and bake in a water bath at 325°. When set cool. Top with rest of sugar and brown.
887	Crème Caramel	6 Eggs		qt Whole Milk	ea Vanilla Bean			ea Yolks	oz Sugar	1.5 qt	Bring the sugar, milk and vanilla to 180°. Temper in eggs. Portion into caramel lined cups and bake in a water bath at 325°. When set cool. Refrigerate 12 hrs. Unmold.
888	*Caramel*			tsp Lemon Juice			oz Water		oz Sugar	8 port	Combine all ingredients. Caramelize in a copper pot and portion 1 oz into 8 each 4 oz ramekins. Allow to cool.
889	Ice Cream	8 oz Egg Yolks	1 ea Vanilla Bean	pint Milk	pint Cream				oz Sugar	1 qt	Bring the sugar, milk, cream and vanilla to 180°. Temper in eggs. Whisk over a double boiler until it reaches 165°. Refrigerate overnight. Churn in ice cream maker to directions. Freeze to 12°
890	Meringue			lb Egg White		lb Sugar				5 cup	Combine both and heat to 110°. Whip on high speed to desired peak texture.
891	Mousse	9 ea Eggs	Flavoring As Desired	qt Heavy Cream					oz Sugar	6 cup	Separate eggs. Mix half sugar with yolks. Half with the whites. Warm both to 110° and whip separately. Add flavor to yolks. Whip cream. Fold yolks &cream. Fold in whites last. Portion in glasses, chill
892	Pastry Cream	6 ea Eggs		qt Milk	tsp Vanilla Extract		oz Cornstarch	oz Butter	oz Sugar	1 qt	Bring the sugar and ¾ of milk and vanilla to a simmer. Mix cornstarch with rest of milk. Thicken the hot mixture. Temper in eggs. Heat to 160°. Add in butter and cool in shallow pan.
893	Parfait	15 oz Yolks	10 oz Flavor	qt Heavy Cream-whipped	tsp Vanilla				oz Sugar	6 cup	Mix eggs and sugar. Whisk over a double boiler. Cool to 80°, add in flavor. Fold in cream. Portion and freeze in glasses.
894	Pots au Crème-Blanc	¼ oz Vanilla	2 oz Sugar	pint Milk	pint Cream	ea Egg Yolks	oz White Chocolate	oz Eggs		1 qt	Lightly caramelize the sugar. Add in the dairy, temper in eggs and chocolate. Portion. Bake in a water bath at 325° for 20 min. Chill
895	Vanilla Sauce	9 oz Yolks		qt Half And Half	tsp Vanilla Extract				oz Sugar	5 cup	Bring the sugar, dairy and vanilla to a simmer. Temper in eggs. Heat to 165°. Whisk over a double boiler until the sauce coat a spoon. Cool over an ice bath.
896	Whipped Cream			qt Whipping Cream	tbsp Vanilla Extract	oz Sugar				1.5 qt	Make sure the cream is very cold. Combine and whip in cold bowl to the desired texture.

Bavarian Cream

No.	Name		1	1	2	3	4	8	Yield	Method of Preparation
897	Basic		quart Half and Half / quart Cream	tsp Vanilla / oz Gelatin	oz Sugar			ea Egg Yolk / oz Water	3 qt	Step 1. Bring the sugar, dairy and vanilla to a simmer. Temper in eggs. Heat to 160°. Whisk over a double boiler until the sauce coats a spoon. Step 2. Bloom the gelatin in water, dissolve in warm vanilla sauce. Cool the mixture to 90°. Whip the cream to a soft peak. Fold the whipped cream into the sauce. Portion & refrigerate for 2 – 3 hours. Unmold and serve Bavarians Cold with sauce and garnish.
898	Cappuccino	6 oz Sugar / ½ oz Gelatin	pint Milk / tsp Instant Espresso	pint Cream	oz Kahlua	oz Water	ea Eggs		1 qt	Bring sugar, milk, and kahlua to a simmer. Dissolve espresso. Temper in eggs. Heat to 160°. Whisk over a double boiler until the sauce coats a spoon. Bloom the gelatin in water, dissolve in warm kahlua sauce. Cool the mixture to 90°. Whip the cream to a soft peak. Fold together. Portion & refrigerate for 2 – 3 hours. Garnish with ground cinnamon.
899	Chocolate	1.5 oz Liqueur / ½ cup Sugar	tsp Vanilla Extract	tbsp Gelatin	cup Milk		ea Yolks / oz Bittersweet Chocolate shaved		6 cup	Bring sugar, milk, and vanilla to a simmer. Temper in eggs. Heat to 160°. Whisk over a double boiler until the sauce coats a spoon. Bloom the gelatin in liquor, dissolve in sauce. Add in the shaved chocolate and melt. Cool the mixture to 90°. Whip the cream to a soft peak. Fold the mixture together. Portion & refrigerate for 2 hrs.
900	Chocolate Mint	12 oz Chocolate Shavings / Green Food Coloring as needed	oz Gelatin	qt Cream	pint Vanilla Sauce			oz Mint Liquor	3 qt	Warm the vanilla sauce. Bloom the gelatin in liquor, dissolve in warm sauce. Cool the mixture to 90°. Add in coloring to preference. Whip the cream to a soft peak. Fold the mixture together then fold in the shaved chocolate. Portion & refrigerate 2 hrs.
901	Pear	5 ea Egg Yolks / 6 oz Sugar	pint Milk / pint Pear Puree	pint Cream	tbsp Gelatin	oz Pear William Liqueur	oz Egg Whites	oz Pear Concentrate	1 qt	Bring half the sugar, milk, and vanilla to a simmer. Temper in egg yolks. Heat to 160°. Whisk over a double boiler until the sauce coats a spoon. Bloom the gelatin in pear William liquor, dissolve in pear sauce. Stir the pear concentrate and puree into the sauce. Cool to 90° Whip the cream to a soft peak. Whip the egg whites with remaining sugar. Fold the cream into the sauce mixture. Fold in meringue. Portion & refrigerate for 2 hrs.

Bavarian Cream

#	Name			1	1	2	3	4	8	Yield	Method of Preparation
902	Pina Colada	2 oz Coconut Water	6 oz Pineapple Rum	cup Cream of Coconut	oz Gelatin	cup Vanilla Sauce		cups Heavy Cream		2 qt	Warm the vanilla sauce. Bloom the gelatin in rum, dissolve in warm sauce. Cool the mixture to 90°. Add in the coconut. Whip the heavy cream to a soft peak. Fold the mixture together. Portion & refrigerate.
903	Quark (non egg)	¾ oz. Gelatin	4 oz Liquor or Rum	qt Greek Yogurt	pint Cream	ea Lemon Juice			oz Sugar	6 cup	Bloom the gelatin in the liquor or rum and lemon juice. Warm the yogurt and sugar to 90°. Melt the gelatin mixture and mix into the yogurt. Whip the cream and fold it into the yogurt. Portion into glasses filled with berries. Refrigerate for 2 hours.
904	Raspberry	4 oz Water	4 oz Liquor	qt Cream	oz Gelatin	oz Sugar	cup Raspberry pureed and strained		oz Vanilla Sauce	5 cup	Warm the vanilla sauce. Bloom the gelatin in liquor and water, dissolve in warm sauce. Cool the mixture to 90°. Add in the raspberry puree. Whip the heavy cream to a soft peak. Fold the mixture together. Portion & refrigerate for 2 – 3 hours.
905	Strawberry	12 ea Yolk	1.5 oz Gelatin	cup White Wine / oz Lemon Juice	qt Cream	pint Strawberry Puree		oz Water / oz Grand Marnier Liquor	oz Sugar	2.5 qt	Bloom the gelatin in water. Make a sabayon with the eggs, wine and sugar over a double boiler. Melt the gelatin in the sabayon. Combine the strawberry puree, liquor, and lemon juice. Whip the cream to soft peaks. Fold the strawberry mixture with the sabayon and cool to 90°. Fold in the whipped cream. Portion & refrigerate.
906	White Chocolate	½ cup Sugar	1 ½ oz Liquor	tsp Vanilla Extract	oz Gelatin	cup Milk	cup Cream	ea Yolks	oz White Chocolate shaved	6 cup	Bring sugar, milk, and vanilla to a simmer. Temper in eggs. Heat to 160°. Whisk over a double boiler until the sauce coats a spoon. Bloom the gelatin in liquor, dissolve in sauce. Add in the shaved chocolate and melt. Cool the mixture to 90°. Whip the cream to a soft peak. Fold the mixture together. Portion & refrigerate for 2 – 3 hours.
907	Verbena Lemon	6 oz Sugar	½ oz Gelatin	pint Milk		tbsp Lemon Verbena Leaves or Lemon Grass finely chopped	oz Water	ea Eggs		1 qt	Bring sugar, milk, and leaves to a simmer. Cover and steep for 5 minute. Remove leaves. Temper in eggs. Heat to 160°. Whisk over a double boiler until the sauce coats a spoon. Bloom the gelatin in water, dissolve in warm sauce. Cool the mixture to 90°. Whip the cream to a soft peak. Fold the mixture together. Portion & refrigerate for 2 – 3 hours.

Mousses

			1	1	2	3	4	8	Yield	Method of Preparation
908	Basic	Flavoring to Taste	pint Cream			oz Sugar	ea Eggs		3 cup	Separate eggs. Mix half sugar with yolks. Half with the whites. Warm both to 110° and whip separately. Add flavor to yolks. Whip cream. Fold yolks & cream. Flavor as desired. Fold in whites last. Portion in glasses, chill for several hours.
909	Chocolate	9 ea Eggs 9 oz Sugar	qt Cream	lb Bittersweet Chocolate Melted					2 qt	Separate eggs. Mix half sugar with yolks. Half with the whites. Warm both to 110° and whip separately. Add chocolate to yolks. Whip cream. Fold yolks & cream. Fold in whites last. Portion and chill.
910	Chocolate Coconut	5 oz Sugar	oz Coconut Extract	qt Cream			oz Coconut Rum	12 oz Bittersweet Chocolate-Shaved	7 cup	Make a sabayon with the eggs, rum, extract and sugar over a double boiler. Add in the chocolate and melt. Whip the cream to soft peaks. Fold in the whipped cream. Portion, chill.
911	Chocolate Grand Marnier		tsp Vanilla pint Cream	tbsp Gelatin	oz Simple Syrup	oz Grand Marnier Liqueur	oz Sugar	8 ea. Yolks 8 oz Bittersweet Chocolate Shaved	3 pint	Make a sabayon with the eggs, syrup and sugar over a double boiler. Bloom the gelatin in liquor and vanilla. Add to sabayon and melt. Add in the chocolate and melt. Whip the cream to soft peaks. Fold the whipped cream into the chocolate mixture. Portion and chill.
912	Coffee	4 oz Yolks 5 oz Sugar	qt Cream	oz Instant Coffee		tbsp Water	oz Butter	8 oz Bitter Sweet Chocolate	3 pint	Make a sabayon with the eggs and sugar over a double boiler. Dissolve the coffee in warm water. Melt the chocolate and butter. Whip the cream to soft peaks. Mix the coffee into the sabayon. Fold in the melted chocolate and cool to 85°. Fold in the whipped cream. Portion and chill.
913	Fruit		cup Cooked Fruit Puree	cup Sugar	oz Rum	cup Cream	drops Vanilla Extract	8 ea Egg Whites	3 pint	Bring the sugar and egg whites to 110°. Whip until it forms medium peaks. Whip the cream. Fold the fruit, rum and vanilla into meringue. Fold in cream
914	Grand Marnier	12 ea Yolks 1 tbsp Vanilla	cup Water	cup Sugar		3 cup Cream		8 oz Grand Marnier Liqueur	3 pint	Bring the sugar and water to 260°. Place the yolks in a mixer and whip. Slowly add in the hot syrup and whip. Add the Gran Marnier and whip until cool. Whip the cream and powdered sugar with vanilla until it forms soft peaks. Fold cream into eggs. Portion.

131

Mousses

No.	Mousse			1	1	2	3	4	8	Yield	Method of Preparation
915	**Key Lime**	¼ cup Sugar			ea Lime zested	tbsp Gelatin	oz White Wine	ea Egg Yolk	¼ cup Key Lime Juice	1 qt	Bloom the gelatin and wine. Combine the egg yolk, sugar, and lime juice and zest. Whip over a double boiler until it reaches 135°. Melt the gelatin in the yolks.
				pint Cream	cup Sour Cream	tbsp Sugar		ea Egg White	8 oz Condensed Milk		Blend the sour cream and condensed milk and mix into the yolks. Whip the cream and fold it in. Whip the egg whites and sugar and fold in. Portion and chill.
916	**Kiwi**			cup Pureed and Strained Fresh Kiwi	cup Sugar	oz Grand Marnier Liqueur	cup Cream	tsp Gelatin	8 ea Egg Whites	3 pint	Bloom the gelatin and liquor. Bring the sugar and egg whites to 110°. Whip until it forms medium peaks. Melt the gelatin and add to the meringue. Whip the cream. Fold the fruit puree into the meringue. Fold in cream. Portion and chill
917	**Lemon**	¾ oz Gelatin	14 oz Egg White	cup Lemon Juice	cup Sugar	tbsp Lemon Zest	drops Yellow Food Color		1.5 qt Cream	2 qt	Bloom the gelatin and juice. Bring the sugar and egg whites to 110°. Whip until it forms medium peaks. Melt the gelatin and add to the meringue. Whip the cream. Fold the zest and color into the cream. Fold the cream into meringue. Chill
918	**Milk Chocolate**	2 oz Corn Syrup				lb Milk Chocolate – shaved	cup Cream		8oz Milk	3 pint	Heat the milk and syrup and pour over the milk chocolate. Cool to 80°. Whip cream and fold the chocolate in. Portion and chill
919	**Praline**	12 oz Bittersweet Chocolate	7 oz Butter	cup Milk	cup Yolks	cup Cream			8 oz Praline Paste / 12 oz Sugar	5 pint	Bring the sugar and milk to a simmer. Temper the yolks in and cook to 140°. Cool to 100° and mix in the praline paste. Melt the chocolate and butter together and blend with the praline mixture Cool to 80°. Whip the cream. Fold into praline. Chill.
920	**Raspberry**			cup Raspberry Puree	cup Sugar	oz Raspberry Liquor	cup Cream		8 ea Egg Whites	3 pint	Bring the sugar and egg whites to 110°. Whip until it forms medium peaks. Whip the cream. Fold the raspberries and liquor into meringue. Fold in cream. Portion and chill
921	**Strawberry**	1 tbsp Gelatin		cup Pureed Frozen Strawberries	cup Sugar	oz Grand Marnier Liqueur	cup Cream		8 ea Egg Whites	3 pint	Bloom the gelatin and Gran Marnier. Bring the sugar and egg whites to 110°. Whip until it forms medium peaks. Melt the gelatin and add to the meringue. Whip the cream. Fold the puree into the meringue. Fold in cream. Portion and Chill.

Frozen Desserts

#	Recipe		1	1	2	3	4	8	Yield	Method of Preparation
922	Chocolate Gelato	1.75 pint Cream	gallon Milk	oz Vanilla Extract	lb Sugar	oz Bitter Chocolate	oz Milk Powder	oz Glucose	1.5 gal	Combine all ingredients and heat to 150°. Cool to 35° for 12 hour. Freeze according to manufacturers directions in a gelato or ice cream machine- freeze to 18°
923	Yogurt Sorbet	12 oz Yogurt / 7 oz Sugar			9 oz Water	oz Dextrose	oz Glucose	oz Cream Cheese / oz Sour Cream	1.25 qt	Place all ingredients in a blender and mix until smooth. Add in the items on this line and stir well. Store overnight. Freeze according to manufacturers directions in an ice cream machine- freeze to 15°
924	Lime Sorbet	10 oz Sugar	pint Water			oz Milk Powder		oz Lime Juice	1.25 qt	Bring the milk powder, sugar & water to 150°. Add in the lime juice. Chill to 35 °. Freeze according to manufacturers directions in an ice cream machine- freeze to 15°
925	Lemon Sorbet	1 lb Sugar	pint Lemon Juice		pint Water	tbsp Lemon Zest	tbsp Glucose		1.75 qt	Heat all of the ingredients to 150°. Cool to 35° Freeze according to manufacturers directions in an ice cream machine- freeze to 15°
926	Neutral Gelato	10 oz Sugar	qt Milk		oz Glucose	oz Milk Powder	oz Cream		1.5 qt	Combine all ingredients and heat to 150°. Cool to 35° for 12 hour. Freeze according to manufacturers directions in a gelato or ice cream machine- freeze to 18°
927	Praline Semifreddo	4 oz Praline Masse		pint Whipped Cream	4 oz Glucose		oz Pastry Cream	oz Meringue	1 qt	Warm the glucose in a microwave to 100°. Add in to the pastry cream and praline masse. Fold in the cream then the meringue. Portion and freeze to 20°.
928	Soufflé Glace- Classic	15 ea Yolks / 14 oz Egg White	qt Cream		12 oz Sugar		oz Grand Marnier Liqueur		2 qt	Combine the yolks and half the sugar with the Gran Marnier and whip over a double boiler until it reaches 120° and is light and foamy. Prepare and meringue from the remaining sugar and egg whites. Whip the heavy cream and fold into the whipped egg yolk mixture. Fold in the meringue. Portion and freeze to 18°.
929	Soufflé Glace Bourbon	½ cup Bourbon	cup Sugar	tsp Vanilla Extract	tbsp Gelatin			ea Eggs	1 qt	Separate the eggs. Soak the gelatin in the bourbon. Combine the yolks and half the sugar with the bourbon and whip over a double boiler until it reaches 120° and is light and foamy. Prepare and meringue from the remaining sugar and egg whites. Whip the heavy cream and fold into the whipped egg yolk mixture. Fold in the meringue. Portion and freeze to 18°.

Ice Cream

				1	1	2	4	8		Quart	Method of Preparation
930	Amaretto	5 oz Amaretto Liqueur	1 ½ pints Milk	lb Almonds	pint Cream		oz Sugar	oz Brown Sugar	9 ea Egg Yolk	1.25	Cook egg, dairy, and sugar to 150°. Cool to 35°. Add flavorings and freeze according to manufacturers directions in an ice cream machine. Toast and grind almonds mix in.
931	Cappuccino		½ tsp Cinnamon	pint Milk	pint Cream	tbsp Instant Espresso		oz Sugar	1 ea Vanilla Bean	1	Cook vanilla bean, dairy, and sugar to 150°. Add the cinnamon and espresso to the warm mixture. Cool to 35°. Remove the vanilla bean and scrape the seeds into the ice cream. Freeze according to manufacturers directions in an ice cream machine.
932	Coffee					tbsp Coffee Bean		oz Sugar			Caramelize sugar and add in the freshly ground coffee.
		1 Vanilla Bean		pint Milk	pint Cream	oz Sugar				1.25	Cook vanilla bean, dairy, coffee flavoring (above) and sugar to 150°. Strain the mixture through a chinois fine to remove coffee grounds. Cool to 35°. and freeze according to manufacturers directions in an ice cream machine.
933	Cherry Vanilla		1 tbsp Grenadine	pint Milk	pint Cream	tbsp Rum	oz Dried Cherry	oz Sugar	1 ea Vanilla Bean	1	Cook vanilla bean, dairy, and sugar to 150°. Cool to 35°. Add flavorings and freeze according to manufacturers directions in an ice cream machine. Soak cherries in warm rum and add to ice cream in the first 5 minutes of freezing.
934	Chocolate	9 ea Yolks		pint Milk	pint Cream	tbsp Cocoa Powder	oz Dark Chocolate	oz Sugar	1 ea Vanilla Bean	1	Cook vanilla bean, egg, dairy, and sugar to 150°. Stir chocolate and cocoa powder into the warm mixture. Cool to 35°. Freeze according to manufacturers directions in an ice cream machine.
935	Cinnamon	1 tbsp Cinnamon	1 tbsp Cinnamon	pint Milk	pint Cream	tsp Cinnamon Schnapps		oz Sugar	1 ea Vanilla Bean	1	Cook vanilla bean, dairy, and sugar to 150°. Cool to 35°. Add flavorings and freeze according to manufacturers directions in an ice cream machine.
936	Frangelico	8 ea Yolks	10 oz Sugar	ea Vanilla Bean	pint Cream	pint Milk	oz Frangelico			1.5	Cook vanilla bean, egg, dairy, and sugar to 150°. Cool to 35°. Add flavorings and freeze according to manufacturers directions in an ice cream machine.

Ice Cream

No.	Name			1	1	2	4	8		Quart	Method of Preparation
937	Macadamia	12 oz Sugar	2 oz Honey	pint Cream	pint Milk	tsp Vanilla Extract		oz Macadamia Nuts – chopped	12 ea Egg Yolk	1	Cook egg, dairy, honey, and sugar to 150°. Cool to 35°. Add flavorings and freeze according to manufacturers directions in an ice cream machine. Toast nuts and add to the ice cream.
938	Pistachio	12 oz Pistachio-chopped	5 cup Milk	cup Sugar	tsp Almond Extract	cup Cream	drops Green Food Coloring		12 ea Egg Yolk	2	Cook egg, dairy, and sugar to 150°. Cool to 35°. Add flavorings and freeze according to manufacturers directions in an ice cream machine. Toast nuts and add to the ice cream.
939	Rum Raisin	¾ cup Sugar		cup Spiced Rum			oz Dark Rum	oz Raisin			Soak the raisins in rum and sugar overnight. Drain and reserve liquid for ice cream.
				pint Cream	pint Milk	tsp Vanilla Extract			12 ea Egg Yolk	1	Cook egg, dairy, and sugar to 150°. Cool to 35°. Add reserved liquid and freeze according to manufacturers directions in an ice cream machine. Stir the raisins into the ice cream.
940	Strawberry	1 ea Vanilla Bean		pint Milk	pint Cream		oz Strawberry Puree	oz Sugar	1 lb Strawberries – sliced	1.5	Cook vanilla bean, dairy, and sugar to 150°. Cool to 35°. Add strawberry puree and freeze according to manufacturers directions in an ice cream machine. Stir strawberries into ice cream.
941	Vanilla Bean	1 tsp Vanilla Extract		pint Milk	pint Cream			oz Sugar	1 ea Vanilla Bean	1	Cook vanilla bean, dairy, and sugar to 150°. Cool to 35°. Add flavorings and scrape the vanilla bean seeds into the mixture. Freeze according to manufacturers directions in an ice cream machine.
942	Vanilla – Orange Blossom Honey			pint Milk	pint Cream	tsp Orange Zest		oz Honey-Orange Blossom	1 ea Vanilla Bean	1	Cook vanilla bean, dairy, and honey to 150°. Cool to 35°. Add flavorings and scrape the vanilla bean seeds into the mixture. Freeze according to manufacturers directions in an ice cream machine.
943	White Chocolate Raspberry Ripple	7 ea Yolks	6 oz White Chocolate	pint Milk	pint Cream		oz Melba Sauce	oz Sugar	1 ea Vanilla Bean	1	Cook vanilla bean, egg, dairy, and sugar to 150°. Stir chocolate into the warm mixture. Cool to 35°. Freeze according to manufacturers directions in an ice cream machine. Stripe in the melba sauce.

Chefs Note: It is very important to follow the proper sanitation procedures in the use of an ice cream or gelato machine, follow the local health code laws and refer to manufactures directions on the use and care of the machine. After the the ice cream is churned, dispense into clean containers, harden to 10° to 14° F for service or store -15° F for future use.

Traditional Pies

#	Item	1	2	3	4	Yield	Method of Preparation
944	All Purpose Pie Dough	1 oz Salt pint Ice Water	lb Shortening	lb Pastry Flour		12 Crusts	Rub the Shortening into the flour. Bottom crust- rub until coarse texture. Short Flake- rub until fat is size of peas, Long Flake- rub until fat is size of walnuts. Mix in salt and water. Portion 8 oz.
945	Flakey Dough	1¾ cups All Purpose Flour tsp Salt	tsp Sugar	oz Butter-Unsalted sliced thin	oz Ice Cold Water ¼ cup Shortening	2 Crusts	Mix flour, salt and sugar. Toss flour with butter and breakup the shortening and butter until they are the size of beans. Add to water to mixture and knead until dough forms a ball. Divide in half, roll into 2 balls, wrap and chill for 1 hour.
946	Graham Cracker Crust	¼ tsp Cinnamon	tbsp Brown Sugar	cup Graham Cracker Crumbs	oz Sugar 6oz Melted Butter	2 Crust	Toss all ingredients together and press into a pie pan. Using another pie pan that is the same size press and mold the crust to evenly fill the pie pan. Either prebake for a cream filling or fill and bake for a custard.
947	Apple – Filling	30 # IQF Apple Slices oz Nutmeg tbsp Salt	oz Cinnamon	64 oz Can Apple Juice	lbs Sugar 1# 3 oz CLEARJEL®	39 lb	Mix clear gel with ¼ of the sugar and 1 quart of liquid. Place remaining liquids, spices, salt and sugar in a 4 gallon kettle. Bring to a boil. Whisk the CLEARJEL® mixture into the liquid and heat to thicken. Bring to a full boil, and mix in frozen fruit.
948	Apple- Granny Smith	8 ea Granny Smith tbsp Lemon Juice	oz Sugar tsp Cinnamon	tbsp Brown Sugar tbsp Butter	tsp Cornstarch pinch Salt	Serves 8	Toss all dry ingredients together. Peel and slice apples ½" thick. Toss with dry ingredients and juice. Place in pie shell, drizzle melted butter over top. Cover with 2nd crust. Cut vents. Bake 400° 60 – 70 minutes. Cool for 1 hour before serving.
949	Blueberry Filling	lb Sugar	quart IQF Blueberry	oz Lemon Juice	cups Blueberry Juice 8 oz CLEARJEL®	3 quarts	Mix CLEARJEL® with ¼ of the sugar and 1 quart of liquid. Place remaining liquids, and sugar in a 4 gallon kettle. Bring to a boil. Whisk the Clear Jel mixture into the liquid and heat to thicken. Bring to a full boil, and mix in frozen fruit
950	Cherry Filling	30 # IQF Cherries cup Lemon Juice	quarts water tsp salt	cups Cherry Juice	lbs Sugar 1# 8 oz CLEARJEL®	40 lb	Mix clear gel with ¼ of the sugar and 1 quart of liquid. Place remaining liquids, salt and sugar in a 4 gallon kettle. Bring to a boil. Whisk the CLEARJEL® mixture into the liquid and heat to thicken. Bring to a full boil, and mix in frozen fruit
951	Fruit Pie	cup Juice oz INSTANT CLEARJEL®	ea Pie Crusts	oz Sugar	cups Fruit	Serves 8	In a bowl toss INSTANT CLEARJEL® and sugar together first. Add fruit and toss, add juice last and allow to set for 10 minutes. Use to fill between two pie crusts. Cut vents and bake 400° for 45 min to 1 hour. Sugar and thickener amount depends upon the type of fruit and its sweetness.
952	Key Lime	12 oz Key Lime Juice doz Egg Yolks	tbsp Lime Zest	drop Green Coloring	cups Sweet Cond. Milk	Serves 8	Whisk yolks into milk, then whisk in color and juice with zest. Fill 2 ea 9" graham cracker crust lined pie or tart pans. Bake 350° for 18 min. When cool top with whipped cream rosettes.
953	Lemon Meringue	2 tbsp Butter ¼ tsp Salt cup Sugar pinch Salt	ea Egg Yolks	ea Lemons-Juice and Zest	tbsp CLEARJEL® drop Yellow Color 1 pint Water	Serves 8	Combine sugar, salt, CLEARJEL® Whisk into water and bring to a boil until thickened. Temper into egg yolks and zest. Heat 2 minutes. Whisk in butter and finish with juice and color. Pour into pre-baked shell. Top with ½ recipe of Basic Meringue 857. Bake 10 minutes 350°, until brown
954	Peach Filling	# 10 can Peach Slices	cups Peach Nectar	cups Sugar	oz CLEARJEL®	7.5 lb	Mix clear gel with ¼ of the sugar and all the liquid from the can. Place remaining liquids and sugar in a 4 gallon kettle. Bring to a boil. Whisk the CLEARJEL® mixture into the liquid and heat to thicken. Bring to a full boil, and mix in fruit. Cool
955	Pecan	7 oz Corn Syrup ¼ tsp Salt cup Light Brown Sugar	tsp Vanilla cups Pecan Halves	tbsp Flour cup Pecan Pieces	ea Eggs 6 oz Butter	Serves 10	Melt butter and sauté pecan pieces lightly, add syrup, sugar, vanilla and salt and mix well. Mix in eggs. Fold in pecan halve last. Fill prepared deep pie or tart shell. Toss pecan halves in bowl to pick up left over filling then arrange on top. Bake 350° for 40 minutes. Allow to cool 2 hours before serving.
956	Pumpkin	2/3 cup Maple Syrup cup Cream tsp Cinnamon	cups Pumpkin Puree	tbsp Dark Rum	ea Eggs slice Ginger ¾ tsp Nutmeg	Serves 10	Heat rum and ginger slices to 180°. Allow to steep for 30 minutes. Strain rum into syrup. Blend syrup with remaining ingredients. Pour into a deep 10" pie pan lined with pie dough. Bake 350° for 45 minutes, or until filling is set and crust is light golden brown. Cool 2 hrs.

All recipes that include CLEARJEL® are for cooked applications. INSTANT CLEARJEL® does not require precooking and may be added directly to fruits for pies.

Regional Pies

#	Item			1	2	3	4	8	Method of Preparation
957	Amish Funeral	2 cup Raisins	2 oz Sugar; ½ tsp Salt	cup Light Brown Sugar; cup Water	2 tbsp Butter; tsp Vanilla	tbsp Bread Flour; ea Eggs	oz Buttermilk	oz Pie Dough	Roll and place the dough in a 9 inch pie pan. Blind Bake. Separate eggs. Mix brown sugar with salt and flour. Whip egg yolks with vanilla. Add flour mixture and mix well. Add buttermilk and mix. Bring raisins and water to a boil. Slowly add the hot liquid to the batter while mixing. Pour the raisins in pie shell. Top with batter. Whip egg whites and sugar. Top pie with meringue. Bake 30 minutes 325°.
958	Banana Cream	3 ea Bananas Sliced	¼ cup Cornstarch	cup Sugar; cup Cream	tsp Vanilla		ea Egg Yolks	oz Milk	Blend cornstarch, ½ of sugar, salt, and yolks. Warm remaining sugar, cream and milk to 170°. Slowly whisk the wet into the dry. Place in a sauce pot and heat to a boil. Strain into bowl and add vanilla and butter. Fold in sliced bananas. Pour into a pre-baked pie crust. Cool 4 hours. Top with whipped cream. Garnish– glazed banana slices
959	Butterscotch		1/3 cup Cornstarch	cup Dark Brown Sugar; cup Cream	tsp Vanilla; oz Salted Butter	tbsp Scotch	ea Egg Yolks	oz Milk	Blend cornstarch, ½ of sugar, salt, and yolks. Warm remaining sugar, Scotch, cream and milk to 170°. Slowly whisk the wet into the dry. Place in a sauce pot and heat to a boil. Strain into bowl and add vanilla and butter. Pour into a prebaked pie crust. Cool 4 hours. Top with whipped cream. Garnish with Butterscotch Morsels
960	Chocolate Cream	2/3 cup Sugar	pinch Salt	tsp Vanilla; cup Cream	tbsp Dutch Cocoa; cup Milk	tbsp Cornstarch	ea Egg Yolks	oz Bittersweet Chocolate	Blend cornstarch, ½ of sugar, salt, and yolks. Warm remaining sugar, cocoa, cream and milk to 170°. Slowly whisk the wet into the dry. Place in a sauce pot and heat to a boil. Strain into shaved chocolate, mix and add vanilla. Pour into a prebaked pie crust. Cool 4 hours, top with whipped cream. Garnish with shaved chocolate
961	Coconut Cream	1 cup Toasted Coconut	¼ cup Cornstarch	cup Sugar; cup Cream	tsp Vanilla; oz Butter	tbsp Coconut Rum	ea Egg Yolks	oz Milk	Blend cornstarch, ½ of sugar, salt, and yolks. Warm remaining sugar, rum, cream and milk to 170°. Slowly whisk the wet into the dry. Place in a sauce pot and heat to a boil. Strain into bowl and add vanilla and butter. Fold in coconut. Pour into a prebaked pie crust. Cool 4 hours. Top with whipped cream. Garnish with toasted coconut.
962	Coconut Custard	1 cup Toasted Sweetened Coconut		cup Milk	cups Heavy Cream	tsp Vanilla	oz Sugar; ea Eggs	ea Egg Yolks	Blind bake a pie shell for 10 minutes. Whisk eggs, yolks, sugar in bowl. Heat milk and cream to 130°. Slowly add liquid into dry until blended. Pour coconut into pie shell, and then pour custard on top. Bake 325° for 25 minutes, until custard is set. Cool 2 hours.
963	Kentucky Derby	6 oz Chocolate Chip	6 oz Chopped Walnuts	cup Sugar; oz Bourbon	ea Eggs	oz Flour	oz Butter-melted	oz Pie Dough	Roll and place the dough in a 9 inch pie pan. Combine eggs, sugar, and bourbon. Whisk in flour then butter. Mix in chocolate and nuts. Pour in pie shell, bake 350° 45 min.
964	Shoo-fly	1 tsp Baking Soda	1 ½ tsp Cinnamon	cup Warm Water; cup Molasses	cup Flour	oz Butter-chopped	oz Brown Sugar	oz Pie Dough	Roll and place the dough in a 10 inch pie pan. Mix the liquids with baking soda. Add the rest, mix and pour into shell. Bake in a 360° oven for 45 min. Allow to cool 30 min
965	Strawberry Rhubarb			ea Lemon-Zest	cups sliced Strawberries	cups Rhubarb Stalks ¼"	tbsp INSTANT CLEARJEL®	oz Sugar	Mix sugar and INSTANT CLEARJEL® together. Toss all ingredients together. Pour into a 9" pie dough lined pie pan. Top with flakey dough and seal edges. Brush crust with buttermilk, as needed. Bake 350° for 1 hour. Cool 2 hours
966	Sweet Potato	½ tsp Cinnamon	½ tsp Nutmeg	pint Cooked Sweet Potato; tsp Vanilla	ea Eggs; oz Dark Rum	oz Salted Butter-melted	oz Light Brown Sugar	oz Milk	Rice the warm potatoes, mix in butter, sugar. Whisk everything else together and blend with potatoes. Pour into a 9" pie dough lined pie pan. Bake 350° for 50 minutes. Cool 2 hours before serving. Make sure to not use fresh dug potatoes, they are too starchy.

Each of these formulas yields one 9-inch pie or 8 portions

Tarts and Quiche

#	Item		1	2	3	4	8	Yield	Method of Preparation
967	Tart Dough	2.5 cups All Purpose Flour	tsp Salt	tbsp Sugar		oz Ice Water	oz Butter sliced	24 oz	Pulse the flour, salt, sugar and butter in a food processor until it is coarse in texture. Pour into a bowl. Add the water and knead by hand to form a ball. Portion 8 oz for a 9"crust, and 10oz for a 10"crust. Chill until needed. Unless noted all recipes on this page use this recipe.
968	Apple Almond Tart	½ recipe 854 Frangipane	tbsp Lemon Juice	oz Sugar	Large Granny Smith Apples (Peel, core, and thinly slice)	oz Apricot Glaze		Serves 6	Roll out dough and line a greased 11" Fluted Tart Pan. Spread out Frangipane evenly to coat bottom. Toss the apples with sugar and lemon. Arrange in a spiral over the filling. Bake at 350° for 30 minutes, crust should be brown. Melt and brush glaze over the apples. Cool 2 hours.
969	Bakewell Tart	8 oz finely ground Almonds / 2 oz Jam	cup Sugar	oz All Purpose Flour	ea eggs / oz sliced Almonds	tsp Lemon Zest	oz Butter	Serves 6	Roll out tart dough and line a greased 10" Fluted Tart Pan. Blind bake at 375°. When cool spread out cherry or raspberry jam to coat bottom. Cream the butter and sugar; add the egg slowly then ground nuts, flour, and zest, mix until smooth. Fill tart. Garnish with almond slices. Bake at 350° for 20 minutes.
970	Chocolate Pecan Rum Tart	6 oz Light Corn Syrup / ¾ tsp Vanilla	cup Brown Sugar	oz Bakers Chocolate-grated	ea Eggs / Tbsp Dark Rum	oz Salted Butter / oz Pecan Halves	oz Pecan Pieces	Serves 8	Roll out tart dough and line a greased 10" x 1 ¾" Fluted Tart Mold. Blind bake 10 minutes to set dough. Melt butter and sauté pecan pieces for 10 seconds. Add chocolate, remove from heat. Whip eggs with sugar, syrup, extract, rum. Mix with chocolate and fold in pecan halves. Pour into tart and arrange the pecan halves on top. Bake at 350° for 40-50 minutes. Cool 2 hours.
971	Lemon Chess Tart	5 ea Eggs	oz Melted Butter	oz Cream	tbsp Flour / tbsp Lemon Zest	oz Lemon Juice	oz Sugar	Serves 6	Roll out tart dough and line a greased 10" Fluted Tart Pan. Blind bake at 375°. Whisk eggs and sugar to blend. Add the rest and mix until smooth. Pour in crust. Bake 350° for 30 minutes. Cool 2 hours, top with powdered sugar,
972	Linzer Tart	1 recipe # 1075 Linzer Dough	ea Egg White	oz Powdered Sugar (Garnish)			oz Raspberry Jam	Serves 8	Roll out dough into 2ea 10" circles. Place first disk in 10" ring mold. Dock and blind bake for 10 minutes at 375°. Allow to cool. Brush the baked disk with egg white. Place 2nd disk on a cake circle. Use an 8" cutter to remove the center. Cut the center into strips. Pipe the jam in the tart. Decorate the jam with a lattice of dough. Brush with egg white. Bake 350° for 30 minutes. Dust.
973	Quiche Breakfast	1 recipe 865 Savory Custard	cup Ham diced	cups Cheese shredded	oz Bacon crumbled	tbsp Chives sliced	oz Pâte Brisée	Serves 8-10	Grease and line a 9 inch spring form pan with dough. Mix all ingredients with the savory custard. Pour into pan, spread out ingredients. Bake at 375° for 20 minutes. Then bake at 325° until custard is set. Allow to cool for 1 hour
974	Quiche Florentine	1 recipe 865 Savory Custard	ea Shallot Minced	cups Fontina diced	tbsp Butter / tbsp Flour	cups Fresh Spinach	oz Pâte Brisée 861	Serves 8-10	Chop spinach. In a sauté pan melt butter and sweat shallots. Wilt spinach and chill. Mix in flour to absorb moisture. Grease and line a 9 inch spring form pan with dough. Mix all ingredients with the savory custard. Pour into pan, spread out ingredients. Bake at 375° for 20 minutes. Then bake at 325° until custard is set. Cool 1 hour
975	Quiche Lorraine	1 recipe 865 Savory Custard		cups Bacon Lardon		oz Gruyere Cheese grated	oz Pâte Brisée 861	Serves 8-10	Grease a 9 inch spring form pan with rendered bacon fat and line pan with Pâte Brisée. Mix all ingredients with the savory custard. Pour into pan, spread out ingredients. Bake at 375° for 20 minutes. Then bake at 325° until custard is set. Cool for 1 hour
976	Tarte Tatin	8-9 oz Leftover Puff Pastry Scraps	cup Sugar	oz Calvados		oz Butter	ea Golden Apples	Serves 6	Peel and core apples. Quarter apples. Toss with Calvados. Heat a 9" x 2" Copper Tatin pan, and coat with butter. Sprinkle ¾ of sugar in pan and remove from heat. Arrange apples in pan very tightly and gently caramelize for 25 -30minutes. Roll out dough and place over apples to seal. Bake 400° for 20 min. Flip over on to a platter. Serve with Crème Chantilly or Ice Cream

Hot Desserts

#	Recipe		1	2	3	4	8	Yield	Method of Preparation
977	**Apple Walnut Crisp**	½ cup Walnuts / ¼ cup Honey	cup Flour / Cup Rolled Oats	tsp Cinnamon	cups Diced Apple	oz Melted Butter	oz Brown Sugar	Serves 10	In a bowl combine oats, walnuts, sugar flour and butter. Place ½ this mixture in a casserole. Toss apples, honey, and spice. Place in casserole, top with rest of the oat nut. Bake 350° for 45 min. Serve with vanilla ice cream.
978	**Austrian Crepes**	7 oz Bread Flour	cup Milk / tbsp Sugar	tbsp Butter-melted	ea Eggs	oz Cream		8 ea	Combine the dry ingredients. Combine the milk and eggs. Whisk wet into dry. Whisk in melted butter last. Portion 2 oz of crepe batter into a 10 inch pan. Brown both sides.
979	**Basic Crepe Batter**	½ tsp Salt	oz Sugar / ea Egg Yolk	ea Eggs	tbsp Butter	oz All Purpose Flour	oz Milk	20 ea	Combine the dry ingredients. Combine the milk and eggs. Whisk wet into dry. Whisk in melted butter last. Portion 1 oz of crepe batter into an 8 inch pan. Brown on both sides.
980	**Bananas Foster**	½ tsp Cinnamon / ½ ea Lemon	oz Banana Liqueur	oz Butter	oz Dark Rum	ea Bananas-split	oz Brown Sugar	Serves 8	Heat the pan. Warm the butter and sprinkle the brown sugar over. Rub the pan with the lemon on a fork. Squeeze the juice. Add the bananas, brown. Remove from flame, flambé. Sprinkle flames with cinnamon. Over ice cream.
981	**Brown Betty** Pears and Peaches are great in this recipe as well	¾ cup Sugar	tsp Cinnamon	cups Ginger Snaps		ea Granny Smith Apples	oz Butter	Serves 8	Melt butter, use 2 oz of butter and ¼ cup sugar. Place in baking dish. apples add spice and sauté peeled diced apples. Combine crumbs, remaining sugar and butter in a bowl. Use to top apples, bake 350° 20 minutes.
982	**Chocolate Soufflé**	6 oz Sugar	qt Milk			oz Butter	oz Bread Flour	Serves 12	Combine the items on this line and bring to a boil while whisking. Remove after thickened.
		6 oz Chocolate				ea Yolks			Add in the chocolate and melt. Stir the mixture in the pot and place over a bowl of ice to help cool it off. Add in the yolks when cool.
		16 ea Egg White				oz Sugar			Preheat the oven to 350°. Butter and sugar 12 large ramekins. Whip the eggs slightly and sprinkle in sugar. Whip to medium peaks. Fold in the chocolate batter. Bake for 15–20 minutes. Dust with powdered sugar, serve immediately, offer sauce tableside.
983	**Crepes Normandy**	½ tsp Cinnamon	oz Calvados	ea Apples	oz Butter	oz Brown Sugar	oz Cider	Serves 4	Heat the pan. Warm the butter and sprinkle the brown sugar over. Add the apples and cider and sauté. When reduced add calvados Carefully place over the flame and flambé. Sprinkle flames with cinnamon. Fill 8 crepes with this mixture and serve.
984	**Crepes Suzette**	1 oz Brandy	oz Orange Zest / oz Sugar	1 oz Grand Marnier Liquor		oz Butter	oz Orange Juice	Serves 4	Heat the pan. Sprinkle the sugar on the pan and caramelize. Add the zest and some of the juice. Simmer. Add the rest of the juice and reduce. Place the 8 crepes in the liquid and warm. Remove from heat and add the alcohol. Carefully place over the flame and flambé. Fold the crepes and plate. Add the butter to finish.

Hot Desserts

#		1	2	3	4	8	Yield	Method of Preparation
985	**Cherries Jubilee**	½ ea Lemon / 1 shot Kirshwasser	cup Bing Cherries pitted / tsp Cornstarch	oz Cherry Liqueur	tbsp Sugar		Serves 4	Mix the cornstarch and cherry liqueur to marinate the cherries. Heat the pan. Sprinkle the sugar over the pan and caramelize. Rub the pan with the lemon on a fork. Squeeze the juice. Add the cherries carefully place over the flame and flambé with kirsch. Simmer until thick. Serve over ice Cream.
986	**Dessert Omelet**	6 ea Yolks / 6 ea Whites	cup Milk	oz Bread Flour	oz Butter	oz Cream	Serves 4	Combine the wet ingredients. Whisk wet ingredients into the flour until smooth. / Whip the egg whites until soft peaks. Fold into batter. Portion into buttered omelet pans and fill with jams or fruit. Fold and finish in oven. Top with Anglaise.
987	**Fritter Batter**	12 oz All Purpose Flour	oz Sugar / Tbsp Orange Juice	ea Eggs	oz Apple Juice		1 lb	Combine all the wet ingredients and whisk in the flour. Dredge fruit in powdered sugar and dip into batter. Portion into 350° fat and fry until golden brown. Remove and serve.
988	**Grand Marnier Soufflé**	3 oz Grand Marnier	pint Milk	oz Bread Flour	oz Sugar	8 ea Yolks / 8 ea Whites	Serves 6	Combine sugar, flour and milk. Warm to 180° while whisking. Remove and temper in yolks. Add the Gram Marnier. Cool until needed. / Whip the egg whites and fold into the batter. Bake in a 350° water bath pan for 20 minutes.
989	**Topen Palatschinken** (Sweet Cheese Crepes)	14 oz Bakers Cheese / 4 oz Raisins	cup Cream / Lemon Zest	oz Sugar	oz Butter / oz Sugar	oz Yolks / oz Whites	1 qt	Mix all of the line items until smooth / Prepare a meringue and fold into the cheese mixture. Add the raisins and zest. Portion into Austrian Crepes (recipe number 978) and top with Anglaise. Bake until brown and serve hot.
990	**Strudel Dough**	10 oz Bread Flour	tsp White Vinegar / ea Egg	oz Oil		oz Warm Water	1 lb	Prepare straight dough. Mix for 6 minutes on 2nd speed. Rest for 30 minutes. Pull dough to 60" square on a floured pastry cloth.
991	**Strudel – Apple Cherry**	¼ tsp Nutmeg / 1 cup Dried Cherries	tbsp Cinnamon / cup Ground Vanilla Wafer	lbs Apples- peel and slice	oz Hazelnut Flour	oz Sugar / oz Melted Butter	Serves 8	Toss apples sugar, flour, spices and cherries. Allow to sit covered for 1 hour. Follow recipe # 990. Brush with ½ of the butter, Sprinkle ground wafer. Then apple mixture over ¼ of the dough. Roll, butter, bake 375°-20 minutes
992	**Vanilla Soufflé Base**	6 ea Yolks	Pint Milk / ea Vanilla Bean	tbsp Cornstarch	oz Bread Flour	oz Sugar	Serves 6	Warm the milk with sugar and vanilla to 170°. Make a paste with yolks dry ingredients. Temper liquid into paste. Return to heat to thicken. Remove and cool.
993	**Vanilla Soufflé per portion**	2 ea Egg Whites	Kitchen Spoon Of Base	tbsp Sugar			Serves 1	Prepare a meringue from eggs and sugar. Fold into the base. Flavor with 1 oz of liqueur (optional). Portion into a 4 inch round soufflé cup that has been buttered and sugared. Bake in a 365° oven for 12 – 15 minutes.

Dessert Sauces

Item		1	1	2	3	4	8	Yield	Method of Preparation
994	Anglaise		tsp Vanilla	cups Half and Half	oz Cream	tbsp Sugar	oz Egg Yolk	2.5 cups	Combine the cream and eggs in a bowl. Place the half and half, sugar and vanilla in a pot and bring to simmer. Temper the hot into cold. Place over a double boiler and whisk until thickened. 160°. Cool over an ice bath.
995	Butterscotch	cup Milk	tsp Vanilla	tbsp Flour	tbsp Salted Butter	oz Cream	oz Brown Sugar	12 oz	Combine the cream and flour. In a sauce pan heat the brown sugar and melt. Once melted slowly add the milk and bring to simmer. Add the vanilla. Temper the cream mixture into the sauce. Thicken over medium heat add butter.
996	Caramel	cup Cream		tbsp Butter	oz Corn Syrup	oz Sugar		12 oz	Combine the syrup and sugar in a sauce pot and caramelize over high heat. Remove from heat when brown. Slowly add cream & butter.
997	Chocolate	cup Cream	tbsp Butter	tbsp Sugar		oz Bittersweet Chocolate		12 oz	Bring the cream and sugar to a boil. Chop the chocolate. Pour the hot cream over the chocolate. Stir until melted. Add in the butter and stir until smooth. Cool before using
998	Cinnamon Apple	shot Rum / oz Apple Butter	ea Lemon-juiced	tsp Cinnamon	oz Sugar	tsp Butter	oz Apple Cider	1 cup	Combine the cider, sugar, lemon and cinnamon. Whisk over medium heat and bring to boil. Remove and finish with rum and butters. Serve warm or cool.
999	Frangelico	oz Frangelico Liqueur	oz Chocolate-shaved	cup Vanilla Sauce or Anglaise		tbsp Toasted Hazelnuts		1 pint	Warm the vanilla sauce and pour over the chocolate to melt. Add in the frangelico and cool. Ground nuts are an optional texture
1000	Fruit Coulis	lb Fruit	oz Cornstarch	ea Lemons	oz Orange Juice		oz Sugar	1 pint	Peel the fruit. Combine with the sugar and lemon juice. Bring the fruit to a simmer. Puree the mixture. Combine the cornstarch and orange juice. Thicken puree with slurry. Cool.
1001	Hard	tbsp Lemon Juice			oz Dark Rum	oz Sugar	oz Butter	12 oz	Combine all ingredients with a paddle in a mixer and slowly mix until soft. Turn to high speed and whip the butter until light. Pipe the butter into rosettes. Use to finish hot desserts.
1002	Lemon	tbsp Cornstarch	tbsp Salted Butter	drop Egg Shade Color	ea Lemons	oz Sugar	oz Water	12 oz	Juice and zest the lemon. Combine with sugar, water, cornstarch and salt. Whisk and bring to a simmer. Once thickened finish with butter and egg shade. Chill before using.
1003	Melba	oz Sugar	pint Raspberry	oz Chambord				1 pint	Crush the raspberries add sugar and boil. Strain the sauce and add the chambord
1004	Raspberry			oz Sugar	oz Burgundy		oz Raspberries	1 cup	Simmer the sugar and wine. Add raspberries, puree and strain.
1005	Strawberry	lb strawberry	Orange juiced	oz Sugar	tsp Grand Marnier			1 pint	Simmer the strawberries, sugar and orange juice. Puree and strain. Add Grand Marnier
1006	Sabayon			oz White Wine	oz Yolks / oz Sugar	oz Whip Cream		1 pint	Whip eggs, wine, and sugar over double boiler. For cold sauce cool egg, fold in whipped cream.
1007	Toffee	cup Sugar		tbsp Lemon			oz Butter	20 oz	Boil sugar and butter until it begins to caramelize. Remove from heat, stir in cream then lemon juice
1008	Zabaglione			oz Sugar	oz Marsala	ea Yolks		1 cup	Whip eggs, wine, and sugar over double boiler until light and foamy. Serve warm.

Cake Batters

ID	Name				1	2	3		Yield	Method of Preparation
1009	**Angel Food** Yields 2 each			lb Egg White	tsp Cream of Tartar			8 oz Sugar	2.5 lb	Combine the eggs, tartar, and sugar in a clean bowl. Warm to 100° and whip to medium peaks.
		7 oz Cake Flour	½ tsp Salt	tsp Almond Extract				8 oz Confectionary Sugar		Sift the flour, salt and sugar together and fold into meringue with extract. Portion and bake in a 350° oven.
1010	**Baum Kuchen**	1lb 11oz Sugar		lb Almond Paste			lb Butter		20 lb	Cream the almond paste and sugar first. Then add the butter. Cream until light.
		1lb 12.5 oz Cake Flour	¾ oz Baking Powder					1.5 lb Cornstarch		Add the flour, powder and cornstarch and mix until smooth
		2lb 11.5 oz Egg Yolk	7.5 oz Rum	tbsp Vanilla Extract	tsp Cardamom	Lemon Juice and Zest				Add the items on this line and mix until smooth. Make sure there are no lumps.
		4lb 3.5 oz Egg White					lb Sugar			Prepare a meringue and fold into the batter. Use this batter in a baum kuchen machine of bake in layers on a sheet pan under a broiler.
1011	**Carrot** Yields 5 ea	18 ea Eggs	5 cup Oil					5 ¼ lb Sugar	20 lb	Blend oil and sugar. Whip in eggs.
		3 ½ lb All Purpose Flour	¼ cup Cinnamon	oz Bakery Blend # 1101	tbsp Salt	oz Baking Soda	1lb Crushed Pineapple	5 cup Buttermilk		Add the dry ingredients and mix well. Add the pineapple and buttermilk. Mix.
		½ oz Baking Powder	1 ½ lb Coconut				1lb Carrot grated	1 ½ lb Walnut		Mix in the remaining ingredients. Scale 1/2 gal per 10" pan bake at 350° for 25 - 35 min or until an inserted toothpick is clear when removed.
1012	**Cheesecake** Yields 2 ea	12 oz Sugar	1 oz Lemon Juice	tbsp Vanilla Extract	pinch Salt		1lb Cream Cheese	6ea Eggs	2 ea	Cream the sugar and cream cheese until smooth. Gradually add the eggs and mix until smooth with remaining ingredients. Portion into 10" greased and graham cracker crumb lined pans. Bake at 375° for 30 - 45 minutes in a waterbath. Open the door of the oven and allow the cheesecakes to rest for 30 minutes before refrigerating
1013	**Chocolate Sponge** Yields 5 ea	30 ea Eggs	30 oz Sugar					8oz Cornstarch	5 ea	Combine the eggs and sugar in a mixing bowl and warm to 100° over a pot of warm water, stir the eggs to warm evenly. Whip the eggs with an electric mixer on high speed until it reaches it maximum volume. Mean while sift all the dry ingredients together 3 times and melt the butter.
		17 oz Cake Flour	½ tsp Baking Soda	stick Butter-Melted (4 oz)						When the eggs are fully whipped fold the dry ingredients into the eggs without loosing its volume. Fold the butter in last. Portion into 10" cake pan and bake at 350° for 20 – 25 minutes.
1014	**Fudge Cake** Yields 6 ea	1.5 lb Butter	6 lb Brown Sugar			1lb Baker Choc	1lb Sour Cream	2 oz Baking Soda	20 lb	Melt the chocolate over a double boiler. Cream the butter and sugar until light in texture.
		24 ea Eggs	3lb 6 oz Cake Flour			oz Baking Powder	pint Boiling Water	½ oz Salt		Add the eggs and sour cream to the butter and mix well. Add the chocolate and mix well. Add the, dry ingredients and mix. Mix the water in last. Portion into 10" prepared cake pans. Bake in a 340° oven for 30 -40 minutes or until an inserted toothpick is clear when removed.

Cake Batters

Code	Recipe	Ingredients					Yield	Method of Preparation
1015	**Joconde Sponge** **Yields 1 sheet pan**	6 oz Powdered Sugar				8 oz Ground Nuts / oz Cake Flour	2 lb	Sift the flour and sugar together twice then mix in the finely ground nuts.
		10 oz Whole Eggs						Whip the eggs and mix into the dry ingredients to form a smooth batter.
		6 oz Egg Whites		tbsp Sugar		1 ¾ oz Melted Butter		Prepare a meringue from the egg whites and sugar and fold into the batter. Fold the butter in last. Spread over prepared sheet pan and bake at 350 ° until set.
1016	**Joconde Garnish Paste**	1 oz Powdered Sugar	oz Butter	ea Egg White		1 oz Flour	5 oz	Make a paste with the sugar, flour and butter. Soften with the egg white. Color as desired with cocoa powder or dry coloring as desired.
1017	**Lady Fingers** **Yields 5 Dozen**	13 ea Egg Yolk	7oz Sugar tsp Vanilla			12 oz Cake Flour	60 ea	Warm the egg yolks and sugar and whip with vanilla until light in texture. Fold the sifted flour into the whipped egg yolks.
		13 ea Egg White	6 oz Sugar					Make a meringue from the egg whites and sugar and fold into the batter. Pipe the batter on to powder sugar dusted parchment lined sheet pans. Bake at 350° for 10 – 12 minutes or until light golden brown.
1018	**Pound Cake - English** **Yields 4 ea**		1lb Butter	lb Sugar	tsp Vanilla		4 lb	Cream the butter and sugar until light in texture with the vanilla extract.
		½ tsp Salt	1lb Eggs	1lb Cake Flour	tsp Baking Powder			Gradually add the eggs to the butter and sugar and mix well. Sift the dry ingredients together and add to eggs. Portion into 1 lb loaves and bake in a 340° until golden brown and set. Approximately 45 minutes or until an inserted toothpick is clear when removed
1019	**Pound Cake** **1 lb 12 oz Cakes**	4 lb Powdered Sugar	4lb Butter	tbsp Vanilla Extract			8 lb	Cream the butter and sugar until light in texture with the extracts.
		20 Eggs		tbsp Rum Extract	cups Milk	¼ oz Baking Powder		Gradually add the eggs to the butter and sugar and mix well. Sift the dry ingredients together and add to eggs. Add the milk in last and mix for 4 minutes on low speed. Bake at 350° for 12 minutes then reduce temperature to 325° until an inserted toothpick is clear when removed.
1020	**Sacher Torte** **Yields 2 ea 10" cakes**	9 oz Egg Yolk	8 oz Sugar			8 oz Butter	3 lb	Cream the butter and sugar until light in texture. Gradually add the eggs to the butter and sugar and mix well.
		12 oz Egg White	4 oz Sugar					Make a meringue from the egg whites and sugar and fold into the batter.
		3 oz Cake Flour	4 oz Ground Almonds		oz Cocoa Powder			Fold the dry ingredients into the batter without loosing its volume. Bake at 340° for 35 – 40 minutes or until an inserted toothpick is clear when removed

Cake Batters

No.	Item			1	2	3		Yield	Method of Preparation
1021	**Savarin, Babka** — Portion 1lb 8 oz	12 oz Milk	1 ½ lb Bread Flour		oz Sugar		6 oz Yeast		Dissolve the yeast is 100° water. Combine with the other items on this line to form a batter. Cover and place in a warm area of the kitchen to form a sponge.
		4lb Bread Flour	10 oz Sugar	1 ½ oz Salt		1lb Butter Melted	3lb 8oz Eggs	12 lb	Combine everything except for the butter and knead into dough for 7 minutes. Add the butter last. Form into 1.5 lb loaves into buttered ring pans. Proof then bakes at 375°.
1022	**Sponge** — Yields 5 ea	30 ea Eggs	30 oz Sugar						Combine the eggs and sugar in a mixing bowl and warm to 100° over a pot of warm water, stir the eggs to warm evenly. Whip the eggs with an electric mixer on high speed until it reaches it maximum volume. Mean while sift all the dry ingredients together 3 times and melt the butter.
		8 oz Cornstarch	22 oz Cake Flour	tbsp Vanilla extract			10 oz Melted Butter	5 ea	When the eggs are fully whipped fold the dry ingredients into the eggs without loosing its volume. Fold the butter in last. Portion into 10" cake pan and bake at 350° for 20 – 25 minutes.
1023	**Sour Cream** — Yields 3 half sheet pans	2 lb Butter	tbsp Vanilla Extract	qt Eggs	lb Sugar	2 tsp Salt			Cream the butter and sugar together. Add eggs and other items gradually. Whip until fully incorporated.
		4 tsp Baking Powder	qt Sour Cream		tsp Baking Soda	lb Cake Flour		11 lb	Sift the dry ingredients and add to the batter. Mix on first speed then add the sour cream. Mix until smooth.
1024	**Roulade Sponge** — Yields 4 ea	12 oz Sugar	30 ea Yolk		tsp Vanilla Extract				Warm the egg yolks and sugar and whip with vanilla until light in texture.
		12 oz Sugar	30 ea Whites						Make a meringue from the egg whites and sugar and fold into the egg yolks.
		11 oz Cake Flour					8 oz Cornstarch	4 ea	Sift the flour and cornstarch together 3 times. Fold into the above mixture and spread on to 4 sheet pans. Bake at 350° for 12 – 15 minutes.
1025	**Sheet** — Yields 3 ea	1 lb 6oz High Ratio Shortening					7lb Sugar		Add the dry ingredients to the creamed mixture. Mix slowly until it is smooth. Gradually add the eggs then the milk last. Spread on to 2 sheet pans and bake at 350° until golden brown or until an inserted toothpick is clear when removed.
		1lb 6oz Butter	oz Vanilla Extract	pint Eggs	qt Milk	oz Salt	5 oz Baking Powder	18 lb	
		6lb Cake Flour							

1. To prepare a pan for baking. Grease pan with shortening or butter. Line pan with parchment paper. Grease the pan again. Then dust the pan with flour. Shake pan and tap out the excess flour.
2. Always preheat oven before beginning mise en place for a cake batter.
3. In most cases allow the cake to cool for several hours before finishing, and decorating.

Torte and Entremet Components

No.	Component		1	1	2	3	4	8	Yield	Method of Preparation
1026	Chocolate Peanut Filling		cup crushed Feuilletine #851				oz Milk Chocolate	oz Peanut Butter	20 oz	Melt the chocolate. Mix in peanut butter. Add crushed cookies. Spread and cool.
1027	Coconut Biscuit	7 oz Butter	pinch Salt	ea Egg	oz Desiccated Coconut	oz Powdered Sugar	oz Cake Flour		18 oz	Cream the butter and sugar until light in texture. Add in coconut, egg, and salt. Mix well. Mix flour in last. Portion and spread. Bake at 350° until crisp. Use as a layer in a torte, petite gateaux or entremet to add texture.
	Crème	pint Milk / oz Cornstarch / 1 ¾ oz Butter	ea Vanilla Bean		oz Sugar		oz Egg Yolk	ea Gelatin Leaves		Heat the half the milk, sugar, and vanilla. Place the rest of the milk, egg yolk, gelatin and cornstarch in a bowl. Whisk the hot milk into the egg mixture. Whisk over a double boiler until thickened. Remove from heat and whisk in the butter. Cool.
1028	Crème Chiboust							oz Heavy Cream	2.5 lb	Whip the heavy cream to a soft peak. Fold into the above crème.
		5 oz Honey				oz Egg White				Bring the honey to a boil. Place the egg whites in a mixing bowl with whip. Slowly add the honey and whip to make a meringue. Fold the meringue into the crème.
1029	Dacquoise	5 oz Sugar / 1 ¾ oz Powdered Sugar	pinch Salt	tsp Dry Egg White			5 oz Almond Flour	oz Egg White	20 oz	Fold in the almond and powdered sugar. Pipe onto a silicon mat and bake at 360° until crisp. Use as a layer in a torte, petite gateaux or entremet to add texture.
1030	Japonaise	pint Egg White / 1 tbsp Vanilla	lb Crushed Hazelnuts		lb Sugar				4 lb	Warm the sugar and egg whites to 110° and whip the meringue to a soft peak with vanilla. Fold in nuts. Pipe into disks and bake at 250° until dry and crisp.
1031	Lemon Jam	cup Apricot Jam	ea Scraped Vanilla Bean		oz Lemon Juice		ea. Lemons Sliced-seeded	oz. Sugar	1.25 lb	Blanch the lemons in boiling water. Remove seeds. Puree all the ingredients together until smooth then simmer to reduce. Chill and spread
	Lemon Mousse Filling	10 oz Half And Half					oz Sugar	ea Egg Yolks		Heat the milk and sugar to 170°. Whisk into egg yolk and whip. Cool to 85°.
1032		6 oz Sugar				ea Gelatin Leaves	oz Lemon Juice	ea Egg Whites	2.5 lb	Bloom the gelatin in the lemon juice. Warm to melt. Combine the egg whites and sugar and heat to 110°. Whip to make a meringue. Whisk the gelatin in to the yolk mixture. Fold the meringue into the yolk mixture. Portion between cake slices and freeze to set.

Torte and Entremet Components

ID	Name	1	1	2	3	4	8	Y	Method of Preparation
1033	**Lemon**	5 oz Sugar	1 tbsp lemon zest		oz Egg Yolk	oz Soft Butter			Cream the butter and sugar together in a small mixer with a whip then whip. Add in the lemon zest and egg yolk. Whip until well blended.
	Sugar Biscuit	½ oz Baking Powder					oz Cake Flour	1.25 lb	Sift the flour and baking powder together then add to the above mixture. Spread into the desired disk size on a silicon mat. Bake at 350° until crisp. Use as a layer in a torte, petite gateaux or entremet to add texture.
1034	**Sugar Biscuit**	pinch Salt	ea Egg White		oz Powdered Sugar	oz Cake Flour	oz Butter	1 lb	Cream the butter and sugar together in a small mixer. Add in the egg white and salt and blend well. Add in the flour and mix until blended. Spread on to a buttered pan and bake at 350° until crisp. Use as a layer in a torte, petite gateaux or entremet to add texture.
1035	**Tiramisu Filling**	ea Egg Yolk	oz Marsala Wine	oz Cream Cheese	oz Sugar	oz Cream	oz Mascarpone Cheese	1 lb	Make a sabayon with the egg yolk and wine. Whip the cream cheese and mascarpone. Whip the cream. Fold all ingredients together.
1036	**Tropic**	2.5 oz Glucose	pinch Salt	oz Butter	oz Mango Puree	oz Passion Fruit Puree	oz Sugar	1.5 lb	In a small heavy bottomed pot caramelize the sugar and glucose to a medium brown color. Add in the salt and purees gradually.
	Caramel		ea Banana diced						Bring to a boil and add in butter, add banana and cool. Thinly spread in between layers of the cake or torte to change the flavor profile.
1037	**Vacherin**	2.5 cup Egg Whites	pinch Cream Of Tartar	tsp Vanilla Extract			oz Sugar		Prepare a soft peak meringue from the eggs, cream of tartar and sugar. Add the vanilla in last.
		1.5 cup Bread Flour						2.25 lb	Sift the bread flour over the meringue and fold in. Pipe into the desired disk size and slowly bake at 200° until crisp. Use as a layer for entremet glace or tortes.
1038	**Walnut Almond Crisp**	7.5 oz Ground Walnut	lb Sugar			oz Ground Almond	oz Egg White	2 lb	Warm the egg whites and sugar to 110° and whip to soft peaks. Fold the ground nuts in. Pipe on to silicon mats and bake at 300° until crisp. Use as a layer in a torte, petite gateaux or entremet to add texture

Icings, Buttercreams and Glazes

			1	1	2	3	4	8	Yield	Method of Preparation
1039	Almond Honey Glaze	6 oz Almonds	ea Lemon Zest	oz Glucose	oz Sugar	oz Honey	oz Butter		1 lb	Bring all ingredients to a boil. Add almonds and simmer until light brown. Pour over a yeast raised cake. Bienstich – Bee Sting
1040	Buttercream		lb Powdered Sugar	ea Egg White	drop Lemon Juice	drops Extract	oz Shortening	tbsp Butter	1.5 lb	Cream the sugar and fats. Add in the rest and whip until light and fluffy.
1041	Caramel Glaze		pint Water	lb Sugar	oz Glucose				5.5 lb	Boil the sugar, glucose and water until caramelized.
			pint Water	oz Gelatin	cups Cream					Bloom the gelatin in water. Slowly add the cream to the caramelized sugar. Then add the gelatin and water. Melt.
1042	Chocolate Ganache- Soft	5 ½ oz Chocolate	pint Cream						21 oz	Chop the chocolate. Bring the cream to a boil, pour over chocolate. Stir then cool.
1043	Chocolate Ganache-Medium	11 oz Chocolate	pint Cream						26 oz	Chop the chocolate. Bring the cream to a boil, pour over chocolate. Stir then cool.
1044	Chocolate Ganache – Hard	lb Chocolate	pint Cream						32 oz	Chop the chocolate. Bring the cream to a boil, pour over chocolate. Stir then cool.
1045	Chocolate Ganache Glaze	¾ oz Glucose	oz Butter			oz Dark Chocolate	oz Cream		9 oz	Chop the chocolate. Bring the other ingredients to a boil, pour over chocolate. Stir until blended then cool.
1046	Chocolate Glaze	6 oz Water			oz Apricot Glaze	oz Cocoa Powder	oz Glucose	oz Sugar	40 oz	Bring the items in this line to a boil.
		9 ¼ oz Dark Chocolate	1 oz Gelatin					oz Milk		Bloom the gelatin in milk. Add the apricot and cocoa powder to the boiled sugar and blend. Add the milk, blend in chocolate.
1047	Coffee Glaze		pint Cream	oz Sugar	lb Milk Chocolate	oz Butter	oz Coffee Bean		3.25 lb	Bring the cream ground coffee &sugar to 160°. Strain over chocolate, stir and cool.
1048	Cream Cheese Icing	10 oz Powdered Sugar	lb Cream Cheese	tbsp Vanilla Extract				oz Butter	2 lb	Cream the cheese, butter and sugar together then whip with extract.
1049	French Buttercream		recipe Swiss Buttercream #1052	recipe Crème Chiboust # 1028					5 lb	Prepare both recipes except for the whipped cream in the chiboust. Blend the butter cream with the chiboust.
1050	Fudge Icing	1 cup Corn Syrup	lb Sugar	cup Brown Sugar				oz Water	3.5 lb	Bring the items on this line to 239° in a copper pot.
			lb Powdered Sugar	tbsp Vanilla Extract		oz Butter		oz Baking Chocolate		Pour the boiled sugar over the chocolate in a mixing bowl to melt. Cream in the powdered sugar. Whip in butter last.
1051	Milk Chocolate Whipped Cream	26 oz Milk chocolate		qt Cream					3.75 lb	Melt the chocolate, fold soft whipped cream into chocolate to temper, and mix.
1052	Swiss Buttercream		lb Butter	lb Sugar	tsp Extract		oz Shortening	oz Egg White	2.5 lb	Whip fats and extract together. Warm the egg whites and sugar to 135°. In a clean bowl whip the egg whites and sugar to medium peaks. Make sure meringue is 90° Whip both together with flavorings.

Confections

#	Name		1	1	2	3	4	8	Yield	Method of Preparation
1053	Caramel Walnut Squares	14 oz Condensed Sweet Milk	lb Brown Sugar	cup Corn Syrup	drops Vanilla Extract	cup Walnuts		oz Salted Butter	3 lbs	Heat butter in a 2 quart sauce pot. Add sugar and syrup to melt. Slowly add the milk and simmer to 235°. Add nuts and stir until the mixture reaches 245°. Add vanilla, pour into buttered pan, cool. Recipe by my Dad- Frederick Julius Tiess
1054	Cherry Nut Bark	12 oz Chopped Milk Chocolate	lb Dried Cherries	lb Hazelnut – toasted	lb Dark Chocolate			oz Chopped White Chocolate	5 lb	Place everything except for the dark chocolate in the refrigerator for 20 minutes. Melt and temper the dark chocolate. Add the cooled Ingredients, spread over a textured silicon mat. Allow to set. Break
1055	Chocolate Caramel	1 ½ cup Honey		pint Cream	cup Sugar				2.5 lb	Bring all of the ingredients on this line to a boil. Cook until it reaches 255°.
			lb Dark Chocolate-chopped							Cool the above mixture to 120° and add in chopped chocolate, pour and cool to 85°. Pour into a pan to cool overnight. Portion into squares and coat with chocolate.
1056	Chocolate Praline Filling		lb Milk Chocolate					oz Praline Paste	1.25 lb	Melt the chocolate and place in an electric mixer with the praline paste. Mix and cool. Cool overnight. Coat with chocolate.
1057	Coconut Rum Filling		lb White Chocolate-chopped		oz Rum	oz Cream	cup Shredded Coconut		2 lb	Bring cream to a boil. Add the remaining ingredients. Stir and cool overnight. Portion into balls and coat with chocolate.
1058	Fudge – Chocolate	20 oz Dark Chocolate	can Evaporated Milk (13 oz)	lb Butter		tsp Vanilla	cups Sugar	oz Nuts	4 lb	Boil the sugar and milk to 238°. Pour over chocolate and butter. Add rest and cool 2 hours.
1059	Fudge- Peanut Butter	¼ lb Butter	can Evaporated Milk (13 oz)	cup Peanut Butter			cups Sugar	oz Marshmallow	3lb	Boil the sugar and milk to 238°. Pour over all other ingredients. Cool in a mixer. Pan
1060	Krokant	tbsp Glucose		cup Almond Slices			oz Cream	oz Sugar	1.75	Heat sugar and glucose to light brown, add the cream very slowly. Add the nuts and simmer until almonds are light brown. Cool
	Cream		lb Butter Cream #1040						1 lb	Place the above mixture in a mixer to break up the almonds and soften the caramel. Mix in the butter cream. Pipe this mixture into tempered chocolate molds.
1061	Marshmallow	¼ tsp Salt	tbsp Gelatin	oz Vanilla	cup Corn Syrup	cup Sugar	oz Powdered Sugar	oz Water	50 ea	Bloom gelatin and water. Heat sugar, salt, syrup to 243°. Place gelatin in mixer, slowly add hot syrup. Add vanilla or other flavoring. Whip 16 minutes on high. Dust pan with sugar. Pour in the mixture and set for 4 hours. Slice.
1062	Nut/Rice Crunch		lb Sweetened Praline Paste		cups Crisp Rice Cereal				1.25 lb	Whip the praline paste so that is very soft. Mix in the rice cereal. Cool overnight and portion into balls. Coat with chocolate.
1063	Pecan Caramels	1 ½ cup Honey		pint Cream	cup Sugar		tbsp Butter		3.5 lb	Bring all of the ingredients on this line to a boil. Cook until it reaches 255°.
			lb Pecans							Chop pecans. Add to caramel and cool.
1064	Truffle Filling		oz Liqueur	lb Chocolate	tsp Glucose	tbsp Butter	oz Cream		1.5 lb	Boil cream and glucose, add to grated chocolate. Stir, add liqueur and butter. Cool

Cookies

#	Name				1	2	3	4	8	Yield	Method of Preparation
1065	**Anisette Toast**	3/4 cup Oil	1 tsp Anise Extract	4½ cup Flour	cup Sugar tsp Vanilla	tbsp Water		ea Eggs tsp Baking Powder		4 dozen	Cream the oil and sugar with the eggs. Add in the liquids. Add the sifted dry ingredients and mix well. Form into 4 small loaves bake at 325° until golden brown and firm. Cool for 3 hours. Slice the loaves, toast in oven until light golden brown.
1066	**Biscotti**	11 oz Butter 3/4 oz Baking Powder	1½ lb Sugar	2½ lb Cake Flour	tsp Almond Extract	tsp Vanilla		cups Garnish	ea Eggs	6 dozen	Cream the butter and sugar with the eggs. Add in the liquids. Add the sifted dry ingredients and mix well. Form into 4 small loaves bake at 325° until golden brown and firm. Cool for 3 hours. Slice the loaves, toast in oven until light golden brown.
1067	**Biscotti Chocolate** Use chocolate, nuts, dried fruit for garnish	2¼ lb Sugar	3½ lb Cake Flour	1¼ oz Baking Powder	lb Butter	tsp Vanilla	cup Garnish	ea Egg Yolks oz Milk	ea Eggs oz Cocoa	6 dozen	Cream the butter and sugar with the eggs. Add in the liquids Add the sifted dry ingredients and mix well with garnish. Form into 4 small loaves bake at 325° until firm. Cool for 3 hours. Slice the loaves, toast in oven until crisp.
1068	**Brownie Cups**	6 oz Baking Chocolate 1¾ cup All Purpose Flour	3/4 cup Butter	5 ea Eggs	tsp Salt cup Nuts chopped	tsp Vanilla tsp Baking Powder	cup Sugar			4 dozen	Melt the chocolate and butter. Whip the eggs and sugar in a mixer on high speed until light and fluffy. Fold the melted chocolate & butter into the eggs. Sift the dry ingredients together. Add into the eggs. Mix in nuts last. 1 oz portion into greased (24) mini muffin tin. Bake 325° 15 minutes.
1069	**Butter Walnut** Tiess Family Christmas Cookies	1 ea Egg	3/4 cup Walnut	1 tsp Baking Powder	cup Powder Sugar tsp Vanilla Extract	cup Flour			oz Butter	2 dozen	Cream the butter and sugar with the eggs until light. Mix the dry ingredients together and combine with the mixture and extract. Add in the nuts. Drop the cookies on to a buttered pan, top with maraschino cherry. Bake at 350° until golden brown.
1070	**Chocolate Chip**	2/3 cup Sugar pinch Salt	2/3 cup Brown Sugar 2¼ cup Flour	2½ cup Chocolate Chips	tsp Baking Soda tsp Vanilla Extract	ea Eggs			oz Butter oz chopped Walnuts (optional)	4 dozen	Cream the butter and sugar with the eggs until light and fluffy. Mix the dry ingredients together and combine with the mixture and extract. Add in the nuts. Drop the cookies, quarter size, on to a buttered pan. Bake at 365° for 10 minutes.

Cookies

Item				1	2	3	4	8	Yield	Method of Preparation
1071 Chocolate Cherry Nut	1 ½ lb Chocolate							oz Butter		Melt the chocolate and butter
	5 oz Eggs	12 oz Bread Flour	1 oz Cocoa Powder	tsp Salt	tsp Baking Powder		oz Sugar		8 dozen	Cream with sugar, cocoa powder, and eggs. Add dry ingredients and mix well.
	6 oz Dry Cherries						oz Hazelnut - chopped	oz White Chocolate Chips		Add the nuts, cherries, and chips. Mix well. Drop the cookies, quarter size, on to a buttered pan. Bake at 350° 12 min.
1072 Chocolate Chunk Nut	½ cup Brown Sugar	1 cup Walnut	1 tsp Salt	cup Butter	tsp Vanilla		tbsp Peanut Butter	oz Dark Chocolate	8 dozen	Cream the butter and sugar with the eggs until light and fluffy. Mix in the dry ingredients with eggs
	2 ½ Cup flour			tsp Baking Powder	ea Egg		oz White Chocolate	oz Milk Chocolate		Fold 1d in nuts, chocolate. Spread on a buttered pan like brownies. Bake 325° for 25 min. Cool for 20 minutes – cut warm
1073 Gingersnaps	2 ½ cup Brown Sugar	4 ½ cup Flour		tsp Baking Soda	pinch Salt	ea Egg		oz Butter	6 dozen	Cream the butter and sugar with the eggs until light and fluffy.
	¼ cup Dry Ginger	1 ½ tsp Cinnamon	¼ tsp Nutmeg	pinch Baking Powder						Mix in the dry ingredients with the eggs. Pipe the cookies 3 inches apart. Bake at 350 ° for 10 minutes. This dough can also be used for gingerbread. Cool overnight and roll out, cut and bake at 325° until firm and brown.
1074 Lemon	1 cup Butter	¼ tsp Salt		cup Sugar	tbsp Lemon zest				6 dozen	Cream the butter and sugar with the eggs until light and fluffy. Add the zest, juice and extract with the flour and baking soda. Mix well
	1 oz Lemon Juice	1 tsp Baking Soda		tsp Vanilla	cup Flour			oz Powdered Sugar		Pipe the batter on to buttered pans and bake at 400° until golden brown. Cool and dust with powdered sugar.
1075 Linzer	¼ tsp Clove	¾ tsp Cinnamon		lb Butter	cup Hazelnut	cup Flour	ea Egg Yolk		4 dozen	Grind the hazelnuts to flour. Cream the butter and sugar with the eggs until light and fluffy. Add all the dry ingredients. Wrap and chill. Roll out and cut into circles. Two pieces per cookie. Remove the center of half the cookies. Bake at 350° until golden brown. Cool and sandwich with raspberry jam. Dust with sugar.
	2 tsp Lemon Rind	3 tbsp Cocoa		pinch Nutmeg	tsp Vanilla					
1076 Macaroon Almond	2 ½ lb Almond Paste	2 ½ lb Sugar		pint Egg Whites					6 dozen	Cream the almond paste and sugar. Mix in the whites then whip until smooth. Pipe. bake at 350° 12 min
1077 Macaroons Coconut	1 ¾ lb Egg White	5 oz Desiccated Coconut	6# Shredded Coconut		tsp Vanilla Extract		lb Sugar		6 dozen	Combine the eggs, sugar and warm to 106°. Fold in the remaining ingredients. Portion with a number 40 scope on to a parchment lined sheet pan 5x6 bake at 350° until golden brown.

150

Cookies

Item					1	2	3	4	8	Yield	Method of Preparation
1078	Macaroon- New York	12 oz Egg White	12 oz Sugar	pinch Salt	oz Flour	tsp Vanilla	oz Corn Syrup	oz Desiccated Coconut	oz Shredded Coconut	6 dozen	Combine the eggs, sugar and syrup. Warm to 100°. Whip to form a semi firm meringue. Fold in the remaining ingredients. Scoop on to a parchment paper lined pan. Bake at 350° until golden brown.
1079	Oatmeal	12 oz Brown Sugar ¼ oz Baking Soda	12 oz Pastry Flour ½ oz Baking Powder	12 oz Oats 2 oz Milk	tsp Salt	ea Egg tsp Vanilla	oz Molasses		oz Butter oz Raisin	6 dozen	Cream the butter and sugar with the eggs until light and fluffy. Mix the dry ingredients together and combine with the mixture and extract. Add in the raisins. Drop the cookies, on to a buttered pan. Bake at 365° for 10 minutes
1080	Peanut Butter	2 ea Egg 1 ½ tsp Baking Soda	1 ½ cup Brown Sugar	2 tsp Vanilla	lb Butter cup Peanut Butter	tbsp Honey tbsp Corn Syrup	cup Flour		oz Chopped Peanuts	4 dozen	Cream the butter and sugar with the eggs until light and fluffy. Mix the dry ingredients together and combine with the mixture and remaining ingredients. Drop the cookies on to a buttered pan. Mark, bake at 375° 10 min
1081	Pecan Sandies	¼ cup Brown Sugar pinch Salt	2/3 cup Sugar	1 tbsp Milk	lb Butter		cup Pecan	tsp Vanilla cup Flour			Cream the butter and sugar until light and fluffy. Mix the dry ingredients together and combine with the mixture and remaining ingredients. Drop the cookies on to a buttered pan. Bake at 325° 15 min
1082	Scottish Lemon	12 oz Butter ½ tsp Salt		1 tsp Vanilla	cup Powdered Sugar	oz Caster Sugar	cup Flour	ea Lemon zest		4 dozen	Cream the butter and sugar until light and fluffy creaming. Mix the dry ingredients together and combine with the mixture and remaining ingredients. Form into logs or rolls. Chill overnight, slice, top with sugar. Bake at 350° for 12 minutes.
1083	Speculaas	12 oz Powdered Sugar ¾ tsp Cardamom	5 oz Sugar ¾ tsp Clove	tbsp Lemon zest	lb Butter lb Pastry Flour		oz Egg	tsp Cinnamon	oz Flour	8 dozen	Cream the butter and sugar until light and fluffy creaming. Mix the dry ingredients together and combine with the mixture with rest.. Roll out the dough and press into speculaas molds. Cool for 1 hour. Unmold and refrigerate overnight. Bake at 375° until brown.
1084	Spritz	12 oz Almond Paste ¾ tsp Salt	6 oz Sugar 5 oz Egg		tsp Vanilla			oz Bread Flour	oz Cake Flour	6 dozen	Cream the butter and sugar with the almond paste until light. Add the eggs and whip. Combine the dry and mix until blended. Pipe and bake at 375° until golden brown.

Bar Cookies

Item	Item			1	1	2	3	4	8	Yield	Method of Preparation
1085	Cake Brownies	4 ¼ oz Cocoa	2 tsp Salt	lb Sugar	lb Shortening	oz Milk Powder			oz Corn Syrup	½ sheet pan	Combine and mix for 5 minutes on second speed, scrape down sides.
			14 oz Water	lb Bread Flour	tsp Baking Powder	ea Eggs		tsp Baking Soda			Add eggs and mix. Combine water with baking soda, add and mix. Sift rest and mix in. Bake at 375° 30 min
1086	Chocolate Coconut	24 oz Butter	1 ½ cup Brown Sugar	cup Sugar	tbsp Vanilla		cups Flour		ea Eggs	Full Sheetpan	Cream butter and sugar. Add the vanilla and eggs, blend well. Add salt and baking soda and blend again.
		24 oz Choc Chips	1 ½ tsp Salt	lb Coconut shredded		tsp Baking Soda	pints Oats				Add in oats, chips and coconut. Mix well Bake on a lined greased pan at 360° for 45 minutes.
1087	Fudge Brownies	1 tbsp Vanilla	1 ½ lbs Eggs	lb Bakers Chocolate	lb Butter / lb Walnuts	oz Semi Sweet Chocolate	lb Sugar	oz Cake Flour	oz Shortening	½ sheet pan	Melt shortening, butter and chocolates over double boiler. Whip eggs, sugar, flour, and vanilla for 10 minutes. Add half of the melted mix and mix. Add other half with nuts and mix. Pour on line greased pan. Bake 350° 40 min
1088	German Chocolate Brownies					cup Pecans chopped		oz Heavy Cream	oz Coconut Flakes	½ sheet pan	Prepare 1 recipe of the cake brownies that are baked with pecans folded in. Follow the same procedure as the turtle brownie topping. Mix the coconut into the caramel and add cream.
1089	Lemon Bars	5 each Lemon -juice and zest	½ cup Bread flour	cup Sugar (1st)	lb Butter		cups Sugar (2nd)	cups All Purpose Flour	ea Eggs	½ sheet pan	Prepare a cookie dough base by creaming the butter and 1st sugar, and then add in All purpose flour. Roll and bake on a greased pan for 15 minutes at 350°. Prepare filling by blending 2nd sugar with bread flour, add egg and mix in with lemon juice and zest. Pour into shell and bake for 20 – 25 minutes, powder sugar
1090	Oatmeal Breakfast	2 ½ cups Milk Powder	2 tbsp Vanilla	tbsp Baking Powder	tsp Cinnamon	oz Honey	cup Peanut Butter	cup Oatmeal	ea Ripe Banana	½ sheet pan	In a food processor puree everything except for oatmeal. Mix oatmeal in with spatula. Place on lined greased pan and bake in a 350° oven for 25 min.
1091	Praline Pecan Squares	1 tsp Salt	14 oz Sugar	lb Honey	lb Light Brown Sugar	lb Butter	lb Pecans	oz Dark Brown Sugar	oz Cream	½ sheet pan	Bring the butter and sugars to a boil for 7 minutes. Add honey and boil 4 minutes. Add in pecans and cream simmer 1 minute. Pour into prebaked short crust, Cool 12 hrs.
1092	Toffee Blondies	½ tsp Baking Soda	2 tsp Salt	quart All Purpose Flour	lb Butter	tsp Baking Powder	Ea Eggs	cups Brown Sugar	each Heath Bars chopped	½ sheet pan	Cream together sugar and butter. Add in vanilla and eggs and blend. Combine dry ingredients and mix in. Add in candy last. Bake on a greased lined pan at 350° for 35 minutes.
1093	Turtle Brownies	½ tsp Salt		cup Heavy Cream	cup Corn Syrup	cups Sugar	tsp Vanilla	oz Water	oz Pecan Halves	½ sheet pan	Prepare 1 recipe of the fudge brownies w/o nuts. Once cooled top with this mixture- Combine sugar, salt, syrup, water boil for 15 minutes or until light brown, temper in cream and vanilla. Top caramel pecans.

American Spices and Rubs

Ingredients ↓	1094 BBQ	1095 Chili	1096 Cajun	1097 Rotisserie	1098 Key West	1099 Tex Mex	1100 Savory Roast	1101 Bakery Blend	1102 Steak Rub	1103 Grilling Spice
Allspice					1 tbsp			2 tsp		
Caraway							1 tsp			
Cardamom								2 tsp		
Cayenne	½ tsp		1 tsp	1 tsp			¼ tsp			½ tsp
Celery Salt				4 tbsp						
Chili Powder										
Ancho		1 ½ oz				¼ cup				
Dark	4 tsp									½ tsp
Chipotle		¼ oz								
Cinnamon								1 cup		
Cloves								¼ tsp		
Coriander		¼ tsp						1 tsp		
Cumin	2 tsp	½ oz								
Fennel Seeds							1 tsp		1 tsp	
Ginger- fresh					4 oz			1 oz		
Mustard	1 tsp									
Nutmeg								1 tbsp		
Paprika	½ oz		1 tbsp	½ cup		½ cup	1 tbsp			1 tsp
Pepper										
Black	1 tsp		¾ tsp	½ cup	3 tbsp	3 tbsp	1 tbsp		2 tbsp	1 tsp
White			¾ tsp							
Basil							2 tsp			
Marjoram				6 tbsp						
Oregano	1 tsp	1 tsp	½ tsp	4 tbsp			1 tsp			
Parsley									1 bunch	
Rosemary				½ cup			1 tsp		2 tbsp	
Sage							2 tsp			
Thyme	1 tsp		1 tsp	6 tbsp	¼ cup		2 tsp		2 tbsp	1 tsp
Curry Powder	1 tsp			3 tbsp						
Old Bay Seasoning ®			2 tsp	3 tbsp						2 tsp
Garlic- minced		1 tbsp							1 tbsp	
Kosher Salt	¼ oz	2 tsp	3 tsp	2 lb		3 tbsp	5 oz		1 tbsp	1 tbsp
Sugar	2 tsp		1 tsp			3 tbsp		2 cups		
Olive Oil									2 oz	
Granulated Garlic	1 tsp		2 tsp			2 tsp	2 tsp			1 tsp
Onion					1 ea					
Tabasco®					1 tsp				½ tsp	
Soy					½ cup				2 tsp	
Key Lime Juice					½ cup					
Yields	3 oz	2.5 oz	1.5 oz	2.5 lb	1 pint	7 oz	9 oz	3 cup	5 oz	1 oz
Use to Flavor Of	5 lb	2 qt	3 lb	45 lb	5 lb	8 lb	20 lb	10 lb	5 lb	2 lb
	Beef Chicken Pork	Chili Beans Stew	Chicken Fish Seafood	Chicken Beef Pork	Shrimp Fish Scallop	Beef Pork	Pork Beef Lamb	Dough	Beef Lamb Pork	Fish Steak Chicken

Curry Rubs and Pastes

Recipe

Ingredients ↓	1104 Lamb Blend	1105 Tandoori Rub	1106 Curry Spice	1107 Garam Masala	1108 Saambar Spice	1109 Punjabi Masala	1110 Bese Bel	1111 Meen Fish	1112 Dhal Stew	1113 Korma Stew
Allspice										½ tsp
Cardamom										
Green	1 tsp	1 tbsp		10 pod						6 pod
Black						2 tbsp				
Cayenne		½ tsp							½ tsp	½ tsp
Ground Chilies			1 tbsp		2 tbsp		¼ cup			
Cinnamon	½ tsp		1 tbsp	1 stick		2 stick	4 ea			
Cloves				1 tsp		1 ½ tsp	6 ea			
Coriander Seed		3 tsp	¼ oz	1 tbsp	¼ cup	¼ cup	¼ cup			2 tbsp
Cumin	1 tsp	1 tbsp	¾ oz	1 tbsp	1 ½ tsp	¼ cup	3 tbsp			
Fenugreek			1 tsp	1 tsp	1 ½ tsp		3 tbsp			1 tsp
Ginger- fresh	¾ oz	2 oz	1 tbsp	1 tbsp						1 oz
Mace						½ tsp		1 tbsp		
Mustard Seed			1 tsp						1 tsp	
Nutmeg	¼ tsp			½ tsp						
Pepper										
Ground Black	1 tsp				1 ½ tsp					1 tsp
Cracked Black				2 tsp		3 tbsp				
Saffron		½ tsp								1 tsp
Turmeric	½ tsp		¼ oz		2 tbsp			1 tsp	1 tsp	
Bay Leaf				2 ea		4 ea				
Cilantro										1 bunch
Mint	1 oz fresh									
Garlic- minced	¾ oz	4 clove	1 tbsp	1 tbsp					2 clove	4 clove
Kosher Salt	1 tsp		1 tsp	2 tsp				2 tsp	1 tsp	1 tsp
Sugar										1 tsp
Ghee	1 tbsp							2 oz	1 oz	2 oz
Onions minced	4 oz							1 cup	1 cup	2 ea
Yogurt	4 oz	8 oz							1 cup	1 pint
Limes	1 ea	2 ea						2 ea		
Dal					3 tsp		1/3 cup		1 cup	
Yellow split pea					2 tsp		¼ cup			
Curry leaves							2 tbsp			
Coconut Flake							2/3 cup			
Chilies								4 ea	2 ea	1 ea
Coconut Milk							8 oz			
Yields	12 oz	14 oz	3 oz	½ cup	½ cup	¾ cup	2 cup	3 cup	3 ½ cup	3 cup
Use this spice or rub to season of	2 lb Lamb	3 lb Chicken Lamb	4 lb Chicken Fish	3 lb Beef Lamb	4 lb Fish Chicken	5 lb Lamb Beef	6 cup Mixed Veg	3 lb Fish	3 cup Liquid	4 lb Lamb Beef
Method of Preparation	Grill Stew	Grill Bake	Grill Stew	Grill Stew	Stew	Stew	Stew	Stew	Stew	Stew

154

Mexican and Caribbean Spices and Rubs

Recipe

Number→ Ingredients ↓	1114 Jamaican Jerk	1115 Bahaman Jerk	1116 Antiguan Curry	1117 Rum Jerk	1118 Havana Rub	1119 Bistek Rub	1120 Pollo Loco	1121 Picante Creole	1122 Ancho Rub	1123 Aruba Rub
Allspice	1 tsp		¾ tsp	2 tsp					½ tsp	
Cayenne				2 tsp	½ tsp			1 tsp		
Chili Powder			½ tsp			1 tsp	1 tsp			1 tsp
Ancho						½ tsp		1 tsp	2 oz	
Chipotle						1 tsp		2 tsp		
Cinnamon	1 tsp			1/2 tsp			½ tsp	1/4 tsp	¼ tsp	
Cloves							¼ tsp			
Coriander									1 tbsp	
Cumin			1 ½ tsp			1 tsp	1 tsp	1 tsp	2 tbsp	
Curry Powder			3 tsp		½ tsp					
Ginger- fresh	2 tbsp		2 tsp	1 tbsp						
Mustard	¼ cup									
Nutmeg				½ tsp						
Paprika			3 tsp			2 tsp	2 tsp			1 tsp
Pepper										
Black					1 tsp		2 tsp	2 tsp		1 tsp
Cracked Black						2 tsp				
White		1/2 tsp						½ tsp		
Cilantro					2 oz	1 bunch	1 bunch			1 bunch
Epazote						1 tsp		2 tsp		
Goya Sazon®					1 pack	2 pack	1 pack		1 pack	
Oregano		1 tsp				1 tsp	1 tsp	2 tsp		1 tsp
Thyme	1 tsp	1 tsp			1 tsp					½ tsp
Orange Juice					¼ cup		1 cup			
Scallions	2 ea		3 ea							
Limes	2 ea			4 ea		1 ea	3 ea			3 ea
Jalapeño		1 ea				1 ea	2 ea		6 ea	2 ea
Habanero	2 ea		1 ea				1 ea			
Poblano						1 ea				
Serrano					2 ea	2 ea				
Vinegar	1/4 cup				1 oz					
Garlic- minced	6 clove	2 clove	1 clove	3 clove	6 clove	5 clove	6 clove	2 clove	2 clove	3 clove
Kosher Salt	1 tsp	1 tsp	1 tsp		1 tbsp	1 tbsp	1 tbsp	1 tbsp		1 tbsp
Rum		1 tbsp		1 cup						
Brown Sugar	2 tbsp		1 tsp	½ cup					¼ cup	
Olive Oil	½ cup				2 oz	2 oz	1 oz		¼ cup	1 oz
Onions				1 cup						
Red Onions		1 cup								¼ cup
Yields	1 ½ cup	1 ¼ cup	½ cup	3 cup	¾ cup	1 cup	2 cup	½ cup	1 cup	¾ cup
Use to season of	3 lb Chicken Fish	3 lb Fish	1 lb Chicken Goat	3 lb Chicken Pork	4 lb Pork Chicken	4 lb Beef	6 lb Chicken	2 lb Fish Shrimp	4 lb Chicken Beef	3 lb Fish
Method of Preparation	Grill	Grill	Grill Stew	Grill	Grill	Grill	Grill	Grill Sauté	Grill	Grill

Punches and Cocktail Mixes

	Item		1	1	2	3	4	8	Yield	Method of Preparation
1124	Bloody Mary Mix	1 tbsp Tabasco	gal Tomato Juice	tsp Black Pepper	tsp Celery Salt	tbsp Worcestershire	ea Lemons Juiced	oz Cocktail Sauce	1 Gallon	Whisk all ingredients together. Refrigerate overnight and strain. Per portion 1 shot of Vodka to 6 oz mix, shake, ice, celery garnish.
1125	Cafe Diablo	2 stick Cinnamon	peel Lemon / tbsp Sugar	peel Orange	oz Brandy	oz Cointreau	tbsp Cloves	shots Espresso	6 Demitasse Cup	Stud the lemon and orange peels with cloves. Attach forks to the ends of the peels. Place in flambé pot with sticks. Add alcohol warm to 120°. Flambé and dust with sugar. Add espresso.
1126	Champagne Punch	1cup Water	cup Sugar	pint Orange Juice	bottle Champagne	oz Grand Marnier	ea Lemons-Juiced, Zest	oz Cognac	Serves 12	Prepare syrup from zest, sugar and water. Strain and chill. Mix all chilled ingredients. Garnish with citrus slices.
1127	Christmas Punch	1 ea Lemon and Orange	bottle Red Wine	bottle Dark Rum	cups Sugar	cup Hot Water	bag Orange Pekoe tea	ea Clove	Serves 20	Steep tea in water for 10 minutes with clove studded orange, and sugar Remove tea bags Juice lemon and combine with rest
1128	Collins Mix		cup Water			oz Lemon Juice	oz Sugar	Juniper Berries	12 oz	Boil sugar, water, juniper for 2 minutes and strain. Add juice and chill. For 1 portion stir 2 oz mix, 2 oz Gin, and 3 oz club soda. Cherry garnish with a slice or orange
1129	Daiquiri Mix	5 cups Sugar	cup Lime Juice	cup Water	quarts Fruit				1 Gallon	Dissolve sugar and water. Puree fruit and juice. Blend, chill. Strawberry or Banana. 1 Portion blend 6 oz mix, .2 oz rum, 1 cup ice
1130	Egg Nog	1 tbsp Cinnamon	pint pasteurized Egg Yolk	qt ½ +1/2 / tsp Nutmeg	cup Sugar / tbsp Vanilla	pint Heavy Cream	oz Grand Marnier	oz Bourbon	3 quarts	Combine egg yolk with spice, sugar, extract, and alcohol. Whisk in half and half cream and 1 pint of heavy cream. Whip remaining cream to a soft peak. Fold nog into cream. Refrigerate overnight. Garnish with additional cinnamon.
1131	Margarita Mix		cup Agave Nectar	cup Orange Juice	cup Lime Juice		oz Warm Water		28 oz	Pour nectar in pitcher. Use warm water to rinse cup measure, mix well. Blend in juices. 1 portion shake 5 oz mix 1oz Grand Marnier, 2 oz Tequila. Salt rim garnish, wedge lime.
1132	Pina Collada Mix		cup Coconut Milk	pint Pineapple Juice		cups Fresh Pineapple		oz Coconut Cream	48 oz	Puree all ingredients together and chill. For 1 portion blend 6 oz of puree, 1 cup crushed ice, 1.5 oz white rum, and 1 oz dark rum. Pineapple and Cherry garnish
1133	Rainbow Punch		qt Rainbow Sherbet	liter Sprite		pint Fruit Punch	slice Lemon	slice Orange	Serves 15	Prepare ice ring with citrus slices and water. Mix punch with soda. Float sherbet scoops + ring.
1134	Sour Mix	2 ea limes and lemons	cup Key Lime Juice	tbsp Powdered Egg white	pint Water	cup Sugar	oz Corn Syrup	oz Lemon Juice	80 oz	Slice citrus. Boil water, sugar, syrup and citrus for 5 minutes. Cool and strain. Whisk in rest and chill. 1 Portion 2 oz mix to 2 oz Spirit. Shake with 1 cup crushed ice. Cherry Garnish
1135	Spiced Cider Punch	6 stick Cinnamon	gal Apple Cider		ea Orange			ea Cloves	Serves 12	Stud the orange with cloves and cinnamon. Warm cider to 130°. Add oranges. Steep 1 hour.
1136	Summer Sangria		cup Orange Juice	ea sliced Oranges	bottle Red Wine	ea Peaches Sliced	oz Grenadine	oz Brandy	Serves 12	Mix all ingredients together and chill for 8 hours.
1137	Wassail	¾ cup Sugar	qt Cranberry Juice	qt Apple Juice	ea Lemons Sliced	stick Cinnamon	Bottles Red Wine	oz Calvados	Serves 20	Boil apple juice, lemon slices cinnamon and sugar. Add the rest and heat to 120.
1138	White Sangria		ea sliced Lime	ea sliced Lemon	bottle White Wine	ea Apples Parisienne	oz Triple Sec	oz Vodka	Serves 12	Mix all ingredients together and chill for 8 hours.

Emergency Preparations – Quick response solutions to feed 50 to 500 people in 3 hours or less. (Hold and Serve all preparations at 140° or higher)

	Item	1/2	1	2	3	4	10	Portion Size	Method of Preparation
1139	Brown Beans and Ham	lb Bacon Fat	gallon Water	lb Onion diced	lb Smoked Ham Pieces	lb Dry Pinto Beans		Yields 50 6 oz Portions	Place beans, ham and water covered in steamer for 1 hour. In a 5 gallon kettle sweat the onions and fat until very tender. Add beans and stock- Simmer 1 hour, shred ham. Serve with cornbread and diced onion
1140	Brunswick Stew	gallon Celery diced	gallon Onion diced / cup Cajun Spice Blend	lb Diced Bacon	# 10 Can Diced Tomato w/ Green Chili	Ea 2.5 lb box Frozen 5 Way Veg	lb Cooked Deboned Chicken	Yields 100 6 oz Portions	In a 20 gallon kettle, render bacon, sweat onions and celery. Add tomatoes, plus 2 can of water. Add spice and simmer for 30 minute. Add veg simmer 15 minute. Add Chicken, heat to 185°, season to taste. Serve with biscuits.
1141	Chicken and Biscuits	gallon Celery diced	gallon Onion diced / quart Flour	lb Butter	gallon Chicken stock	ea 2.5 lb box Frozen 5 Way Veg	lb cooked Deboned Chicken	Yields 100 6 oz Portions	In a 20 gallon kettle, melt butter, sweat onions and celery, add flour and cook for 10 minutes. Add Chicken stock, a sachet of herbs and simmer 30 minutes. Add in veg and chicken, simmer 20 minutes, season to taste, Serve with biscuits
1142	Chicken Jambalaya	gallon Celery diced / lb Butter	gallon each Onion and Peppers diced / cup Cajun Spice Blend	# 10 Can Diced Tomato w/ Green Chili	lb diced Smoked Sausage	lb Converted Rice	lb cooked Deboned Chicken	Yields 50 10 oz Portion	In a tilt skillet or large braiser with lid, sweat onions, celery and peppers in butter. Add in sausage and rice with 1 gallon of water or chicken stock; add tomatoes, spice and chicken. Cover and gently simmer or braise for 25 minutes. Season to taste
1143	Arroz con Pollo	gallon Green Pepper diced	gallon Onion Diced / cup chop Garlic — oz Goya Sazon® / pint olive Oil	# 10 can Salsa or Sofrito	ea 2.5 lb boxes Frozen Peas	lb Converted Rice	lb Roasted Chicken Thighs (50)	Yields 50 12 oz Portion	In a tilt skillet or large braiser with lid, sweat onions, garlic and peppers in oil. Add in sofrito or salsa and rice with 1 gallon of water or chicken stock, Sazon and chicken. Cover and gently simmer or braise for 25 minutes. Finish with steamed green peas. Season
1144	Chili	50 lb Bag Onion diced	Case #10 can Dark Red Kidney Bean / Case #10 Can Pinto Beans — 60 lb case Ground Meat	# 10 can Diced Green Chili / 32 oz jar Garlic	20 oz container Dark Chili Powder / #10 can Tomato Puree	#10 can Refried Bean / #10 can Corn	# 10 can Diced Tomato w/ Green Chili	Yields 500 8 oz Portions	In a 50 gallon kettle or tilt skillet brown the ground meat. Add in the diced onions and spices with 3 gallon water or stock. Add in refried beans, mix and simmer. Add in remaining ingredients and simmer for 2 hours over medium low heat. Season with salt, cumin, sugar to taste. Serve with cornbread or with fried corn tortilla chips. Offer additional chili sauce, jalapeños, and cheese.
1145	Beef and Rice Casserole	cup Beef Base	gallon Onion diced / Ea 5lb box Frozen Corn	5 lb chub ground beef	Ea 2.5 lb boxes Frozen Peas	lb Converted Rice	each Large Carrots diced	Yields 50 12 oz portions	In a tilt skillet or large braiser with lid, brown the ground beef then sweat onions. Add in rice with 1 gallon of water, beef base and carrot Cover and gently simmer or braise for 15 minutes. Add veg cover and cook for 10 more minutes. Season to taste
1146	Pasta Bolognese	gallon Parm Cheese grated	gallon Whole Milk / Pint Flour — lb minced Garlic	gallon Mirepoix small dice	gallons Marinara or Tomato Sauce	ea 5lb Chub Ground Meat	lb Penne or Macaroni	Yields 100 10 oz portions	In 1 large kettle brown the ground meat, add in mirepoix, garlic. Add in flour to make a roux, add milk to simmer for 10 minutes. Add in tomato sauce simmer 10 minutes. In a separate kettle cook the pasta in 15 gallons of boiling salted water until al dente. Drain and mix into the sauce. Finish with cheese.

Emergency Preparations – Quick response solutions to feed 50 to 500 people in 3 hours or less. (Hold and Serve all preparations at 140° or higher)

Item			1	2	3	4	10	Portion Size	Method of Preparation
1147 Pork Burgoo	2 gallon Tomato Sauce	gallon Onion diced	ea 5lb box Frozen Corn	ea 2.5 lb boxes Frozen Okra	ea 2.5 lb boxes Frozen Peas	gal Potato diced cooked	lb Ground Pork	Yields 50 12 oz portions	In a tilt skillet or large braiser with lid, brown the ground pork then sweat onions. Add the tomato sauce, with ½ can water. Cover and gently simmer or braise for 15 minutes. Add veg cover and cook for 30 more minutes. Season with thyme, pepper and salt. Add the potatoes in last
1148 Red Beans and Rice	½ gallon Celery diced	gallon Onion diced	cup Cajun Spice Blend	lb Bacon diced	#10 Can Diced Tomato w/ Green Chili	#10 can Red Beans	lb Smoked Sausage	Yields 100 6 oz Portions	In a 20 gallon kettle, render bacon, sweat onions and celery. Add tomatoes, plus 1 can of water. Add spice and simmer for 30 minute. Add beans and sausage. Serve over rice
1149 Turkey Noodle Soup	8 oz Butter	gallon Celery diced	5 lb Box Noodles	gallon Onion diced	ea Turkey Breasts cooked diced	ea 2.5 lb box Frozen 5 Way Veg	gal Turkey Stock or Broth	Yields 100 6 oz Portions	In a 20 gallon kettle, melt butter, sweat onions and celery. cook for 10 minutes. Add stock, a sachet of herbs and simmer 30 minutes. Add in veg and noodles, simmer 10 minutes, season to taste, add turkey last heat to 165°. Serve with rolls and biscuits
1150 Ziti- Baked	10 lb Ground Meat or bulk Italian Sausage	quart Eggs	gallon Ricotta Cheese	lb Parmesan Cheese grated	gallons Marinara or Tomato Sauce	lb Mozzarella grated	lb Penne or Macaroni	Yields 100 10 oz portions	In 1 large kettle brown the ground meat, add in tomato sauce simmer 10 minutes. In a separate kettle cook the pasta in 15 gallons of boiling salted water until al dente. Drain and mix into the half of the sauce. Mix ricotta with eggs and parmesan, season with basil, oregano and garlic salt. Layer pasta with ricotta mix, top with sauce and mozzarella cheese. Bake in oven until it reaches 185° and brown.

Checklist

Flatware kits w/napkin _____
Styro Clamshell, Plate _____
Side Towels _____
Beverage Cups _____
Beverages _____
Ice Coolers w/Ice _____
Chafing Dishes _____
Sterno® _____
Serving Utensils _____
Sanitizer Wipes _____
Cambro® - Hotbox _____

Hand Sanitizer _____
Service Gloves _____
Hairnet _____
Potable Water _____
Matches _____
Fire Extinguisher _____
First Aid Kit _____
Utility Knife _____
Flashlight _____
Cell Phone _____
Ware washing Supplies _____

Classical Cuisine Preparations

	Item	1	2	3	4	Use	Method of Preparation
1151	**Agnes Sorel**	10 oz Sauce Supreme recipe 74	Tbsp Chopped Parsley	oz. Julienne Cooked Beef Tongue	oz. Julienne Mushroom	Sauce	Melt mushrooms in butter, add a few drops of sherry, warm tongue, add parsley and season.
1152	**Algérienne**	cup. Eggplant Macedoine; Paprika, Salt, Pepper	Tbsp Mince Garlic; ea. Tomatoes Concasse	oz. Brunoise Onion	ea. Chicken Breast; 2 Tbsp butter	Chicken	Season, dredge, sauté in olive oil, add veg, simmer and finish with butter.
1153	**Alexandra**	cup Chiffonade Butter Lettuce	Tbsp Whole Butter		ea. Chicken Quenelles	Garnish	Use ¼ recipe 229 with pinch of Turmeric for the Quenelles, rewarm with lettuce and butter.
1154	**Allemande**	10 oz Sauce Supreme recipe 74	cup Julienne Mushroom	oz. Whole Butter		Sauce	Prepare sauce, melt mushrooms in butter, season. Sauce item then garnish with julienne mushrooms.
1155	**Alsacienne**	cup Sauerkraut recipe 566	Tbsp Chopped Parsley	lb. Gold Potatoes - Tourne	Portions Sausage recipe 263	Garnish	Prepare 2-inch sausages, sheep's casing. Serve with Sauerkraut and cooked, buttered potatoes. Finish with parsley.
1156	**Amandine**	½ cup White Wine	Tbsp Chopped Parsley	oz. Almond Slivers	oz. Clarified Butter; 4 Tbsp butter	Garnish	Shallow fry almonds in clarified butter, drain and save butter for sauté. Deglaze sautéed protein with wine, mount in butter, add parsley and almonds, season.
1157	**Américaine**	cup Sauce Americaine recipe 73	oz. Whole Butter	ea. Cooked Lobster	Sprig Chervil	Lobster	Blanch lobster 2 minutes then prepare sauce Americaine from shells. Butter poach lobster medallions. Use as a garnish with chervil.
1158	**Ancienne**	6 oz Fish Mousseline recipe 229	Tbsp. Brunoise Truffle	Tbsp. Lobster Caviar	oz. Crayfish; 10 oz Sauce Nantua recipe 73	Fish	Prepare mousseline, fold in crayfish, truffle and caviar. Use to chemise fish or timbale, sauce under.
1159	**Andalouse**	¾ cup Sautéed Brunoise Eggplant	ea. Tomatoes Concasse	oz. Rice Pilaf	ea. Sweet Pimento	Garnish	Blanch peel Pimento, add tomato to eggplant and reduce dry, add rice and peas. Stuff pimentos then reshape using cheesecloth.
1160	**Anglaise**	lb. Gold Potatoes - Tourne	Tbsp Chopped Parsley		4 Tbsp butter	Potato	Carefully cook tourne potatoes until tender, toss with butter and parsley and season with salt and white pepper. Use as garnish.
1161	**Ardennaise**	½ cup Stock; tsp Juniper	cup Diced Onion	oz. Diced Bacon	oz. Butter; 2 Tbsp Chop Parsley	Potato	Prepare fondant potato disk, render bacon in butter, sauté onions then remove. Brown fondant, add stock. Season, juniper, braise with rest.
1162	**Basquaise**	4 Portions Poulet Sauté Basquaise recipe 495; ea. Roasted Green Pepper-Julienne	Tbsp Minced Garlic; ea. Tomatoes Concasse	Tbsp. Minced Onion	Portion Pomme Anna; 1½ oz EVOO	Chicken	To prepare the tomato fondue. Melt onions and garlic, add tomato, season with thyme. Add peppers and simmer. Use atop the portions of Pomme Anna to accompany the Chicken Basquaise.
1163	**Bayonnaise**	½ cup Minced Onion; oz. Serrano Ham-Brunoise	cup Sliced Mushrooms; oz. Petite Basque Cheese-Grated	Tbsp. Butter	ea. Tomatoes; Chopped Parsley and Chive	Garnish	Peel tomatoes, shape into cups. remove seeds and reserve juice, concasse inner pulp. Sauté ham, onion, mushroom in butter, add concasse, juice, season, fill cup. Top with cheese and bake, herb garnish.
1164	**Bénédictine**	½ cup cream	Clove Garlic; Tbsp. Chopped Truffle	oz. EVOO	oz. Salt Cod	Garnish	Soak cod overnight. Poach 5 minutes and flake. Heat oil, cream, garlic and puree with cod, season, add truffle to brandade.
1165	**Bercy**	1 oz White Wine; Tbsp Lemon Juice	Tbsp Minced Shallot; Tbsp Chopped Parsley	Tbsp Nouilly Prat	ea. Sole Filet; 4 oz butter	Fish	Season, fold filet. Lay in buttered dish. Warm wines, shallot, juice, baste liquid on top, season. Top with Tbsp of butter. Garnish.
1166	**Berny**	½ recipe 557; cup Ground Almond	lb. Gold Potatoes Shape-large olives	Tbsp. Brunoise Truffle		Potato	Prepare duchesse, mix in truffle, form into corks. Standard bread with ground almond coating. Fry until golden brown, season. Pomme William can be made the same way without the truffle. The croquette is shaped into a pear shape.
1167	**Berrichone**	Pint Chicken Stock	lb. Gold Potatoes	Tbsp Chopped Parsley	oz. Bacon Diced; ½ cup Brunoise Onion	Potato	Render bacon, sauté onions. Mix with stock lay in casserole with potatoes, cover, bake, season, garnish with parsley.
1168	**Bizontine**	Portions Braised Lettuce recipe 553	cup Cauliflower Puree recipe 551		Portions Duchesse recipe 557	Garnish	Form duchesse into croustade in small buttered tins. Pipe in a firm cauliflower puree, served with braised little gem or baby romaine.
1169	**Bonne Femme**	½ cup White Wine; ½ ea. Lemon Juiced	Tbsp Chopped Parsley; Tbsp Beurre Manie	oz. Chopped Mushroom	ea. Sole Filet; 4 oz Fish Fumet	Fish	Melt 2 oz of butter in casserole, line with chopped mushroom. Season & fold filet, place over mushroom, add wine, lemon, stock. Bake in oven until firm, thicken, season, nappe, glaze, garnish.

All recipes equal 4 portions, the use column specifies the application.

Classical Cuisine Preparations

No.	Item	1	2	3	4				Use	Method of Preparation
1170	Bordelaise	1 ½ cup White Bordeaux	Sprig Basil tbsp Tarragon	cup Mirepoix	ea. Cooked Lobster	oz. Brandy	oz. Whole Butter	3 ea. Egg Yolk	Lobster	Blanch lobster 2 minutes. Save legs, knuckle and claw shells once shucked cut tail in half. Sauté shells in 1 oz butter with mirepoix, add wine and brandy, flambé and reduce nappe, strain. Reheat lobster with herbs, thicken with egg yolk. Nappe sauce over.
1171	Boulangère	1 sprig Rosemary	Tbsp Chopped Parsley		lb. Gold Potatoes - Tourne -8 ea.		2 oz. Butter	ea. Cipollini Onions	Potato	Lightly fry the potatoes and onions until brown then finish in oven with stock and herb alongside roasted chicken until tender, season, and garnish with parsley
1172	Bouquetière	4 ea. Cauliflower Florets	cup Diced Haricot Vert	cup Green Peas	oz. Butter	oz. Hollandaise Recipe 58	Portion Oval Cut Carrot & Turnip Recipe 550	4 Portion Chateau recipe 1186	Garnish	Prepare root vegetables. Blanch green veg and reheat with remaining butter and season. Arrange vegetables by separating colors, nappe hollandaise over the cauliflower.
1173	Bourgeoise		oz. Whole Butter	oz. Bacon- diced	ea. Carrots		ea. Pearl Onions		Garnish	Trim carrots to look like garlic cloves, halve onions, glaze both and refresh in bacon infused butter. Serve with roasted chicken.
1174	Bourguignonne	12 ea. Pearl Onion and Button Mushroom- Saute	cup Pinot Noir	cup Fish Fumet	Tbsp. Beurre Manie	oz. Demi-Glace	Portion Fish	1 sachet of Fennel, Thyme, Pepper	Fish	Combine sachet, wine, and fumet. Simmer covered. Season and braise fish with mushroom and onion, remove, add Demi reduce then thicken with beurre manie. Add chopped parsley to garnish and nappe.
1175	Brabaçonne	¼ tsp Sugar	tsp. Lemon Juice		Head Endive	tsp. Chopped Parsley	1 cup Stock		Garnish	Place all items in pot, except parsley and braise until tender, finish with parsley and seasoning.
1176	Bréhan	ea. Cauliflower Florets	Tbsp Chopped Parsley		oz. Hollandaise Recipe 58	oz. Fava Bean Puree	ea. Artichoke Bottoms	4 portions Fingerling	Garnish	Prepare artichokes barigoule recipe 548. Fill with puree, cook cauliflower, nappe hollandaise, Roast potato finish with parsley.
1177	Bressane	See method recipe 230	Tbsp Flour	ea. Truffle	oz. Foie Gras	oz Ground chicken thigh	Dash of Cognac	2 Tbsp Cream	Chicken	Follow method for recipe 230 with these amounts. Slice 4 slices of truffle soak in cognac and mince rest, fold in. Truffle slice under skin and pipe farce. Roast.
1178	Bretonne	1 sachet d' espice	cup White Beans- Soak	cup Mirepoix- small dice	oz. Bacon Lardon- small dice	Tbsp Butter	cups Stock	1 Tbsp Chopped Parsley	Garnish	Sauté bacon, add mirepoix, sachet and stock and simmer 20 minutes. Strain and reserve. Add beans to liquid and simmer gently until very tender, reduce liquid, season add parsley.
1179	Bruxelloise		oz. Butter				portions Brussel Sprouts	4 Portions Anglaise recipe 1160	Garnish	Fabricate Brussel Sprouts and blanch until tender. Shock. At service reheat and toss with butter, season. Serve with potatoes
1180	Cardinal	Pinch Cayenne	cup Fish Stock	cup Cream	ea. Lobster Shells	oz. Whole Butter	oz. Béchamel recipe 40	2 oz. White Wine	Sauce	Sauté shells in butter, deglaze with wine and add the stock. Simmer slowly, strain and combine with béchamel and cream, simmer to thicken. Season
1181	Catalane	1 sachet d' espice	ea. Onion small dice	cup Rice- use short grain Spanish Rice	Tbsp. Butter	cups Stock	Clove Garlic minced	¼ cup Brunoise Red Pepper	Rice	Sauté rice with butter add pepper, onion, and garlic. Add stock, sachet, bring to simmer, braise in oven until tender, finish parsley.
1182	Célestine	Tbsp Pearl Tapioca	tsp Finely Chopped Truffle		oz. Chicken Mousseline 229	ea. Crepes- recipe 3	Cups Consommé recipe 4		Soup	Thicken consommé with soaked tapioca. Layer truffle mousse between 3 crepes and press, bake between silpat. Cut 1 inch round disks of crepe to garnish.
1183	Champenoise	1 tsp. Minced Shallot	Tbsp. Dijon Mustard	Tbsp. Fine chop Fines Herb	oz. Champagne Vinegar		oz. Grapeseed Oil		Dressing	Prepare simple vinaigrette starting with mustard and vinegar first, add shallot, drizzle in oil. Season with salt and fresh black pepper. Finish with herbs.
1184	Charcuterie	1 tsp. Minced Shallot	Tbsp. Whole Grain Mustard	oz. Brunoise Cornichons	oz. Champagne Vinegar		oz. Salad Oil	1 Tbsp. Chopped Parsley	Dressing	Prepare simple vinaigrette starting with mustard and vinegar first, add shallot, drizzle in oil. Season with salt and fresh black pepper. Finish with cornichons and parsley.
1185	Chasseur	10 oz Sauce Chasseur recipe 44			oz. Clarified Butter	oz. White Wine	ea. Chicken Breast		Chicken	Season and dredge chicken, brown in butter then remove excess fat. Deglaze with wine and pan roast until cooked. Add in sauce and simmer, adjust season
1186	Chateau		Tbsp Chopped Parsley		lb. Gold Potatoes Tourne.	oz. Clarified Butter	Tbsp butter		Potato	Carefully sauté tourne potatoes until brown in clarified butter. Finish in oven until tender toss with butter and parsley and season with salt and white pepper

All recipes equal 4 portions, the use column specifies the application.

Classical Cuisine Preparations

	Item		1	1	2	3	4	4	Use	Method of Preparation
1187	Chevalière	10 oz Sauce Nantua recipe 73	cup Crawfish Meat	cup Mushroom quarters	oz. Nouilly Prat	oz. Fish Mousseline recipe 229	ea. Sole Filet	8 ea. Oyster	Fish	Combine mousseline with ½ crayfish, fill sole filets. Poach sole and mushroom add oysters. Add crayfish to sauce, garnish with truffle.
1188	Chimay	cup Glacage Royale recipe 56	ea. Chicken Breast Torchon	Tbsp. Fine Julienne Truffle	oz. Duxelle Recipe 10			1- quart Chicken Stock	Chicken	Poach a truffle infused torchon of chicken breast is stock. Allow to relax, reduce liquid for sauce. Top each medallion with duxelle and glacage to reheat.
1189	Chinonaise	4 Portions Anglaise Potato recipe 1160			Cups Chicken Stock	oz. Forcemeat	ea. Savoy Cabbage Leaves		Garnish	Blanch leaves and shock. Fill with forcemeat and braise with stock, serve with potatoes.
1190	Choisy	2 oz Fish Veloute recipe 76	Tbsp. Whole Butter	Tbsp. Fine Chopped Parsley	cup Chiffonade Butter Lettuce	oz. Stock	8 ea. Chateau Potatoes		Garnish	Quickly wilt lettuce in stock, remove, reduce liquid, add veloute and butter. Finish with parsley, use along with potatoes.
1191	Clamart	½ cup tiny Pearl Onions	oz. Butter	cup Shelled Peas	cup Chiffonade Lettuce		Tart Shells	4 ea. Macaire recipe 559	Garnish	Blanch peas and onions, sauté with lettuce and butter. Season, fill shells. Serve with Macaire Potatoes
1192	Colbert	4 ea. Quail Egg				oz. Brunoise Spring Vegetable	Cups Consommé recipe 4		Soup	Reheat consommé. Blanch all vegetables separately and shock. Poach quail egg. Garnish consommé with spring vegetables and poached egg.
1193	Commodore	4 ea. Fish Quenelle recipe 229	Pint Mussels		oz. Butter	oz. White Wine	4 ea. Portions Poached Fish	4 ea. Crayfish Croquette	Fish	Poach mussels in wine, remove and thicken with butter. Refresh quenelles in liquid then plate with a border of sauce.
1194	Crecy	3 ea. Egg Yolks	ea. Shallot	ea. Egg	Tbsp Basmati Rice	ea. Carrots- Peel, chopped small	oz. Cream	1 oz Butter	Garnish	Sauté shallot and carrot with rice, add in ½ cup water and simmer until fully cooked and dry. Puree until smooth with cream, pass through sieve. Combine with eggs and season. Portion into soufflé cups and bake in waterbath until firm.
1195	Créole	½ clove minced Garlic	Tbsp. Chopped Parsley		tsp. Brunoise Chile Pepper	oz. Roasted Pepper Julienne	4 ea. Portions Fish	4 ea. Tomatoes stuffed with rice	Fish	Season fish with salt, pepper, cayenne. Dredge and pan fry. Remove and add garlic, chiles, parsley, nappe over fish. Garnish with peppers on top and stuffed tomatoes as an accompaniment.
1196	Daumont	1 cup Sauce Nantua recipe 73	cup Crawfish Salpicon		oz. Nouilly Prat	oz. Fish Mousseline recipe 229	ea. Sole Filet	4 ea. Mushroom Fluted	Fish	Combine mousseline with ½ crayfish. Prepare paupiettes Shallow poach in oven. Add crayfish to sauce. Saute mushroom in butter.
1197	Dauphine		cup Pâte au Choux Recipe 17	cup Duchesse Potato Recipe 9	Tbsp Potato Starch				Potato	Prepare both recipes and chill, mix with starch. Place in pastry bag with straight tip. Pipe into cork shapes, standard bread and fry to order. Pomme Champignon is shaping the preparation into small mushrooms before frying.
1198	Demidoff	1 pint Chicken Stock	ea Julienne Carrot, Turnip, Celery	each Chicken prepared for Poulet Sauté	oz. Demi Glace	oz. Madera	each Petite slices of Smoked Ham and Truffle	1 cup White Wine	Chicken	Season and brown chicken in butter. Deglaze with wine and remove liquid, strain fond. Add stock, simmer veg until tender. Prep poulet saute, use all liquids then finish with veg, truffle, ham.
1199	Diable	1/3 cup Panko	oz Melted Butter	Tbsp. Chopped Dill	Tbsp. Dijon		ea. Salmon Portions		Fish	Combine panko, butter, dill and season. Season fish and brush with Dijon, coat with crumb mixture and broil until golden brown.
1200	Diablotin	4 slices of French Bread	Pinch Cayenne	oz. Parmesan	oz. Sauce Mornay recipe 63		Cups Consommé recipe 4	¼ tsp Paprika	Soup	Reheat thickened consommé. Combine cheese, cayenne, paprika. Toast bread cover with cold mornay, top with cheese, broil to golden brown, float crouton on top
1201	Diane		oz. Brunoise Celeriac	oz. Pearl Barley	oz. Pheasant Mousseline recipe 229		Cups Consommé recipe 4		Soup	Use ground pheasant for consommé flavor, make quenelles from mousseline. Garnish with blanched celeriac and cooked rinsed barley.
1202	Diplomate	¼ recipe 69- no Tarragon	Tbsp Brunoise Truffle	ea. Lobster Claw Salpicon	oz. Nouilly Prat	oz. Fish Mousseline recipe 229	ea. Sole Filet	4 oz Fish Fumet	Fish	Combine mousse with ½ truffle, fill fillet. Poach in funet and wine. Add ½ truffle to sauce - fold in salpicon on lobster, serve under
1203	Doria	Chervil Pluches	oz. Petite Parisienne Cucumbers	oz. Parmesan- fine grate	oz. Mousseline recipe 229	oz. Pâte Au Choux recipe 17	Cups Consommé recipe 4		Soup	Prepare quenelles from mousseline. Combine pate au choux and cheese. Pipe into small balls. Reheat consommé, fry choux balls, drain fat, add garnish ala minute at the table it possible.
1204	Dubarry		oz. Butter	Tbsp. Chopped Parsley			ea. Cauliflower (Large Florets)		Garnish	Blanch Cauliflower until very tender, shape into balls with cheesecloth. Reheat and flavor with seasoning, butter and parsley.

All recipes equal 4 portions, the use column specifies the application.

Classical Cuisine Preparations

#	Item		1	1	2	3			Use	Preparation
1205	Dugléré	1 cup Duglere Sauce recipe 50	oz. Butter		oz. White Wine		ea. Bass Filet		Fish	Season fish, pan sear, deglaze with wine. Add sauce and simmer.
1206	Espagnole	1 Tbsp. EVOO	cup Sauce Espagnole recipe 51	oz. Iberico Ham Brunoise	oz. Sherry	oz. Tomato Concasse	ea. Chicken Thigh	½ cup Dice Roasted Pepper	Chicken	Season thighs, brown skin side down in oil. Defat, deglaze, add concasse, sauce, ham and peppers. Serve with small grilled onion rings.
1207	Favorite	oz. Butter	oz. Butter		cup Veal Stock	ea. Celery Heart	ea. Artichoke Heart	8 ea. Chateau recipe 1186	Garnish	Braise celery heart in stock, reduce nappe. Fabricate hearts. Sauté artichoke. Serve with potato.
1208	Fermière	1 cup Matignon recipe 3	oz. Brunoise Country Ham		oz. Dry White Wine	Tbsp Butter	Portions Dark Meat Chicken	2 Tbsp Fines Herb chopped	Chicken	Fabricate chicken, season, brown, defat, deglaze. Lay over matignon, ham and bake until fully cooked. Finish with butter, herb.
1209	Financière	1 cup Sauce Madère recipe 61	Tbsp Brunoise Truffle		oz. Madeira Wine	oz. Butter	ea. Chicken Breast	1 Sprig Thyme, 1 quarter Shallot	Chicken	Season chicken, brown and rissole with butter, thyme shallot. Remove all. Deglaze with wine, add rest, simmer, refresh chicken.
1210	Flamande	4 Portions Tourne Carrots and Turnips			cup Braised Savoy recipe 567	oz. Smoked Beef Sausage	ea. Savoy Cabbage Leaves	4 Portions Anglaise Potato	Garnish	Use method from recipe 550 for carrot and turnips. Blanch leaves and fill with 567 and diced sausage, reheat at service. Serve with Pommes Anglaise.
1211	Florentine		oz. Melted Butter		cup Creamed Spinach recipe 552		ea. Small Tomato- Peeled		Garnish	Trim top of tomato, to make a cup remove seeds, juice. Pipe in Florentine, brush outside with butter, season, then bake in oven.
1212	Fondante		Sprig Thyme	Slice Shallot	oz. Butter	oz. Veal Stock	ea. Golden Potato		Garnish	Shape potatoes into thick disk, like a hockey puck. Brown in butter to golden brown, rissole with herb, shallot. Braise in oven, season.
1213	Florian	8 Cipollini Onion			Head Baby Gem Lettuce Recipe 1175		Portions Fondante Recipe 1212	8 ea. Tourne Carrot	Garnish	Use baby gem for 1175, glaze carrots and onions, serve with fondant potato.
1214	Forestière	4 portions Parisienne recipe 1264	cup Chanterelles	cup Morels	cup Cepes	oz. Veal Stock	oz. Butter	2 tbsp Thin Slice Chive	Garnish	Brush and fabricate mushrooms, sauté in butter, add stock and simmer until dry. Finish with seasoning and chive, serve with Pommes Parisienne.
1215	Française	½ cup Tiny Pearl Onions	oz. Butter	cup Shelled Peas	cup Chiffonade Lettuce		ea. Duchesse Nest Recipe 557		Garnish	Pipe duchesse, recipe 9 into nests and bake. Blanch peas and onions, sauté with lettuce and butter. Season, fill nests.
1216	Gastronome	12 ea. Cork Shaped Potatoes	Drop Truffle Oil		oz. Butter			12 thin Truffle Medallions	Garnish	Partially cook potatoes in salted water, cool, dry and sauté in butter. Add truffle and garnish each cork with a truffle medallion.
1217	Galette	12 oz Duchesse recipe 9	ea. Egg yolk	oz. Milk	Tbsp. Clarified Butter				Potato	Create disks 1½ inch thick, 2½ inches wide. Place in buttered pan, brush with egg milk wash. Use knife to decorate top in a cross hatch pattern, bake.
1218	Georges V	1 tsp Fine Chopped Truffle	oz. Julienne Celeriac	oz. Pearl Barley	oz. Pheasant Mousseline recipe 229		Cups Consommé recipe 4		Soup	Use ground pheasant for consommé flavor. make quenelles from mousseline with truffle. Garnish with blanched celeriac and cooked rinsed barley.
1219	Grand-Duc	½ pound Asparagus Tips			oz. Mornay Sauce 63		ea. Croustades	ea. Truffle Slices	Garnish	Brown croustades in butter. Coat with chilled mornay and bake in oven. Blanch shock and reheat asparagus to order in butter, arrange on croustades and garnish with truffle.
1220	Grenobloise	½ cup Beurre Blanc 42	oz. White Wine	oz. Capers	Tbsp Lemon Juice	Tbsp Butter	Portions Fish	Chopped Parsley	Fish	Season and sear fish in butter, remove. Deglaze with wine, add capers, remove from heat and whisk in beurre blanc, finish with parsley.
1221	Grimaldi	4 ea Royale Dariole recipe 1281	oz. Julienne Celeriac	oz. Sundried Tomato Strips	oz. Julienne Peeled Celery		Cups Consommé recipe 4		Soup	Infuse consommé with dried tomato, strain. Sous Vide Celery 185° 15 minute. Place celery over dariole, pour consommé around custard at table.
1222	Grecque	¼ recipe 182 no rosemary					ea. Fish Steaks		Fish	Marinate fish for 30 minutes. Pan fry, sear or grill at service. Serve with small amount of fennel slaw, recipe 320
1223	Hélène	4 ea Royale Dariole recipe 1281	oz. Parmesan- fine grate	oz. Sundried Tomato Strips		oz. Pâte Au Choux recipe 17	Cups Consommé recipe 4		Soup	Infuse consommé with dried tomato, strain. Combine pate au choux and cheese. Pipe into small balls bake until golden brown. Serve with dariole royale.
1224	Henri IV	4 Portions Noisette Recipe 1259	cup Watercress Leaves		Tbsp Butter		ea. Artichoke Bottoms		Garnish	Fully prepare artichoke bottoms. Wilt watercress and fill cups, garnish with noisette potatoes.

All recipes equal 4 portions, the use column specifies the application.

Classical Cuisine Preparations

#	Item		1	1	2	3	4		Use	Method of Preparation
1225	Hollandaise	12 oz Fish Fumet recipe 33	Cup Hollandaise Sauce recipe 58				Portion Salmon		Fish	Season and poach salmon in fumet over low heat, remove drain, serve with hollandaise sauce.
1226	Hongraise	½ cup Onion – Fine Dice	tsp Hungarian Paprika	oz. Panko	ea. Small Baking Potatoes-			2 oz. Butter	Garnish	Clean, brush with oil and salt potatoes and bake. Place onion, butter, paprika in a covered dish and bake with potatoes until tender. Cut potato remove and rice potatoes. Drain butter over panko. Combine onions, potato, season stuff skins, top with crumbs and bake until golden brown.
1227	Impériale				oz. Beurre Blanc recipe 42	oz. Crayfish Tails	ea. Fish Filets	4 ea. Truffle Slices	Fish	Poach fish, top with crayfish tossed in beurre blanc and truffle.
1228	Indienne	2 Tbsp Curry recipe 1107	cup Apple Juice	ea. Apple Julienne	oz. Butter	Tbsp Brunoise Red Pepper	ea. Chicken Breast	1 cup Cream	Chicken	Season chicken breasts with toasted curry spice. Poach with butter in immersion circulator. Strain liquid into juice and reduce with cream, add julienne, brunoise. Serve with timbale of basmati rice.
1229	Infante	ea. Sweet Pimento, Julienne	Chervil Pluches	Tbsp Tapioca	oz. Boiled Arborio Rice		Cups Consommé recipe 4		Soup	Thicken consommé with tapioca and strain. Garnish with 1 tbsp rice, 1tbsp pimento.
1230	Isabelle	Tbsp Fine Julienne Truffle	Tbsp Muscat Wine		oz. Petite Pois	oz. Mousseline recipe 229	Cups Consommé recipe 4		Soup	Prepare quenelles from mousseline. Reheat consommé and garnish with quenelles, blanched peas and truffles cooked in Muscat wine.
1231	Italienne	½ cup Brunoise Onion	Pint Chicken Stock	oz. Butter	oz. Grated Parmesan		oz. Arborio Rice		Rice	Sauté onions slowly until golden brown, add rice then slowly add stock. When al dente finish with parmesan cheese.
1232	Ivan	3 oz. Brunoise Golden Beet	Tbsp. Plum Wine		oz. Beet Juice, fine strained	oz. Boiled Forbidden Rice	Cups Consommé recipe 4		Soup	Sous vide beets for 45 minutes at 185°. Boil rice until tender, rinse. Reheat consommé with beet juice. Garnish to order.
1233	Japonaise	3 oz. Brunoise Sunchokes	Tbsp. Plum Wine	oz. Fine Julienne Snow Peas		oz. Boiled Sushi Rice	Cups Consommé recipe 4		Soup	Sous vide sunchokes for 45 minutes in wine at 185°. Boil rice until tender, rinse. Reheat consommé with beet juice. Blanch snow peas at last moment. Garnish with all items at the last moment.
1234	Jardinière	3 oz. Cauliflower Tiny Florets	ea. Large Carrot Allumette	ea. Turnip Allumette	oz. Butter	oz. Green Peas	oz. Haricot Vert 1 ½ "bias		Garnish	Blanch all veg separately then sauté with butter, season to taste.
1235	Joinville	1 oz Whole Butter	cup Sauce Normande recipe 74	Wedge Lemon	tsp. Brunoise Truffle	oz. Diced Mushroom Cap- white only	Portions Fish	4 ea. Prawns	Fish	Peel prawns, make butter from shells. Flavor mushrooms with lemon. Poach fish in a fumet. Gently heat prawns and mushrooms. Drain leftover butter and whisk into warm sauce, truffle garnish.
1236	Juliette	4 ea. Poached Quail Egg		oz. Ditalini Pasta	oz. Petite Pois		Cups Consommé recipe 4		Soup	Boil pasta until tender, rinse. Blanch peas last minute and use with pasta and egg as garnish reheated consommé. Pour consommé at table.
1237	Languedocienne	1 ½ cup Diced Eggplant	cup Tomato Concasse	Clove Garlic	cup Cepes- brushed and sliced	oz. Butter		2 oz. Sauce Madére 62	Garnish	Peel and salt eggplant, rinse. Sauté cepes in butter with garlic and eggplant. When brown remove garlic, add tomato, sauce, reduce.
1238	Lorette		cup Pâte au Choux recipe17	cup Duchesse Potato recipe 9	Tbsp Potato Starch				Potato	Prepare both recipes and chill, mix with starch. Place in pastry bag with straight tip. Pipe into half-moon portions on to greased parchment. Deep fat fry 350°
1239	Louisianne	Ripe Plantain - Sliced or Sweet Potato Cups	ea. Red Pepper - Diced	ea. Green Pepper - Diced	oz. Cream	Ears Corn		1 ea. Green Onion Sliced	Garnish	Boil corn, remove kernels, milk the cobb. Make creamed corn from cream, milk, corn then add peppers and simmer. Finish with green onion. Season. Griddle plantain and use for sides of a tian on the presentation or make potato cup.
1240	Lyonnaise			lb Julienne Onion	Tbsp Chopped Parsley	ea. Russet Potato	oz. Clarified Butter		Potato	Simmer potato with jacket until tender. Cool several hours. Peel and slice into circles, brown in butter. Season and garnish with parsley. Caramelize onions, make napoleon with onion and potato. reheat at service.

All recipes equal 4 portions, the use column specifies the application.

Classical Cuisine Preparations

#	Item			1	2	3	4	Use	Method of Preparation
1241	Madame Brazier			Tbsp Parsley	tsp Fresh Tarragon	oz. Duxelle recipe 10	Portions Dark Meat Chicken	Chicken	Debone thighs and make a forcemeat from the legs. Season with tarragon and parsley and fold in Duxelle. Form between two thighs and pan roast with a weight on top to hold flat. Rest and slice into four portions.
1242	Macédoine	ea. Large Carrot Macédoine		ea. Turnip Macédoine	oz. Butter	oz. Green Peas	oz. Haricot Vert Macédoine	Garnish	Blanch all veg separately then sauté with butter, season to taste.
1243	Madère	1 Sprig thyme, 1 quarter shallot	oz. Whole Butter		oz. Madeira Wine	oz. Clarified Butter	ea. Chicken Breast	Chicken	Season chicken, brown and rissole with clarified butter, thyme, and shallot. Remove fat. Deglaze with wine, add sauce, simmer, finish with whole butter and season.
1244	Madrilène	Chervil Leaves		oz. Sundried Tomato Strips	Tbsp Fine Dice Peeled Tomato		Cups Consommé recipe 4	Soup	Infuse consommé with dried tomato, strain, season with a pinch of cayenne. Garnish with exact cut tomato that has been held in seasoned water, and chervil.
1245	Marengo	ea. Whole Chicken 3.5 lb. / Clove Garlic Crushed	¾ cup White Wine	cup Mushroom Caps	ea. Tomato Concasse	oz. Crushed Tomato	Sliced Truffle and Chopped Parsley / ea. Eggs, Crayfish, Heart Shaped Butter Fried Croutons	Chicken	Prepare chicken for Poulet sauté. Season and brown in oil, brown mushrooms, remove excess fat. Deglaze with wine, add tomato and garlic, arrange so dark meat is above sauce, simmer use cartouche. When done remove breasts from bone and split in half lengthwise. Finish with truffle and parsley. Garnish with poached crayfish, fried egg and crouton.
1246	Marinière	20 ea. Mussels cleaned		cup White Wine	Pinch Saffron	oz. Butter	Tbsp Minced Shallot / 2 Tbsp Parsley	Garnish	Heat pan and add mussels, shallot, wine, and saffron. When mussels begin to open remove from shell and add tomato, reduce, add butter and parsley, season.
1247	Marquise	¼ recipe Duchess 9	Tbsp Tomato Paste	oz. Whole Butter			Egg Yolk Wash	Potato	Expand tomato into butter then combine with duchesse. Pipe to form a patty shell then brush with egg wash before baking. Use as a socle for other elements.
1248	Marseillaise — In place of a whole chicken 4 portions of dark meat can be used.	ea. Whole Chicken 3.5 lb. / Clove Garlic - Split	¾ cup White Wine	Lemon Half	oz. Fine Slice Green Pimento	ea. Small Tomatoes-Quartered	2 Tbsp. Chopped Parsley	Chicken	Prepare chicken for Poulet sauté. Season and brown in oil, remove excess fat. Deglaze with wine, add tomato, pimento and garlic. Arrange so dark meat is simmering in sauce and breast is above sauce, simmer with cartouche. When done remove breasts from bone and split in half lengthwise. Finish with parsley.
1249	Maryland	½ cup Fritter Batter Recipe 755 – no clams	ea. Banana	Ear Sweet Corn	Tbsp Horseradish	oz. Lean Bacon Rashers	10 oz Sauce Béchamel Recipe 40 / ea. Chicken Breasts	Chicken	Season and standard bread chicken. Combine corn kernels with batter. Steep horseradish into sauce. Griddle bananas and bacon. Fry chicken and corn fritters. Serve the chicken topped bacon, banana, sauce under, fritters on side.
1250	Meunière	½ cup Beurre Blanc 42	oz. White Wine		Tbsp Lemon Juice	Tbsp Butter	Chopped Parsley / Portions Fish	Fish	Season, dredge and brown fish in butter. Deglaze with wine, remove from heat and plate fish. Whisk in beurre blanc, finish with parsley, nappe over fish.
1251	Mexicaine — In place of a whole chicken 4 portions of dark meat can be used.	ea. Whole Chicken 3.5 lb.	¾ cup White Wine	cup Tomato Jus		oz. Tomato Fondue*	Large Mushroom Caps / 4 ea. Grilled Red Pimento	Chicken	Prepare chicken for Poulet sauté. Season and brown in oil, brown mushrooms, remove excess fat. Deglaze with wine, add tomato jus, meat is simmering in sauce, simmer, use cartouche. When done remove breasts from bone and split in half lengthwise. Fill mushroom with fondue, served with grilled pimento.
1252	Mikado			oz. Sundried Tomato Strips	Tbsp Macédoine Peeled Tomato	oz. Poached Chicken	Cups Consommé recipe 4	Soup	Infuse consommé with dried tomato, strain. Garnish with exact cut tomato that has been held in seasoned water and macedoine chicken.

* Tomato Fondue- 1 ea tomato concasse, 2 oz whole butter, 1 sprig thyme, 1oz white wine. Slowly melt the tomato over low heat in the butter, wine, and thyme. Season to taste.

All recipes equal 4 portions, the use column specifies the application.

Classical Cuisine Preparations

	Item		1	1	2	3	4		Use	Method of Preparation
1253	Milanese	½ cup Brunoise Onion	Pint Chicken Stock	oz. Butter	oz. Grated Parmesan	Tbsp White Wine	oz. Arborio Rice	1 tsp Saffron	Rice	Sauté onions slowly until tender, add rice and saffron then slowly add stock. When al dente finish with wine and parmesan cheese.
1254	Montpensier	8 oz Asparagus Tips	ea. Truffle-Shaved			oz. Butter	ea. Chicken Breast		Chicken	Standard bread seasoned chicken and fry in butter until fully cooked. Blanch asparagus and arrange on top. Shave truffle over and nappe with brown butter.
1255	Nantua	½ Recipe 73 Sauce Nantua	lb. Crayfish			oz. Butter			Garnish	Boil crayfish, shuck meat, use shells to prepare sauce. Butter poach meat. Nappe sauce over.
1256	Newburg	½ Recipe 299 Sauce Newburg	ea. Lobster			oz. Butter	ea. Bouchee		Garnish	Dispatch and blanch lobsters, shuck meat, use shells to prepare sauce. Butter poach meat. Nappe sauce over lobster that has been rewarmed in bouchee.
1257	Niçoise	Tbsp Capers	oz. Minced Olive	ea. Anchovy Filet	oz. Lemon Juice	Tbsp Tomato Water	oz. Olive Oil	1 Egg Yolk	Dressing	Prepare an emulsified dressing with mashed anchovy, yolk, oil, water, juice. Add in rest. To dress salad, rub the bowl with a clove of garlic first. Season to taste.
1258	Normande In place of a whole chicken 4 portions of dark meat can be used.		ea. Whole Chicken 3.5 lb.	lb. Pippin Apples-peeled and sliced	oz. Calvados	oz. Butter			Chicken	Prepare chicken for Poulet sauté. Season and brown in butter. Remove chicken, sauté apples. Arrange so dark meat is on bottom of terrine and breast is above. Sprinkle with calvados and place apples on top. braise with cartouche. When done remove breasts from bone and split in half lengthwise. Serve in terrine.
1259	Noisette		oz. Chopped Parsley		lb. Gold Potatoes	oz. Butter			Potato	Peel potatoes. Use a Parisienne scoop to shape potatoes. Brown in butter and finish in oven if needed, season and finish with parsley.
1260	Nouvelle		cup Beurre Blanc recipe 42		cup Sorrel Leave		ea. Salmon Tranche		Fish	Make sure fish is flat, place on broil pan. Season. Broil and serve over a bed sorrel leafs and ¼ cup of beurre blanc. Created by Troisgros Brothers.
1261	Orientale	4 Portions Rice Pilaw recipe 1269	cup Sauce Supreme 74	Pinch Saffron	cup Diamond Cut Nappa Cabbage	oz. Tomato Puree	ea. Chicken Breast	½ cup Diced Pimento	Chicken	Season and dredge chicken, lightly brown in butter. Remove and add cabbage until tender. Infuse saffron into sauce supreme, coat cooked chicken with sauce then top with cabbage. Serve over pimento flavored rice.
1262	Orléanaise In place of a whole chicken 4 portions of dark meat can be used.	¾ cup Red Wine	ea. Whole Chicken 3.5 lb.	oz. Clarified Butter	oz. Whole Butter	oz. Demi Glaze	oz. Veal Stock	Pearl Onions and Fluted Mushroom	Chicken	Prepare chicken for Poulet sauté. Season and brown in clarified butter, brown mushrooms and onions and remove. Deglaze with wine, add stock and demi. arrange so dark meat is simmering in sauce and breast is above sauce, simmer use cartouche. When done remove breasts from bone and split in half lengthwise. Finish sauce with whole butter.
1263	Orly		Bunch Parsley	cup Tomato Sauce 75	oz. Chopped Onion	oz. Clarified Butter	ea. Chicken Breast	½ Lemon	Chicken	Use lemon, parsley stem and onion to marinate the chicken. Wipe, dredge and pan fry in butter. Fry parsley until crisp. Sauce under and parsley on top.
1264	Parisienne		oz. Chopped Parsley	oz. Butter	lb. Gold Potatoes				Potato	Peel potatoes use a Parisienne scoop to shape potatoes. Gently cook potatoes in salted water. Toss with butter, season and finish with parsley.
1265	Parmentier	½ cup White Wine	ea. Whole Chicken 3.5 lb.	Tbsp Chopped Parsley	Tbsp. Whole Butter		oz. Veal Stock	1 lb Oval Shaped Potato Parisienne	Chicken	Prepare chicken for Poulet sauté. Season and brown in butter, brown potatoes and remove. Deglaze with wine, add stock. Arrange so dark meat is simmering in sauce and breast is above liquid, place potatoes around and braise with cartouche. When done remove breasts from bone and split in half lengthwise. Finish sauce with parsley.
1266	Périgueux	1 Tbsp Chopped Truffle	cup Mousseline recipe 229	cup Sauce Périgueux rec 65	oz. Melted Butter		ea. Chicken Breast		Chicken	Fill heart shaped breasts with truffle mousseline. Brush with melted butter and bake covered until fully cooked, nappe with sauce over

All recipes equal 4 portions, the use column specifies the application.

Classical Cuisine Preparations

Item			1	2	3	4		Use	Method of Preparation
1267 Périgord	½ cup Madeira Wine	ea. Whole Chicken 3.5 lb.	oz. Clarified Butter	oz. Whole Butter		oz. Demi Glaze	8 each Truffles – Olive Shaped	Chicken	Prepare chicken for Poulet sauté. Season and brown in clarified butter. Deglaze with wine, add demi. Arrange so dark meat is simmering in sauce and breast is above meat. When done remove breasts from bone and split in half lengthwise. Finish sauce with whole butter.
1268 Piémontaise	½ cup Brunoise Onion	Pint Chicken Stock	oz. Butter	oz. Grated Parmesan	Tbsp Chopped White Truffle	oz. Arborio Rice		Rice	Sauté onions slowly until golden brown, add rice then slowly add stock. When al dente finish with parmesan cheese and truffle.
1269 Pilaw	1 ea. Bay Leaf	oz. Minced Onion	cup White Stock	Tbsp Butter		oz. Basmati Rice		Rice	Use half butter to sauté onion, add rice to coat. Add hot stock braise for 15 minutes. Rest 5 minutes and fluff in remaining butter and season
1270 Polignac		cup Sauce Supreme	Tbsp Julienne Truffle	oz. Julienne Mushroom		ea. Chicken Breast	1 oz Butter	Chicken	Dredge and shallow fry seasoned chicken. When cooked remove and sauté mushroom, and truffle. Nappe sauce over chicken and garnish.
1271 Portugaise — In place of a whole chicken 4 portions of dark meat can be used.	½ cup White Wine	ea. Whole Chicken 3.5 lb. / Clove Garlic - Crushed	oz. Minced Onion	ea. Tomato Concasse	oz. Sliced Mushroom	ea. Duxelle Stuffed Tomato	1 Tbsp. Chopped Parsley	Chicken	Prepare chicken for Poulet sauté. Season and brown in oil, brown onions and mushrooms, remove excess fat. Deglaze with wine, add concasse and garlic. Arrange so dark meat is simmering in sauce and breast is above meat, simmer, use cartouche. When done remove breasts from bone and split in half lengthwise. Finish with parsley. Garnish with tomato and chateau potatoes
1272 Printanière	1 cup Chiffonade Sorrel	ea. Large Carrot Batonnet	ea. Turnip Batonnet	oz... Butter	oz. Green Peas	oz. Haricot Vert Diamond Cut		Garnish	Blanch all veg separately then sauté with butter and sorrel, season to taste.
1273 Provençale	1 clove Garlic	cup Grape Tomatoes- Peel	oz. EVOO	oz. Pitted Nicoise Olives	Wedge Lemon	Portions Bass		Fish	Season and pan sear fish, add tomatoes, garlic and olives, dress with lemon and slowly heat until fish is cooked, Remove garlic, add parsley, garnish on top.
1274 Rabelais	1 tsp Fine Chopped Truffle		oz. Parmesan- fine grate	oz. Partridge Mousseline recipe 229	oz. Pate Au Choux recipe 17	Cups Consommé recipe 4		Soup	Use ground pheasant for consommé flavor, make quenelles from mousseline. Prepare cheese profiteroles. Garnish with truffles heated in madeira
1275 Rachel	4 ea. Royale- Asparagus - Dice	Recipe 1277 4 Dariole	oz. Parmesan- fine grate	oz. Asparagus Tips	oz. Pate Au Choux	Cups Consommé recipe 4		Soup	Prepare cheese profiteroles. Blanch asparagus, dice chicken royale. Garnish bowl with elements and pour reheated consommé at the tables.
1276 Ravigote	¾ cup Sauce Ravigote recipe 69	Tbsp Nouilly Prat		ea. Dover Sole	oz. Butter		8 oz Jumbo Lump Crab	Fish	Filet fish. Season, dredge and brown in butter. Deglaze and remove. Combine ¼ cup of ravigote and crab. Stuff between the two filets, top with sauce and reheat in oven at service.
1277 Reine Royale		Tbsp Butter	ea. Yolk	ea. Egg	oz. Diced Mushroom	oz. Veloute	4 oz Milk	Garnish	Sauté mushrooms until brown. Dab off fat, combine with rest and portion into 4 dariole. Bake in waterbath until fully cooked.
1278 Régence		¼ tsp Truffle Oil	Tbsp. Sherry Vinegar	Tbsp EVOO				Dressing	Prepare truffle vinaigrette for micro greens Season with salt and pepper
1279 Richelieu		¼ recipe 97 Maître D' Hotel Butter	ea. Truffle- Shaved		oz. Butter	ea. Chicken Breast		Chicken	Standard bread seasoned chicken and fry in butter until fully cooked. Shave truffle over and nappe with melted Maître D' Hotel butter.
1280 Rossini		cup Sauce Madère recipe 61	ea. Small Truffle	oz. Foie Gras	oz. Madeira Wine	ea. Chicken Breast	1 oz Butter	Chicken	Dredge and shallow fry seasoned chicken remove and sear four slices of Foie Gras, place on chicken. Deglaze with madeira and reduce add sauce nappe with sliced truffle.
1281 Royale		¼ recipe 25 Royale						Garnish	Prepare royals by gently warming the custard to your body temp, slowly bake in a hot water bath until firm. May use molds or cut after it is chilled for consommé.

All recipes equal 4 portions, the use column specifies the application.

Classical Cuisine Preparations

Item	1	2	3	4		Use	Method of Preparation
1282 Saint-Florentin		oz. Brunoise Ham	oz. 1 inch Vermicelli	Portion Duchesse recipe 9		Potato	Blanch vermicelli and dry. Combine duchesse with ham. Shape into corks, dip them in egg wash then vermicelli before frying to order.
1283 Saint-Germain	cup Fresh Peas	oz. Cream	oz. Sauce Béarnaise recipe 38	ea. Chicken Breast	1 oz. Butter	Chicken	Season and dredge chicken, lightly brown in butter and fully cook. Remove chicken then add peas and cream to pan. Puree until smooth. Place chicken over peas, and sauce on top.
1284 Souvaroff	1 sheet Puff pastry cup Sauce Madère recipe 61 Tbsp Julienne Truffle	oz. Foie Gras	oz. Madeira Wine	ea. Chicken Breast	Egg yolk wash	Chicken	Prepare an individual ballottine of chicken stuffed with foie gras. Arrange in individual terrines and top with truffle and sauce Cover with puff pastry, brush with yolk. Bake until well browned and fully cooked.
1285 Stanley — In place of a whole chicken 4 portions of dark meat can be used.	11 oz. Julienne Onion ea. Whole Chicken 3.5 lb cup Cream	oz. Whole Butter	Large Mushrooms- Julienne and Sauteed	Portions Rice Pilaw recipe 1269	Cayenne and Madras Curry Powder	Chicken	Prepare chicken for Poulet sauté. Season and lightly cook in butter. Remove chicken, sauté onions. Add cream with a pinch of cayenne and curry to taste. Arrange so dark meat is on bottom and breast is above. Braise with cartouche. When done remove breasts from bone and split in half lengthwise. Puree and strain sauce arrange chicken with sauce on top with mushrooms, over Pilaw.
1286 Turque	1 ea. Bay Leaf oz. Minced Onion cup White Stock	Tbsp Butter	oz. Tomato Fondue*	oz. Long Grain Rice		Rice	Use butter to sauté onion, add rice to coat. Add hot stock; and baked covered for 18 minutes. Rest 5 minutes and stir in tomato fondue.
1287 Verneuil	5 oz. Colbert Butter recipe 92 ea. Artichoke ea. Lemon	oz. Chopped Onion	oz. Clarified Butter	ea. Chicken Breast	Artichoke and Parsley Puree	Chicken	Use lemon, parsley stem and onion to marinate the chicken. Make puree from artichoke leaves and parsley. Boil artichoke bottom in lemon water and slice thin. Warm in pan with Colbert butter. Arrange chicken over puree with artichokes and Colbert on top.
1288 Véronique	½ cup Beurre Blanc recipe 42 cup Peeled Green Grapes	Tbsp Noilly Prat	Tbsp Butter	ea. Sole Paupiette	1 oz Fish Forcemeat	Fish	Prepare paupiette with fillet and trimmings from sole. Brush with butter and drizzle wine, bake in oven. Nappe with sauce, add grapes last second and serve.
1289 Vichy	Recipe Carrot Vichy 550 ea. Whole Chicken 3.5 lb	oz. Whole Butter		oz. Veal Stock		Chicken	Prepare chicken for Poulet sauté. Season and brown in butter. Remove excess fat Arrange so dark meat is on bottom of terrine and breast is above. Place carrot vichy over chicken, braise with cartouche. When done remove breasts from bone and split in half lengthwise. Serve with carrots on top.
1290 Victoria	½ Recipe 73 Sauce Americaine ea. Lobster ea. Truffle		oz. Butter			Garnish	Dispatch and blanch lobster, shuck meat use shells to prepare sauce. Butter poach meat. Nappe sauce over and garnish with truffle.
1291 Washington	½ Recipe 1286 Turque Rice – no tomato ea. Whole Chicken 3.5 lb		Ear Corn-blanched	oz. Cream		Chicken	Prepare a ballottine of chicken with corn kernels from 1 cob and rice as a stuffing. Poele in oven. Make a creamed corn puree for under the slices.
1292 Wolseley	½ lb. Asparagus Tips cup Mousseline recipe 229 cup Sauce Supreme recipe 74	oz. Melted Butter		ea. Chicken Small Double Breast Supreme		Chicken	Fill heart shaped supreme with mousseline. Brush with melted butter and bake covered until fully cooked, nappe with sauce supreme, garnish with asparagus.

* Tomato Fondue- 1 ea tomato concasse, 2 oz whole butter, 1 sprig thyme, 1oz white wine. Slowly melt the tomato over low heat in the butter, wine, and thyme. Season to taste.

Recipes and dishes in the classical preparations have been crossed referenced using the following sources. Check out Our Youtube Channel - chefreference.

100 Styles of French Cooking, Karl Wurzer. Grosset and Dunlap. 1981
Classical Cooking the Modern Way, 2nd ed. Eugene Pauli. Van Nostrand Reinhold. 1989
Dictionnaire de l' Académie des Gastronomes, Prisma Paris 1962
Larousse Gastronomique(American Edition) Jennifer Harvey Lang, ed. Crown 1988
Le Guide Culinaire. A. Escoffier, Wiley and Sons, Inc 1979
Mastering the Art of French Cooking Julia Child, Knopf 1963
The Hotel Butcher, Garde Manger, and Carver. Frank River. Hotel Monthly 1916

All recipes equal 4 portions, the use column specifies the application.

Culinary Terminology

A

A la broche- (Fr) to roast on a spit over a fire

A la carte- (Fr) Dishes which are made to order and individually priced.

A la minute-(Fr) Cooked to order

A la- (Fr) In the style of. I.e. *A la Normande*

A.P. Weight- As Purchased Weight -before the trimming process

Aal–(Gm) - eel

Aam- (In) Mango

Abats- (Fr) - Offal. Examples: Liver, Kidney

Abernethy Biscuit- (Br) Scottish shortbread cookie flavored with caraway seed.

Aboyeur- Fr- the person who calls out the orders to the cooks. Also known as the expeditor.

Acarajé -(La) Brazilian field peas with dry shrimp

Acciuga -(It) Anchovy

Accompaniments - Items offered separately with a dish of food

Acetic 1. Spoilage from bacteria that causes the wine to have the aroma of vinegar. 2. The acid in vinegar.

Achaar-(In)-Pickle

Achiote -(La) Annatto Seeds used for coloring food yellow

Acidulated Water- water and vinegar or lemon juice which is used to prevent oxidation of vegetables, or to help coagulate proteins.

Adobado- Philippino paste or sauce made from chilies, vinegar, and other seasonings. Used as a seasoning for pork, goat and chicken.

Adobo -(La) Marinade or spice rub for meats

Adovada-(Sp)- Marinated and stewed.

Adrak-(In)-Ginger

Aerate- Sifting dry ingredient, adding pressurize gas, whipping ingredients into a form to incorporate air.

Affumicato -(It) Smoked

African Mirepoix- Aromatic base of very hot chilies, tomatoes, and onion.

Aging- The tenderization of meat by maintaining it at temperatures of 34° to 36° for an extended period of time

Aglio -(It) - Garlic

Agnello- It- Lamb

Agnolotti –(It)-half round ravioli.

Agrodolce -(It) Sweet and sour

Agrumes –(Fr)- Citrus fruit

Aigre -(Fr)- Sour

Aiguillette- Long, thin slices of poultry breast. The term is mainly used for duck

Ail- (Fr) Garlic.

Aile- (Fr) Wings of poultry and feathered game.

Aioli- Fr - A cold egg and oil emulsion with olive oil and garlic, similar to a mayonnaise.

Aji -(La) Peruvian hot chile.

Ajo- (Sp) Garlic

Akami (Jp) Portions cut from the back of tuna that are lean, used for sushi.

Akrot-(In)-Walnut

Al Carbon- (Sp) grilled or containing meat.

Al Dente- (It) "to the teeth". The cooking of pasta resulting in a firm texture.

Al Forno- (It) baked in the oven.

Al Pastor- (La) (It) Shepherd style cooking. Cooked over a grill or on a sp(It)

Albarelle -(Fr)- Boletus mushroom. These mushrooms grow on chestnut trees

Albondigas- (Sp) Pork and beef meatballs served with a spicy tomato sauce for tapas.

Albumin- the protein source of egg whites.

Alcapurria-(Cr)- Ground plantain and yucca are made into a dough then filled with spiced meat, shaped into a croquette then fried

Alfredo-(It) A pasta sauce made from butter and parmesan cheese. Adapated versions use a cream base with the addition of garlic.

All'aglio e Oilio -(It) Garlic and olive oil flavoring for pasta

Allemande -(Fr) "German style" sauce. Veloute with a liaison

Alligator Pear - Avocado

Almond Paste- finely ground almonds that are made into a paste and then emulsified with powdered sugar and glucose.

Aloyau de boeuf -(Fr) Top sirloin of beef that is usually roasted.

Alsacienne-(Fr) From the Alsace region of France.

Alumette -(Fr) 1. Matchstick cut 1/8" x 1/8"x2 ½". Term used for potatoes. 2.Thin strips of pastry

Amande - (Fr)- Almond

Amandine-(Fr) Dish made with crisp almonds.

Amontillado -(Sp) Darker sherry that is typically dry

Amrood- (In)- Guava

Amuse Gueule- (Fr)- Savory tasting portion of food offered as a gift before the meal to welcome the guests.

Amuse-bouche –(Fr) "amuse the mouth"; small plated appetizer given to the guest.

Ananas - (Fr)- (Gm)- Pineapple

Anar- (In) Pomegranate

Anchoïade -(Fr) A puree of anchovies, garlic and olive oil that is used as dip for raw vegetables and bread.

Ancienne -(Fr) -ancient style.

Anda-(In)- Egg

Andouille- 1.(Fr) - A pork sausage that smoked then boiled .2. (Cr) Cajun version is very spicy and served in gumbo.

Angelica- (It)-Stalks from fennel- like plants are candied and used primarily to garnish pastries.

Angels on Horseback- (Br) Bacon wrapped oysters that are grilled and served over toast points.

Anglaise-(Fr) English style. Plain cookery

Anguille- (Fr) Eel

Anjeer- (In)- Fig

Annatto Seed- achiote seeds that are used to color and spice Latin American dishes. Example: Pasteles from Puerto Rico are yellow because of this.

Antipasto- (It) before the pasta. Antipasto items include cured meats and salamis, olives, marinated vegetables, and cheese.

Apfel -(Gm)- Apple

Apfelsine –(Gm)- Orange

Appellation d' Origine Contrôlée (AOC)- (Fr) A protected designation of the wines and food products origin

Appellation- (Fr)- This term is used to identify wine from a demarcated region.

Apperail-(Fr) Prepared mixture.

Arepa- (La)-Thick maize pancakes filled with meat, common for breakfast in Columbia and Venezue(La)

Argenteuil -(Fr) An area known for the production and use of asparagus in preparations.

Arista -(It) Pork loin

Aromates- (Fr) Aromatic herbs or spices.

Arrabbiata -(It) "Angry" spicy tomato sauce

Arroser -(Fr) To baste a product that is roasting.

Arrosto –(It) - Roast

Arrowroot- Used like cornstarch this root leaves sauces with a glossy finish.

Arroz con Pollo-(Cr)- National dish of Cuba, chicken and rice.

Arroz- (Sp) rice.

Artichaut - (Fr)- Artichoke

Asada- (La) Grilled, as in Carne Asada or grilled beef.

Asado-(Sp) Roasted or broiled meat

Asafetida-(In)- Fennel like spice used in South Indian cuisine

Asopao-(Cr)- Traditional chicken or seafood and rice soup that is very much like a Gumbo. Flavored with onions, olives, tomato, cilantro, paprika and cured pork.

Asperge - (Fr)- Asparagus

Aspic- (Fr) - Clarified meat stock and gelatin used for pates and head cheese.

Assemblage-(Fr)- the blending of grape varietals to develop balance in the finished wine.

Assorti- (Fr) An assortment

Astringent- the dry, tannic attributes found in wine. Very common in underdeveloped wines.

Asturiana-(Sp)- Ablood sausage from the Asturias region of Spain

Athole Brose- (Br) Oatmeal milk with honey and whisky served as a creamy beverage.

au -(Fr) -Prepared with

> **au beurre-**(Fr) With butter
> **au bleu-**(Fr) -1. to cook meat very under done.2. The poaching of trout in a vinegar solution to turn it blue.
> **au four-**(Fr) Baked in an oven.

Continued

au gratin-(Fr) To brown on top, food covered with a sauce, sprinkled with bread crumbs and baked or placed in a salamander. Pomme de terre au gratin

au jus-(Fr) Served with natural juices and drippings from a roast.

au lait-(Fr) With or of milk

au maigre -(Fr) dishes prepared without meat

au natural -(Fr) dishes prepared simply and plainly without any extras

au vin blanc -(Fr) With white wine

Aubergine- -(Fr) eggplant.

Aurora-(Fr) - cream sauce that has tomato puree or concassé added to (It)

Auslese- (Gm)- "Select Harvest" wine category.

Autolysis- the deterioration of yeast cells.

Avgolemano- (Gr) Egg and lemon soup from Athens.

Azafrán-(Sp) Saffron, the best comes from La Mancha.

B

Baba au Rhum –(It)- A small yeast cake made from a sweet rich dough that is then soaked with a rum after it is baked.

Baba Ganoush- (Le) Roasted and pureed eggplant dip.

Babka- (Yd)- Dense yeast bread flavored with chocolate or cinnamon

Bacalao- (Sp) -Salt cod

Baccala- It- Salt Cod **Backhendl**–

(Gm)- roasted chicken **Badaam**-

(In) Almond

Baekenhofe- (Fr) - An Alsatian stew made of marinated beef, pork and lamb, layered with mashed potatoes, bacon, and fried leeks.

Bagel- (Yd)- Boiled and baked bread ring

Bagna Cauda –(It) A "warm bath" made of anchovies, olive oil, and garlic used as a dip for bread and raw vegetables

Baguette- (Fr) Long and narrow French bread.

Baharat- (Ar)- Spice blend of black cardamom, black pepper, allspice, cassia bark, nutmeg, cumin, coriander, cloves and dried chilies.

Bain-marie-(Fr) A container of simmering water used for holding hot foods.

Bak Tong Go -(Ch)- Steamed sweet rice pudding cake.

Baked Alaska- A frozen dessert made of sponge cake filled with ice cream and decorated with meringue. The dessert is then placed in a hot oven to brown the meringue before the ice cream can melt.

Baking Powder- A chemical leavening agent which combines an acid with bicarbonate of soda.

Baklava- (Gr) A very sweet Turkish -Greek dessert made of layers of fillo filled with a mixture of ground pistachios and walnuts. The pastry is sliced, baked, and finished with honey syrup flavored with lemon, cinnamon and cloves.

Bakr aka Gost-(In)-Mutton

Balandėliai-(Eu) -Lithuanian cabbage rolls filled with lamb and rice.

Balkabağı Çorbasi-(Tu) – Pumpkin soup flavored with sweet spice and leeks, finished with yogurt.

Ballotine-(Fr) - A forcemeat filled poultry leg or wing that is shaped into a ball then braised or roasted. A ballottine may be served hot or cold.

Balsamic Vinegar- vinegar made from the juice of trebbiano grape that is heated and aged in wooden barrels which concentrates the sweet flavor through evaporation.

Bamia Bi-Lahm- (Ar) – Lamb, okra and tomato stew from the Middle East.

Banane - (Fr)- Banana

Banh Canh- (Se)-Vietnamese thick noodle (udon) pork soup with ground fish cakes, Vietnamese ham, finished with cilantro.

Banh Mi- (Se)-Vietnamese baguette sandwich with various meat fillings and flavored with cucumber, pickled vegetables, cilantro.

Bao -(Ch)- Very light wheat bun filled and steamed.

Barbecue- To cook over an open fire, above direct flame. From the Carib Barbacoa

Barbunya- (Tu) – Barlotti beans, Roman Beans

Barde- (Fr) -the covering of meat with strips of bacon or fat that are used add flavor and retain moisture

Bari Mirch-(In)- Green pepper

Barigoule- (Fr)- Cooking in olive oil and lemon juice to prevent oxidation and add flavor. Typically used for artichokes

Baron of Beef- Br-. A spit roasted double sirloin of beef. Carved off the backbone when served.

Barquette-(Fr) **-** A small oval boat shaped pastry dough that is baked then filled with sweet or savory ingredients.

Basmati- (In) Aromatic long grain rice .

Basquaise-(Fr) - in the style of Basque region of Spain and France. These dishes often include tomatoes, ham, and sweet or hot pimentos and garlic.

Baste- The process of using liquid or drippings from a roasted item to enhance the flavor and moisten while cooking.

Batidos -(La) Smoothie or milkshake

Bâtonnage-(Fr)- the stirring of barrel fermented wine to reduce hydrogen sulphide in order to improve flavor.

Bâtonnet-(Fr) - A knife cut that produces food that has the dimensions of ¼ x ¼ x 2 ½ -3".

Batter- A preparation of a liquid and eggs bound with flour that can be used for cakes and for coating foods.

Bau Yew -(Ch) Abalone

Bavarian Cream - Sauce Anglaise that is flavored and folded with whipped cream and gelatin This preparation is poured into moulds or used as a cake filling or pastry filling.

Bayonnaise-(Fr) From Bayonne France, an area famous for cured pork and ham products.

Béarnaise-(Fr) -a butter emulsion sauce that is prepared similar to a hollandaise sauce but with that is flavored with tarragon and chervil.

Beat-to bring a mixture to smooth texture by constant motion of a spoon or paddle.

Béchamel-(Fr) - A white mother sauce made from roux, milk and a clove studded onion. This thickened sauce can be used as filling, or as the base for soufflés, or as the topping for moussaka or pasticcio.

Beerenauslese- (Gm)- "Selected Grapes" wine category. This refers to the degree of ripeness, color and richness developed by botrytis.

Beignet-1. (Fr) – fritter. 2. (Cr)- small square donut topped with generous amount of powdered sugar, served with Café au Lait.

Belle Helene- (Fr) - a dessert that features poached pears, ice cream, and chocolate sauce.

Benedictine-(Fr) Cod brandade garnish.

Benne - Sesame seeds from Africa.

Bercy-(Fr)- A garnish term of dishes that contain wine, shallot and herbs.

Berliner Pfannkuchen-(Sw)-Jam filled doughnut from Berlin

Berner Plat-(Sw)- "Butchers Plate" a generous portion of smoked meat, tongue, sausage, sauerkraut, potatoes, green beans served with mustard.

Besan-(In) Chick pea flour

Best End- (Br)- Rack of Lamb

Betterave - (Fr)- Beets

Beurre Blanc-(Fr) - An emulsified sauce made of a wine or vinegar reduction blended with softened butter. Used to accompany fish, vegetables, and poultry dishes.

Beurre fondue -(Fr) -Melted butter and stock

Beurre manie-(Fr) -Equal quantities of butter and flour mixed to a smooth paste; used for thickening small quantities of sauce.

Beurre noir-(Fr) Blackened or burned butter.

Beurre noisette-(Fr) Brown butter that has a nutty flavor.

Beurre-(Fr) - Butter

Bhat ya Patnijokra- (In) Soybeans

Bhatura-(In)-Bread

Bhindi- (In)- Okra

Bhoona-(In)- expanding the flavor of spice in hot fat.

Bhuna-(In)-Pan fried

Bhunana-(In)-Roast

Bialy- (Yd)- Bagel type of roll that is baked only without a hole, center is filled with onions.

Bibim- (Kr) Soba noodles with vegetable and kim chi in a sweet and spicy sauce.

Bienenstich-(Gm)- "Bee sting Cake"- Sweet yeast dough filled with a crème chiboust. Topped with a layer of honey caramelized almonds.

Bier-(Gm)- Beer

Bing Tong -(Ch)-Sugar

Birchermüesli-(Sw)- Whole grain cereal soaked overnight with milk, yogurt, or juice then served with fresh or dried fruit

Biryani-(In)- Baked rice with vegetables, meat.

Biscotti- (It) Twice baked Italian cookies flavored with anise seed, almonds, or chocolate, served with espresso or cappuccino.

Bisque- (Fr)A thick cream soup made from the puree of shellfish thickened with rice.

Bistec-(Cr)- Butterflied steak marinated with lemon, olive oil and pepper then grilled. Served with black beans and rice in Cuba.

Bistecca- (It) - Steak

Blanc de Blancs-W. (Fr) – "White of Whites"- white wines made from white grapes, chardonnay grapes.

169

Blanc de Noirs- (Fr) – "White of Blacks" white wines made from black grapes, pinot noir grapes.

Blanc Mange 1. -(Fr) Pudding made from milk, cream, almonds and gelat(In) 2. (Br) – Pudding made from milk, sugar and cornstarch

Blanc-(Fr) 1. White 2. A cooking liquid of water, lemon juice, flour and salt. White

Blanch -To plunge into boiling water or oil to partially cook.

Blanchir-(Fr) blanching

Blanco- (It) -White

Blanquette-(Fr) A white stew, typically veal or fowl that has been blanched

Blend- The combination of two or more ingredients which are mixed until they are consistent.

Blind Bake-(Br) baking a pie or short crust with weights or a covering to prevent leavening

Blinis-(Eu) A yeast leavened small pancake made of buckwheat flour. These pancakes are traditionally served with caviar and sour cream.

Blintz-(Yd)- crepe filled with cottage cheese, and often served with fresh fruit or fruit preserves.

Bloom- 1. To dissolve gelatin in cold water so that when melted it does not cloud or clump. 2. A cocoa fat separation on chocolate.

Blown Stage-cooking equal parts sugar and water until it reaches112 ºC, 234 ºF

Bò kho-(Se)-Vietnamese beef curry with tomato, ginger, garlic, shallot, and lemongrass.

Bocconcini -(It) Small bits of food, typically small mozzarella balls

Bodega- (Sp) Winery

Body- Wine term which describes the weight of the wine across the palate. Examples; light body – Proscecco, medium body- Pinot Noir, full body Cabernet.

Bœuf - (Fr)- Beef

Bøfsandwich- (Sc)- Danish hamburger served with brown gravy on a bun with grilled onions.

Boil-To cook in liquid at 212º (at sea level).

Bok Bang-(Ch)-Pancakes served with Moo Shu

Bok Cho -(Ch)-White rice vinegar

Bok Choy -(Ch)- A small green vegetable in the cabbage family.

Bok Ker -(Ch)- Eggplant

Boletus- A type of wild mushroom like porcinis.

Bollito Misto- (It) stew made of meat, and zampone, boiled in broth. Served with pickled onions, cornichons, and mustard.

Bollito- (It) To Boil

Bolognese -(It) Ragu sauce of meat, tomato, mirepoix and milk

Bombe-(Fr) An ice cream specialty of different flavors made in a round mould with layers of cake and topped with a meringue.

Boniato -(La) South American sweet potatoes

Bonne Femme-(Fr) Garnish of potatoes, bacon, onions and mushrooms for meat, rustic style.

Boquerones-(Sp)- Vinegar -marinated white anchovies.

Bordeaux blend- this wine must contain at least two of the following varietals Cabernet Franc, Cabernet Sauvignon, Carmenère, Malbec, Merlot, and Petit Verdot. The purpose it to provide consistency in the production of wine from year to year.

Bordeaux- (Fr) A wine region divided by the banks of the Gironde estuary and more particularly the banks of the Dordogne and Garonne rivers. Wine produced on the left bank are primarily blended with Cabernet Sauvignon, whereas the right bank is blended with Merlot.

Bordelaise-(Fr) - The cuisine of Bordeaux. Usually a brown sauce that includes marrow, shallots and red wine. Fish dishes with this name will be cooked with white Bordeaux wine

Böreks- Stuffed Turkish savory pastries

Borscht- (Eu) -A peasant soup from Eastern Europe containing beets and beef. The cold version is served with sour cream.

Boston Cream Pie- Sponge cake baked in a pie shell, split in half and filled with pastry cream, topped with confection sugar or chocolate fondant.

Bot Gok -(Ch)-Star anise

Botifarra-(Sp) Much like the white boudin this Catalan pork sausage is flavored with fennel and black pepper with a hint of cinnamon.

Botrytis Cinerea- A fungus that helps to dehydrate the grape so that the wines level of sugar increases.

Bouchée-(Fr) Small patty shells made from puff pastry. Boucheé a la Reine

Boucherie-(Cr)- An autumn event in which animals are communally slaughtered and processed to maximize utilization of every part of the animal, traditionally pigs.

Boudin- 1. (Fr) - Smooth textured sausages made from veal, pork, or chicken for the white versions. Made with blood and starch for the black version. 2.(Cr) –Hot and spicy version thickened with rice.

Bouillabaisse-(Fr) - A fisherman's stew made in Provence from fish scraps flavored with fennel leeks and tomatoes. Served with toasted bread and rouille.

Bouillé-(Fr) To boil

Bouillon-(Fr) Broth made of veal, beef or chicken.

Boulanger- (Fr) -Baker.

Boulette- (Cr) – Haitian meatballs served with fried plantains.

Bouquet – term used in the assessment of a wines aroma or nose.

Bouquet garni-(Fr) Parsley, thyme, bay leaf, garlic tied into a bundle and added to stocks for flavoring.

Bouquetiere-(Fr) "flower girl" arrangement of vegetables.

Boureka- (Yd)- baked savory pastry wrapped with fillo dough

Bourgeoisie-(Fr)- middle class, not haute style

Bourguignon-(Fr) - in the style of Burgundy. Dishes will include red or white burgundy wines, white mushrooms, pearl onions, and cured bacon.

Bourride- (Fr) a fish stew from southern France. The fish broth is strained and thickened with rouille.

Bracha- (Yd) Blessing over the meal

Braciole- (It) Well-seasoned slow roasted shoulder

Braesaola -(It) Shaved dried beef filet served for antipasti or in a salad

Braise- the method of browning meat and vegetables in a small amount of fat to caramelize and retain moisture. Cooking is continued with a moderate amount of liquid in a covered marmite in the oven until the item is fork tender.

Bran- The outer shell of grains like wheat, which are high in fiber.

Brandade- (Sp) Salt cod pureed with olive oil and potatoes.

Branzino -(It) Sea bass

Brasato- (It) -to braise

Bratkartoffeln- (Gm) Pan fried yellow gold potatoes with bacon, onions, and parsley.

Brawn- (Br) – A type of headcheese.

Breading-The process of coating a food item in flour, eggs, and bread crumbs before frying or baking.

Break- the term used to describe an item that has experienced fat separation.

Bresaola- (It) Thin sliced of cured beef which is prepared for scecondo piatto which is the traditional meat course.

Bretonne-(Fr) Served with Brittany style white beans.

Brigade System-(Br) refined by Chef Auguste Escoffier this staffing system clearly defines job tasks and responsibilities.

Brine-A curing liquid flavored with salt, aromatics, sugar.

Brioche-(Fr) - A sponge dough flavored with butter and eggs that is baked in a fluted tin

Broche (la) -(Fr) A roasting spit for whole pieces of meat.

Brochette-(Fr) prepared on a skewer.

Brodetto- (It) Fish soup

Brodo -(It) Broth

Broil-To cook with direct heat over the food product so that it browns the top in order to gratinee.

Brombeeren –(Gm)- blackberries

Brot –(Gm)- bread

Broth- A meat flavored stock or liquid.

Brouillé -(Fr) Scrambled, as the process for scrambling eggs

Brulé- (Fr) Topped with a layer of dark caramelized sugar.

Brunoise-(Fr) -A fine dice either 1/8" square or 1/16" square.

Bruschetta- (It) Grilled slices of bread brushed with olive oil and fresh garlic. This version of Italian Toast is commonly topped with marinated diced tomatoes.

Brut-(Fr) Dry usually refers to a Champagne that is not sweet, but very dry.

Bruxelloise -(Fr) From Brussels Belgium, with Brussels sprouts and olive shaped potatoes.

Bubble and Squeak-(Br) Leftover pan fried vegetables from a roast dinner, usually with cabbage and potato.

Bucatini- (It) A hollow form of spaghetti served with a Sauce Bolognese.

Buffet- A assortment of hot and cold foods, used to visually stimulate the appetite.

Bulgogi- (Kr)- Marinated barbecued beef or meat.

Bulgur- Cracked whole wheat used for tabouleh salad.

Bún Riêu-(Se)-Vietnamese soup of crab, pork, noodles, tomato finished with greens, bean sprouts, green onion, mint, sorrel, and limes.

Bündnerfleisch- (Sw) cured and air-dried beef that is thinly sliced and served with hearty bread.

Buñuelo-(Sp)- Doughnut created by Sephardic Jews to celebrate Hanukkah.

Burgundy- (Fr) A wine region in the eastern part of France famous for both white wines made from Chardonnay, and red wines made from Pinot Noir.

Buri Sushi – (Jp) Mature yellowtail fish

Burnt Ends- Crispy ends of a bbq beef brisket

Burrata- (It) – "Buttered" a type of cheese that has an outer layer of fresh mozzarella and an inner creamy filling of fresh curd blended with cream.

Burridda -(It) Fisherman's stew

Burrito- (La)- Wrapped closed end sandwich made of a tortilla filled with meat or beans, topped with a tomato-based sauce. Tex-Mex and California version are filled with a variety of beans, rice, salsa, cheese, sour cream, guacamole.

Burro -(It) - Butter

Butter Chicken- (In)- Makani style chicken from Punjab. Tandoori chicken that is refreshed in a sauce of onions, butter and tomato with spices.

Buttercream- An icing made from butter and or shortening, sugar and eggs.

> 1. **American-** Shortening is whipped with confectionary sugar.
> 2. **French-** Hot syrup is added to egg yolks and whipped to make a sabyon, then whipped butter is added with flavoring.
> 3. **German-** Rich pastry cream is blended with whipped butter and flavoring.
> 4. **Italian-** An Italian meringue is made by adding a steady stream of hot syrup to egg whites while whipping, when cooled the mixture is blended with whipped butter and flavoring.
> 5. **Swiss-** Sugar and egg whites are heat then a Swiss meringue is prepared, when cooled whipped butter and flavoring are added.

Butterfly- horizontal slicing of an item to double the surface area.

Buttermilk- The product that is left over from the production of butter, high in lactic acid it has a sour flavor.

C

Ça marche-(Fr) – "order in"

Cabrales- (Sp) -a variety of blue cheese from Spain from Asturias.

Cacciatore- (It) Hunters stew of game tomato, wine, peppers and mushrooms. Commonly used for chicken.

Café au Lait-(Cr)-Chicory coffee with steamed milk

Caille- (Fr)- Quail

Cajeta-(La)-Similar to Dulce de Leche but made from goats' milk.

Cajun-(Cr)- French Canadians that settled in the bayou area of the Mississippi delta. Robust flavors, rustic cooking techniques that utilize ingredients that are locally sourced is the cornerstone of the cuisine.

Calabacita-(Sp) A squash used in Latin American dishes.

Calabaza-(Cr)- Squash based stew from the Carribean

Calamari- (It) "squid".

Calçot-(Sp) Small leeks that are grown in the spring commonly grilled.

Caldo Gallego-(Sp) A Galacian stew of beef, beans and green cabbage.

Caldo Verde- (Pt) soup made from kale, broth, potatoes, olive oil and sausage.

Callaloo-(Cr) -Leafy greens simmered with coconut and spice

Calvados- (Fr)An apple brandy from Normandy.

Calzone- (It)-A half-moon shaped savory turnover filled with cheese, meat and vegetables.

Campagne- Country style forcemeat

Canapé-(Fr) -a small open face sandwich made of a base, spread, nourishing element, and garnish served as a Hors d' oeuvre.

Canard- (Fr) Duck

Canela -(La) Cinnamon

Caneton- (Fr) Duckling

Canh chua la giang (Se)-Vietnamese sour soup of fish, sour greens (la giang), shallot, garlic, chile, fish sauce and tomato.

Canh ga nau mang- Se-Vietnamese soup of chicken with bamboo

Cannelloni- (It) Pasta tubes that are filled with meat, cheese or fish. The tubes are then sauced and baked until golden brown with cheese on top.

Cannoli- (It) A crisp pastry cylinder filled with sweetened ricotta cheese, nuts, and dried fruit

Caper Berries - The fruit that develops from the flowers of the Capernium Plant.

Capers- The unopened flower bud of the Capernium Plant. The buds are preserved in salt and vinegar and used in dressings, sauces, and as a condiment.

Capicolla- (It)-A spiced and pressed Italian pork shoulder ham.

Capon- A castrated chicken that has very plump breasts.

Caponata-(It)- a spread or cold salad containing eggplant, raisins, celery, ripe tomatoes, and pine nuts seasoned with red wine vinegar and extra virgin olive oil.

Capra- (It) Young Goat

Caprese -(It) In the style of Capri, tomato salad with basil and buffalo mozzarella

Caquelon- Sw- enameled cast iron pot for fondue.

Carambola-(Cr)- Star fruit

Caramel Stage-cooking equal parts sugar and water until it reaches192 ºC, 377 ºF

Caramel-boiled sugar that has been allowed to brown

Caramelize-(Fr) -1. To melt sugar until it turns to a brown liquid. 2. To complex the flavor of a product by heating the outer layer until brown.

Caramelization- to develop flavor of a product by browning the exterior with heat.

Carapulcra- (Sp) -Peruvian dish of pork, potatoes, cumin and peanuts cooked in Inca clay pots.

Carbonara- (It) Pasta sauce made of pancetta, eggs, and parmesan cheese.

Carbonic Maceration- Fermentation is produced in the whole cluster of grapes by carbon dioxide.

Carbonnade A Flemish braised beef steak braised in Chimay beer.

Cardoon- A artichoke type of vegetable that looks like celery ribs

Carne-(Sp) Meat

Carnitas- (La)-Mexican fried meat tidbits. Pork is fried in oil, cinnamon, chilies, and oranges until fork tender. Served on toasted corn tortillas with Pico de Gallo

Carpaccio- (It) very thin slices of raw beef and drizzled with olive oil, mayonnaise, lemon or parmesan cheese served for Antipasto.

Carpet Bag Steak-(Br)- Tender steak that has a pocket filled with a plump oyster seasoned with Worcestershire sauce before it is grilled

Carré- (Fr) Rack. Knife cut ¾" dice.

Carte du jour - (Fr) Menu of the day

Cartellate- It- Thin strips of dough, fried, drizzled with honey

Cartouche - (Fr) Round cover of greaseproof paper for shallow poaching/

Casserole An earthenware dish with a lid, also the dish of food cooked in it

Cassis A liqueur made from blackcurrant

Cassoulet- (Fr) - A casserole of white beans, duck confit, lamb, pork, and sausage.

Caul Fat- The fat lining a pig's stomach which can be used to hold together forcemeats and roulades.

Cava-(Sp) Sparkling wine from Spain

Cavatelli -A gnocchi made from ricotta cheese.

Cave- (Fr) Cellar

Caviar- Sturgeon eggs that have been salted to preserved them. Caviar should only be served with toast points or blinis, sour cream and lemon.

Cazuela -(La) Chilean hearty meat stew cooked in a dish of the same name.

Çebiç-(Tu)- Whole roasted kid or lamb with garlic and herbs

Ceci - (It) Chickpeas

Celeriac- The root of celery.

Center of the Plate- this term refers to the main featured item or point of sale that focuses on the guest perceived nutritional and economical value.

Cepes- A wild mushroom with a meaty texture from the boletus family.

Cervena-New Zealand farm raised venison.

Ceviche- (La)/(Cr)- Seafood or fish are marinated with citrus to denature the protein which firms the texture then flavored with chili, onion and cilantro.

Ćevapčići- (Eu) – Croatian beef and pork kebab links that are charcoal grilled.

Chai- (In) Hot tea

Chaku-(In)- Knife

Challah- (Yd)- Braided egg bread developed by Ashkenazi Jews for celebrations including Passover and Shabbat, Sabbath. A three-braided loaf symbolizes the creation, the exodus, and the messianic periods. A six braid represents the six days we work. The twelve braid represents the twelve showbreads in the temple.

Chalupa- (La)- Boat shaped masa dough that is fried and filled with meat and topped with onions, smoked chilies and salsa

Champenoise-(Fr)- Champagne Method

Champignon -(Fr) - white button mushrooms.

Chan Bao -(Ch)- Bun filled with minced BBQ pork, green onion & oyster sauce.

Chana Masal-(In)- Popular vegetarian curry made with chick peas

Channa Dal-(In)- Yellow split peas, chick peas in some regions

Chanterelle- A trumpet shaped wild mushroom with a golden color.

Chantilly cream- (Br) Whipped cream and sugar.

Chantilly-(Fr) - Lightly sweetened whipped cream.

Chao Fan-(Ch)- Fried rice

Chapatis- (In)- Whole wheat flat-bread made like a tortilla

Chapelure-(Fr) Bread crumbs made from dried baguettes.

Chappan Kaddoo- (In) Summer squash or zucchini

Chaptalization- Increasing the amount of alcohol in the wine by adding sugar while the wine is fermenting.

Char Siu -(Ch)- "Burned Fork" Typically pork that is marinated then smoked to give a BBQ flavor.

Char Siu Bao -(Ch)- BBQ pork bun

Charain- (Yd)- Spicy horseradish sauce.

Charcuterie- (Fr) A general term for any pork preparations that are ground, cured, smoked, or processed. Items include hams, sausages, , pates, and rillettes.

Charlotte-(Fr) – 1. a mould with cake or lady fingers and filled with a Bavarian cream. 2. A hot dessert with buttered strips of bread in a mold that is filled with fruit then baked.

Charlotte Royal (Fr) Charlotte that uses jelly rolls**.**

Charlotte Russe (Fr) – Charlotte that uses lady fingers.

Charros- (Sp) Cowboy Style

Chasseur-(Fr) Hunter style, mushrooms, tomato and tarragon flavored brown sauce.

Château- (Fr) An estate that produces wine in France.

Chateaubriand -(Br) Head of the beef tenderloin named after Francois Rene Chateaubriand, the French Minister to the Court of St. James. The three muscles represent the Holy Trinity. Roasted then carved tableside served with two sauces

Chaud-(Fr) Hot

Chaud-Froid-(Fr) - roasted meat served cold, topped with a veloute, garnished and glazed with aspic.

Chauffant-(Fr) -Bain Marie of hot salted water used for reheating foods.

Chawal- (In) Long grain rice

Cheeni-(In)- Sugar

Chef de communard-(Fr) -the cook responsible for all staff meals.

Chef de Cuisine-(Fr) - Executive Chef or head chef in charge of the kitchen.

Chef de entremetier-(Fr) -the person responsible for all vegetables, starch and hot appetizer dishes. In some kitchens, they will also complete the preparation for hot desserts.

Chef de friturier-(Fr) -the person responsible for all fried and pan-fried dishes.

Chef de garde manger-(Fr) -the person responsible for all aspects of the cold kitchen. Literally the "keeper of all foods to be consumed".

Chef de grillardin -(Fr) –the person responsible for all grilled and broiled dishes.

Chef de nuit-(Fr) -this person is responsible for the ala carte dishes. He or she will also close out the room service shift after the dining room is closed.

Chef de partie-(Fr) -the person responsible for a certain department.

Chef de patissier-(Fr) –the person responsible for all pastries, confections, entremets, and desserts.

Chef de poissonnier-(Fr) -the person responsible for all handling, storing, and preparation of fish and seafood.

Chef de potage -(Fr) -the person responsible for all soups, and stocks.

Chef de rang-(Fr) -the head waiter of the dining room.

Chef de rotisseur-(Fr) -the person responsible for all roasted and braised dishes.

Chef de saucier-(Fr) -the person responsible for all sauce, sautéed entrees. In some cases, this person is a type of Sous Chef.

Chef, Sous -(Fr) –the person who is second in command under the Chef de Cuisine. Responsible for scheduling.

Chef Tournant-(Fr) -the person who relieves other on their day off. Rounds Chef.

Chemical Leavener- A chemical reaction from the combination of acid and alkaline in the form of bicarbonate of soda, cream of tartar and baking powder. The gas that forms leavens quick breads, cookies and cakes.

Chemiser -(Fr) To line or coat a mold before adding filling to aid in the appearance.

Chervil- an aromatic herb has curly, dark green leaves with a slight anise flavor.

Cheung Fun -(Ch)- Steamed rice paper rolls.

Chevre- (Fr) Goat's milk cheese.

Chiacchiere-It- thin fried dough dusted with powdered sugar.

Chiboust-(Fr) - pastry cream filling for the Gâteau Saint-Honor, made of pastry cream, Italian meringue and gelatin

Chicharrón-(Sp)- Crispy fried pigskin snacks.

Chicken à la Maryland – (Fr)- Fried chicken served with corn oysters or fritters, sautéed bananas and a sauce supreme. Sometimes topped with batter fried onion rings and rashers of bacon.

Chicory- 1.A type of bitter lettuce 2.(Cr)- dried herb used to flavor coffee.

Chiffon Cake – Whipped egg white are folded into a batter of egg yolks, sugar, flour, and oil.

Chiffonade-(Fr) - A fine julienne of herbs, or lettuce greens.

Chilaquiles- (Sp)-Mexican fried corn tortillas simmered in chilies, tomatoes, and garlic made into a sauce.

Chimichanga-(La) –deep fat fried burrito, served with either sour cream, salsa, and guacamole or a queso sauce.

Chimichurri- (La) Raw sauce made with parsley, chili pepper, oil, garlic, oregano and vinegar. Typically served with grilled meats and vegetables.

Chinese Mirepoix- Aromatic base of ginger, garlic and scallion.

Ching Cha -(Ch)-Green tea

Chinois -(Fr) A cone shaped strainer, also known as china cap.

Chipolata-(Fr) Small pork sausages, similar in flavor to Italian sweet sausage.

Chipotle- A dried and smoked jalapeno.

Chiqueter-(Fr) To lightly score the cut edges of puff pastry to ensure it rises evenly.

Cho Mein -(Ch)- thick wheat noodles, served in a soup like udon.

Choccolata- It- Chocolate

Chocolate Liquor- Unsweetened chocolate.

Chok- Se-Thai breakfast rice porridge

Cholent- (Yd)-slow cooked stew with to be served on the Sabbath. Whole eggs are cooked in the stew overnight for breakfast while the bean-based stew is consumed after temple service for lunch

Cholia-(In)- Garbanzo beans

Chongqing Huo Guo-(Ch)- Hot pot with very spicy broth, numbing chilies.

Chop- 1. To roughly cut into small pieces with a knife. 2.A sliced portion of meat on the bone from the loin

Chopped tomatoes.

Chorizo-(Sp)- A cured Spanish pork sausage ranging in seasoning from mild and sweet to hot.- (La) A raw pork sausage ranging in seasoning from mild and sweet to hot.

Choron-(Fr) - A Béarnaise sauce with reduced tomatoes.

Chot llaichi-(In)-Green cardamom

Chou - (Fr)- Cabbage

Chou de Bruxelles - (Fr)- Brussels sprout

Chou-fleur - (Fr)- Cauliflower

Choucroute-(Fr) - Alsatian dish of sauerkraut, sausages, and smoked meats which has been seasoned with garlic, caraway seeds, juniper berries and braised in white wine.

Chow Fun-(Ch)- Very wide rice noodles, typically served in a brown sauce.

Chow Yau -(Ch)-Soy sauce, dark

Chow-chow-1. A vegetable relish flavored with vinegar, mustard and sugar. 2. (In) Chayote squash

Christmas Pudding- Steamed pudding made of beef suet, dried fruits, crumbs. Set ablaze with brandy and surrounded with holly, served with hard sauce.

Christophie-(Cr)- Chayote squash stewed with coconut milk

Chub- a 1 to 10lb plastic tube of ground meat preparation packaged to reduce oxidation

Chuen Guen Pay -(Ch)-Eggroll wrappers

Chun Yao Bang -(Ch)- Fried onion pancakes.

Chun Guen -(Ch)-Spring rolls

Churrasco- (La) Grilled meat commonly served with Chimichurri.

Churros- (Sp) Fried Pâté à Choux stick dipped in sugar.

Chutney- cooked fruit relish, made with vinegar, sugar and spices.

Chutoro - (Jp) Portions cut from the upper belly which have a moderate amount of fat used for sushi.

Ciboule - (Fr)- Scallion

Ciboulette - (Fr)- Chives

Çiğ köfte-(Tu)- Minced raw lamb or beef with kirmizi biber, spices, garlic, tomato and onion. Shaped into small raw meatballs.

Cioppino- (It) A San Francisco fish and shellfish stew flavored with white wine, garlic, and tomato, spiced with chilies.

Cipaille- (Br) – Canadian wild game pie. Similar to a Tourtiere pork pie.

Citron - (Fr)- Lemon

Civet-(Fr) A blood thickened brown stew of game, usually hare.

Clafoutis-(Fr) - A cherry and cheese cake tarte.

Clamart-(Fr) A dish served with a fresh pea puree.

Clarified butter- Whole butter melted on low heat until it separates from the milk solids. The fat is removed, strained, and heated until clear.

Clarify -To remove the impurities

Clear Flour- the outlayer of the wheat endosperm is ground into a flour used for bread production

Clotted Cream- The cream that forms on top of unpasteurized cream used for scones at tea.

Clouté -(Fr) Studded

Cloying- A wine term used in wine tasting to describe a wine that lacks balance or acidity.

Club Sandwich- Triple decker sandwich filled with sliced turkey lettuce and tomato on one layer then bacon lettuce and tomato on the attaching layers, the bread is toasted then spread with mayonnaise. Held together with frilled toothpicks and cut into quarters.

Çoban Salatasi-(Tu)-Shepherds salad of cucumber, hot peppers, onion, tomato, garlic, olive oil, parsley and lemon.

Cobb Salad- A bed of salad greens topped with rows of diced; turkey, tomato, hard-boiled egg, avocado, blue cheese and bacon. Created at the Brown Derby in Hollywood,, it was dressed tableside with a creamy vinaigrette flavored with mustard and Worcestershire.

Cobbler-(Br)- A hot dessert made with fruit and either a batter -based or a short dough crust.

Cochon- (Fr) Pork

Cock-a-Leekie- Scottish soup made of chicken, leeks, and barley.

Cocotte -(Fr) Porcelain or earthenware shallow dish, used for cooking

Coeur à la Crème-(Fr) - "the heart of the cream". Fromage blanc with cream and sugar.

Colbert-(Fr) A compound butter made with wine, tarragon, and butter.

Combine-To mix ingredients to a homogenous product.

Commis -(Fr) Apprentice cook

Compote-Br Stewed sweetened fruit

Compound Butter- a flavored butter used to enhance a finished product. e.g. Maitre d' Hotel Butter.

Concassé-(Fr) -rough chop

Conchiglie- shell shaped pasta

Condiment - pre-prepared sauce like ketchup, mayonnaise, Worcestershire used to enhance. The flavor of a dish.

Conejo Cazadora- (Sp) – Rabbit braised with Serrano ham, onions, tomato, mushrooms, and white wine.

Confectioners' Sugar- Powdered sugar made with sucrose and cornstart(Ch)

Confit-(Fr) – to preserve a product by cooking slowly in fat. e.g. preserved duck or goose meat that is braised in its own fat until tender.

Confiture-(Fr) - fruit preserves.

Connoisseur -(Fr) Expert

Consommé-(Fr) - A clarified broth or stock

Contorno -(It) Vegetable side dishes that are served just after the Secondi or entree

Contrefilet -(Fr) -Boneless strip loin of beef.

Coo-coo-(Cr)- Caribbean style polenta or grits

Coppa-(It)- a form of salami from the shoulder of pork that is cured, cooked and dried.

Coq au Vin-(Fr) -Old chicken, or hen braised in wine.

Coquille St Jacques- (Fr)-Scallops are served in a shell casserole with a Duchess border. The sauce is made from a mushrooms, shallots, white wine and cream that nappes the scallops. It is topped with shredded Gruyere cheese before it is baked or broiled.

Coquille- (Fr) -Shell

Coquito-(Cr)- Coconut Nog from Puerto Rico

Cordon -(Fr) - thin line of sauce to border a plate.

Corked- A wine term that describes the poor condition due to improper storage, handling whereby the cork has permitted a fungus to grow in the bottle or on the cork.

Cornichon- (Fr) -a tiny sour pickle used to accompany cured meats.

Côte- (Fr)- Slope, a wine term to describe the gradual elevation in regard to the terroir of the vineyard.

Côte-(Fr) – **1.** Rib chop from the loin, 2. Sides

Cotechino-(It)- fine ground sweet pork sausage.

Côtelette-(Fr) **Cutlet** from the loin, loin chop

Cotijo-(La) Feta like cheese used to flavor tacos, beans, soups

Couche- Couche-(Cr)-Fried cornbread topped with milk and sugar served for breakfast.

Coulibiac- (Eu) -A savory pie like a salmon made with sliced of salmon, boiled eggs, cabbage and mushrooms

Coulis-(Fr) – A puree of fruit or vegetables

Country Style- " Campagne" a course textured forcemeat.

Coupe-(Fr) - portioned serving bowl.

Courgette- (Fr) zucchini

Court bouillon-1. (Fr) A solution of white wine or vinegar, water and aromatics in which food is poached. 2.(Cr)- a rich spicy vegetable and tomato broth used to flavor gumbos, etouffe, and fish.

Couscous-(Ar) a dish containing large ground semolina kernels that are steamed until tender, also the name of the dish it is served

Couverture- (Fr) – Sweet chocolate with no additional cocoa butter added. Good for covering, dipping, and molding chocolates.

Coxinha- (La) Fried croquette of minced chicken, shaped like a leg.

Crackling- (Br)-Crisp rendered skin

Cracknel- (Br) hard crisp biscuit

Creaming- Creaming is simply the mixing together of fat and sugar to form a smooth paste with the purpose of distributing the fat and sugar evenly while also aerating the dough

Crècy -(Fr) The use of carrots

Crema Catalana- (Sp) -a custard with a very thin burned sugar crust. Similar to Crème Brulee

Crémant-(Fr) Sparkling wine that is produced outside of the Champagne region of France.

Crème Anglaise-(Fr) -Custard sauce of scalded milk, egg yolks, vanilla and sugar.

Crème Bavarois-(Fr) –Light dessert of crème anglaise, whipped cream and bloomed gelatin flavored with fruit purees, chocolate, or liqueurs.

Crème Brûlée (Fr) – Rich custard with a layer of caramelized sugar on top.

Crème Caramel-(Fr) – Plain custard baked in a caramelized sugar line mold, when chilled the sugar forms and syrup. Served syrup side up.

Crème Chiboust-(Fr) –Pastry cream lightened with whipped cream or whipped egg white, flavored with orange zest and liqueur.

Creme Chibouste- (Fr) Pastry cream blended with Italian meringue.

Crème Fouetteé- (Fr) Whipped cream

Crème Fraiché- (Fr) A Heavy Cream based sour cream. May be purchased or made by combining 1-part heavy cream to 1-part sour cream and allowing it to develop under refrigeration 2 - 3 days before using.

Crème Patisserie-(Fr) - pastry cream made from scalded milk, egg yolks, sugar, vanilla and thickened with flour.

Crème-(Fr) - Cream

Cremolata -It- Italian ice with fruit pieces

Crémeux- (Fr) "Creamy"- is a sauce anglaise mixed with chocolate and used for a filling. A fruit crémeux can be made with a fruit puree and white chocolate.

Creole-(Cr)- People of Spanish, French and Western African origin who settled in the Caribbean and Louisianna. These people combined the culture of their cuisines with others to develop a unique style of cooking.

Crêpes -(Fr) - Thin pancakes

Crêpes al la reine -(Fr) - Thin pancakes filled with poached chicken, mushrooms and sauce supreme.

Crêpes Normande -(Fr) - Thin pancakes with apple filling and sauce anglaise.

Crêpes Suzette -(Fr) - Thin pancakes with sweet orange and brandy sauce.

Crepinette-(Fr) - small sausage covered with caul fat or a layer of forcemeat surrounding a tender cut of meat with caul fat.

Crespelle- (It) Crépe that is used instead of pasta for lasagna manicotti and cannelloni.

Crevette - (Fr)- Shrimp

Crianza- (Sp)- Wine term for the ageing of wine in oak.

Critical Control Points- key areas of control in the receiving, storing, handling, preparation and service of food as prescribed by HACCP.

Croissant- Laminated dough made from butter, flour, yeast formed into a crescent shape.

Croque Madame-(Fr) – Toasted Brioche bread is layered with Bayonne ham and Mornay sauce with Dijon mustard. Top with additional sauce and Gruyere cheese. Gratinee then top with fried egg.

Croque Monsieur-(Fr) – Toasted French Bread is layered with Bayonne ham and cheese béchamel, grain mustard Top with additional sauce and Gruyere cheese and gratinee.

Croquembouche-(Fr) **French** wedding cake or dessert made up of cream filled profiteroles, shaped in a cone with caramel.

Croquette-(Fr) Molded or shaped food preparation breaded and deep fat fried until it becomes golden brown.

Cross Contamination- the transfer of bacteria from one source to another that can result in a food borne illness.

Cross Contact- contaminating food from person to product.

Crostata -(It) Sweet or savory tart

Crostini- (It) Toasted slices of bread that has been brushed with olive oil. Served with marinated tomatoes, chopped liver, or tapenade.

Croustade- (Fr) – Baked pastry case

Croûte -(Fr) –crust

Crouton- (Fr) -toasted or fried pieces of bread which can be used as a base for canapés or as a garnish for soups or salads.

Cru- (Fr) "growth" from a singular vineyard.

Crudite-(Fr) - A finger food of various raw vegetables served with a creamy dip.

Crudo -(It) Raw

Cruller- twisted yeast raised doughnut, coated with cinnamon sugar or confectionary sugar.

Crumpets- (Br) Small English Muffins served at Tea.

Crushing- breaking the grape's skin so that the juice is exposed to the skin to develop flavor and color.

Csirkepaprikás-(Eu) Chicken paprikash from Hungary.

Cuban Mirepoix- Aromatic base of onion, cubanella peppers, and garlic.

Cubano- (Cr) Cuban pressed sandwich filled with roast pork, ham, Swiss cheese, pickle, mustard and salami.

Cuire al nap (Fr) -Coating the back of a spoon a la nappe.

Cuisse -(Fr) Leg of -from the section below the thigh of poultry.

Cumberland Sauce-(Br) An English sauce made of currant jelly, lemon, orange and port wine

Curing Salt- a blend of sodium chloride and sodium nitrite used to preserve meat and inhibit some forms of bacteria growth.

Curry -Indian dish known as a Kari that includes vegetables, meats and spices that are cooked until tender.

Custard- a basic preparation of eight eggs to a quart of dairy used for savory and sweet preparations.

Cuttlefish- a mollusk similar in appearance to squid.

Cuvée- (Fr) "blend" term used in the production of wine.

D

Daab-(In)- Fresh coconut

Dacquoise-(Fr) - torte made of nut flavored meringues layered with whipped cream.

Dahi-(In)-Yogurt

Dal- (In)-dried beans, split peas, and lentils

Dan Dan Noodles-(Ch) -Szechwan chili spiced egg noodles with preserved vegetables and crispy minced pork.

Danger Zone- refers the temperature range that food can grow the greatest number of bacteria in a short time. The range is from 41° to 140° however some laws follow 41° to 135°. Find out the standard of your local public health officer.

Dariole-(Fr) A small round mold or timbale

Darné -(Fr) A center cut slice of a whole round fish, a thick straight slice.

Dashi- A Japanese preparation that is used like a fish stock. It is made with dried bonito and kombu seaweed.

Daube-(Fr) - A stew of meat with wine, broth, herbs and vegetables.

Dauphine-(Fr) - fried potato puffs made of 2 parts of duchesse potatoes and 1 part of Pâte à Choux.

Dauphinoise-(Fr) - potato gratin with heavy cream and garlic, topped with Gruyere cheese.

Ddukbokki- (Kr)- spicy rice and fish cake stew.

Découper- (Fr) To cut with scissors, a knife or a pastry cutter.

Décuire- (Fr) To stop the process of caramel from cooking by adding liquid to prevent it from hardening (e.g. cream, butter).

Deep Fat Fry- The process of cooking a product submerged in fat that is between 325°- 350°.

Deglaze- (Fr) To dilute pan juices with stock, or wine or to release the caramelized particles from the pan.

Degraisser -(Fr) - To skim the fat from a stock.

Dejeuner (Fr) Dinner

Demi -(Fr) Half

Demi-glace -(Fr) -A reduction of half Espagnole sauce and half fond de veau.

Demi tasse (Fr) Half cup

Demi-Sec – Fr "medium dry" a wine that is slightly sweeter than a dry wine.

Démouler- (Fr) To remove from the mold.

Deschear (Fr) -To remove unwanted moisture or humidity through heat.

Desi Makkan-(In) Butter made from yogurt

Desosser -(Fr) –fabricating meats from the primal cuts.

Détrempe- (Fr) A paste made from water and flour; used for puff pastry.

Devil's Food Cake- chocolate cake with a higher percent of baking soda which turns the cake slightly red.

Dhingri-(In)- Mushroom

Diable-(Fr)- Devil, hot and spicy

Dieppoise-(Fr) Mussel garnish or mussel-based dish.

Dijonnaise-(Fr) - Dijon mustard as the main flavor ingredient for a sauce, vinaigrette or preparation in the style of Dijon France.

Dim Sum- (Ch) Snacks or lunch dishes in China which include egg rolls, shrimp toast, fried and steamed dumplings.

Dinde- (Fr) Turkey

Diplomat Crème- (Fr)/(Sw)- Whipped cream and vanilla cream or pastry cream combined and used as a filling.

Dirty Rice-(Cr)- Highly seasoned pilaf of trinity (celery, onion, green pepper), livers, giblets. Some versions include sausage or bacon.

Disgorgement- The removal of the yeast in the neck of the bottle of a sparkling wine.

Disjoint-To segment poultry into pieces at the joints.

Dissolve-To put into a solution so that the original form is no longer visible.

Ditalini- (It)-Short pasta tubes.

Dragon Juice- Hot pepper oil

Doboschtorte –(Gm)- A seven-layer cake with mocha butter cream and caramel.

Docking- Piercing a dough to inhibit physical leavening.

Dolce -(It) -Candies and desserts

Dolma- (Gr) Stuffed grape leaves. Filled with cooked rice, lamb, and onion. These bundles are cooked and packed in olive oil and lemon slices.

Don -(Ch)- Chicken egg

Don Mein -(Ch)- Fresh egg noodles

Dönar Kebab- (Tu) Skewered layers marinated beef, roasted vertically. Used for pita sandwiches.

Dong Koo -(Ch)- Dried black mushrooms

Doodha-(In)-Milk

Doong Quar -(Ch)- Winter melon

Dorer- (Fr) To egg wash.

Dosage-(Fr) The addition of wine and additional sugar to a sparkling wine.

Dosai-(In)-Rice or lentil pancakes that are filled with potato or vegetable

Dow -(Ch)- Bean curd

Dow Gok -(Ch)-Yard Long beans

Dow Sa -(Ch)- Sweet black beans

Dow Sai -(Ch)- Sweet bean paste.

Dow See -(Ch)- Fermented black beans

Dow Sha -(Ch)- Red bean paste

Drained Weight- the strained weight of canned fruit

Dredge-To dust or coat a product with flour.

Drippings-(Br)-Fat and juice which are collected from roasting meat.

Du Barry-(Fr) The use of cauliflower in a dish.

Du jour-(Fr) Of the day, i.e. Soup of the Day.

Duchesse-(Fr) - potato purée that is flavored with butter, egg yolk, parmesan, nutmeg, salt and white pepper.

Dulce de Leche-(Cr) Sweetened milk is slowly cooked until maillard browning occurs and the consistency is very thick.

Dun Tat -(Ch)- Sweet custard tart served at the end of Dim Sum

Dung Fun-(Ch)- "Winter noodle"- made from various starches, cellophane noodles.

Dust-To lightly coat with either flour or sugar.

Duxelles-(Fr) -A filling made from cooked mushrooms, shallots, wine and parsley

E

E.P. Weight- Edible Portion Weight- the trimmed weight.

Eau - (Fr)- Water

Ebi Sushi -(Jp) – Poached Shrimp over rice

Éclair – a Pâte à Choux paste that is piped into sticks, baked, then filled with diplomat cream and topped with fondant or chocolate.

Écumer - (Fr)- To foam.

Een Sigh –(Ch)- Cilantro

Egg Cream- A soda fountain drink of whole milk, chocolate syrup and seltzer water, does not contain eggs or cream.

Eggwash- A mixture of eggs and milk used to seal and coat pastry items for the purpose of even browning.

Ei –(Gm)- egg

Eintopf –(Gm)- stew

Eis –(Gm)- ice

Eisbien- (Gm) Salt cured pork hock

Eiswein- (Gm) Ice wine

Émietter - (Fr)- To crumble

Émincer-(Fr) To cut into very thin strips for the purpose of sautéing.

Emmental- Sw- Swiss cheese from Emme valley

Empanada-(Sp)- Turnover filled with savory items.

Emulsify- The process of combining a fat into another product which allows the fat to be suspended in the product. e.g Mayonnaise

Enchilada- (La)- Filled corn tortilla then topped with a tomato and chili pepper-based sauce before it is baked.

Endosperm- The starchy inner portion of the wheat kernel.

Énfourner- (Fr)- To put into the oven

Engadiner Torte-(Sw)- Short dough discs are alternately layered with sweet almond filling, kirsch buttercream then topped with ground almond and sugar crumb.

Enginar- (Tu) - Artichokes

Ensalada- (Sp) -Salad

Ente–(Gm)- Duck

Entrecôte -(Fr) - boneless portioned steak from the strip lo(In)

Entrée-(Fr) The main course or dish, usually protein based.

Entremet- Fr- served between course, small dessert.

Épépiner - (Fr)- To remove the seeds

Épinard--(Fr) Spinach

Éplucher - (Fr)- To peel

Erbsen –(Gm)-Peas

Erdbeeren –(Gm)- Strawberries

Escabeche- 1. (Sp)-A well seasoned marinade used to flavor and preserve food by pickling. 2. Cr- Fresh fish pickled in vinegar and hot chilies.

Escalope-a very thin cutlet of meat.

Espagnole Sauce-(Fr) –Spanish Style. A brown veal sauce flavored with ham and tomato.

Essayer-(Fr) -To taste, to sample

Essig –(Gm)- vinegar

Estragon-(Fr) Tarragon.

Étaler - (Fr)- To spread out evenly.

Étendre au rouleau - (Fr)- To roll out dough flat

Etouffé -(Fr) To stew or slowly cook in a brown roux thickened sauce. To smother.

F

Faafar- (In)- Buckwheat greens originating in the Himalayas.

Fabada-(Sp) Cannelini bean and chorizo sausage stew.

Fabes-(Sp) Fava Beans

Fagioli -(It) Beans

Faisander - (Fr)- To hang game

Falafel- (Le) Parsley and garlic spiced ground chickpea balls that are fried until crispy.

Fan –(Ch)-Cooked Rice

Far Joo –(Ch) –Red Chilies

Far Jui –(Ch) Star anise

Far Sang –(Ch)-Peanuts

Far Sung Yow -(Ch)-Peanut oil

Far Woo Jiao –(Ch)-Black pepper

Farce-(Fr) Stuffing of forcemeat.

Farfalle- (It)-Bowtie pasta

Fårikål-(Sc)- National dish of Norway. Mutton and cabbage stew simply flavored with black pepper.

Farro -(It) Spelt grain

Fasülye-(Tu) – Bean

Fatteh- (Ar)- Fried pita bread topped with yogurt and garlic chick peas.

Fava Bean- A very large flat type of lima bean.

Feijoada Completa-(Pt)- Brazilian cassoulet made with black beans, sausage, bacon, ham, accompanied with rice, greens, oranges and pico de gallo

Fenugreek- the main flavor in curry powders. It is a very hard seed with a mustard color.

Fermentation- the reaction of yeast and sugars that produces carbon dioxide and alcohol gases. In wine production, after yeast is introduced to sugar in grapes the carbon dioxide and alcohol stabilize the juice.

Fermiere-(Fr) Farmers wife, flavored with ham.

Fettuccine- (It)-Flat long narrow pasta noodles.

Feuilletage -(Fr) -Puff pastry

Fideos-(Sp) Very thin and short vermicelli like noodles.

Fideuá- (Sp) A paella made from fideos.

FIFO- first in first out process of rotating stock.

Filé -(Cr)- powdered sassafras leaves used to thicken gumbo.

Filet- 1. boneless cut of fish. 2.To cut meat away from the bone. 3. A steak portion cut from the tenderloin

Financière-(Fr) -banker's style. Very rich dishes.

Fines Herbes-(Fr) - Chopped fresh tarragon, parsley, chervil and chives mixture.

Fining- the clarification of wine to separate sediments in the production.

Finish- a wine tasting term to describe how the affects the palate after it has been swallowed.

Finnan Haddie-(Br)- Scottish smoked haddock, cooked with milk.

Fino -(Sp) Dry and pale fortified wine from various regions of Spain

Fish fumet-Reduced fish stock lightly flavored with white wine.

Five Spice Powder- A Chinese spice mix of star anise, cinnamon, white pepper, clove, and anise.

Five Way Veg- Commercial blends of IQF Frozen Vegetables -comprised of Corn, Peas, Carrot, Lima Beans, and Green Beans. Packed in 2.5lb boxes or 20lb cases

Flabby- this describes a wine which lacks acidity.

Flæskesteg- (Fr)-Danish roasted pork with a generous layer of crispy fat on top. Served with rødkål, braised red cabbage.

Flamande-(Fr) -Flemish style, dishes cooked with beer.

Flambé -(Fr) To flame with alcohol

Flan-(La) an egg custard baked in a shallow dish with caramel.

Flauta- (La) "Flute". Corn tortilla filled with various meats then fried until crisp, aka Taquito. Commonly topped with guacamole.

Fleisch-(Gm)-meat

Fleuron-(Fr) Small flower crescents of puff pastry.

Flint- a way to describe the minerality of some wines.

Flor- (Sp) Flower, a layer of yeast that develops over sherry in a wine barrel which prevents oxidation.

Florentine-(Fr) 1. In the style of Florence, the use of spinach as a filling 2. A almond candy cookie.

Foaming- whipping eggs to incorporate air.

Focaccia- (It) flatbread flavored with olive oil, herbs, onions and salt.

Foie - (Fr)- Liver

Foie Gras-(Fr) - force fed ducks and geese that produce an engorged liver that has the consistency of butter.

Foncage- (Fr) To line the bottom and sides of a baking mold or pan with dough.

Foncer-(Fr) To line the base of a stew pan with slices of ham or bacon

Fond de Veau (Fr) concentrated veal stock.

Fond (Fr) Lightly concentrated meat stock.

Fondant- 1. Sugar Icing 2. Coated with butter then baked with stock.

Fondante -3" long, Château -2" long, Olivette -1" long

Fondre -(Fr)-To melt

Fondu - (Fr)- Melted

Fondue-1. verb – to melt (Sw) 2. Melted Swiss cheese preparation and served with bread.2. A Swiss style of cooking in a pot at the table in oil, the product is cooked in hot fat until the desired degree of doneness.

Fonduta- (It) fondue made of Fontina cheese.

Foo Gaw -(Ch)- Bitter melon

Foo Yong- (Ch) – Flat omelet flavored with bean sprouts, green onions, mushrooms, meat or shrimp, cabbage and served with a brown garlic sauce.

Forcemeat. -Chopped or pureed meat, fat and seasoning used for stuffing or dumplings.

Formaggio -(It) Cheese

Fortified Wine- the addition of spirit to a wine to increase the level of alcohol and to stop fermentation.

Foul Meddamas- (Ar)- Breakfast of fava beans, egg, olive oil, onion, garlic and lemon. Served from streetcars' with baladi (flatbread).

Foyot-(Fr) - a variation of a béarnaise sauce with the addition of a reduced meat glace.

Fragola-(It)- Strawberry

Framboise-(Fr) Raspberry

Française-(Fr) French style.

Frangipane- (Fr) 1. An almond flavored batter of butter, eggs, flour, and almond paste. 2. A type of panada made from butter eggs and flour.

Frappé-(Fr) –Chilled

Fresco -(It)- Fresh

Friandises -(Fr) –Assortment of Petit fours, Truffles, and cookies.

Fricandeau- (Fr) Veal that that is simmered with white wine, mushrooms, vegetables and finished with cream.

Fricassee- 1.(Fr) A white stew of chicken or veal. 2.(Cr)-various proteins are browned in a pan, a roux is made from the fat, then a thick gravy is made, the main item is then added back to gravy before serving with rice.

Frijoles Charros- (La) Pinto beans stewed with bacon, onion, garlic and seasoning. Commonly severed like a soup. Translates to cowboy beans.

Frijoles Negros- (La) Black beans that are typically stewed with ham hock, onion, garlic and seasoning.

Frijoles- (Sp) Beans

Frikadelle -(Gm)- Meat balls

Frikadeller -(Sc)- Danish pan-fried meatballs
Frite-(Fr) - fried.
Frittata- (It) Flat open omelet.
Fritto Misto-(It) mixed fried platter of food served as a hot antipasto.
Friture -(Fr) Deep fryer
Frogmore Stew- Low country Carolina preparation of shrimp, smoked sausage, onions, corn, and potato.
Froid -(Fr) Cold
Fromage -(Fr) Cheese
Frucht -(Gm)- fruit
Fruits de mer-(Fr) -"Fruits of the Sea" Shellfish.
Frutta-(It)-Fruit
Frutti di mare-(It)- Seafood
Fugu- Edible Japanese blowfish.
Fukusa Sushi- (Jp) Sushi which is wrapped in a rice crepe.
Full English- (Br)-English breakfast served with a sunny side up egg, white and black pudding, sausage, side bacon, mushrooms, grilled tomato, baked beans and toast and a potato cake.
Fumé-(Fr) **-** Smoked
Fumet -(Fr) The essence or concentrated flavor
Fun-(Ch)-Shrimp and pork filling for dumpling
Fun Gwor -(Ch)- Rice paper filled with chicken, pork, and shrimp
Fung Jaw -(Ch)- Steamed chicken feet in black bean sauce.
Fusilli- (It)-Spiral shaped pasta
Futomaki Sushi -(Jp) Large sushi roll.

G

Ga Lei -(Ch)- Curry flavored
Gai -(Ch)- Chicken
Gai Dun Go -(Ch)- Light sponge cake.
Gai Lan -(Ch)- Broccoli
Gai Yick -(Ch)- Chicken wing:
Gai-(In)- Cow
Gajak-(In)- Milk fudge flavored with sesame seed
Galanga- A root spice related to ginger, which has a flavor similar to cough medicine.
Galantine-(Fr) -A poultry which is boned and filled with forcemeat, and variety meats, wrapped and shaped into a log, poached and chilled in stock and served cold as an appetizer.
Galette- (Fr)- pancake or small round cake
Gamberetto, Gamberi-(It)- Shrimp
Ganache- cream made from varied amounts of chocolate to scalded cream. The higher the ratio the less percent of cream in the mixture.
Gans–(Gm)- Goose
Ganth Gobhi- (In) - Kohlrabi
Garam Masala- (In) A blend of hot spices used in Northern Indian cuisine.
Garde-manger-(Fr) - "The keeper of the foods to be eaten". The person in charge of all dishes that are designed to be consumed cold.
Garni –(Fr) To garnish
Garnish-to accent the presentation of an item without taking away the item's critical attributes.
Gastrique (Fr) A sauce base comprised of caramelized sugar, vinegar, demi glace and a primary flavor like a fruit, jam, or liquor.
Gâteau -(Fr) -A multi layered and filled cake.
Gaufre (Fr) - Waffle
Gaufrette-(Fr) - waffle cut fried potatoes.
Gawn Don Mein -(Ch)- Dried egg noodles
Gazpacho-(Sp)- Cold pureed vegetable soup made from fresh ripe tomatoes, vinegar, and olive oil, with diced raw onions, cucumbers, and peppers. Garnished with croutons and hard-boiled eggs.
Gebackene Forelle- (Gm) – Swiss style trout that has been filled with lemon and herbs then baked with carrots and potatoes.
Gee Yuk -(Ch)-Pork and water chestnut filling for dumpling.
Gefilte-(Yd)- Ground fish and matzah meal ball that is boiled.
Gehun-(In)-Wheat
Gelato-(It) a soft and silky Italian ice cream made from whole milk and eggs.
Gemüsen-(Gm) - Vegetables
Genoise- (Fr) - A rich sponge cake.
Genovese -(It) In the style of Genoa. e.g. Pesto Genovese
Germ -the plant's embryo
Ges Nadziewana Owocami- (Eu) Duck or Goose filled with apples and prunes then roasted.
Geschnetzeltes –(Gm)- Cutlet
Gewürz -(Gm)-spice

Gewürztraminer- grape varietal originally from Germany that has spice flavor used for white wine.
Ghee- (In)-Clarified butter from Water Buffalo Milk
Giardiniera- (It) "Garden", vegetable preparation
Gibelotte -(Fr) A buttery rabbit stew with onions and potatoes
Glacé -(Fr) 1.-A glaze. 2. Frozen
Glace de Viande-(Fr) - Stock reduced to a very thick consistency, used to flavor sauces.
Glatt- (Yd)- type of kosher meat whereby the lungs were healthy
Gliadin- protein wheat flour that gives gluten elasticity.
Gluten- The protein found in wheat flours.
Glutenin- protein wheat flour that gives gluten strength.
Gnocchi- (It) Pasta dumpling usually made from potatoes.
Gobi-(In)-Cauliflower
Gỏi Cuốn Tom Thịt - Se-Vietnamese spring rolls of shrimp, pork, noodles and vegetables served with a peanut sauce.
Gok -(Ch)- Deep fried glutinous rice dumpling.
Gołąbki-(Eu)- Polish stuffed cabbage filled with pork simmered with tomato, bacon and onion.
Golubtsi- (Eu)- Polish stuffed cabbage filled with rice, ground veal, beef and pork simmered in a light tomato sauce.
Gone Tong Gow -(Ch)-Shang Hai soup dumpling with pork and shrimp
Gordita- (La)- "Chubby" Masa pastry filled with various meat and cheese.
Gordita- (La)- two thick tortillas are sandwiched with a savory filling, sealed then quickly fried.
Gorgonzola -(It) Blue cheese made from cows' milk, Northern Italy
Gougère-(Fr) - cheese flavored pate au choux that is baked into cigar shapes.
Goujon -(Fr) - strips of a flat fish fillet.
Goulash-(Eu) A Hungarian soup or stew of meat, peppers, onions and tomatoes seasoned with paprika and bay leaves.
Gourmet- (Fr) - one who appreciates great food and great wine.
Goûter - (Fr)- To taste
Gow Choy -(Ch)-Chives
Graisse –(Fr) Excess or leftover fat
Gran Reserva- (Sp) The highest quality level of Rioja wine.
Grana Padana -(It) Hard cheese from Northern Italy, cows' milk
Granchio-(It)- Crab
Grand Cru- (Fr) "Great Growth", the highest quality level wine from Burgundy.
Grand Vin- (Fr) "Great Wine", a high-quality level designation for wine from Bordeaux.
Granita-(Sp)- Coarse textured fruit ice.
Granita (It)- Fruit ice that has a smooth texture.
Gras-(Fr) - Fat, plump
Gratin Forcemeat -a farce made from a mixture of raw and seared or fully cooked product. This causes it to have less shrinkage.
Gratinée -(Fr) To brown on top under a salamander or broiler
Gratis – A Latin word which means Free of charge
Gravalax- (Sc)-cured salmon filets that have been flavored with dill and anise. Other spellings include gravad lax, gravlachs and gravlox.
Grecque- (Fr) A marinade of lemon, garlic, herbs and olive oil
Green- a wine tasting term to describe unripe grapes.
Gremolata- It chopped mix of parsley, garlic, and lemon peel.
Grenadine –(Fr) Small slice of veal filet which is larded with kidney and lumbar fat.
Grenouille- (Fr) Frogs legs
Grill- to cook a food item over a grid; the heat is from under the grid so that carmelization occurs in lines.
Grinder- American sandwich of crispy bread filled with various Italian cold cuts, provolone and vegetable fillings and vinaigrette, origin New England.
Grissini- (It) Crunchy bread sticks.
Groseille- (Fr) "Berry", i.e. strawberry, raspberry
Grosse pièce- (Fr) "large piece" used as a centerpiece.
Grüenkohl-(Gm) Kale
Gruyère Sw- a nutty flavored Swiss type of cheese used for fondue and French onion soup.
Guacamole- (Sp) A dip of avocados seasoned with onions, tomatoes, chilies, and cilantro.
Gugelhopf-(Sw) Yeast based Bundt cake flavored with raisins and rum.
Gulab Jaman-(In)- Doughnuts soaked in rose syrup
Gulasch-(Gm)- Viennese Goulash is similar to the Hungarian goulash but is finished with chopped lemon zest, caraway seeds, dill pickles and sour cream.
Gumbo- 1.(Cr)-A Creole soup made with seafood, okra and file powder served over steamed or boiled rice. 2.(Ar)– Okra

Guo Bao Rou-(Ch)- Sweet and sour sauce over batter fried strips of pork.
Guo tie-(Ch)- Dumplings that are pan fried.
Gup Guy -(Ch)- Clams
Gurken-(Gm)- Cucumbers
Gwa Jee Choy -(Ch)- Watercress
Gyro-Gr- pronounced (Yeer ro). Forcemeat of lamb/ beef that is roasted on a vertical spit, served on pita. The forcemeat can also be sliced thin, then griddled to order.

H

HACCP- Hazard Analysis and Critical Control Points established by NASA.
Haché -(Fr) Finely chopped or minced
Hackbraten –(Gm)- Meatloaf
Hak Mi Cho -(Ch)- Black rice vinegar.
Haldi-(In)-Turmeric
Halva-1. (In)-Sweets pastes like marzipan made nuts, vegetable, fruit. 2.(Yd) made from sesame paste
Ham Sui -(Ch)-Vegetable and pork filling for dumpling
Hamachi Sushi- (Jp) Yellowtail
Hamantaschen- (Yd)- Triangle shaped pastry served during Purim
Har -(Ch)- Prawn, shrimp
Har Mi -(Ch)-Dried small shrimp
Har Peen -(Ch)-Shrimp crackers that puff when fried.
Hara Dhania-(In)- Cilantro leaves
Hard Ball Stage-cooking equal parts sugar and water until it reaches 128 ºC, 262 ºF
Hard Crack Stage-cooking equal parts sugar and water until it reaches156ºC, 313 ºF
Hard Sauce -(Br) -Confectioner's sugar and butter sauce.
Har Gow -(Ch)- Shrimp and bamboo shoot dumpling
Haricot- (Fr) Bean
Harissa- spice mixture containing chilies, cumin, garlic, coriander, and olive oil.
Hase-(Gm)- Rabbit
Hasselbacken-(Sc)-Swedish style potato sliced thinly half way through then topped with butter and seasoning before they are baked.
Haute -(Fr) High class
Havuç-(Tu) Carrots
Haxe–(Gm)- Leg of meat. Lamb, veal.
Hechsher- (Yd)- Kosher certification label on food to ensure the standard of quality established under the Jewish law.
Herbaceous- a wine tasting term to describe the herbal aroma of wine.
Hero- American sandwich with hot filling, meatballs, eggplant, chicken, or veal parmigiana, or sausage and peppers. Originally from the New York
High Ratio Cake- when the amount of sugar equals or exceeds the amount of fat in the batter.
Himbeeren –(Gm)- Raspberries
Hirame Sushi- (Jp) Halibut
Ho Fun- (Ch) -wide flat rice noodle.
Ho Lon Dow -(Ch)-Snow peas
Hongroise-(Fr) Hungarian Style -flavored with paprika and bay leaves.
Ho Yau Jeung -(Ch)-Oyster sauce
Honig-(Gm)- Honey
Hoagie- American sandwich with various cold cuts, cheese and vegetable fillings and vinaigrette and or condiments, origin Philadelphia.
Hoang Dow -(Ch)- Red beans
Hoisin -(Ch) sweet sauce used in Chinese cooking made from soybean flour, chilies, red beans, and five spice.
Holishkes-Yd- Cabbage rolls filled with veal. Two cabbage rolls are served during Sukkot to resemble the Torah.
Hollandaise Sauce- an emulsified sauce made from clarified butter and egg yolk . Originally from Holland it is flavored with fresh lemon juice or white wine vinegar.
Holländerli- (Sw) – Small oval tart made from puff pastry filled with lightly sweetened frangipane
Holubtsi-(Eu) – Cabbage rolls filled with pork,buckwheat, serve with smetana a type of sour cream.
Holy Trinity -Equal parts of diced onions, celery and green pepper used as a mirepoix for many Creole and Cajun dishes
Horchata- (La)- Beverage made from rice, nuts or grain Sweetened and served hot or cold
Horn Har Jeung -(Ch)-Shrimp sauce
Horn Yee -(Ch)- Dried fish
Horn Don -(Ch)- Salted eggs

Hors d'oeuvres-(Fr) "Outside of the work". Small bite size appetizers.
Hoşmerim-(Tu) Warm cheese pudding with lemon and cardamom
Hotatagai Sushi- (Jp) Scallops
Hôte - (Fr) Host
HP Sauce- (Br)- "House of Parliament" sweet spicy sauce flavored with tamarind and molasses.
Hủ Tiếu- (Se)-Vietnamese seafood and pork soup flavored with dried shrimp, dried squid, and daikon. Typically served with fish balls, Thai BBQ pork and hard-boiled eggs.
Huevos Rancheros- (La)- Fried eggs over toasted corn tortillas, with a tomato, chilie, and onion sauce served with refried beans, rice, and guacamole.
Huevos- (Sp)- Eggs
Hühnerbrust-(Gm)- chicken breast
Hui Guo Rou-(Ch)- "Twice cooked pork", roasted, sliced then stir fried with ginger, chili paste, and soy, peppers and scallion.
Huile - (Fr) Oil
Huitre - (Fr) Oyster
Hummer -(Gm)- Lobster
Hummus- (Ar) Chickpea, tahini, lemon and garlic puree dip
Hung Cha -(Ch)- Black tea
Hun tun (Ch)- Dumplings that are wontons.
Huo Guo-(Ch)- "hot pot"- a simmering broth is centered in the table with raw protein, greens, noodles, and dumplings. The customer cook their own food in the fondue type of preparation at the table, typically in groups.
Hwa Jo-(Ch)-Szechwan pepper
Hy -(Ch)- Crab:

I

Iç Pilavi-(Tu)- Rice pilaf with liver, nuts and currants
Ice Wine- grapes are picked while they are frozen, the process concentrates the sweetness because the water is frozen. Typically, Riesling and Vidal grape varietals are used.
İçli Köfte-(Tu)- Rice balls filed with meat, then fried.
Ika Sushi- (Jp) Squid
Ikura Sushi- (Jp) Salmon roe
Imam Bayildi -(Tu) Stuffed eggplant -filled with peppers, onions, tomatoes and spices
Imbiber- To absorb liquid; syrup etc.
Imli-(In)-Tamarind
Indian Mirepoix- Aromatic base of garlic, ginger, curry leaf, and onion.
Indienne-(Fr) Indian Style -with curry.
Indochina Mirepoix-Aromatic base of shallot, chilies, and garlic.
Integrale -(It) Whole wheat
Invert Sugar- a mixture of levulose and dextrose to improve hydration of cakes.
Involtino-(It)- Roulade
Irmika Helvasi –(Tu) Semolina pudding with cinnamon and nuts.

J

Jaew bong (Se)-Laotian basic salsa of shallot, galangal, garlic, cilantro, chile, and fish sauce.
Jaew isan (Se)-Laotian anchovy sauce flavored with shallot, galangal, garlic, lemongrass, chile, kaffir lime, and tomato
Jafran-(In)-Saffron
Jalepeño-(La) Medium hot chile from Mexico
Jambalaya- (Cr)-A dish made from rice, tomatoes, peppers, onions, and ham. The dish may include oysters, chicken, andouille sausage, and shrimp for additional flavors.
Jambon- (Fr) Ham
Jamón-(Sp) Cured ham, the best is known as Iberico de Pellota as the black pigs are fed acorns and the ham is cured for three years. Serrano comes from Andalusia.
Japonaise- Merinque disks with crushed nuts added.
Jardinière - (Fr) Garden vegetables cut into batonnet used to garnish grilled or braised dishes.
Jaun- (In) Barley
Javatri-(In)- Mace
Jean Dui -(Ch)- Sesame seed flavored dumplings filled with bean paste.
Jee Ma Yow -(Ch)- Sesame oil
Jee Ma -(Ch)-Sesame seeds
Jee -(Ch)- Pork
Jeow Yau -(Ch)-Soy sauce, heavy
Jerez-(Sp) Sherry made from Palomino grapes. Fino is dry and Pedro Ximénez is very sweet.
Jinga-(In)- Shrimp

Jit Cho -(Ch)- Red rice vinegar.
Joghurt-(Gm)- Yogurt
Johannisbeeren-(Gm)- Currants
Joulupöytä-(Sc)- "Yule table"- a variety of dishes that make up the traditional Christmas meal including ham, lutefisk, gravalax, herring and casseroles made from carrot, rutabagas, liver, and potatoes
Jow Har Gok -(Ch)- Shrimp Dumpling
Julep- Farsi name for a drink that contains mint.
Julienne-(Fr) To cut into thin sticks. Either 1/8" x 1/8" x 2" or a Fine Julienne 1/16 "x 1/16 "x 1"
Jus lié- (Fr) A jus that has been slightly thickened with cornstarch or flour.
Jus- (Fr) Juice

K

Kabinett- (Gm) -denotes the lower level of ripeness found in wines, riper than table wines.
Kaeng chuet (Se) Clear Thai soup of pork or chicken broth with minced pork, glass noodle, tofu, vegetables and seaweed.
Kaeng khiao wan- (Se) -Thai green curry flavored with Thai mirepoix and coconut milk.
Kaeng matsaman- (Se) -Thai yellow curry flavored with Indian spices.
Kaeng phet- (Se) -Thai red curry flavored with Thai mirepoix and coconut milk and red chile.
Kaffee–(Gm)- Coffee
Kajoo- (In)-Cashew
Kala Jeera-(In)- Black cumin seeds
Kalbfleisch –(Gm)-Veal
Kalbi- (Kr) BBQ Beef short ribs.
Kåldolmar-(Sc)- Swedish cabbage rolls filled with pork and rice.
Kali Mirch-(In)- Ground black pepper
Kamarakh- (In)- Carambola fruit
Kani Sushi- (Jp) Crab meat
Kani-kamaboko Sushi- (Jp) Artificial crab meat
Karei Sushi- (Jp) Flounder
Karela – (In) – Bitter melon
Karem ka Saag- (In) Kale from Kasmir
Karniyarik-(Tu)-Eggplant stuffed with ground lamb
Karotten –(Gm)- Carrots
Kartoffel–(Gm)- Potato
Kartoffelkloesse- (Gm) Potato Dumplings
Käse –(Gm)- Cheese
Kasha- (Yd)- Buckwheat groats made like a pilaf
Kasher- (Yd)- To make a cooking implement or kitchen kosher
Kashrut- (Yd)- Kosher dietary laws
Kassler Rippchen –(Gm)- Smoked pork ribs
Katahal- (In)- Jackfruit
Katsuo- (Jp) Bonito fish.
Kebab- skewered meat, fish, or vegetables grilled over a fire.
Keema-(In)-Minced meat curry
Kefir- 1. A fermented camel's milk drink flavored with salt or spices. 2. Variety of lime leaves used for tea.
Khao mok- (Se)-Thai curried biryani
Khao phat- (Se)-Thai fried dish with various meat or seafodo, pineapple, coconut, and vegetables.
Khao soi- Se-Thai curried noodle soup with coconut
Khao tom mat- Se-Thai sticky rice and coconut dessert steamed in banana leaves.
Kheer-(In)- Rice pudding with dried fruits and nuts
Kheera-(In)- Cucumber
Khopra-(In)- Coconut
Kibbeh- (Ar) Bulgur and beef fritter. Minced meat is packed inside of the dough. Football shaped and fried
Kibbi- (Le) Bulgur and lamb fritter. Minced meat is packed inside of the dough. Ballshaped and fried
Kimchi- (Kr)-Fermented vegetable dish with seasoning.
King Cake-(Cr)- A version of the Galette des Rois, the kings cake traditionally used to celebrate the epiphany. The creole version is associated with Mardi Gras and is a rich yeast bread topped with green, gold and purple sugar with a plastic baby Jesus baked in the dough. The person who finds Jesus traditionally buys the next cake.
Kirmizi Biber- (Tu)-dried ground mild chili pepper.
Kirsch- Clear distilled cherry brandy.
Kisir -(Tu)-Bulgur patties flavored with mint, onions, garlic and chili that are fried in olive oil.

Kjøttboller-(Sc)- Coarse ground meatballs from Norway that are served with a brown sauce with cream and nutmeg.
Klopse-(Gm)-Meat balls
Kneidlack- (Yd)- Matzah balls usually served in a chicken soup.
Knish- (Yd)- Savory handheld pastry filled with potato.
Knoblauch-(Gm)- Garlic
Knödel -(Gm)- dumpling
Koeksister -Gm – braided doughnut soaked in a honey syrup.
Kofta-(In)- Deep fried vegetable or meat balls
Köfte-(Tu) Meatball
Konbu -(Jp) A large edible seaweed used in Japanese cooking
Konditorei-(Gm)- Pastry shop.
Konfitür-(Gm)-Jam
Kosher- (Yd)- adherence to the strict rabbinical dietary law as described in Leviticus.
Köttsoppa-(Sc)- meat soup of simmered beef with root vegetables and potatoes.
Köy Peyniri –(Tu)-Village cheese, can use simple farmers cheese.
Krapfen –(Gm)- Doughnuts
Kreplach- (Yd)- Triangle shaped dumpling served in soup
Kromeskis -(Eu) - Croquettes made with meat or fish, origin is Poland.
Kroppkakor- (Sc) Bacon filled dumplings served with lingonberries.
Kuchen-(Gm)-Cake
Kugel- (Yd)- Sweet or savory baked noodle pudding
Kugelhopf- (Gm) -A yeast leavened coffee cake shaped like a crown flavored with currants or golden raisins and almonds.
Kulfi-(In)-Ice cream flavored with fruits and nuts
Kümmel-(Gm)- Caraway
Kung Pao -(Ch)- Dragon juice is used to stir fry the protein and vegetables, then numbing peppercorns are added with peanuts or cashews.
Kurodai Sushi- (Jp) Snapper
Kuy teav- (Se)-Cambodian noodle soup with braised pork and broth, noodles, sometimes offal and shrimp.
Куриша Kiev- (Eu) Chicken is filled with butter and parsley, shaped, breaded then fried until golden brown

L

Lachs- (Gm).- Salmon
Ladyfinger- Thin dry sponge cookie used is dishes like tiramisu
Lagniappe-(Cr)- Serendipitous flavor surprise or added component.
Lahsun-(In)-Garlic
Lait- (Fr) Milk
Laitue - (Fr)- Lettuce
Lal Mirch-(In)- Cayenne pepper
Lamian-(Ch)- Fresh noodles that are pulled into many strands.
Lamm –(Gm)-Lamb
Lampone-(It)- Raspberry
Landjäger-(Sw)- Thin dried sausages carried by hikers in the Alps to snack on.
Langouste- (Fr) Small spiny lobsters.
Langoustine- (Fr) prawns from warm waters that look like crawfish.
Langue - (Fr) Tongue, tongue shaped
Lapin- (Fr) Rabbit
Lar Dew Din -(Ch)-Chili sauce
Lard - 1. Rendered and clarified pork fat. 2. (Fr) To insert strips of fat into lean cuts of meat.
Lardon - (Fr) Batonnet of thick streaky bacon.
Lasagna- (It)-Sheets of pasta layered with tomato sauce Bolognese and a ricotta cheese mixture, baked au gratin
Lassi- (In)- Buttermilk
Latke- (Yd)- Potato pancake served during Hanukkah.
Latte-(It)- Milk
Lattuga-(It)- Lettuce
Lauki ya Doodhi- (In)-Snake squash
Leber -(Gm)-Liver
Lebkuchen- (Sw) – Gingerbread biscuits with a crisp glaze.
Lechon-(Sp)- Whole roasted suckling pig with citrus and spices.
Lees- Dead yeast cells, seed and pulp on the bottom of a wine barrel.
Legs- wine tasting term to describe how the wine clings to the glass.
Légume - (Fr) Vegetable
Leitão Assado à Bairrada- (Pt)- Roasted suckling pig, loin portion with crispy sk(In) Basted with lemon and orange.
Lekkerbekje- (Gm) Fried fillet of haddock, served with a sauce Ravigote.
Lendensteak-(Gm)- Sirloin steak
Lepre-(It)- Hare

Lévered - (Fr) paste of flour and water used for sealing pastry crusts.
Liaison - (Fr) A final thickener of egg yolks and cream.
Lievito-(It)- Yeast
Limone-(It)- Lemon
Linguiça- Pt- Portuguese cured garlic sausage.
Linguini –(It) oval shaped pasta cut into long strips which is commonly served with seafood.
Linzer torte- Austrian pastry made of a nut flavored short dough filled with raspberry jam and topped with a lattice dough on top.
Lo Bak -(Ch)- Chinese daikon radish
Lo Han Jai-(Ch)- "Buddha Delight" – vegetarian dish of Chinese mirepoix, snow peas, mushroom, bamboo shoots, tofu, cellophane noodles, in oyster and soy sauce.
Lo Mein-(Ch)- "stirred noodles" – typically flavored with soy, proteins and vegetables.
Lobhai Dal- (In) –Black-eye peas
Lokum-(Tu)- Classic Turkish delight- a gummy rose fudge with pistachios coated with confectioners' sugar.
Lombo-(It)- Loin
Lomo -(Sp) Cured pork loin
Longanissa -(Sp) Highly spiced pork sausage flavored with vinegar.
Loong Har -(Ch)- Lobster
Loot Jee -(Ch)- Chestnuts
Lop Chong-(Ch)-Hard cured sausage
Lop May -(Ch)- Bacon
Lörtsy- (Sc) -Finnish half-moon pie filled with apples or savory meats.
Lox- (Yd)- salt cured salmon.
Lozenge- Diamond shaped cut for garnish.
Luscious- a wine tasting term describe the balance in sweet wines.
Lutfisk- (Sc) – Lye fish. Cod is soaked in lye for several days which changes to a jellylike texture. Served with bacon, boiled potatoes, and green peas and a cream sauce.
Luzerner Chugeli- (Sw) Bombe shaped puff pastry shell filled with veal, meatballs, mushrooms, apples, and onions in a thick veloute.
Lyonnaise - (Fr) A garnish of sautéed onions. In the style of Lyon.

M

Ma Tio -(Ch)- Water chestnuts
Macaire- - (Fr) potato pancake with grated cheese, chives and bacon.
Macaron- (Fr) – Sweet almond meringue cookie sandwich filled with buttercream, ganache, or jam.
Macaroon-(Yd) A sweet biscuit made of nuts or coconut, sugar and egg whites.
Macchi-(In)-Fish
Macédoine - (Fr) -1. 1/4" dice. 2. a mixture of dried fruits or vegetables.
Macerate- to soaking fruits in sugar, wine, liquors, or a syrup so that they absorb the flavor of the added item and release some of their flavor to form a liquid.
Machaca-(La) Shredded dried beef preparation.
Madeleine- (Fr) Shell shaped cookie flavored with almonds and lemon zest that is then dipped in chocolate.
Madhu-(In)-Honey
Madras-(In)- Spicy curries from Southern India
Magnum- a wine bottle that contains 1.5 liters.
Magret- (Fr)- breast meat from a foie gras producing Barbary duck.
Maguro Sushi- (Jp) Tuna
Mai Fun -(Ch)- Rice noodles
Maillard Reaction -the browning of low sugar foods. This process begins at 310°.
Maiale-(It)- Pork
Maison - (Fr) House
Maître d' Hotel Butter- a compound butter flavored with lemon and chopped parsley, used to flavor fish and grilled meats.
Maize-(La) Corn
Maki Sushi- (Jp) – a layer of rice on the outside with a filling wrapped with
Makka-(In) Corn
Malai-(In)-Cream
Malolactic Fermentation – the conversion of malic acid into lactic acid which softens the acidity in the wine.
Manakeesh- (Ar)- Flatbread pizza topped with meat or cheese and seasoned with zaatar.
Manchego -(Sp) Sheep's milk cheese from La Mancha
Mandelbrot- (Yd) Biscotti like cookies
Mandeln-(Gm)- Almonds

Mandolin - (Fr) Tool used for slicing vegetables and fruits into slices or stick.
Mandoo- (Kr) Pan fried meat filled dumplings
Manzanilla -(Sp) Light fortified wine from the south of Spain that has the flavor of chamomile.
Manzo-(It)- Beef
Maque Choux-(Cr)- A creamed corn preparation with onions, spice and tomato, corn kernels and corn milk.
Marc- what remains once the liquid is removed after the wine fermentation of crushing.
Mardi Gras-(Fr)- Fat Tuesday, the last celebration before Lent.
Marengo-(Fr) Garnish of coddled eggs, crayfish and tomatoes named after the battle of Marengo.
Marinade- a flavorful liquid made of oil, acid and aromatics.
Marinara -(It) Tomato sauce flavored with olive oil, garlic and parsley
Marinate-To immerse raw meat, poultry fish or vegetables in a marinade in order to prevent excess drying during the cooking process.
Mariniére-(Fr) Boatman style, flavored with wine and shallots for mussels.
Marmitako -(Sp) Basque fisherman's stew
Marmite - (Fr) Stockpot
Marron- (Fr) Sweetened Chestnuts
Marshmallow- Confection made from meringue and gelatin
Marzipan-almond paste, sugar and egg whites shaped as fruits or vegetables or figurines
Masa Harina-(La) Dried corn that is made into a flour for tamales.
Masala-(In)- A blend of spices
Mascarpone- (It) triple cream cheese used for tiramisu.
Mashgiach- (Yd)- A kashrut overseer or supervisor to ensure that the correct process has been taken to meet the dietary law.
Masu Sushi- (Jp)Trout
Matambre-(La) Stuffed and rolled flank steak from Argentina.
Mateca-(La) Lard
Matelote- (Fr) Fish stew made with freshwater fish, Riesling and thickened with cream and egg yolks.
Matignon-(Fr) A braised mirepoix with ham used to flavor poêléed dishes.
Matjes –(Gm) - herring
Matzah Brei-(Yd)- Passover breakfast of scrambled eggs and crumbled matzah.
Matzah-(Yd)- Unleavened bread used to celebrate Passover.
Maultaschen –(Gm)- Ravioli
Mayonnaise- (Fr) A cold sauce emulsion made of egg yolks, vinegar, seasoning and oil.
Medallion- (Fr) -Small round cuts of beef, lamb or veal tenderloin.
Medium Crack Stage-cooking equal parts sugar and water until it reaches147 ºC, 297 ºF
Medium Soft Ball Stage-cooking equal parts sugar and water until it reaches124 ºC, 255 ºF
Mee Chha- Se-Cambodian egg noodles with beef, vegetables and thick beef sauce.
Mee Kantang- Se-Cambodian wide noodles with beef, eggs, oyster sauce and greens
Mee Sua Cha- Se-Cambodian cellophane noodles with garlic, vegetables and oyster sauce.
Meeresfrüchte –(Gm)-Seafood
Meetha-(In)-Sweet
Mein -(Ch)- Noodles
Mein Fun -(Ch)- Thin wheat noodles
Mela-(It)- Apple
Mélange - (Fr) Mixture
Melanzana-(It)- Eggplant
Melba- a raspberry dessert sauce. This sauce is served over peach halves with vanilla ice cream for Peach Melba, named after Dame Nellie Melba.
Melt- to liquefy solid fat by heating
Menu - Fr A bill of fare
Menudo-(La)- A Hispanic soup of tripe, meat broth, chilies and hominy.
Meringue- (Fr) - Whipped egg whites with sugar used to lighten mousses, cakes, and pastry creams.
Meringue Chantilly- (Fr) Baked méringue shells filled with whipped cream.
Meringue Glacé-(Fr) Baked méringue shells filled with ice cream.
Merluzzo-(It)- Cod
Mesclun- (Fr) - This is a mix very young lettuces and greens
Methi-(In)-Fenugreek seeds
Méthode Champenoise- (Fr) The traditional method of Champagne production which includes a second fermentation in the bottle, riddling the

bottles lees to collect the sediment, once removed a dosage is added to adjust sweetness and top off the bottle before final corking and cage closure.

Meunière - (Fr) -in the style of the miller's wife, a sauce made from brown butter and lemon.

Mì hoành thánh- (Se) -Vietnamese pork wonton and noodle soup with shrimp, fried shallot and green onion.

Midye Tavasi-(Tu)- Beer batter fried mussels served with a walnut, breadcrumb, olive oil and lemon sauce.

Mien -(Ch)- Brown bean sauce

Migas -1. (Sp) Chopped fried bread 2. La- Eggs and leftover bread for breakfast.

Mignon - (Fr)small, delicate

Mignonette- (Fr) 1. Coarsely ground pepper .2. Small round pieces of meat or poultry.

Milanaise-(Fr) In the style of Milan. Garnish of macaroni, mushroom, tongue, truffle and veal fond.

Milch-(Gm)- Milk

Milchig –(Yd)-dishes that contain dairy and must be served from a dairy kitchen.

Mille-Feuille- - Fr "thousand leaves" -puff pastry preparations.

Millésime-(Fr) - vintage

Mincemeat-(Br)- mixture of candied fruit, wine, spices, and beef suet or beef fat.

Minestra -(It) Soup

Minestrone- (It) Broth soup with beans, pasta and vegetables.

Mirch-(In)- Chile

Mirepoix- (Fr) A mixture of Carrots, Onions and Celery, used to enhance the flavor of meats and sauces. The ratio is twice as much onion as carrots and celery.

Mirepoix Blanc- (Fr) -A mirepoix that substitutes the carrots with leeks.

Mirin- A sweet non-alcoholic sake.

Mise en bouteille- (Fr) - bottled

Mise en place - (Fr) -"everything in its place"- Preparation prior to cooking

Misir Ekmeği- (Tu)- Cornbread leavened with yeast.

Miso-(Jp)- fermented soy bean paste used in Japanese sauces and soups.

Misua-(Ch)- Very thin salted wheat noodles

Mofongo-(Cr)- Fried mashed plantains flavored with seafood, meat, or vegetable broths and fried pork skins

Mohinga- Se-Burmese catfish and vermicelli soup flavored with fish sauce, lemongrass, green onion and garlic. Commonly served for breakfast..

Mojito-(Cr) Cocktail of rum, lime juice and mint

Mojo- (Pt) Sauce made from citrus, vinegar, olive oil, salt, garlic, cumin, paprika and cilantro.

Mole Coloradito Oaxaqueño- (La) Braised chicken with sauce made from Mexican chocolate, spices, sesame seeds, almonds, onions, garlic and Oaxacan Chilies like arbol, guajillos, and ancho.

Mole- (Sp) Mexican sauce made with chilies, cumin, coriander, cinnamon, nuts, seeds, and chocolate stewed with chicken, turkey, and pork.

Mollee-(In)-Fish simmered in coconut milk with chilies

Momo (Ch)- Dumplings that are purse shaped.

Mondongo-(Cr) Puerto Rican dish of mashed plant

Monté au Beurre - (Fr) To finish by whisking butter into a preparation. "To lift with butter"

Montmorency -(Fr) Variety of cherries from a region near Paris.

Moo Goo -(Ch)- White mushrooms

Moo Shu-(Ch)- Pork that is stir fried with Chinese mirepoix soy, sherry, and hoisin.

Moong Dal-(In) Mung beans

Moong Phali-(In)- Peanuts

Moqueca-(Pt) Fish Stew

Morcela-(Pt) Black pudding sausage

Morel- wild mushroom with hollow honeycombed cap.

Mornay - (Fr) - Cheese flavored béchamel sauce.

Moros y Cristianos- (Cr) Black beans and white rice, Typical in Cuban Cuisine. A dish celebrated in Spain to remember the Spanish triumph over the Moors (African Muslims) during the 15th century.

Moules - (Fr)- Mussels

Moussaka- (Gr) Casserole of eggplant and lamb flavored with tomatoes and onions. This is all topped with a feta cheese flavored béchamel and baked until brown.

Mousse - (Fr) A dish of cooked puréed foods, whipped egg whites and whipped cream.

Mousseline- - (Fr)a hollandaise sauce with unsweetened whipped cream. **Moutarde** - (Fr)- Mustard

Muffuletta- (Cr) – Large round sesame sandwich filled with ham, salami, mortadella ,Swiss and provolone cheeses, and olive salad.

Mulligatawny- "Fire Water" A curried soup with lentils and rice. It is finished with coconut milk in the south or yogurt in the north

Mung -(Ch)-Bean sprouts

Murgh Mahal-(In)-Butter chicken with tomato and cream, mild flavor

Mushy Peas- (Br)-Marrowfat peas simmered with a pinch of baking soda then mashed and seasoned.

Muskatnuß -(Gm)- Nutmeg

Mussaman- (Se) Thai yellow curry made with turmeric and spices coconut milk, potatoes, peanuts, vegetables and typically seafood or chicken.

N

Naan-(In)-Flatbread baked in a tandoori oven

Nachtisch –(Gm)- Dessert

Nage- (Fr)- An aromatic crustacean broth.

Ñame-(Cr)- Yam

Nantua- - Fr -dishes containing crayfish.

Napolean (Fr) – Dessert made with layers of puff pastry, pastry cream and fondant glaze.

Nappage-(Fr) Apricot glaze used to finish pastries with a shiny glaze.

Nappé-(Fr) To cover an item with a sauce.

Narangi-(In)- Orange

Natilla-(La) Sweet custard

Navarin- (Fr) - French stew made with lamb and onions, potatoes, turnips, and savory herbs.

Navet - (Fr)- Turnip

Naw May Fun -(Ch)- Glutinous rice flour

Neembu-(In)-Lemon or lime

Négociant (Fr) - Merchants who source wine from the vineyard. After these wines are mature they bottle the wines.

Neige- (Fr) Snow –e.g. Oeufs a la Niege are meringue quenelles poached in a simple syrup.

Ngau -(Ch)- Beef

Ng Heung Fun -(Ch)- Five Spice

Natilla-(La) Sweet custard

Niçoise-- (Fr) -dishes containing garlic, Niçoise olives, anchovies, tomatoes, artichokes and green beans.

Nigella-(In)-Onion seeds

Nigiri Sushi- (Jp) Slice of raw fish or other topping on top of seasoned vinegar rice.

Nocciola -(It) Hazelnuts

Noce-(It)- Nut

Nockerl- (Gm)- A type of Austrian Spatzle cut from a wooden board.

Noisette- (Fr) "nut". A nut sized cut of venison or lamb from the neck meat. Description of a nutty flavor or color,

Noodle- a ribbon of egg-based pasta.

Nopale-(La) Cactus

Nori - dry sheets of processed seaweed used to wrap sushi.

Norimake Sushi- (Jp) Filled roll with nori seaweed on the outside

Normande- (Fr) In the style of Normandy, the use of apples.

Nosh- (Yd)- To snack

Nougat -chewy candy made from sugar, honey and almonds.

Nouille - (Fr)- Noodle

Noyau- (Fr) The pit from stone fruits

Nudeln -(Gm)- noodles.

Nuoc cham- (Se) -Vietnames basic sauce of lime, vinegar, sugar, garlic, chile, fish sauce and water

Nuoc leo- (Se) -Vietnamese ground peanut sauce with pork, garlic, fermented soy paste, sugar, chile, and lime. Served with grilled meat.

Nuoc mam- Se-Vietnamese fermented fish sauce.

Nutella- (It) A creamy paste of chocolate and hazelnuts.

O

Ochsenschwanzsuppe –(Gm)-Oxtail soup

Oenologist (Fr) - term for wine professional who understands the process of product and balancing that wine with food.

Oeuf -(Fr)- Egg.

Ohno khao swe- (Se)-Burmese curried noodle soup with coconut milk.

Oie - (Fr)- Goose

Oignon - (Fr)- Onion

Öl –(Gm)- Oil

Oloroso -(Sp) Rich and dark Sherry with the highest alcohol content.

Onion Piqué Onion studded with cloves

Opp -(Ch)- Duck

Orechiette- (It) "Little Ears" shaped pasta

Orge - (Fr)- Barley

Orzo - (It)- A pasta preparation that is shaped like barley or rice.

Oseille - (Fr)- Sorrel, a lemon-flavored green leaf herb.

Oshizushi - (Jp) Sushi rice and other ingredients formed using a mold.

Osso Buco - (It) braised veal shanks served with risotto milanaise and gremolata.

Othello - (Fr) – petite spherical sponge cake filled with diplomat cream and glazed with fondant.

Otoro Sushi - (Jp) Very Fat Tuna

Ouzo - (Gr) Anise flavored liquor

P

Paella – (Sp) Valencian rice and shellfish dish prepared in a flat pan with chorizo sausage, poultry and saffron.

Pai Guck - (Ch)- Steamed spare ribs with brown sauce.

Paillard - - (Fr) Thin tender cut of meat that is lightly pounded and sautéed or grilled.

Pain - (Fr)- Bread

Pain d' Epicé - (Fr) Gingerbread

Pain Perdu - (Cr)- American style French toast topped with syrup.

Pakora - (In)- Chick pea batter used to coat for fried meats, vegetables.

Palak – (In)- Peppery spinach

Palak Paneer - (In)- Popular dish of Indian cheese in spinach curry

Paling in Groen - (Gm) – Belgian eels simmered in a parsley lemon sauce.

Palmier - (Fr) a puff pastry cookie that is rolled in sugar that looks like palm leaves.

Pan - (Fr) Bread

Pan Bagnat - - (Fr) A sandwich from Nice filled with onions, anchovies, black olives, and tuna, then flavored with extra virgin olive oil.

Pan Sear - The process of cooking a food product in an uncovered pan with little or no fat, to caramelize the item.

Panada - (Fr) Binding paste of liquid, starch, and or eggs used for forcemeats

Pancetta - (It)-Cured and rolled pork belly rendered for its fat to flavor dishes.

Pane - (It)- Bread

Paneer - (In)- Fresh cheese

Panforte - (It-) Dense fruit and nut torte

Pani Puri - (In) Fried puff-pastry balls served with spiced water, potatoes, onion and chick peas.

Panissa - (It) – Piedmontaise risotto with red beans, lardo, onions and red wine.

Panjeon - (Kr)- Scallion and egg pancake

Panna Cotta - (It) Gelatin thickened cream dessert

Panna - (It)- Cream

Pannetone - (It) yeast-based cake flavored with raisins, candied fruits, and almonds or pistachios traditionally served at Christmas

Panzanella - (It) toasted bread tossed with vegetables and vinaigrette served as a salad.

Papas - (La) Fried potatoes

Papeeta - (In)- Papaya

Pappardelle - (It) Wide flat noodles.

Paprikash - (Eu) Paprika flavored stew with sour cream

Paratha - (In) – Buttered layered bread that is griddled

Pareve - (Yd)- a food that is neither meat nor dairy and that it may be served with either.

Parfait - (Fr)- 1. Semi frozen mousse. (Br) A ice cream sundae with syrup.

Paris- Brest – (Fr) Ring shaped choux with almonds filled with praline whipped cream and dusted with confectionary sugar. Names after the original French bicycle race.

Parisienne - - (Fr) 1. In the style of Paris. 2. Ball shaped fruit and vegetables.

Parmentier - (Fr)1. dishes that use potatoes. 2. A knife cut that is a ½" dice.

Parmigiano-Reggio - (It) Hard cheese from Parma, Parmesan.

Passerillage - (Fr) - the process of drying the grapes on the vine to increase the level of sugar.

Passito - (It) -the process of drying the grapes on or off the vine to change the flavor or color of the wine.

Pasta e Fagioli - (It) bean and pasta soup

Pasta - (It) - A paste made from flour eggs and water that is shaped many different ways.

Pastaciotti - (It)- small tart filled with almonds and mascarpone.

Pasteles - (Cr)- Tamale made from corn or plantains that are filled with various meets depending upon the country and wrapped in a banana leaf. Common dish during Christmas to remember that Mary swaddled Jesus.

Pasticcio – 1. (It)- Pâté 2. (Gr)- A pasta casserole with spiced ground meat and béchamel.

Pastilla - (Ar) Moroccan pie that is made with poultry and pignolis. The turnovers are wrapped in fillo dough and baked then dusted with sugar and spice. Piñon in Puerto Rico

Pastillage - (Fr)sugar paste used for decoration. Made from confectioners' sugar, cornstarch and gelatin

Pastólon - (Cr)- Sweet plantain lasagna with layers of ground beef and eggs from the Dominican Republic.

Patata - (It)- Potato

Patatas Bravas - (Sp) -sautéed potatoes served in a spicy tomato sauce.

Pâté - (Fr) A forcemeat cooked in a fat lined mould.

Pâte - (Fr) Paste

Pâte à Choux - - (Fr) Cooked batter made from water or milk, butter, and eggs. Used for pastries and for pommes dauphine.

Pâte Brisée - (Fr) Short crust pastry dough made with butter and eggs. **Pâte Feuilletage** - - (Fr) Laminated dough, puff pastry.

Pâte Sablée - (Fr)sweetened biscuit dough used for tarts or cookies.

Pâte Sucrée - (Fr)A sweetened short dough that is used for tarts and tartlets.

Patisserie - (Fr) Pastry or Pastry Shop.

Patlican Ezmesi – (Tu)-Charcoal smoked eggplant with garlic, lemon, and yogurt.

Patlican Musakkasi – (Tu)- Layered eggplant dish with spiced lamb baked with a béchamel.

Paupiette - (Fr) stuffed, rolled fillet of fish

Pay Don - (Ch)- Preserved eggs

Paysanne - (Fr) knife cut that is ½" x ½" x 1/8" either square or triangle

Pêche - (Fr)- Peach

Pecorino Romano - (It) Hard Cheese made from sheep's milk

Peler - (Fr)- To peel

Peler à vif (Fr)-To remove the peel and outer membrane of a citrus fruit with a knife.

Pellicle - the forming of dry skin on the outside of a protein in improve smoke absorption.

Penne - (It)- Quill shaped pasta.

Pepe - (It)- Pepper used to spice a dish.

Peperonata - It -Sautéed and seasoned peppers and onion preparation used for antipasti or as a flavoring element.

Peperoncino - (It)- Chili Pepper

Peperone - (It)- Bell Pepper

Périgourdine - (Fr) With truffles, Madeira wine and Foie Gras.

Pernil - (Cr)- Roasted pork shoulder with annatto, garlic, onions and pepper from Puerto Rico

Persil - (Fr)- Parsley

Persillade - (Fr) - mix of chopped parsley and garlic used to flavor breadcrumbs or to finish a dish.

Pesce - (It)- Fish

Pessadik or Pesachdik - (Yd)- Kosher for Passover.

Pesto - (It) Ligurian "paste" made of fresh basil, garlic, olive oil, pine nuts and parmesan cheese.

Petha - (In) – Winter melon

Pétillant (Fr)- Sparkling wine

Petit fours glacé - (Fr) Bite sized cakes coated with fondant and decorated

Petit fours sec - (Fr) Bite sized cookies that are filled and served at the end of the meal.

Petit pois - (Fr)- Peas

Petti - (It) Young poultry breast

Pfannkuchen – (Gm)- Pancakes

Pfeffer – (Gm)-Pepper

Pfirsiche – (Gm)-Peaches

Pflaumen – (Gm)- Plums

Phalian - (In)- Asparagus beans aka yard bean

Phở - Se-Vietnamese soup of meat broth, raw or cooked beef, rice noodles, herbs. The hot liquid quickly cooks the shaved raw beef.

Phoa - (In) Rice flakes

Phyllo - (Gr) – Paper thin sheets of dough that are then layered with butter and used for preparations like baklava and spanakopita.

Piaza - (In)- Onion

Picadillo - (Cr)- Spicy Cuban hash made with olive and raisins.

Picado - Sp- Spicy stewed beef for burrito or tacos

Pico de Gallo - (Sp) "rooster's beak" raw salsa made of fresh tomatoes, chilies, and red onions.

Pide - (Tu)- Large loaves of pita bread.

Pièce de resistancé - (Fr) The main course or focus of a meal

Pièce Montée - (Fr)- a large sculpted centerpiece used to draw the attention.

181

Piémontaise-(Fr) Piedmont style preparation of porcini mushrooms and truffle.

Pignoli -(It) Pinenuts

Pilaf- Braised rice dish, pulao, pilav, pilao.

Pilze –(Gm)- Mushrooms

Pimentón -(Sp) Smoked Spanish paprika.

Pina-(La) Pineapple

Pinnekjøtt-(Sc)- Cured and smoked ribs of lamb or mutton dish are reconstituted then steamed with birch wood then served with mashed rutabagas and steamed potatoes. A traditional Christmas dish.

Pintade- (Fr) Guinea Fowl

Piquant -1. (Fr) -Sharp flavor. 2.(Cr) Spicy Creole sauce.

Piqué-(Fr) **Studded**

Piquillo -(Sp) Sweet red peppers from Navarro Spain

Pirasa- (Tu) Leeks.

Piroshki-(Eu) -Small Russian meat and pastry appetizers.

Pissaladière-(Fr) Pizza from the French Riviera made from caramelized onions, garlic, black olives and anchovies.

Pista-(In)-Pistacio

Pisto Manchego- (Sp) -Braised squash, peppers and tomato dish.

Pita Bread- Flat round bread originally from the Middle East, Asia Minor.

Pithiviers -(Fr) Sweet or savory frangipane is filled between two layers of puff pastry, glazed with egg wash and decorated by a knife this is then portioned after it is baked.

Piyaz- (Tu) – bean salad

Pizza -(It) Open face pie from Naples

Pizzaiolo -(It) Fresh tomato sauce from Naples

Pizzelle- It- crisp waffle cookie.

Plat du jour –(Fr) Plate of the day.

Plin- (It) – Pinched ravioli from Torino served with sage butter.

Po Boy – (Cr) American sandwich of a light crispy baguette filled with fried seafood or roast beef, origin New Orleans. Filled with BBQ brisket or smoked sausage in Texas.

Poach-To slowly cook in a liquid that is between 150º - 180º.

Poblano- (Sp)- Dark Chile Pepper that has a mild flavor used in "Chilies Rellanos". When dried this chile is called Ancho.

Poêlé-–(Fr) 1. Butter covered roast. 2.Tender cuts of meat or poultry that are roasted with their own juices and a Matignon while being covered.

Poğaça-(Tu) Feta cheese turnover pastry

Poilâne-(Fr)- the name of a Boulangerie that has produced Round naturally fermented 2 kilo sourdough bread, the original 1932 sour is still in use.

Poire - (Fr)- Pear

Poireau - (Fr)- Leek

Poisson - (Fr)- Fish

Poivrade-(Fr) Peppercorn based sauce used to flavor game or meats.

Poivre - (Fr)- Pepper

Poivron - (Fr)- Bell pepper

Poivron pimenté - (Fr)- Chili pepper

Polenta –(It) A dish using ground cornmeal, stock, milk, cooked like a porridge.

Pollo-(It)-(Sp) Chicken

Polonaise- (Fr) "Polish Style" hard-boiled egg and bread crumb mixture for vegetables.

Polpa-(It)-Octopus

Polpetta -(It) Meatballs, Variety of croquettes found in Venice.

Pomme - (Fr)- Apple

Pomme de terre - (Fr)- Potato

Pommes Anna - (Fr)- Spiral pan fried potato cake.

Pommes Duchesse - (Fr)- Mashed potato preparation with egg yolk, butter, parmesan cheese, salt, white pepper and nutmeg used as a base recipe for many other potato dishes

Pomme Fondant- (Fr)- Potato disk that is browned in butter then baked with small amount of stock and aromatics to develop the flavor.

Pomodoro-(It)- Tomatosauce

Ponzo-(Jp) Citrus based soy dipping sauce.

Porchetta -(It) Stuffed and seasoned whole roasted pig

Porcini -(It) Hearty mushroom also known as cepes

Poronkäristys- (Sc) Sautteed reindeer strips served with potatoes and lingonberries.

Posole- (Sp) Mexican soup of hominy, onions, tomatillos, garnished with avocado, lime, oregano, crispy pork skin, and fresh white cheese.

Posset (Br) – Lemon cream curd

Potage(Fr)Thick Soup

Potpourri (Fr) –A variety of flavors applied to a stew.

Poularde- (Fr) -Fattened Chicken

Poulet–(Fr) Fryer or Broiler Chicken. Poulet Saute see recipe 495

Pousse-café- (Fr)- a cocktail made from a variety of liqueurs with different densitys which results in a layered appearance.

Poussin–(Fr)- Baby chicken

Poutine-(Fr)- National dish from Quebec of French fries, cheese curd, and brown gravy

Praline- 1. (Fr) Hazelnut candy or truffles. 2.(Cr)- American pralines are made from cream caramel and pecans.

Premier Cru- (Fr) "First Growth" the highest quality level wine from Bordeaux. In Burgundy this is the level just below Grand Cru.

Pressing- applying pressure to extract the liquid from grapes or olives.

Prestige Cuvée- (Fr) – the finest blend from a Champagne producer. e.g.- Armand de Brignac, Dom Pérignon, Cristal.

Prik nam pla- Se- Thai sauce made with bird chile and fish sauce

Primo Piatto-(It)- First Course -Pasta, Risotto, Soup **Printanier**– (Fr) Garnish of spring vegetables.

Profiteroles–(Fr) Bite size pate au choux balls.

Prosciutto -(It) Ham

Prosecco-(It) Wine that is made from glera grapes. Produced as a sparkling wine- Spumante, semi sparkling – Frizzante, or still wine – tranquilo.

Provençale -(Fr) From Provence, Garnish of mixed vegetables and garlic.

Provolone -(It) Sharp semi firm cow's milk cheese

Pruning- removing the undesirable canes and shoots from the gnarly vines to produce a stronger root system for the next growth.

Puff Pastry – a thousand layers of dough and fat make up this laminated multipurpose dough.

Pulla-(Sc)-Finnish sweet dough bread with cardamom, raisins, and almonds.

Pulled- slow cooked meat that is literally pulled into strands. i.e. Pulled pork

Pullman Loaf- Box car shaped loaves of bread baked in mold to form a perfect rectangle

Pulses- Dried vegetables that grow in pods like lentils and peas.

Pumate- (It) Sundried tomatoes.

Pumpernickel Dark rye bread with molasses

Pupusa-(La) Thick corn tortilla filled with meat or cheese

Puree-A smooth paste of fruits or vegetables.

Purloo- Thick stew of seafood, chicken or game with rice

Puttanesca- (It) Pasta sauce flavored with tomatoes, capers, onions, anchovies, black olives, and crushed red pepper flakes.

Q

Quahog- chowder or large clams.

Quark-(Gm) A soft cheese that tastes like yogurt, made from skim milk.

Quatre-epices (Fr) Spice mixture of ginger, nutmeg, cloves, and white pepper.

Quenelles(Fr)-Three-sided or oval forcemeat dumplings of fish, poultry, veal, vegetable or starch. Shape is commonly be used for creams and dessert elements like ice cream.

Quesadilla- (La)- Tortilla filled with cheese, meat, or vegetables then griddled.

Quiche–(Fr) Flat custard tart. e.g Quiche Lorraine is made with bacon and gruyere cheese.

Quickbread -a bread, muffin, or scone that is leavened with baking soda or baking powder.

Quwarmah Al Dajay- (Ar)- Kuwaiti curried chicken flavored with turmeric, lime, ginger, black pepper, nutmeg, paprika, cumin, cardamom, and baharat.

R

Raclette-(Sw)-Style and type of Alpine cheese melted under a broiler or near a hearth then "scraped" over boiled potatoes and cornichons.

Radicchio- red chicory lettuce that can be mild to bitter in flavor.

Raft- the term used to describe the coagulation of the proteins in clarification of a consommé that rises to the top of the pot.

Ragoût-(Fr) Stew

Rai-(In)-Mustard seeds

Raisin - (Fr)- Grape

Raisin sec - (Fr)- Raisin

Raita-(In)- Cool dip made with cucumber, mint, cilantro and yogurt

Rajma Dal- (In)- Kidney beans

Rakfisk-(Sc) – Fermented raw trout

Ramekin –(Fr) Small porcelain mould

Ramollir - (Fr)- To soften

Ramp- Wild onion from the Appalachian mountain range.

Rancheros- (Sp) Ranch Style

Ras-el-Hanout- (Ar)- North Africa spice mixture of turmeric, ginger, cardamom, cumin seeds, coriander seeds, and nutmeg

Ratatouille–(Fr) A vegetable stew of eggplant, onions, peppers, zucchini, tomatoes, herbs, garlic, and olive oil.

Ravioli- (It) Stuffed pasta that is shaped either round or square. Usually filled with meat, cheese or other ingredients.

Recaito-(La) Cooking base of onion, vinegar, spices, garlic, cilantro

Rechauffé –(Fr) To reheat

Red Beans and Rice-(Cr)-Dark red kidney beans are simmered with sausage or ham then served over boiled rice. Typical dish served on Monday nights in New Orleans.

Redeye Gravy- Prepared from the pan juices of fried ham and black coffee and spiced with cayenne.

Reduce- To concentrate the flavors in liquid by simmering moderate heat.

Refritos- (Sp) Refried

Reh–(Gm)-Venison

Reis–(Gm)- Rice

Rindfleisch- (Gm)- Beef

Rellenas- (Sp) -Stuffed

Rémoulade-(Fr) A mayonnaise that is flavored with cornichons, mustard, anchovies, capers and herbs

Remuage (Fr)-riddling

Render-To change solid fat to liquid fat slowly with heat.

Reserva- 1. (Sp)- aged 3 years in Spain for reds and 2 years for whites. 2. (Pt)- slightly higher alcohol content in Portugal

Residual Sugar- refers to leftover unfermented sugar in the wine which is an indication of sweetness.

Reuben Sandwich- Corned beef with Swiss cheese, Russian dressing, sauerkraut, and mustard is layered between rye bread and grilled.

Ribolitta-(It) White bean soups flavored with vegetables, bread, cheese

Rickey- Originally prepared with Bourbon, soda water, lime juice and a lump of sugar it was adapted to for soda fountains during prohibition.

Ricotta -(It) Fresh whey that is cooked to form this fresh cheese.

Riddling- force the yeast cells into the neck of the bottle by twisting and lightly shaking the bottle while it is in racks or mechanically on gyropalettes.

Rinderrouladen -(Gm)- round steak pounded thin and typically used for a roulade, filled with carrot, pickle and mustard then braised.

Rigatoni –(Fr) Large pasta tubes with ridged sides.

Rijsttafel- Dutch for "rice table". A pilaf prepared with a variety of sambals and curries made from seafood, meats, and vegetables, served with fruits, and chutneys.

Rillette–(Fr)- spiced pork spread similar to American potted meat cooked in fat.

Ripasso- the lees from a batch are refermented with freshly press wine to increase flavor and color.

Ripieno-(It)- Stuffed

Risi e Bisi- (It) Rice with Peas

Riso-(It)- Rice

Risotto- (It) An Arborio or Carnaroli rice that is served for Il Primo, the first course. It has a creamy texture and is usually finished with cream and or cheese.

Rissoler –(Fr) To fry to a golden-brown color on all sides.

Roast-To cook a product which has been elevated using a dry heat method.

Rockefeller- spinach, mornay, and pernod filling used to flavor oysters. The dish is then layered with hollandaise then browned in a salamander.

Rogan Josh-(In)-Northern Indian meat curry that is bright red

Rognon - (Fr)- Kidney

Rollatini- (It) Roulade, roll

Romesco -(Sp) Roasted pepper and tomato sauce thickened with nuts

Rondeau- (Fr) -two handled shallow pot used for braising.

Rondelle – Vegetable cut that is ½" in diameter by 1/8" thick round

Ropa Vieja- (Cr) Shredded beef stew from Cuba

Rosado- (Sp) Rosé

Rösti- (Sw)- Thick potato pancake made from grated cooked potatoes.

Roti-(In)-Unleavened flat breads

Rôtir - (Fr)- To roast

Rouille–(Fr) "Rust"- Cold sauce made of roasted red peppers, garlic, potatoes or bread and olive oil.

Roulade To roll a thin slice of meat which is filled or stuffed. These products are usually braised, roasted, or breaded and fried.

Roussir - (Fr)- To brown or singe

Roux–1. (Fr) equal parts of fat and flour cooked to various degrees used to thicken various liquids. 2. (Cr) Brown to black roux is used as the base for soups, gumbo and etoufee.

Royale-(Fr) An egg custard garnish.

Rub -a spice blend that is rubbed into a protein to change the flavor, color and texture of an item before it is grilled or smoked.

Ruby- the lowest grade of port wine

Rúgbrauð-(Sc) Dense steamed rye bread from Iceland. Served with butter, liver pate, pickled herring or smoked lamb.

Rugelach-(Yd)- A flakey rolled cookie filled with jam, almond paste, or chocolate.

Rührreier –(Gm)-Scrambled eggs

Ruisleipä-(Sc)-Finnish coarse grain rye bread

S

Saag-(In)- Leafy greens

Sabayon - (Fr) Egg yolks and sweet wine heated over a double boiler while being whipped until creamy.

Sablée–(Fr) - A rich short biscuit similar to shortbread, that it delicate in texture

Sabler (Fr) - Process of mixing butter into flour until sandy consistency; avoids formation of gluten ("Cut-in-Fat method").

Sabzi-(In)- Generic term for curry dishes made from vegetables

Sacher Torte-(Gm)-Viennese hazelnut chocolate cake layered with apricot or whortleberry jam then coated with hard ganache.

Sachet d' épices- (Fr) -Spice sack that is used to flavor liquids, stocks and sauces.

Sacristain- (Fr) -Strips of puff pastry coated with sugar and nuts.

Saft –(Gm)-juice

Sahne –(Gm)- cream, whipped cream

Saignant - (Fr)- Cooked very rare

Saint Honoré- (Fr)- Named for the patron saint of Bakers this torte is built with a layer of puff pastry, a pate au choux ring, and a crème chiboust, garnished with caramel coated profiteroles.

Saison –(Gm)- season

Sake Sushi- (Jp) Salmon

Şakşuka- (Tu)- Fried vegetables in yogurt

Salamander-A broiler, to change the color of an item by browning

Salat -(Gm)- salad, lettuce

Salata-(Gr)- salad

Salchichón -(Sp) Iberico pork sausages that are smoked

Sale-(It)- Salt

Salmis–(Fr) **A** game sauce / stew prepared from the roasted legs and thighs.

Salpicon-(Fr) Diced cooked meat or seafood bound in a white sauce or mousseline.

Salsa -(Sp) Sauce, chopped vegetables and fruits combined to accompany grilled and highly spiced dishes. 2-(It)- Sauce

Salsiccia-(It)- Sausage

Saltah- (Ar) Yemeni brown meat stew flavored with chilies, vegetables, tomatoes and garlic. Served with rice, eggs, and flatbreads.

Saltimbocca- (It) A dish made from slices of veal, layered with prosciutto and sage, sautéed.

Saltpeter -potassium nitrate

Salumi -(It) Cured meats and sausages

Salz –(Gm)- salt

Sambar-(In)-South Indian vegetable lentil broth

Sambuca- (It) Licorice flavored liqueur.

Samlo kako- (Se) -National dish of Cambodia made with ground spices, fish, pork, vegetables- sometimes finished with coconut milk.

Samosa- (In)- similar to an empanada filled with curried potatoes, cauliflower, peas and other assorted vegetables.

Sang Chau -(Ch)-Soy sauce, light

Sang Geung -(Ch)- Fresh ginger root

Saray Lokmasi- (Tu)- Fritters in honey syrup

Sangler- (Fr) To pre-chill a bowl or mold.

Sarsoon ka Saag- (In) Punjabi

Sashimi- Sliced raw fish served with soy sauce and wasabi

Satay- (Se) Skewered meat that is grilled over a flame served with a spicy peanut sauce. Very popular street food in Indonesia, Vietnam and Thailand.

Saucisse (Fr) - Sausage

Sauer- (Gm)- pickled, sour

Sauté-(Fr) 1.To cook quickly, in a small amount of hot fat. "to jump". 2. The process of tossing the product within the pan to cook on all sides.

Sauteuse-(Fr) - sauté pan with sloping sides

Sautoir –(Fr) -sauté pan with straight sides

Savarin-(Fr) -Egg and butter-based yeast dough, baked in a donut shaped mould, the baked ring is then flavored with a rum syrup and filled with pastry cream.

Sazon-(La) A Puerto Rican Seasoned salt with annatto seeds.

Scald-To quickly bring milk to about 200° to change the lactic acid in milk.

Scaloppini -(It) Thin flattened piece of veal or other meats

Scampi- (It) "langoustine'. In the US the term also applies to shrimp.

Schinken-(Gm)- Ham

Schlachtplatte -(Gm)-Cold cuts and sausage platter

Schluferli-(Sw)-Almond lemon and flavored dough puff dough that is fried and finished with sugar.

Schmaltz-(Yd)- Rendered chicken fat used in cooking.

Schnecken -(Gm)-Snails

Schnitzel -(Gm)- cutlet, schnitzel

Schokolade-(Gm)-chocolate

Schwarzwälder Kirschtorte-(Gm)- Black Forest Cake. Layers of chocolate sponge are flavored with kirsch, whipped cream, and cherries. Topped with shaved chocolate.

Schweinefleisch-(Gm) pork

Schweinhaxe-(Gm) Smoked pork shank

Scone- Br-A dried fruit studded biscuit used for tea or breakfast.

Score-To cut thin lines into a food product for the purpose of either rendering fat or lightly cutting the skin layer of vegetables.

Sear- To brown the surface of meat at a high temperature to build flavor.

Seasoned flour -All-purpose flour with salt and pepper or other seasonings.

Sec- (Fr) Dry

Secco- (It) Dry

Secco-(It)- Dry

Secondo Piatto-(It)- Second Course- Meat, Fish, Poultry

Seezunge -(Gm)- sole

Şekerpare-(Tu) Small almond sponge cakes soaked in syrup.

Sel - (Fr)- Salt

Sem- (In) – Butter beans

Semifreddo- (It) "half cold", this is an ice cream or gelato with whipped cream.

Semolina- Durum wheat flour used for pasta and bread.

Senf –(Gm)-mustard

Serviette –(Gm)- napkin

Seviche- (Sp) Raw fish, scallops, or shrimp which is marinated in citrus juice, onions, peppers, and chilies to denature the protein by lowering the pH level.

Sformato- (It)- A molded sweet or savory preparation.

Sha Ho Fun -(Ch)- Rice stick noodles

Shaka Hari-(In)- Vegetarian

Shallot- sharp flavored onion used in French cuisine. When cooked shallots become sweet.

Shan Yee -(Ch)- Eel.

Shao Mai (Ch)- Dumplings that are steamed

Shao Yazi-(Ch)- "Peking Duck"- boiled then air dried ducks are coated with a sherry sugar syrup before being roasted. The final preparation is ladling hot fat over the skin to make it cri(Sp) Carved at the table then served with pancakes, sweet bean sauce and scallion.

Sharifa- (In)- Custard apple

Shawarma-(Le) Spice marinated, skewered and grilled chicken or lamb

Shee Yau -(Ch)- Soy sauce

Shock- To stop the cooking process quickly by immersing in an ice bath.

Sherry-a fortified Spanish wine made from white grapes commonly used in cooking. aka Jerez, Xeres.

Shiro Maguro Sushi- (Jp) Albacore tuna.

Shorba-(In)-Spicy broth

Shortbread- (Br) A buttery cookie from Great Britain, often seasoned with lemon, cinnamon, and ginger and garnished with nuts. The short dough is made from 1 part of sugar, 2 parts of butter and 3 parts of flour.

Shue jia (Ch)- Dumplings that are boiled.

Shoyu- Japanese soy sauce

Shrub- During Colonial American times this became a sweetened vinegar drink, recently used in mixed drinks.

Shuen Moo Jeung-(Ch)-Plum sauce

Sicak Humus-(Tu)- Hot chick pea puree with pinenuts, butter, olive oil.

Sidra-(Sp) Apple cider from Asturias Spain

Sigara Böreği–(Tu)-Farmers cheese filled pastries shaped like cigars that are fried.

Simit-(Tu)- Sesame bread rings

Simmer-To cook a liquid under the boiling point at 185- 200°.

Simple Syrup-A solution of equal weights of sugar and water. The mixture is brought to a boil to dissolve sugar. Can be flavored and used as soaking syrup for cakes.or to mix in alcoholic beverages

Sing Gwa -(Ch)- Okra

Singer- (Fr) The sprinkling of flour over a product that has been cooked in fat to form a roux.

Sippets –(Br)-English term for croutons

Şiş Kebabi-(Tu)- Lamb kebabs with onion, pepper and tomato

Sitaphal-(In) Pumpkin

Siu Pai Guck -(Ch)- BBQ pork spare rib

Slurry- A thickening agent composed of a refined starch and cool liquid.

Smorgasbord- (Sc)Swedish buffet of many hors d'oeuvres for the main meal. A smorgasbord will offer smoked and cured salmon, pickled herring, marinated vegetables, cheeses, cracker breads and open-faced sandwiches.

Smørrebrød-(Sc) – Danish open-faced sandwiches of buttered dark brown bread topped with cold cuts, pickled fish, shrimp, cheese or spreads.

Soba Noodle- Japanese buckwheat noodles.

Soffriggere-(It)- to sauté

Soffrito -(It) Chopped mirepoix and garlic base used for soups and stew

Sofrito-(Cr)-Spanish based tomato sauce used to flavor other preparations like stews and roasts.

Soft Ball Stage-cooking equal parts sugar and water until it reaches 121 °C, 250 °F

Soft Crack Stage-cooking equal parts sugar and water until it reaches 136 °C, 277 °F

Soon -(Ch)- Bamboo dish used for a palate cleanser or as a dessert.

Sorbet -(Fr) Frozen dessert or intermezzo

Soubise -(Fr) Puréed cooked white onions.

Soufflé-(Fr) "to rise above the rim". A light dish made from a base, main flavor and whipped egg whites which is then baked, served hot as an appetizer or dessert.

Soupe - (Fr)- Soup

Sourdough- Naturally leavened bread that is made with a starter that give the bread a sour note.

Soutirage (Fr) -separating wine in a barrel from its sediment.

Souvlaki- (Gr-) Marinated and grilled meat skewers.

Spanikopita- (Gr)- Baked phyllo triangles filled with feta and spinach

Spanish Mirepoix- Aromatic base of tomato, garlic, and onion.

Spatchcock- the process of splitting a small roasting bird in half then spit roasted on flat racks.

Spätlese- (Gm) "late harvest", a level of ripeness for German Wines. Above Kabinet and below Aulese.

Spatzle- (Gm) dropped noodles made from flour, eggs, and milk. (Sw)- same dough that is pressed into noodles.

Speck -1. (Gm)- Bacon. 2. It Alto Adige smoked ham

Spezzatino-(It)- stew of small pieces of meat.

Spiedino -(It) Skewer

Sponge Cake- Whipped eggs and sugar made into a foam, sifted flour and butter are folded in e.g. Genoise and Angel Food Cake

Sponge Toffee-(Br)- honeycomb candy made with baking soda which develops a foam texture.

Spoon Bread- A southern corn bread that has a pudding quality, served hot.

Spotted Dick-(Br)- Traditional English dessert of currants and batter that is steamed.

Stage Method - a mixing method where items are combined in parts or stages, mixing wet ingredients into dry ingredients.

Stamp and Go-(Cr)- Spicy cod fritters sold at the tariff docks

Standard Breading Procedure- the breading of an item by dredging in flour, dipping into an egg wash then coating the item with bread crumb mixture.

Steak and Kidney Pie- (Br) – Beef is stews then finished with prepared kidneys in a brown gravy, packed into deep pies before baking.

Steam -To cook utilizing the vapor produced by boiling water or in a pressurized cabinet above 215°.

Steen- Chenin Blanc in South Africa.

Stock- A flavored liquid from the bones of meat, fish, shellfish, and vegetables which are the base for sauce and soup making.

Stollen-(Gm) Sweet yeast bread filled with dried fruit, nuts and or marzipan.

Stracciatella- It- Soup with threads of eggs

Straight Method -1. Smooth forcemeat that has been ground and then pureed until consistent. 2. Mixing method used in baking where everything goes right into the mixing bowl before the agitation process begins.

Strain -To separate a liquid from the solids with the aid of screen or filter.

Streusel- (Gm)- crumble on top of baked goods made of butter, sugar, spice and flour.

Stroganoff-(Eu) Sauté or braised beef with mushrooms, onions and cream. Served with noodles.

Strong Blow Stage-cooking equal parts sugar and water until it reaches 116 °C, 240 °F

Strong Thread Stage-cooking equal parts sugar and water until it reaches110 °C, 230 °F

Strudel-(Gm)- Austrian pastry dough layered with melted butter with sweet or savory fillings.

Strufoli- It- fried Pâte à Choux balls coated with honey.

Stufare-(It) To stew

Stufato-(It)Stew of large chunks of meat.

Su Jai Bang -(Ch)- Fried yam dumplings filled with BBQ pork and water chestnuts.

Suan La Tang-(Ch)- hot and sour soup with pork broth, roast pork, tofu, vinegar, white pepper, bamboo shoots, wood ear mushrooms, and scallion.

Submarine "Sub"- American sandwich with various Italian cold cuts, provolone and vegetable fillings and vinaigrette, origin New London.

Succo-(It)- Juice

Sucre - (Fr)- Sugar

Sugar crystallization-Results when cooked sugar begins to turn into tiny crystals which can often cause the melted sugar to re-solidify.

Sulphite – an antioxidant used in wine production.

Suon khia- (Se) -Vietnamese caramelized pork ribs flavored with coconut juice, sugar made into a caramel with garlic, shallot, ginger and pepper.

Supli- (It)- Rice croquette

Suppe -(Gm)- soup

Suprême-(Fr) Boneless chicken breast from a fryer or broiler.

Sur Lie- Win Fr.e that has lee contact during the aging process.

Sursild -(Sc)- Pickled herring

Sushi-(Jp) -Bite size serving of vinegar flavored rice with main element.

Süss -(Gm)- Sweet

Süzme -(Tu)- Thick cream cheese like yogurt.

Suzuki Sushi- (Jp) Striped bass

Svinestek-(Sc)- Norwegian roasted pork loin. A thicker layer of fat is left on the roast and when rendered provides a crunchy skin A Sunday meal that served with a sweet pickled cabbage, potatoes, vegetables and gravy.

Sweat To cook in fat under a lid without coloring the food over a low heat.

Sweetbread- (Br)-Thymus gland of veal and lamb named for the sweetmeats (offal) that has a light texture.

Swiss Roll- (Sw) – thin layer of sponge cake filled with Swiss buttercream that is rolled and sliced.

Syllabub- (Br)- A double cream dessert flavored with fruit marinated in liquor.

T

Ta Siew-(Ch)-Smoke roasted pork

Tabasco Sauce- Creole condiment made from a mash of vinegar, Tabasco peppers, and salt.

Table d'hôte-(Fr) "Table of the host" Established menu at a set price.

Tabouleh-(Le) Mediterranean salad of bulgur wheat, tomatoes, parsley, onions, lemon and mint.

Tagine- (Ar)-Moroccan dish of spicy poultry, fish, meat, or vegetables served with cous cous or the vessel it is served in

Tagliatelle- (It) flat pasta similar to fettuccine with a ribbon edge.

Tahini-(Le) -Sesame seed paste or sauce used for hummus and falafel.

Tai Choy Go -(Ch)- Agar-agar

Tairagai Sushi- (Jp) Razor clam

Tako Sushi- (Jp) Octopus

Tamale- (La) Steamed masa harina based dough filled with meat then wrapped in a dried corn husk or banana leaf.

Tamatar-(In)-Tomato

Tamis- (Fr)-drum sieve

Tamiser (Fr) -To sift dry ingredients/to remove lumps using a wire strainer.

Tandoori-(In)- Northern Indian clay oven pit used to roast and bake. Used for baking Naan and other breads. Because of the intense heat the items baked in this oven have to be moved frequently. Proteins are usually skewered on long metal rods.

Tannin- Polyphenol found in grape skins which gives an astringent flavor to red wine, this is softened with time.

Tapas -(Sp) Small appetizer plates that accompany beverages. Cured fish, meatballs, olives, cheeses and thin slices of ham are common over crusty slices of bread.

Tapenade-(Fr) Chopped mixture of cured olives, olive oil, garlic, anchovies, capers, and lemon.

Taramasalata- (Gr) Fish roe sauce similar to a mayonnaise.

Taratur-(Le)- Yogurt sauce flavored with tahini and garlic

Tartar Sauce -Mayonnaise based sauce flavored with capers, minced onion, pickles, lemon and dill. May contain cooked chopped eggs

Tartare- (Gm)-Dish of raw meat or fish which is made from chopped meat or fish, minced onion, eggs, parsley, capers, Worcestershire sauce and Tabasco sauce.

Tarte Jalousie (Fr) – Puff pastry filled with frangipane, brushed with eggwash, layered pears and confectionary sugar then baked.

Tarte Normande (Fr) – short dough filled with frangipane, brushed with eggwash, layered with sliced apples brushed with honey then baked.

Tarte Tatin- (Fr) - upside down caramel apple tart. with puff pastry.

Tartufo-(It)- Truffle

Tasso-(Cr)- Highly seasoned and smoked country style "ham".

Tavşan Yahnisi-(Tu)- Spiced rabbit braised in wine.

Tawny- Port wine which is aged in oak which allows the wine to develop a brown color

Tazuna Sushi -(Jp) "Rainbow roll" a crab filled maki roll with slices of varied fish across the top.

Tchaka-(Cr) Haitian stew of pork feet, scotch bonnets, red beans, corn and pumpkin

Temaki- (Jp) Cone-shaped hand rolls of vinegared rice and fillings.

Temper- combining two elements of different temperatures or consistencies to one homogenous consistency.

Teriyaki- (Jp) Grilled or broiled food with sweet soy sauce.

Terrine-(Fr) - An earthenware dish used for making layered patés or the name of a dish served from the vessel.

Terroir- Climate, soil and terrain conditions which affect the flavor of the wine.

Thai Mirepoix-Aromatic base of lemongrass, galangal, and lime leaf.

Thit xa xiu- Se-Vietnamese BBQ pork, like Char Siu from China

Thon - (Fr)- Tuna

Thread Stage- cooking equal parts sugar and water until it reaches 105ºC, 221ºF

Tikka-(In)- Skewered meats that are marinated before being roasted

Til-(In)-Sesame

Timbale -(Fr) Small round mould used to cook food in

Timpano- (It) -Dough encrusted mold of pasta, eggs, meats, and cheeses

Tiramasu- (It) Sponge cake cookies, ladyfingers, soaked in espresso syrup and layered with mascarpone cheese. Topped off with powdered chocolate or cocoa powder. "Translates to "Pick me up"

Töltött Káposzta-(Eu) -Hungarian pickled cabbage leaves are filled and rolled with pork and paprika and served with sour cream.

Tom kha gai- (Se) -Thai soup of chicken broth, Thai mirepoix, fish sauce, chile, coconut, and oyster mushroom.

Tom yam - Se-Thai sweet and sour soup of shrimp, Thai mirepoix, cilantro, and lime juice.

Tom yum gung- (Se) Thai soup of chicken broth, Thai mirepoix, fish sauce, and shrimp.

Tom yum pa- (Se) -Laotian soup of lemongrass, ginger, chile paste, fish, lime leaf, bird chile, cilantro and mushroom

Tomahawk Steak- Rib Eye steak with entire rib attached.

Tomate - (Fr)- Tomato

Tong -(Ch)- Soup

Tong Geung -(Ch)- Preserved ginger

Tonkatsu- (Jp) dish of thin pork chops breaded with panko and deep fat fried. Served with a sweet ketchup-based soy sauce and shredded cabbage.

Torchon- (Fr)- cheesecloth formed cylinder that is steamed or poached. A log of foie gras that is deveined, cured, and poached. It is sliced and served as an appetizer.

Toro Sushi- (Jp) Fatty tuna.

Torrone- (It) Light nougat with nuts

Torta Rustica- (It) An Italian version of Coulibiac, a pastry filled with trout or salmon, spinach, and eggs that is baked.

Torta- 1. (It) Cake 2. (La) Sandwiches

Torte- German style layer cakes

Tortellini-(It) "Belly Button". Stuffed pasta dumpling shaped like a wonton.

Tortelloni-(It)-Larger tortellini

Tortière-(Fr) – Pork and lard-based pie from Quebec filled with leftovers flavored with cinnamon, clove, and nutmeg and dark beer.

Tortilla- (Sp) "Flat" -1. flatbread of corn or wheat flour, lard and water used for Mexican cuisine. 2. A Spanish an open-faced potato and onion omelet.

Tortoni-(It)- Frozen almond cream dessert

Tostones-(La) Fried then mashed plaintains

Tourné -(Fr) Turned, to shape into seven sided cylinders or olive shaped.

Tournedos-(Fr) Small trimmed steaks of beef tenderloin

Tranche -(Fr) A slice or portion cut of fish.

Trancher-1. (Fr) To carve. 2.(Br) A carved plate or bread bowl that food is served in.

Treyf- (Yd)- not Kosher.

Trifle- (Br)- Layered sponge cake and pastry cream with fruit. This pudding is served in a glass bowl so that the layers are visible.

Tripe- The stomach of sheep or beef.

Trocken- (Gm) Dry

Trockenbeerenauslese- (Gm) "Dried Berry Selection", this contains the highest level of sugar content in the Prädikatswein category system.

Truite (Fr) – Trout

Truites au Bleu (Fr)- Freshly dispatched trout are tied head to tail, so that the presentation is curved, dipped in vinegar, then poached in a court bouillon. Deboned tableside the blue trout skin is removed, the filets are served with Hollandaise sauce.

Truffle--(Fr) An earthy flavored round fungus tuber that grows under the ground near tree roots.

Tuilles-(Fr) "Tile" Paper thin cookies flavored with almond slices, lemon, and vanil(La)

Tulipe- Fr- Hippen paste made into little cups

Turque-(Fr) Turkish Style.

Tuzlanmiş Balik-(Tu) Fish baked in salt crust.

Tzatziki Sauce- (Gr) sauce made from yogurt, garlic, cucumber, olive oil and lemon juice.

Tzimmes -(Yd) Rosh Hashana casserole of fruit, meat and vegetables flavored with honey and cinnamon.

UVW

Udon- (Jp)-Japanese thick wheat noodles.

Udrak-(In)-Ginger

Unagi Sushi- (Jp) Freshwater eel

Uni Sushi- (Jp) Sea urchin

Unilatéral- (Fr)- Grilled only on one side

Uovo-(It)- Egg

Uva-(It)- Grape

Vacherin- A meringue shell that is slowly baked until crisp that is filled with fruit and ice cream.

Vapeur - (Fr)- To steam

Varietal- the particular variety of grape used in wine production.

Vatana- (In) – Green pigeon peas.

Vatapá- (Pt) – Brazilian stew of shrimp, coconut milk, chilies, tomatoes and onions served over rice.

Veau- (Fr)- Veal

Vegan- A person who does not consume animals or the by- products.

Vegetal- a wine tasting term which indicates a cabbage like quality in older pinot noirs.

Velouté- (Fr) A velvety cream sauce or soup.

Vendange Tardive-(Fr) Late Harvest

Vendange-(Fr) Harvest

Verdura-(It)- Vegetables

Verjuice (Fr) - Juice from unripe grapes, apples or sorrel used to flavor other dishes.

Vermicelli- (It) "small worms". Thin spaghetti.

Vichyssoise-(Fr) - A chilled potatoes and leeks soup that is pureed and finished with cream and chives.

Viennoise-(Fr) Garnish of chopped eggs, anchovies, capers, lemons, olives

Villages-(Fr) Wine that is produced from several wine communes in a region to produce a superior product.

Vin Doux Naturel- (Fr) "Wine with Natural Sweetness"

Vinaigre- (Fr)- Vinegar

Vinaigrette-(Fr) Salad dressing of oil, vinegar and herbs.

Vindaloo-(In)-Very spicy curry flavored with vinegar and potatoes

Vintage Port- the highest quality port produced from a single year

Vişneli-(Tu)- Cherries

Vitello Tonnato- (It) Roast veal, served cold with a spicy mayonnaise-based tuna sauce.

Vitello- (It) Veal

Viticulture- related to the management of vines for wine production.

Vol-au -vent-(Fr) Hollow, puff-pastry shell, filled with a salpicon of shellfish or chicken.

Vongole-(It)- Clams

Wallenbergare-(Sc) A ground veal patty bound with egg yolk and coated in breadcrumbs, pan-fried. Classicallyknow as Veal Pojarski or Pozharskie.

Wasabi- Japanese green horseradish used to compliment sushi and sashimi

Wasser –(Gm)-Water

Waterzooi- Belgium's national soup of chicken or fish and assorted vegetables. Finished with a liaison of cream, yolks.

Wein –(Gm)- Wine

Weintrauben –(Gm)- Grapes

Weißkohl –(Gm)-White Cabbage

Wellington- (Br) traditionally beef tenderloin topped with foie gras and duxelles then baked in a pastry crust. Served with a sauce Périgourdine.

Welsh Rarebit-(Br)- Cheddar cheese sauce flavored with ale, dry mustard, black pepper, and Worcestershire sauce. Served over toast.,

Whip-the rapid lifting and beating process to increase the volume by incorporating air into eggs or fat.

White Mirepoix- Aromatic base of leeks, celery, and onion.

Whoopie Pie- A sponge cookie sandwich filled with buttercream. Origin New England.

Wiener Fiakergulash -(Gm) Viennese goulash of beef finished with sourcream, crushed caraway, julienne pickle and lemon zest.

Wiener Schnitzel-(Gm) Thin slices of veal which are breaded with white bread crumbs and pan fried in clarified butter. Garnished with lemons, anchovies, and capers. Finished with a brown butter.

Wirsingrouladen-(Gm)-Pork and bread filled savoy cabbage rolls.

Wong Dow-(Ch)-Yellow bean paste

Woo Dow -(Ch)-Black beans

Worcestershire Sauce- (Br) A condiment or sauce made from anchovies, tamarind, vinegar, molasses, and cloves.

Wun Yee -(Ch)- Cloud ear mushrooms

Wurst –(Gm)- Sausage

Wu Tao Go -(Ch)- Steamed taro pudding cake

XYZ

Xérès-(Sp) With sherry

Xiaolongbao (Ch)- Dumplings that are cube shaped.

Xiu mai- Se-Vietnamese pork meatballs in sweet tomato sauce, common on a Banh Mi, baguette sandwich with pickled vegetables.

Yak a Mein-(Ch)- "one order of noodles" – chicken or beef broth with noodles and vegetables.

Yakisoba- (Jp) Dish of fried noodles, meat, vegetable.

Yakitori- (Jp) dish of marinated grilled chicken skewers.

Yalanci Yaprak Dolmasi-(Tu)- rice stuffed grape leaves

Yang Fun -(Ch)- Seaweed or cellophane noodles

Yao hon- Se-Cambodian hot pot also known as Chhnang plerng. Used for shrimp, beef, vegetables egg or mung bean noodles.

Yaz Türlüsü- (Tu)- Similar to a ratatouille with the addition of artichokes, mint and dill.

Yin War -(Ch)- "Bird's nest" – solidified saliva from birds' nest that is used for soup. **Yo Yee -**(Ch)- Fresh squid

Yorkie -(Br) – Slang for Yorkshire pudding.

Yu Chee -(Ch)-Dried shark's fin used for soup

Yuk -(Ch)-Beef

Zabaglione- (It) Whipped egg yolk and wine-based sauce used for dessert.also know as a sabayon.

Zafferano-(It)- Saffron

Zakuski- (Eu) Appetizers usually served with vodka.

Zampone-(It)- Forcemeat stuffed pig's foot.

Zeppole- (It)- Blimp/Football shaped pate au choux quenelles, fried and topped with powdered sugar

Zest- the grated rind of citrus used to flavor.

Zeytinyağli- (Tu) Chilled preparation – used like a salad.

Zhajiangmian-(Ch)- Noodles are placed in the bowl first with raw vegetables around then hot soybean-based sauce is placed in the center, customer mixes the elements together.

Zimikand-(In) Elephant foot yams

Zingara-(Fr) In the style of gypsies using ham, tongue, mushrooms, truffles, and paprika.

Zitrone –(Gm)- Lemon

Zuccato- It- Glazed ice cream cake

Zuccherare-(It)- Sugar

Zuppa Millefanti- (It) "Soup of a thousand flowers" made from a beef consommé and parsley flavored panada.

Zuppa Pavese-(It) Chicken soup with poached eggs.

Zuppe- (It) Soup

Zürcher Geschnetzeltes- (Sw) Veal strips sautéed with mushrooms and shallots in a white wine, demi cream sauce.

Zwiebel- (Gm)- Onion

Additional resources and references for these terms can be found on our website www.chefreference.com

A

Abatidor- Blast chiller
Abrelatas - Can opener-
Abril-April
Abrir - Shuck (shellfish)
Aceite - Oil
Aceite de girasol - Sunflower oil
Aceite de oliva - Olive oil
Aceituna - Olive
Acelgas - Swiss Chard
Achicoria - Chickory
Aderezo - Dipping suace
Adiós - Goodbye
Afeitarse -Shave(to)
Afilar -Sharpen (to)
Agosto- August
Agridulce (35%) -Chocolate, bitter
Agua -Water
Aguacate -Avocado
Ahumado - Smoked
Ajedrea - Savory (herb)
Ajo - Garlic
A la juliana -julienne
A la minuta- cooked to order
Ala campesina cuadrado- paysanne cut
Albahaca- Basil
Albaricoque -Apricot
Albóndiga - Meatball
Alcachofa- Artichoke
Alcaparras- Capers
Alérgia -Allergy
Alfombra de piso- Floor Mat
Aliño- Seasoning
Almacén- Storage
Almacenamiento - Storage
Almacenar - Store(to)
Almejas - Clams
Almendras -Almond
Almíbar - Syrup
Almuerzo - Lunch
Alubias rojas- Kidney beans
Amargo (50-70%)- -Chocolate, bitter
Amarillo - Yellow
Amasadora -Dough Mixer
Añadir -Add
Añadir en un hilo- Trickle
Ancas de rana- Frog legs
Anchoa - Anchovy
Anfitrión - Host
Anfitriona - Hostess
Anís- Aniseed
Apagar - Turn off
Aperitivo - Appetizer
Apio -Celery
Aplanar -Roll out (to)
Aplastar - Flatten
Arañas - Spider (utensil)
Arándano Azul -Blueberry
Arándano - Cranberry
Armario frigorífico- Refrigerator
Armari caliente - Hot box(catering)
Arreglar-Arrange
Arrocera -Rice cooker
Arroz - Rice
Arroz con leche - Rice pudding
Arveja verde-Green peas
Arveja (s)- Pea(s)
Asadero - Steakhouse
Asado - Roast

Asar - Grill (to)
Asar a la parilla- Broil
Atar -Truss (to)
Atar - Tie (to)
Atrás-Behind
Atún - Tuna
Avena - Oatmeal
Azafrán - Saffron
Azúcar - Sugar
Azúcar en polvo- Confectionary sugar
Azúcar glacé - Confectionary sugar
Azúcar 10X - Confectionary sugar
Azúcar glas - Confectionary sugar
Azúcar Integral - Raw sugar
Azúcar Morena- Light Brown sugar
Azúcar Negra – Dark Brown sugar
Azul- Blue

B

Bacalao salado -Salt cod
Bacalao - Salt cod
Bacalao-Cod
Balsa- Raft for a consommé
Banano-Banana
Banco -Booth
Bandeja - Sheet pan
Bandeja -Tray
Bandeja de sodio-Baking sheet
Bandeja para rostizar - Roast Pan
Baño -Bathroom
Baño maría - Steam table
Banquete -Banquet
Barbacoa -Barbecue
Barbacoa - BBQ grill
Barman-Bartender
Barra - Loaf
Barrer - Sweep (to)
Barril - Keg
Báscula -Scale
Bastones -bâtonnet
Batata - Sweet potato
Batido(a)- Milk shake
Batidor - Whisk
Batidora - Mixer
Batidoras de vaso -Blender
Batir - Whisk (to), Beat ,Whip (to)
Beber - Drink (to)
Bebida- Drink
Berenjena - Eggplant
Berro - Watercress
Biberón dosificador- - Squeeze bottle
Bien cocido- Well-done (degree of
doneness)
Bien hecho - Well-done (degree of
doneness)
Biscuit Americano -Biscuit
Bistec - Steak
Bistec -Beefsteak
Bizcocho -Cake
Bizcoch o de soletilla - Lady fingers
Blanco - White
Blanquear-Blanch
Blondas de papel- Doily
Bocadillo - Sandwich
Bol de cocina- Mixing bowl
Bol de sopa- Soup Bowl
Bola de helado - Ice cream scoop
Bolero - Portion Scoop
Bollería - Sweet pastries

Bollo de pan - Loaf
Bolsa- Bag
Boquillas de pastelería - Pastry tip
Botana - Appetizer
Botella -Bottle
Botella biberón - Squeeze bottle
Botiquín de primeros auxilios – First Aid
Brécol- Broccoli
Bridar- Tie (to)
Brocha de pastelería- Pastry brush
Brocha- Brush
Brocheta- Kebab
Buenas noches - Good evening
Buenas noches - Good night
Buenas tardes - Good afternoon
Buenos días - Good morning
Butifarra- Cured pork sausage

C

Caballa -Mackerel
Cacahuate - Peanut
Café - Coffee
Café -Brown
Café con leche Coffee with milk
Café negro- Black coffee
Café solo- Coffee plain
Cafetería - Diner (restaurant)
Cafeteria-Coffee machine
Calabacín - Zucchini
Calabaza- Pumpkin
Calamar - Squid
Caldo -Broth, Stock
Calentar - Heat (to)
Camarera - Waitress
Camarero – Waiter, Server, Bartender
Camarones - Shrimp
Camote - Sweet potato
Campanas extractoras - Hood system
Canasta de frutas- Fruit Basket
Canela -Cinnamon
Cangrejo - Crab
Cangrejo de río - Crayfish
Capa - Layer
Caracoles - Snails
Caramelizar -Caramelize (to)
Carbohidrato -Carbohydrate
Cardamomo- Cardamom
Carmelo-Carmel Candy
Carne - Meat
Carne de cerdo - Pork meat
Carne de pecho-Brisket
Carne de res- Beef
Carne de salchicha - Sausage (fresh)
Carne picada - Ground beef
Carro -cart
Carro de queso -Cheese cart
Carros calientes - Hot box(catering)
Carta - Menu
Cáscara - Zest
Cáscara - Rind
Cascara - Shell (to)
Casillero- Lockers
Castaña -Chestnut
Catsup - Ketchup
Cazo - Saucepan
Cebolla - Onion
Cebolla lila - Purple onion
Cebolla morada -Purple onion
Cebolla roja- Red onion

Cebollas verdes - Green onions
Cebolletas- Spring onions
Cebollínes - Green onions
Cebollines - Chives
Cedazo - Sieve
Cena - Dinner
Centrifugadora de lechuga - Lettuce spinner
Cepillar-Brush (to)
Cerdo - Pork
Cerdo picado - Ground pork
Cereza -Cherry
Cerveza- Beer
Cesta de frutas -Fruit Basket
Cestas para lavavajillas- Dishmachine racks
Chaira - Sharpening steel
Chalota - Shallot
Champiñón -Mushroom button
Chícharo(s)-Pea(s)
Chile - Chile pepper -
Chillo -Red snapper
Chipirón- Squid
Chipirones- Squid, baby
Chirimoya-Cherimoya
Chirivías - Parsnips
Chocolate agridulce extra amargo (75-80%)-Chocolate, bitter
Chocolate blanco -Chocolate, white
Chocolate caliente -Chocolate, hot
Chocolate con leche -Chocolate, milk
Chocolate en polvo-Cocoa powder
Chocolate oscuro -Chocolate, dark
Chorizo- Cured pork sausage
Chorrear un poco - Trickle
Chorrito - Dash of liquid
Chuleta -Chop (portion of meat)
Chuleta de cerdo - Pork chop
Ciruela - Plum
Ciruela pasa - Prune
Ciruela seca- Prune
Clara de huevo - Egg white
Clarificar -Clarify (to)
Clavos de olor- Cloves
Cocción al minute – cooked to order
Cocedor a baja tmeperatura- Immersion circulator
Cocer a fuego lento-Coddle (to)
Cocer al horno - Bake (to)
Cochinillo- Suckling pig
Cocinar -Cook(process)
Cocinar a fuego lento - Simmer, full
Cocinar al vapor - Steam(to)
Cocinar lento - Simmer, low
Cocinero-Cook(job)
Coco- Coconut
Cocoa en polvo-Cocoa powder
Cóctel -Cocktail
Cóctel de gambas/ camarones - Shrimp cocktail
Codorniz - Quail
Col -Cabbage
Col rizada- Kale
Colador - Strainer
Colador chino de malla -Chinoise (fine sieve) -
Colar - Strain(to)
Coles de Bruselas - Brussel Sprouts
Coliflor -Cauliflower
Colocar-Arrange

Colorante alimentario - Food coloring-
Combinar – Combine (to)
Comensal -Diner (customer)
Comer - Eat
Comida- Food
Comida buffet- Buffet
Comino – Cumin
¿Cómo está usted? -How are you?
¿Cómo le va?-How's life?
Condiment- Seasoning
Condimentar- Season(to)
Conejo- Rabbit
Confitar- Candy (to)
Congelador - Freezer
Conserver - Preserve (to)
Consistencia - Consistency
Contenedor de basura- Trash can
Copa de helado - Ice cream scoop
Copos de maíz- Corn cereal flakes
Corazón de Alcachofa-Artichoke heart
Corazón de cordero - Lamb, heart
Cordel - Twine
Cordero - Lamb
Cordial -Aperitif
Coriandro-Coriander seed
Corta fiambre - Deli slicer
Cortadoras de fiambre- Deli slicer
Cortapastas - Pastry cutter
Cortar -Carve (to)
Cortar -Trim
Cortar en cubitor-Dice
Cortar en lascas/rodajas- Slice (to)
Cortar en lonchas/lascas/rodajas finas - Sliced thin
Cortar-Cut
Corteza - Crust (bread)
Costillas - Ribs
Crema agria- Sour cream
Crema chantilly -Whipped cream
Crema de avena- Oatmeal
Crema de maíz -Polenta, Grits
Crema montada -Whipped cream
Crema- cream
Cremoso -Cream texture
Cristalería - Glassware
Crudo- Raw
Crutones- Crouton
Cuajar - Curdle
Cubertería -Flatware
Cubeta -Hotel Pan
Cubierta- Countertop
Cubiertos- Cutlery
Cubrir – Cover, Coat
Cuchara - Spoon
Cucharada de helado- Ice cream scoop
Cuchara de medir - Measuring spoon
Cuchara medidora - Measuring spoon-
Cuchara perforada - Perforated Spoon
Cuchara perforada - Slotted spoon
Cucharada – Spoonful, Tablespoon
Cucharadita - Teaspoon
Cucharón - Ladle
Cuchillo - Knife
Cuchillo de pan -Knife, serrated bread
Cuchillo de sierra --Knife, serrated
Cuchillo deshuesador - Knife, boning
Cuenco -Mixing bowl
Cuenta por favor -Check please
Culirrubia - Red snapper
Curar -Cure (to)

Cúrcuma -Tumeric
Cuscurro -Crouton

D

Dar la vuelta -Turn
Dátiles- Dates (fruit)
Desglasar - deglaze
Desvenar- devein
Dejar -Put down
Dejar en infusión - Steep
Delantal -Apron
Derretir – Melt, Render (to)
Desagüe- Drain (fixture)
Desayuno -Breakfast
Desbullar - Shuck (shellfish)
Descansar- Rest
Descremar - Skim (to)
Desinfectar- Sanitize(to)
Despensa - Pantry
Despensa- Storage
Desvainar- Shuck (husks)
Detrás -Behind
Detrás de ti -Behind you
Diciembre - December
Dientes de ajo - Garlic Cloves
Dividir - Portion (to)
Dividir en dos - Halve
Doblar - Fold (to) -
Domingo - Sunday
Dorado - Mahi-mahi
Dorar - to brown meat, ground beef
Dosificador- Sauce/Batter portioner
Dulce-Candy
Durazno- Peach

E

Ejotes- Green beans
El bote de basura cubo- Trash can
El cuarto de galón -Quart
Elote - Corn- fresh cobb
Embeber en salmuera- Soak in brine
Embutidos-Cured pork sausage
Emparedado - Sandwich
emulsionar -Emulsify (to)
En temporada -Season (in)
Encantado de conocerle - Pleased to meet you
Encender - Ignite
En cubos-dice
En dados fino -brunoise
En dados mediano – medium dice
En dados pequeño- small dice
En dados y grande- large dice
Encurtir -Pickle (to)
Endulzante - Sweetener
Eneldo - Dill
Enero - January
Enfriar -Chill
Engrasar - Oil (to)
Enjuagar -Rinse (in water)
Ensalada - Salad
Ensalada de atún - Tuna salad
Ensalada simple- Simple salad
Ensalada verde- Green salad
Entrada- Appetizer
Entremeses variados - Hors d'oeuvres
Envasadoras al vacío - Vaccum chamber

Escabechar -Pickle (to)
Escaldar – Scald, Blanch
Escalfar - Poach (to)
Escarole - Chicory
Escarole -Curly endive
Escobilla- Brush
Escobilla de goma- Squeegie
Escurrir- Drain (process)
Espaguetis - Spaghetti
Espalmar- Flatten
Espárragos -Asparagus
Espátula -Spatula
Espátula flexible de pescado - Fish spatula
Especiero - Shaker
Espesar -Thicken (to)
Espeso-Thick
Espinacas- Spinach
Espolvorear - Dust (to), Dredge
Espolvorear- Sprinkle
Esponja abrasiva - Scouring pad
Esponja- Sponge
Estante- Shelf
Estanterías - Rack shelves
Este es -This is
Estirar - Roll out (to)
Estofado- Braise
Estofar -Braise(to)
Estragón - Tarragon
Estropajo - Scouring pad
Estufa -Stove
Expedidor de alimentos -Expeditor
Exprimidor- Juicer
Exprimir - Squeeze
Extinguidor de incendios- Fire extinquisher-

F

Factura - Invoice
Febrero- February
Fécula de maíz - Cornstarch
Fermenter -Ferment
Fiambres -Cold cuts
Fichar -Clock in
Fichar la salida-Clock out
Fideos - Noodles (thin)
Filete -Cutlet
Filete de res- Fillet of beef
Filetear -Filet (to)
Flan de caramelo - Cream caramel custard
Flan- Caramel custard
Florecer- Bloom(to)
Fluir en un hilo- Trickle
Fondo- Stock
Formar - Shape (to)
Formar picos/un pico, firme- Stiff peak
Frambuesa - Raspberry
Frambuesa Negra -Blackberry
Fregadero(a)- Sink (fixture)
Fregar - Scrub
Freidora - Fryer
Freir - Fry (to)
Freir en sartén-pan Fry
Fresa - Strawberry
Friegaplatos - Dishwasher (job)
Frigorífico - Refridgerator
Frijoles -Beans
Frijoles Negros-Black Beans
Frijoles refritos - Refried beans

Frissé- Curly endive
Frito produndo- Deep Fat Fried
Frotarm - Rub
Fruta - Fruit
Fuego alto - High heat
Fuego fuerte - High heat
Fuego-Fire
Fuente -Casserole
Fuentes de agua - Water fountain
Funda -Bag

G

Gabinete -Cabinet-
Galleta Saboyana- Lady fingers
Galleta- Cookie
Galón -Gallon
Gambas - Shrimp-prawn
Garbanzos -Chick peas
Gelatina - Gelatin
Gengibre - Ginger
Gérmenes - Germs
Girar -Turn
Glasear - Glaze (to)
Gluten- gluten
Gofrera -Waffle iron
Golosina -Candy
Gordo -Fat (size)
Gramo - gram
Granada - Pomegranate
Grande- Large
Grasa - Grease (to) ,Fat (food)
Grasa del asado - Drippings
Grifería- Faucet
Gris - Grey
Grissini -Bread stick
Grueso -Thick
Guantes - Gloves
Guardar - Store(to)
Guarnición - Garnish
Guayaba- Guava
Guineo- Banana
Guisantes - Pea(s), Green peas
Guiso - Stew
Guiso de verduras -Vegetable stew
Güisquil- Chayote squash

H

Haba - Fava Bean
Habas -Broad Beans
Habichuelas -Beans
Habichuelas coloradas - - Kidney beans
Habichuelas Negras -Black Beans
Habichuelas verdes - Green beans
Habichuelas verdes- String beans
Hacer cortes - Score
Hambre - Hunger
Hambriento - Hungry
Hamburguesa -Hamburger
Harina - Flour
Hasta luego -See you later
Hecho en la casa- Made on premises
Helado de chocolate- Ice cream, chocolate
Helado de fresa - Ice cream- strawberry
Helado de mantecado- Vanilla ice cream
Helado- Ice cream, Sorbet

Herida - Wound
Hervir- Boil
Hielo - Ice
Hierba - Herb
Hierbabuena- Mint
Hidratar- to bloom as in hydrate
Hígado -Liver
Higienizar - Sanitize(to)
Higo - Fig
Hinojo - Fennel
Hoja - Leaf
Hojaldrado - Flaky
Hojaldre - Puff pastry
Hongo -Mold, Fungus, Mushroom
Hornear -Bake
Horno - Oven
Horno combinación - Combination oven
Horno de convección - Convection oven
Horno microondas - Microwave oven
Horno mixto-Combination oven
Horno y vaporera -Combination oven
Huachinango- Red snapper
Hueso- Bone
Huevera - Eggcup
Huevo - Egg
Huevo batido -eggwash breading process
Huevos cocidos- Eggs, hard boiled
Huevos duros Eggs, hard boiled
Huevos escalfados- Eggs, poached
Huevos fritos - Eggs, fried
Huevos pasados - Eggs, soft-boiled
Huevos rellenos -Eggs-stuffed
Huevos revueltos- Scramblef Eggs

I

Incendios- Fire
Incorporar - Stir (to)
Ingrediente - ingredient
Invierno - Winter
Isotérmico - Thermos Box(Cambro)

J

Jabón- Soap
Jalea - Jelly
Jamón - Ham
Jamones-Cold cuts
Jarra graduada - Measuring pitcher
Jarra medidoras - Measuring pitcher
Jarrete de cordero - Lamb shanks
Jerez - Sherry
Judías verdes - Green beans, String beans
Jueves - Thursday
Jugo -Juice
Jugo de naranja - Orange juice
Jugo de piña - Pineapple juice
Jugo de tomate -Tomato juice
Julio -July
Junio - June

L

Lado - Side
Laminadora de masa -Dough sheeter
Langosta - Lobster
Lápiz - Pencil
Lata -Can
Laurel- Bayleaf
Lava-vajilla- Dishwasher
Lavamanos - Hand sink

Lavaplatos automático - Dishwasher (machine)
Lavaplatos - Dishwasher (job)
Lavar - Wash(to)
Lazos salados -Pretzel
Leche - Milk
Leche de Coco -Coconut milk
Lechecillas - Sweetbreads
Lechón- Suckling pig
Lechuga - Lettuce
Lejía -Bleach
Lengua- Tongue
Lenguado - Sole
Lentamente- Gradually
Lentejas - Lentils
Liar - Truss (to)
Libra - Pound
Libro de cocina- Cookbook
Licuadora -Blender
Licuadora de inmersión - Immersion blender
Lila – Lilac Purple
Lima - lime
Limón - Lemon
Limpiar-- devein
Linterna - Flashlight
Lo siento -Sorry
Lomo de cerdo - Pork loin
longanizas - Sausage
Lubina de mar- Sea Bass
Lunes - Monday

M

Macarrones - Macaroni
Macarrones con queso - Macaroni and cheese
Macarrones gratinados- Macaroni and cheese
Macedonia de fruta - Fruit salad
ensalada de frutas- Fruit salad
Machacar - Mash (to), Flatten
Mantecado de vainilla - Vanilla ice cream
Maduro- Ripe
Magdalena- Cupcake
Magro - Lean
Maicena - Cornstarch
Maíz -Corn
Majado de papas - Potato, mashed
Majar -Mash (to)
Málaga- Sweet wine
Mandarina - Mandarin orange
Mandolina- mandolin
Maní - Peanut
Manitas de cerdo - Pig's Feet
Manteca - Lard (pork), Shortening
Mantecado- Ice cream
Mantel - Tablecloth
Mantelaría- Linen
Mantenedora de calor - Heat lamp
Mantequilla- Butter
Manzana -Apple
Máquina de vacío - Vaccum chamber
Máquinas de zumo – Juicer
Maracuyá -Passion fruit
Marinar - Marinate (to)
Mariposa -Butterfly
Marisco -Seafood

Marmitas- Steam kettles
Marrón -Brown
Martes - Tuesday
Marzo - March
Masa -Dough
Masa batida- Batter
Masa de hojaldre- Puff pastry
Mayo -May
Mayonesa -Mayonnaise
Mazorca - Corn- fresh cobb
Mecero - Server
Mechar - Lard (to)
Medallones- Cutlet
Mediana - Medium (size)
Medidor- Jigger
Medio crudo- Medium rare (degree of doneness)
Mejillones - Mussels
Melaza - Molasses
Melocotón – Peach, Peach color
Melon miel - Honeydew melon
Melón- Cantaloupe
Membrillo - Quince
Menestra de legumbres- Vegetable stew
Menú de la casa- Price fixed menu
Menú de precio fijo - Price fixed menu
Menú degustación- Price fixed menu
Merengue - Meringue
Mermelada - Jam
Mermelada de Albaricoque -Apricot jam
Mermelada de frambuesas -Raspberry jam
Mermelada de fresas - Strawberry jam
Mermelada de naranja - Orange
Mero - Grouper
Mesa - Table
Mesa de trabajo - Work table
Mezclar - Mix (to),Toss, Stir (to), Blend
Miel - Honey
Miércoles - Wednesday
Migas -Breadcrumbs
Mint flavor -menta
Mixto de vapor y calor- Combination Cooking
Molde - Mold, form
Molde de horno- Casserole
Moledora de carne - Meat grinder
Moler - Grind
Molida de cerdo - Ground pork
Molida de res - Ground beef
Molida de ternera - Ground veal
Mollejas de Cordero- Lamb Sweetbreads
Mollejas de res- Beef Sweetbreads
Mollejas de pollo- Gizzard
Mollete English Muffin
Montar -Arrange
Montar- Whip (to)
Mora -Blackberry
Morado- Purple
Morcilla -Blood Sausage, Cured pork sausage
Mortero- Mortar
Mosca - Fly(pest)
Mostaza - Mustard
Mover(se)-Move
Muslo de pollo -Chicken drumstick -
Muslo y cadera - Leg quarter chicken
Muy bien -Fine (response), Very well

N

Nabo - Turnip
Naranja - Orange
Nata -Cream dairy
Nata agria- Sour cream
Nata montada -Whipped cream
Natilla-Custard
Nectarina - Nectarine
Negro- Black
Nevera- Refrigerator
Níscalos - Wild mushrooms
Noviembre - November
Nuez – Nut, Walnut
Nuez de castilla - Walnut
Nuez moscada - Nutmeg
Nuggets de pollo- Chicken Nuggets

O

Oblicuo -oblique
Octubre - October
Olla - Pot
Olla a presión- Pressure cooker
Olla arrocera - Rice cooker
Olla exprés - Pressure cooker
Onza - Ounce
Oporto - Port
Orégano - Oregano
Ostra - Oysters
Otoño -Autumn

P

Palcha -Passion fruit
Paletilla de cordero -Lamb shoulder
Palitos de pan-Bread stick
Palitroque -Bread stick
Palta-Avocado
Pan - Bread
Pan de molde - Sliced bread
Pan integral - Whole Wheat Bread
Pan rallado-Breadcrumbs
Panaderos de chocolate -Chocolate, bake
Panecillo -Bun
Panecillo de matequilla- Rolls
Paño – Towel, Rags
Panquecito - Muffin
Panqueques- Pancakes
Pantalla - Heat lamp
Papa - Potato(Americas)
Papas rostizadas - Potatoes, roasted
Papel toalla - Paper towel
Pargo - Snapper
Pargorojo- Red snapper
Parrilla - Grill (equipment)
Parrillada – Steakhouse
Pasados por agua - Eggs, soft-boiled
Pasapurés- Food Mill
Pasas – Raisin
Pasta-Paste
Pastel – Pie, Cake
Pastinaca - Parsnips
Pata de cordero- Lamb, leg
Patas de cerdo - Pig's Feet
Patata -Potato(Spain)
Patatas a lo pobre - Home fries
Patatas asadas - Potatoes, roasted
Patatas fritas - French fries, Potato chips
Pato - Duck
Pavipollo – Chicken, Large
Pechuga de pollo - Chicken breast

Pedazo – Chunk, Piece
Pelador - Potato peeler
Peladura- Zest
Pelapapas- Potato peeler
Pelar - Peel, Shuck (husks)
Pelo - Hair
Pepinillo - Gherkin
Pepinillos - Pickles
Pepino - Cucumber
Pepitas de pollo-Chicken nuggets
Pequeño -Small
Pera - Pear
Perca- Perch
¿Perdóneme?- Pardon me?
Perejil - Parsley
Perritocaliente - Hot dog
Personal para limpieza-Cleaning crew
Pesar - Scale (to)
Pescado - Fish
Pescado Frito- Fried fish
Pestiños - Fried fish
Picador- Cutting board
Picadora de carne - Meat grinder
Picar- Chop (to)
Pie - Foot
Piel - Skin, Zest
Pierna de cordero - Lamb,leg
Pierna pernil de pollo - Leg quarter chicken
Pimentón dulce - Paprika
Pimienta Cayena - Cayenne Pepper
Pimienta negra - Black pepper
Pimiento - Pepper (spice)
Pimiento rojo - Red pepper
Pimiento verde - Green pepper
Pimiento- Bell Pepper
Piña - Pineapple
Pincel de pastelería- Pastry brush
Pincho- Kebab
Pinchos-Bar food
Piñones - Pinenuts
Pinta - Pint
Pintar -Brush (to)
Pintar con huevo batido- eggwash for brushing
Pintxos -Bar food
Pinzas - Tongs
Piso limpio- Clean floor
Pitahaya- Dragon Fruit
Pizca - Pinch , Dash of solids
Placa de asados- Roast Pan
Plancha - Griddle
Plátano- Plantain, Banana
Platija -Flounder
Plato - Plate
Plato principal - Main dish
Poco a poco - Gradually
Poco hecho- Rare (degree of doneness)
Pollo-Chicken
Polvo de hornear -Baking powder
Ponchar la entrada- Clock in
Ponchar la salida-Clock out
Poner en salmuera-Brine (to)
Porción - Portion
Portapapeles- Clipboard
Postre -Dessert
Potaje - Porridge
Preparer - Prepare (to)
Primavera - Spring
Procesador de alimentos- Food processor

Propina - Gratuity
Proteína - Protein
Puerro - Leek
Pulgada - Inch
Pulpo - Octopus
Puñado -Handful
Puntilla - Knife, pairing
Punto de fusión - Melting point
Purchase-comprar
Puré de patatas - Potato, mashed
Púrpura -Purple

Q

Quemar -Burn
Queso crema -Cream cheese
Queso cremoso-Cream cheese
Queso- Cheese
Quitar- Remove(to)

R

Rábano – Horseradish, Radish
Rabo de buey - Oxtail
Ración - Portion
Racionador- Portion Scoop
Rallar - Grate(to)
Ramita - Sprig
Rape - Monkfish
Raya - Skate
Rebanadora -Deli slicer
Rebanar- Slice (to)
Rebozado- Battered
Rebozar -Coat
Receta - Recipe
Recetario -Cookbook
Recibir -Receive
Reciclar -Recycle
Recogedor -Dust pan
Recogedor de agua- Squeegie
Recoger - Pick up
Redecilla - Hairnet
Reducer - Reduce (to)
Refrescar -shock in an ice bath
Refresco- Soda, pop
Refrigeradora- Refrigerator
Regar con su jugo- Baste
Regresar- Return (to)
Rejilla -Rack (roasting/cooling/baking) r
Rellano- Filling, Stuffed
Rellenar - Stuff (to)
Remojar - Soak (to)
Remolacha- Beets
Remover - Remove(to)
Repisa- Shelf
Repollo-Cabbage
Repostería de la casa - Baked on premises
Requesón- Cottage cheese
Requisición -Requisition
Restregar - Scrub
Revestir - Line
Revoltillo -Eggs, scrambled
Revolver - Scramble (to),Stir (to)
Riñón - Kidney
Róbalo - Haddock
Rociar - Sprinkle
Rodaballo- Turbot
Rodar - Roll into ball
Rodillo- Rolling pin

Roedor -Rodent
Rojo -Red
Rojo inglés - Rare (degree of doneness)
Romero - Rosemary
Ron - Rum
Rondondear - Round (to)
Roner - Immersion circulator
Rosado - Pink
Rosbif - Roast beef
Roscas- Sweet pastries
Ruibarbo- Rhubarb
Rustidera- Roast Pan

S

Sábado - Saturday
Sabor -Flavor
Sacar- Remove(to)
Sal - Salt
Salado -Savory (not sweet)
Salchicha - Sausage
Salchicha americana - Hot dog
Salero y pimentero- Shaker (S &P)
Salmon - Salmon
Salmon a la parrilla - Grilled salmon
Salmon ahumado - Smoked salmon
Salmuera -Brine
Salpimentar- Season(to)
Salsa - Sauce
Salsa bechamel - White sauce (hot)
Salsa de condimentada - Relish
Salsa de soja/soya- Soy sauce
Salsa de tomate -Tomato sauce
Salsa holandesa - Hollandaise Sauce
Salsa tártara- Tartar sauce
Salsa vinagreta - Vinaigrette
Saltear - Saute
Salvia - Sage
Sandía - Watermelon
Sanear -Sanitize(to)
Sardinas- Sardines
Sartén - Frying pan
Sartén basculante- Tilt skillet
Saturega - Savory (herb)
Sazonar - Salt(to), Season(to)
Secar -Dry (to)
Seco -Dry
Seguridad - Safety
Sellar - Seal (to)
Sellar a la plancha -pan sear
Semidulce - Medium sweet
Semilla -Seed
Semilla de alcaravea- Caraway Seed
Semilla de cilantro -Coriander seed
Separar -Disjoint
Separar- Divide (to)
Separarse -Break in emulsification
Septiembre - September
Servilleta - Napkin
Server -Serve(to)
Setas rellanas - Stuffed mushrooms
Setas silvestres - Wild mushrooms
Setas- Mushroom
Sherbet - Sorbet
Sidra -Cider
Sierra de banda- Band saw
Sierra de cinta- Band saw
Sofreír - Lightly fry, Sweat (to)
Solicitor - Request

Solomillo - Sirloin
Sopa -Soup
Sopa de fideos - Noodle soup
Sopa de pollo Chicken soup -
Sopa de verduras - Vegetable soup
Sopa del día - Soup of the day
Sorbete- Sorbet
Sumergir - Dip (to)

T

Tabla de cortar- Cutting board
Tabla de Queso -Cheese board
Tablilla - Shelf
Tajar- Slice (to)
Tallarines - Noodles (wide), Tagliatelle
Tallo -Stalk
Tamíz- Sieve
Tapa – Lid, Cover (to)
Tapadera - Lid
Tapas -Bar food
Tapeo-Bar food
Tapete - Floor Mat
Tapete -Doily
Tapete de silicona- Silpat
Taquillas -Lockers
Tarta de queso - Cheesecake
Taza - Cup
Taza de medir -Measuring Cup
Tazas medidoras - Measuring pitcher
Taza para medir - Measuring cup
Tazón -Bowl
Té - Tea
Templar – to temper- chocolate or egg custard
Tenazas - Tongs
Tenedor - Fork
Tenedor de Trinchar -Carving fork
Término medio-Medium (degree of doneness)
Término rojo- Rare (degree of doneness)
Termómetro - Thermometer
Termostato de inmersión a baja temperature - Immersion circulator
Ternera - Veal
Ternera picada - Ground veal
Tierno - Tender
Tiritas - Strips
Toalla- Towel
Tocino - Pork fat ,Bacon
Tomate -Tomato
Tomillo - Thyme
Tope de mesa- Countertop
Toronja - Grapefruit
Torrijas -French toast
Tortilla de papas- Potato, omelette
Tortilla de patatas- Potato, omelette
Tortilla de setas -Mushroom omelette
Tortilla española- Spanish potato omelette
Tortitas- Panckaes
Tostada - Toast
Tostador(a)- Toaster
Transferir - Transfer
Trapo- Rags
Tripas -Tripe
Triturador - Immersion blender
Triturar - Pulverize (to)
Trozo- Chunk

Trucha - Trout
Trucha ahumada - Smoked trout
Trufas -Truffles
Tuétano - Marrow
Turno -Shift
Turron -Nougat

U

Un cuarto- Medium rare (degree of doneness
Un poco de mantequilla - Pat of butter
Uva - Grape
Uvas pasas – Raisin

V

Vacío -Empty
Vainilla -Vanilla
Vapor - Steam
Varilla- Whisk
Vaso - Glass
Vegano- Vegan
Vegetariano - Vegetarian
Venda -Bandage
Ventana caliente - Heat lamp
Verano -Summer
Verde - Green
Verdura - Vegetable
Vermú -Vermouth
Vermut-Vermouth
Verter - Pour (to)
Vieira -Scallop
Viernes - Friday
Vinagre - Vinegar
Vino - Wine
Vino blanco - Wine,white
Vino rosado - Wine,rosé
Vino tinto - Wine, red
Vinos dulces - Sweet wine
Violeta -Violet Purple
Vitrinas expositoras - Display case
Voltear -Turn over
Volver- Return (to)

Y

Yema - Yolk
Yuca -Cassava

Z

Zanahoria -Carrot
Zapallo - Pumpkin
Zarzamora -Blackberry

Assistance with translations provided
by Chef Daina Soto MSc

A

Add- añadir
Allergy- alérgia
Almond- almendras
Anchovy- anchoa
Aniseed- anís
Aperitif- cordial
Appetizer- botana (Mexico), aperitivo, entrada
Apple- manzana
Apricot- albaricoque
Apricot jam- mermelada de albaricoque
April -Abril
Apron- delantal
Arrange- arreglar, colocar, montar
Artichoke- alcachofa
Artichoke heart- corazón de alcachofa
Asparagus-espárragos
August - Agosto
Autumn - Otoño
Avocado-aguacate, palta

B

Bacon- tocino
Bag- bolsa, funda
Bake-hornear
Bake (to)-cocer al horno
Baked on premises-repostería de la casa,hecho en la casa
Baking powder- polvo de hornear
Baking racks- rejilla
Baking sheet-bandeja
de sodio
Banana-banano, guineo, plátano
Bandage-venda
Band saw- sierra de cinta, sierra de banda
Banquet- banquete
Bar food-pinchos, pintxos (Spain), tapas, tapeo
Bartender-barman, camarero –
Barbecue-barbacoa
Basil-albahaca
Fruit Basket-cesta/canasta de frutas
Bass- lubina (de mar)
Baste- regar con su jugo
Bathroom-baño
Bâtonnet – bastones
Batter- masa, masa batida, pasta, rebozado
Bayleaf- laurel
Beans- frijoles, habichuelas
Beat- batir
Beef- carne de res
Beefsteak- bistec
Beer- cerveza
Beets-remolacha
Behind- detrás, atrás
Behind you- detrás de ti
Bell Pepper -pimiento
Biscuit- Rolls- biscuit Americano or panecillo de matequilla
Black-negro
Black Beans- frijoles negros, habichuelas negras
Black pepper-pimienta negra
Blackberry-mora, frambuesa negra, zarzamora
Blanch- escaldar, blanquear

Blast chiller - abatidor
Bleach-lejía
Blend-mezclar
Blender-licuadora, batidoras de vaso
Blood Sausage- morcilla
Bloom(to) -hidratar
Blue-azul
Blueberry-arándano azul
Boil-hervir
Bone-hueso
Booth- banco
Bottle- botella
Bowl(soup)-tazón, bol de sopa
Braise- estofar, estofado
Bread- pan
Bread stick-palitroque, palitos de pan, grissini
Breadcrumbs- migas, pan rallado
Break -separarse
Breakfast-desayuno
Brine – salmuera
Brine (to) -poner en salmuera, embeber en salmuera
Brisket-carne de pecho
Broad Beans- habas
Broccoli- brécol, broccoli
Broil- asar a la parilla
Broth-caldo
Brown- café /marrón
Brown(to)- dorar
Brown sugar – azúcar morena, azúcar negra, azúcar integral
Brush-escobilla, brocha
Brush (to)-cepillar, pintar
Brussel Sprouts- coles de Bruselas
Buffet- la comida buffet
Bun- panecillo
Butter-mantequilla
Butterfly- mariposa
Burn- quemar

C

Cabbage- col , repollo
Cabinet-gabinete
Cake- pastel, bizcocho
Can - lata
Can opener- abrelatas
Candy- Carmelo, dulce, golosina
Candy (to)- confitar
Cantaloupe- melón
Capers- alcaparras
Caramelize (to) -caramelizar
Caraway Seed - semilla de alcaravea
Carbohydrate-carbohidrato
Cardamom- cardamomo
Carrot- zanahoria
Cart – carro
Carve (to)-cortar
Carving fork -tenedor de trinchar
Cassava - yuca
Casserole- Fuente, or molde (de horno)
Cauliflower- coliflor
Cayenne Pepper - pimienta cayena
Celery- apio
Chayote squash –güisquil, chayote
Check please –la cuenta por favor
Cheese-queso
Cheese board -tabla de queso
Cheese cart- carro de queso

Cheesecake - tarta de queso
Cherimoya –chirimoya, cherimoya
Cherry- cereza
Chestnut - castaña
Chick peas- garbanzos
Chicken - pollo
Chicken breast- pechuga de pollo
Chicken drumstick - muslo de pollo
Chicken- Large- pavipollo
Chicken nuggets - pepitas de pollo,nuggets de pollo
Chicken soup -sopa de pollo
Chicory- achicoria, escarola
Chile pepper -chile
Chill- enfriar
Chinoise (fine sieve) - colador chino de malla
Chives- cebollines
Chocolate, bitter-chocolate agridulce extra amargo (75-80%), amargo (50-70%), agridulce (35%)
Chocolate, dark- chocolate oscuro
Chocolate, hot-chocolate caliente
Chocolate, milk-chocolate con leche
Chocolate, bake -panaderos de chocolate
Chocolate, white- chocolate blanco
Chop (to) -picar
Chop (portion of meat)-chuleta
Chunk- trozo, pedazo
Cider-sidra
Cinnamon - canela
Clams- almejas
Clarify (to)- clarificar
Clean floor - piso limpio
Cleaning crew- personal para limpieza
Clipboard - portapapeles
Clock in – fichar, ponchar la entrada
Clock out - fichar la salida, ponchar la salida
Cloves- clavos de olor
Coat – rebozar, cubrir
Cocktail- cóctel
Cocoa powder- cocoa en polvo, chocolate en polvo
Coconut - coco
Coconut milk- leche de coco
Cod - bacalao
Coddle (to)-cocer a fuego lento
Coffee- café
Coffee machine - cafetera
Coffee with milk- café con leche
Coffee, black-café solo, café negro
Cold cuts- fiambres, jamones
Combination oven- horno mixto, horno combinación (horno y vaporera), mixto de vapor y calor
Combine- combinar
Confectionary sugar- azúcar glas, azúcar glacé, azúcar 10X, azúcar en polvo
Consistency- consistencia
Convection oven - horno de convección
Cook(job)-cocinero
Cook(process) - cocinar
Cookbook – recetario, libro de cocina
Cookie- galleta
Coriander - semilla de cilantro,coriandro
Corn - maíz
Corn cereal flakes - copos de maíz,cereal
Corn- fresh cobb –elote, mazorca

Cornstarch- fécula de maíz, maicena
Cottage cheese- requesón
Countertop – cubierta, tope de mesa
Cover - cubrir
Cover (to) - tapa
Crab - cangrejo
Cranberry - arándano
Crayfish - cangrejo de río
Cream caramel-flan de caramelo, flan
Cream cheese- queso crema,queso cremoso
Cream dairy-nata, crema
Cream texture-cremoso
Crouton-cuscurro, crutones
Crust (bread) - corteza
Cucumber-pepino
Cumin-comino
Cup- taza
Cupcake- magdalena, cupcake
Curdle- cuajar
Cure (to)- curar
Cured pork sausage- embutidos, longaniza, chorizo, morcilla, butifarra
Curly endive- escarole, frissé
Custard- natilla
Cut - cortar
Cutlery- cubiertos
Cutlet – filete, medallones
Cutting board - la tabla de cortar, picador

D

Dash of liquid - chorrito
Dash of solids -pizca
Dates -dátiles
December – Diciembre
Deglaze-desglasar
Deli slicer - cortadoras de fiambre, corta fiambre, rebanadora
Deep Fat Fried- frito produndo
Dessert- postre
Devein-desvenar, limpiar
Dice-cortar en cubitos, en cubos, en dados (fino (brunoise), pequeño, mediano, y grande)
Dill - eneldo
Diner (customer) - comensal
Diner (restaurant) - cafetería
Dinner- cena
Dip, sauce – salsa, aderezo, dip
Dip (to) - sumergir
Dishmachine racks - cestas para lavavajillas/lavaplatos
Dishwasher (job) – friegaplatos, lavaplatos
Dishwasher (machine) - lavaplatos automático, lavaplatos, lava-vajilla
Disjoint- separar
Display case - vitrinas expositoras
Divide (to)- separar
Doily- tapete, blondas de papel.
Dough- masa
Dough Mixer – amasadora
Dough sheeter- laminadora de masa
Dragon Fruit- pitahaya
Drain (fixture)- desagüe
Drain (process) - escurrir
Dredge- espolvorear
Drink -bebida
Drink (verb) - beber
Drippings- la grasa del asado

Dry- seco
Dry (to) - secar
Duck- pato
Dust (to)-espolvorear
Dust pan - recogedor

E

Eat - comer
Egg - huevo
Eggwash- Pintar con huevo batido
Egg white - clara de huevo
Eggcup - huevera
Eggplant - berenjena
Eggs, fried - huevos fritos
Eggs, hard boiled - huevos cocidos, huevos duros
Eggs, poached - huevos escalfados
Eggs, soft-boiled - huevos pasados, pasados por agua
Eggs, scrambled - huevos revueltos, revoltillo
Eggs-stuffed -huevos rellenos
Empty -vacío
Expeditor- expedidor de alimentos
Emulsify (to)- emulsionar

F

Fat (food)- grasa
Fat (size)- gordo
Faucet- grifería
Fava Bean - haba
February - Febrero
Fennel- hinojo
Ferment- fermentar
Fig - higo
Filet (to)- filetear
Fillet of beef - filete de res
Filling- rellano
Fine (response) - Muy bien
Fire-fuego, incendios
Fire Extinquisher- extinguidor de incendios
First-Aid- botiquín de primeros auxilios
Fish - pescado
Fish spatula - espátula flexible de pescado
Flaky- hojaldrado
Flashlight- linterna
Flatten- aplastar, espalmar, machacar
Flatware- cubertería
Flavor- sabor
Floor Mat - alfombra de piso, tapete
Flounder - platija
Flour -harina
Fly(pest) - mosca
Fold (to) - doblar
Food - comida
Food coloring- colorante alimentario
Food Mill - pasapurés
Food processor – procesador de alimentos
Foot - pie
Fork - tenedor
Freezer- congelador
French fries - patatas fritas
French toast- torrijas
Friday - Viernes
Fried fish – pestiños, pescado frito
Frog legs - ancas de rana
Fruit - fruta

Fruit salad - macedonia de fruta, ensalada de frutas
Fry (to)- freir
Fryer -freidora
Frying pan -sartén

G

Gallon- galón
Garlic - ajo
Garlic Cloves - dientes de ajo
Garnish - guarnición
Gelatin - gelatina
Germs- gérmenes
Gherkin - pepinillo
Ginger- gengibre
Gizzard- mollejas de pollo
Glass -vaso
Glassware- cristalería
Glaze (to)-glasear
Gloves- guantes
Gluten- gluten
Good afternoon - Buenas tardes
Good evening- Buenas noches
Good morning- Buenos días
Good night - Buenas noches
Goodbye - Adiós
Gradually – lentamente, poco a poco
Gram - gramo
Grape - uva
Grapefruit - toronja
Grate(to) - rallar
Gratuity - propina
Grease (to) - grasa
Green - verde
Green beans – habichuelas verdes, judías verdes, ejotes
Green onions –cebollínes, cebollas verdes
Green peas – guisantes, arveja verde
Green pepper -pimiento verde
Green salad, simple - ensalada simple, ensalada verde
Grey - gris
Griddle - plancha, fry top
Grill (to) - asar
Grill (equipment) -parrilla, barbacoa
Grilled salmon- salmón a la parrilla
Grind –moler
Ground beef - carne picada, molida de res
Ground pork - cerdo picado, molida de cerdo
Ground veal - ternera picada, molida de ternera
Grouper - mero
Guava- guayaba

H

HAAS Avocado- aguacate
Haddock – róbalo
Hair-pelo
Hairnet- redecilla
Halve -dividir en dos
Ham - jamón
Hamburger - hamburguesa
Handful - puñado
Hand sink - lavamanos
Heat (to) - calentar
Heat lamp - pantalla mantenedora de calor, ventana caliente
Herb - hierba

High heat - fuego fuerte, fuego alto
Hollandaise Sauce - salsa holandesa
Home fries - patatas a lo pobre
Honey- miel
Honeydew melon – melon, melón miel
Hood system -campanas extractoras
Horseradish- rábano
Hors d'oeuvres- entremeses variados
Host - anfitrión
Hostess - anfitriona
Hot box(catering) -carros calientes, armario caliente
Hot dog - perrito caliente, salchicha americana
Hotel Pan - cubeta
How are you?-¿Cómo está usted?
How's life? -¿Cómo le va?
Hunger- hambre
Hungry – hambriento

I

Ice - hielo
Ice cream – helado, mantecado
Ice cream, chocolate - helado de chocolate
Ice cream scoop - copa de helado, cucharada de helado, bola de helado
Ice cream- strawberry - helado de fresa
Ignite -encender
Immersion blender – triturador, licuadora de inmersión
Immersion circulator -termostato de inmersión a baja temperature, cocedora baja tmeperatura, Roner
Inch - pulgada
Ingredient - ingrediente
Invoice- factura

J

Jam - mermelada
January - Enero
Jelly- jalea
Jigger – medidor, jigger
Juice -jugo
Juicer -máquinas de zumo, exprimidor
Julienne- a la juliana
July - Julio
June - Junio

K

Kale – col rizada
Ketchup- catsup
Kebab- brocheta, pincho
Keg- barril
Kidney- riñón
Kidney beans - alubias rojas, habichuelas coloradas
Knife -cuchillo
Knife, boning- cuchillo deshuesador
Knife, pairing- puntilla
Knife, serrated bread- cuchillo de pan, cuchillo de sierra

L

Ladle -cucharón
Lady fingers –bizcocho de soletilla, soletas, vainilla, galleta Saboyana
Lamb -cordero
Lamb, heart - corazón de cordero
Lamb, leg - pierna de cordero, pata de cordero
Lamb shanks - jarrete de cordero

Lamb shoulder – paletilla de cordero
Lard (pork) - manteca
Lard (to)- mechar
Large- grande
Layer -capa
Leaf - hoja
Lean- magro
Leek -puerro
Leg quarter chicken - pierna pernil de pollo, muslo y cadera
Lemon- limón
Lentils-lentejas
Lettuce- lechuga
Lettuce spinner- centrifugadora de lechuga
Lid – tapadera, tapa
Lightly fry- sofreír
Lime - lima
Line- revestir
Linen- mantelaría
Liver -hígado
Loaf – barra, bollo de pan
Lobster - langosta
Lockers – taquillas, casillero
Lunch - almuerzo

M

Macaroni - macarrones
Macaroni and cheese - macarrones gratinados, macarrones con queso
Mackerel – caballa
Mahi-mahi - dorado
Main dish – plato principal
Mandarin orange – Mandarina
Mandolin- mandolina
March - Marzo
Marinate (to) -marinar
Marrow - tuétano
Mash (to) – machacar, majar
May -Mayo
Mayonnaise - mayonesa
Measuring cup- taza para medir
Measuring pitcher - jarra graduada, jarra/tazas medidoras, taza de medir
Measuring spoon - cuchara de medir, cuchara medidora
Meat- carne
Meat grinder- picadora de carne, moledora de carne
Meatball - albóndiga
Medium (size)- mediana
Medium (degree of doneness) -término medio
Medium rare (degree of doneness)- un cuarto, medio crudo
Medium sweet- semidulce
Melt - derretir
Melting point - punto de fusión
Menu - carta
Meringue- merengue
Microwave oven - horno microondas
Milk - leche
Milk shake – batido(a)
Mint -hierbabuena
Mint flavor - menta
Mix (to)- mezclar
Mixer - batidora
Mixing bowl- cuenco, bol de cocina
Molasses - melaza
Mold, fungus – hongo
Mold, form - molde

Monday - Lunes
Monkfish - rape
Mortar- mortero
Move- mover(se)
Muffin (cake)- mollete, panquecito
Muffin (English style)- tortita
Mushroom – setas, hongos
Mushroom button- champiñón
Mushroom omelette - tortilla de setas
Mussels - mejillones
Mustard - mostaza

N

Napkin- servilleta
Nectarine - nectarina
Noodle soup -sopa de fideos
Noodles (wide) - tallarines
Noodles (thin)- fideos
Nougat- turrón
November - Noviembre
Nut - nuez
Nutmeg - nuez moscada

O

Oatmeal - avena
Oblique - oblicuo
October - Octubre
Octopus - pulpo
Oil - aceite
Oil (to)- engrasar
Olive -aceituna
Olive oil - aceite de oliva
Onion-cebolla
Orange- naranja
Orange juice- jugo de naranja
Orange marmalade- mermelada de naranja
Oregano - orégano
Ounce -onza
Oven -horno
Oxtail -rabo de buey
Oysters – ostra

P

Pan Fry- freir en sartén
Pan Sear- sellar, a la plancha
Pancake - panqueques, tortitas
Pantry-despensa
Paper towel- papel toalla
Paprika - pimentón dulce
Pardon me? – ¿Perdóneme?
Parsley- perejil
Parsnips – chirivias, pastinaca
Passion fruit –maracuyá, palcha
Paste- pasta
Pastry brush –brocha/pincel de pastelería
Pastry cutter -cortapastas
Pastry tip - boquillas de pastelería
Pat of butter-un poco de mantequilla
Paysanne - a la campesina cuadrado
Pea(s) – chícharo(s), arveja(s), guisantes
Peach –durazno, melocotón
Peach color - melocotón
Peanut- cacahuate, maní
Pear - pera
Peel - pelar
Pencil – lápiz
Pepper (spice)- pimienta
Perch -perca
Perforated Spoon - cuchara perforada
Pickles- pepinillos
Pickle (to)- encurtir, escabechar

Pick up- recoger
Pie- pastel
Piece -pedazo
Pig's trotters -patas de cerdo, manitas de cerdo
Pinch -pizca
Pineapple - piña
Pineapple juice - jugo de piña
Pinenuts - piñones
Pink - rosado
Pint - pinta
Plantain - plátano
Plate -plato
Pleased to meet you -Encantado de conocerle
Plum -ciruela
Poach (to)-escalfar
Pomegranate -granada
Pork - cerdo
Pork chop - chuleta de cerdo
Pork fat - tocino
Pork loin - lomo de cerdo
Pork meat -carne de cerdo
Porridge- potaje, crema (de maíz, de avena)
Port – oporto
Portion- porción, ración
Portion (to)-dividir
Portion Scoop- racionador, bolero
Pot - olla
Potato(Spain)- patata
Potato(Americas) - papa
Potato, mashed - puré de patatas, majado de papas
Potato, chips -patatas fritas
Potato, omelette - tortilla de patatas/papas
Potato peeler –pelapapas, pelador
Potatoes, roasted - patatas asadas, papas rostizadas
Pound - libra
Pour (to) – verter,
Prepare (to) - preparar
Preserve (to) - conservar
Pressure cooker- olla a presión, olla exprés
Pretzel- pretzel, lazos salados
Price fixed menu - menú de la casa, menú degustación, menú de precio fijo
Protein- proteína
Prune -ciruela seca, ciruela pasa
Puff pastry – hojaldre (masa de hojaldre)
Pulverize (to) - triturar
Pumpkin – zapallo, calabaza
Purchase-comprar
Purple- morado, violeta, púrpura, lila
Put down- dejar

Q

Quail - codorniz
Quart - el cuarto de galón
Quince- membrillo

R

Rabbit- conejo
Rack (roasting/cooling) – Rejilla
Rack shelves -estanterías
Radish- rábano
Raft (consomme)- balsa
Rags – trapo, paño
Raisin – pasas, uvas pasas

Rare (degree of doneness)- poco hecho, término rojo, rojo inglés
Raspberry - frambuesa
Raspberry jam- mermelada de frambuesas
Raw – crudo
Receive- recibir
Recipe- receta
Recycle - reciclar
Red - rojo
Red onion - cebolla roja/lila/morada
Red pepper - pimiento rojo
Red snapper – huachinango (México), pargo rojo/colorado, chillo (Puerto Rico)-culirrubia
Reduce (to) - reducir
Refried beans – (frijoles) refritos
Refrigerator – nevera, refrigeradora, armario frigorífico
Relish- salsa de condimentada
Remove(to) –quitar, sacar, remover
Render (to)- derretir
Request- solicitar
Requisition - requisición
Rest- descansar
Return (to)- volver, regresar
Rhubarb - ruibarbo
Ribs - costillas
Rice - arroz
Rice cooker - arrocera eléctrica/automática, olla arrocera
Rice pudding -arroz con leche
Rind - cáscara
Rinse (in water) – enjuagar
Ripe - maduro
Roast -asado
Roast beef - rosbif
Roast Pan – rustidera, placa de asados, bandeja para rostizar
Rodent- roedor
Roll into ball- rodar
Roll out (to) – aplanar, estirar
Rolling pin - rodillo
Rosemary - romero
Round (to) -rondondear
Refridgerator - frigorífico
Rub – frotar
Rum – ron

S

Safety- seguridad
Saffron- azafrán
Sage - salvia
Salad -ensalada
Salmon - salmón
Salt - sal
Salt cod - bacalao salado, bacalao
Salt(to)- sazonar
Sandwich – bocadillo, sandwich, emparedado
Sanitize(to) – desinfectar, sanear, higienizar
Sardines- sardinas
Saturday - Sábado
Sauce - salsa
Sauce/Batter portioner - dosificador
Saucepan - cazo
Sausage – salchicha, longanizas
Sausage (fresh) -carne de salchicha
Saute-saltear
Savory (herb)- saturega, ajedrea

Savory (not sweet) – salado
Scald -escaldar
Scale – báscula
Scale (to)-pesar
Scallop- Vieira
Score- hacer cortes en
Scouring pad –estropajo, esponja abrasiva
Scarmble (to)-revolver
Scrub –fregar, restregar
Seafood - marisco
Seal (to)- sellar
Sear (to)- sellar
Season (in) – En temporada
Season(to)- salpimentar, sazonar, condimentar
Seasoning – condimento, aliño
See you later -hasta luego
Seed - semilla
September - Septiembre
Serve(to) - servir
Server- camarero, mecero
Shaker- especiero, (S &P) salero y pimentero
Shallot- chalota
Shape (to)-formar
Sharpen (to)- afilar
Sharpening steel - chaira
Shave(to)- afeitarse
Sheet pan - bandeja
Shelf –estante, repisa, tablilla
Shell (to) - cáscara
Sherry- jerez
Shift – turno
Shock-refrescar
Shortening- Manteca
Shuck (husks)- desvainar, pelar
Shuck (shellfish) -desbullar, abrir
Shrimp - camarones
Shrimp cocktail- cóctel de gambas/ camarones
Shrimp-prawn- gambas, camarones
Side - lado
Sieve –tamíz, cedazo
Silpat-tapete de silicona (
Simmer, full- cocinar a fuego lento
Simmer, low- cocinar lento
Sink (fixture)- fregadero(a)
Sirloin - solomillo
Skate -raya
Skim (to)- descremar
Skin - piel
Slice (to)- tajar, rebanar, cortar en lascas/rodajas
Sliced bread -pan de molde
Sliced thin - cortar en lonchas/lascas/rodajas finas
Slotted spoon- cuchara perforada
Small- pequeño
Smoked- ahumado
Smoked salmon - salmón ahumado
Smoked trout- trucha ahumada
Snails - caracoles
Snapper - pargo
Soak (to) - remojar
Soap - jabón
Soda, pop- refresco, soda
Sole - lenguado
Sorbet – sorbete, sherbet, helado
Sorry -Lo siento

Soup -sopa
Soup of the day - sopa del día
Sour cream - nata agria, crema agria
Soy sauce - salsa de soja/soya
Spaghetti - espaguetis
Spanish potato omelette - tortilla española
Spatula- espátula
Spider (utensil)-arañas
Spinach - espinacas
Sponge - esponja
Spoon - cuchara
Spoonful - cucharada
Sprig -ramita
Spring - Primavera
Spring onions - cebolletas
Sprinkle –espolvorear, rociar
Squeegie - la escobilla de goma, recogedor de agua
Squeeze - exprimir
Squeeze bottle- botella biberón, biberón dosificador
Squid -calamar, chipirones, chipirón
Stalk -tallo
Steak-bistec
Steakhouse –parrillada, asadero
Steam-vapor
Steam(to) - cocinar al vapor
Steam kettles -marmitas
Steam table - baño maría
Steep- dejar en infusión
Stew – guiso
Stiff peak – formar picos/un pico, firme
Stir (to) – revolver, mezclar, incorporar
Stock –caldo, fondo
Store(to)- guardar, almacenar
Storage- almacenamiento, almacén, despensa
Stove-estufa
Strain(to) - colar
Strainer - colador
Strawberry - fresa
Strawberry jam - mermelada de fresas
String beans – habichuelas verdes, judías verdes
Strips-tiritas
Stuff (to) - rellenar
Stuffed- relleno
Stuffed mushrooms - setas rellanas
Suckling pig -lechón, cochinillo
Sugar -azúcar (maybe add)
Summer - Verano
Sunday - Domingo
Sunflower oil - aceite de girasol
Sweat (to)- sofreír
Sweep (to) – barrer
Sweet pastries- roscas, bollería
Sweet potato-batata, camote
Sweet wine- málaga, vinos dulces
Sweetbreads –mollejas de res/cordero, lechecillas
Sweetener - endulzante
Sweets- caramelos, dulces
Swiss Chard -acelgas
Syrup -almíbar

T

Table -mesa
Tablecloth- mantel
Tablespoon – cuchara, cucharada

Tagliatelle - tallarines
Tarragon - estragón
Tartar sauce -salsa tártara
Tea - té
Teaspoon – cucharadita
Temper- templar
Tender-tierno
Thermometer- termómetro
Thermos Box(Cambro) – isotérmico
Thick –grueso, espeso
Thicken - espesar
This is- Este es
Thursday - Jueves
Thyme- tomillo
Tie (to)-atar, bridar
Tilt skillet- sartén basculante
Toast -tostada
Toaster- tostador(a)
Tomato - tomate
Tomato juice -jugo de tomate
Tomato sauce- salsa de tomate
Tongs- pinzas, tenazas
Tongue – lengua
Toss- mezclar
Towel – toalla, paño
Transfer - transferir
Trash can - el bote de basura, cubo/contenedor de basura
Tray- bandeja
Trickle- chorrear un poco, (fluir) en un hilo, añadir en un hilo
Trim - cortar
Tripe -tripas
Trout -trucha
Truffles – trufas
Truss (to)- atar, liar
Tuesday - Martes
Tumeric - cúrcuma
Tuna -atún
Tuna salad - ensalada de atún
Turbot- rodaballo
Turn- dar la vuelta, girar
Turn off- apagar
Turn over- voltear
Turnip- nabo
Twine- cordel

V

Vaccum chamber- envasadoras al vacío, máquina de vacío
Vanilla- vainilla
Vanilla ice cream- helado de mantecado, helado/mantecado de vainilla
Veal- ternera
Vegan- vegano
Vegetable - verdura
Vegetable soup -sopa de verduras
Vegetable stew - menestra de legumbres, guiso de vegetales, guiso de verduras
Vegetarian- vegetariano
Vermouth – vermú, vermut
Very well - muy bien
Vinaigrette – (salsa) vinagreta
Vinegar - vinagre

W

Waffle iron- gofrera
Waiter- camarero
Waitress -camarera
Walnut- nuez de castilla, nuez
Wash(to) -lavar

Water- agua
Water fountain- fuentes de agua
Watercress - berro
Watermelon - sandía
Wednesday - Miércoles
Well-done (degree of doneness)- bien hecho / cocido
Whip (to)- batir, montar
Whipped cream –nata/crema montada, crema chantilly
Whisk-batidor, varilla
Whisk (to) - batir
White -blanco
White sauce (hot) -salsa bechamel
Whole Wheat Bread - pan integral
Wild mushrooms – níscalos, setas silvestres,
Wine -vino
Wine,white - vino blanco
Wine, red - vino tinto
Wine,rosé - vino rosado
Winter - Invierno
Wound- herida
Work table - mesa de trabajo

Y

Yellow- amarillo
Yolk - yema

Z

Zest- peladura, cáscara, piel
Zucchini - calabacín

Assistance with translations provided by Chef Daina Soto MSc

Food Safety Study Guide

Common Bacteria Foodborne Illnesses	Incubation Period	Symptoms	Common Cause	Prevention	Type of Illness
Staphylococcus Aureus ⚕ (*Gastroenteritis*) 🍽	1-7 hours	Nausea, vomit Abdominal pain Diarrhea	From infected person to food Grows in high protein foods	Prevent cross contact. Serve food at correct temp.	Intoxication
Clostridium Perfringens (*Gastroenteritis*) 🍽	6-24 hours	Abdominal pain Diarrhea, Nausea	Intestinal tract of animals Protein, Gravy stew-temp abuse	Wash Fruits and Vegetables. Time temperature	Toxin Mediated Infection
Bacillus Cereus 🍽 (*Gastroenteritis*) 🐟	30 minutes to 15 hours	Nausea, vomit Abdominal pain Diarrhea	Soil - rice, seasonings, starch Sauces, pudding, casserole Salads	Time temperature Quick chilling of food Cleaning of Veg	Intoxication
Botulism 🍽 🐟	4 hours to 8 days	Fatigue, Headache Dizziness, can't swallow	MAP packaging Sous Vide Under processed canned foods	Don't use home canned items. Discard bloated cans.	Intoxication
Salmonella 🍽	12-72 hours	Abdominal pain Nausea, vomit Headache, Fever, Diarrhea	Source animals humans, poultry Improper cooking of high protein item	Watch cross contamination and contact Cook proteins to the specified temp	Infection
Shigellosis 🍽 ⚕	1-3 days	Diarrhea-Bloody Headache, fever Lassitude, Dehydration	Human feces Raw Vegetables Mixed foods salads	Hygiene Avoid cross contamination and contact Use safe water, pest free area	Infection
Listeriosis 🍽 🐟	3 - 70 days	Nausea, vomit Fever, backache	Unpasteurized Dairy Products Deli Foods Prepared Salads Ice Cream Machine	Use only pasteurized dairy Avoid Cross Contamination, Clean surfaces	Infection
E. Coli 🍽	2-8 days	Diarrhea, Severe cramps Abdominal pain	Undercooked ground meats Lettuce, Alfalfa	Cook to 165° Use domestic products - USDA	Toxin Mediated Infection
Campylobacteriosis 🐟 ⚕	2- 5 days	Diarrhea, Muscle Pain Nausea, vomit Headache	Raw milk, protein Cross Contact Cattle, Poultry	Use Pasteurized Milk. Wash Hands Proper cooking temperatures	Infection
Vibrio 🐟 ⚕ *Parahaemolyticus*	12 to 24 Hours	Fever, Chills, Diarrhea, Cramp	Shellfish Cross Contact	Proper sources Wash Hands Proper Cooking	Infection

Foodborne Infection- pathogen consumed, grows, causes illness. – Slow Symptom
Foodborne Intoxication- pathogen causes toxin, toxin consumed, illness caused – Fast Symptom
Toxin Mediated Infection – pathogen consumed, toxins develop in digestive tract

Common Viral Foodborne Illnesses	Incubation Period	Symptoms	Common Cause	Prevention	Duration
Hepatis A	10 – 50 Days	Fever, Fatigue Nausea, Loss of Appetite, Jaundice	1. Food handler Contaminates ready to eat food 2. Shellfish	1. Good Hygiene, Sanitize contact surfaces. 2.Approved Source	1 week to several months
Norwalk Virus (*Gastroenteritis*)	1-2 Days	Mild Fever, Nausea, Vomit Diarrhea	1. Fecal contaminated water 2. Shellfish	1. Use chlorinated water, wash hands 2.Approved Source	1 – 3 days
Rotavirus (*Gastroenteritis*)	1-3 Days	Vomit, Diarrhea abdominal pain	1. Ready to Eat Foods. 2. Water and Ice	1. Good Hygiene, proper cooking 2. Chlorinate water	4-8 days

Viral – needs a living host to reproduce, person to person and person to food

Parasites and Fungi– passed to human from host.
  Trichinosis, Anisakiasis, Giardiasis, Cyclosporiasis
Foodborne Contamination-food poison or chemical ingested by human
  Biological =Scrombroid Toxin, Ciguatera Poisoning, Plant and Fungi Toxins
  Chemical = Toxic Metals, Pesticides, Chemical
Physical Contamination- when a foreign object is found in food. Metal, Glass, Plastic

FATTOM- Environments or conditions for Microorganisms to reproduce the quickest are
F- Food *that are potentially hazardous – proteins and carbohydrates*
A- Acidity *level has a ph that is neutral*
T- Temperature *is in the TDZ – Temperature Danger Zone 41°F to 135°F-* **Quickest Growth 70° - 125°F**
T -Time- *the longer the item is in the TDZ the greater the chance for bacteria growth.*
O -Oxygen *–Aerobic require oxygen, Anaerobic requires no oxygen, and Facultative- uses both.*
M- Moisture *is high in potentially hazardous foods*

HAACP – Hazard Analysis Critical Control Point – Systematic way of building information to identify areas of concern related to all areas of food service.
Step 1 Conduct Hazard <u>Analysis</u>
Step 2 Determine Critical Control Points <u>CCP</u>
Step 3 Establish Critical <u>Limits</u>
Step 4 Establish <u>Monitor</u>ing Procedures
Step 5 Identify <u>Correct</u>ive Action
Step 6 <u>Verify</u> System Operates Correctly
Step 7 Set Procedures for <u>Record</u> Keeping

2017 USDA Food Code
TCS (Time- Temp Control for Safety)

  Using an instant read thermometer

Stuffed Meat	165° Instantly
Casseroles	165° for 17 seconds
Ground Meats	155° for 17 seconds
Cured Meats	155° for 15 seconds
Meats *	145° for 15 seconds
Fish	145° for 15 seconds
Fresh Eggs	145° for 15 seconds
Reheated Food	165° for 17 seconds
Microwave Foods	165° hold 2 minutes
Poultry	165° Instantly or 155° for 1 min

* A chart of intact muscle temperatures can be referenced on page 4 for meat preparations with lesser degrees of doneness.

Sanitizing Equations
Chlorine = 50 ppm in [55° - 115° H_2O] x 7 seconds
Iodine = 12.5 – 25 ppm in [75° H_2O] x 30 seconds
Quats = 200 ppm in [75° H_2O] x 30 seconds or longer

REFERENCE CHARTS

Volume to Weight Conversions

Bread Flour	1 cup = 4.75 oz
Brown Sugar, Packed	1 cup = 6 oz
Butter	1 cup = 8 oz
Cake Flour, sifted	1 cup = 3.75 oz
Cornstarch	1 cup = 4.5 oz
Cocoa Powder	1 cup = 3.25 oz
Cornmeal	1 cup = 5.5 oz
Eggs	1 cup = 7.75 oz
Honey	1 cup = 12 oz
Oil	1 cup = 8 oz
Rice	1 cup = 8 oz
Sugar	1 cup = 7 oz

Can Size (Number)	Approximate Volume of Food	Approximate Weight of Food
No. 1 picnic	1 ¼ cups	10 ½ to 12 ounces
No. 300	1 ¾ cups	14 to 16 ounces
No. 303	2 cups	16 to 17 ounces
No. 2	2 ½ cups	20 ounces
No. 2 ½	3 ½ cups	27 to 29 ounces
No. 3	5 ¾ cups	51 ounces
No. 10	3 quarts	6 ½ lbs to 7 lbs 5 ounces

Metric Conversion

Ounces to Milliliters
Multiply ounce by factor of 30

Cups to Liters
Multiply cups by factor of 0.24

Ounces to Grams
Multiply ounce by factor of 28.3

Grams to Ounces
Multiply gram by factor of .0353

Pounds to Gram
Multiply pound by factor of 453.59

Pounds to Kilograms
Multiply pounds by factor of 0.45

Measure Conversion

1 tsp = 1/3 Tbsp

3 tsp= 1 Tbsp

1/2 Tbsp= 11/2 tsp

1 Tbsp= 3 tsp or 1/2 fluid ounce

2 Tbsp = 1/8 cup or 1 fluid ounce

Pinch= 1/8 tsp using two fingers

Dash = 1/4 tsp using three fingers

1/8 cup = 2 Tbsp or 1 fluid ounce

1/4 cup = 4 Tbsp or 2 fluid ounces

Volume to Fluid Ounce

1 cup = 8 ounces
1 pint = 16 ounces
1 quart = 32 ounces
½ gallon= 64 ounces
1 gallon = 128 ounces

CONVERSION AND HYDRATION RATIOS

TBSP to 1 Ounce

1/3 tbsp= 1 tsp

Baking Powder	2
Baking Soda	1.3
Dried Vegetable Flake	6
Flavored Salts	2.3
Granulated Garlic, Onion	3
Herb Flakes	18
Herb Powdered	6
Herb Whole	9.6
Herbs Ground	7
Kosher Salt	3.3
Pepper Ground	4.3
Pepper Whole	4
Saffron	14
Sea Salt	1.6
Seeds	5
Spice Blends	4.3
Spice Powdered	4
Spices Ground	5

Cups to 1 Pound

Bisquit Mix	4
Cornmeal	2.5
Dried Beans	2.5
Flour - All Purpose	3.5
Flour - Bread	3.3
Flour - Whole Wheat	3.8
Flour- Cake	4
Flour- Semolina	2.8
Nuts Chopped	4
Nuts Ground	5
Nuts Sliced	4.8
Nuts Whole	3.8
Rice	2.5
Whole Grains	3

Ounces to 1 Cup

Baking Powder	7
Baking Soda	8.5
Butter	8
Cheese, Hard- Grated	3.25
Cheese, Semi Firm- Shredded	4
Chocolate Chips	5.5
Cocoa Powder	3
Coconut, Shredded	3.75
Cornstarch	4.5
Cream- Heavy	8
Cream- Sour	8.5
Eggs- unshelled	8.5
Fresh- Celery Diced	3.5
Fresh- Tomato, Diced	7
Fresh-Carrot, Diced	5.25
Fresh-Chives, Sliced	1.75
Fresh-Leeks, Diced	3.25
Fresh-Mushrooms, Sliced	2.75
Fresh-Onions, Diced	5
Fresh-Peppers, Diced	5
Fresh-Shallots, Minced	5.75
Fresh-Spinach, Chopped	7
Graham Cracker Crumb	3.5
Honey	12
Milk- Dried Solids	4.25
Panko Bread Crumb	1.75
Salt- Kosher	9
Salt- Sea Salt Fine	10
Sugar- Brown, Packed	7.75
Sugar- Granulated	7
Sugar- Powdered	4
Vegetable Oil	7.75

Volume Grain Hydration Ratio

Liquid to Volume Measure of Grain

Pilaf Method	
Rice- Converted	2
Rice- Basmati	1.5
Rice - Carolina Gold	1.75
Rice- Brown	2.5
Rice- Wild	3
Quinoa	2
Buckwheat	1.5
Farro	2.5
Wheat Berry	4
Barley	4
Millet	1.5
Amaranth	1

Traditional Method	
Cous Cous	2
Polenta	3.5
Risotto	3
Rice - Spanish- Paella	2.75

Rice Cooker	
Rice- Jasmine	1.5
Rice - Sushi, Rinse 3x	1
Rice - Basmati- Biryani	1.25
Rice - Spanish -Paella	1.25
Rice - White , Rinsed 2x	1
Rice- Brown	2
Rice- Wild	2
Quinoa	1.5
Buckwheat	2
Farro	2.75
Bulgur Wheat	1.5
Barley	2.5
Millet	2
Oats Rolled	1.75
Oats Steel Cut	3

Contributions by Thomas DeRosa MBA, CEC

Hotel Pan Portion Scoop Matrix

Pan Size	Pan Depth	Pan Capacity		Portion Size			Portions
		Quarts	Cups	Cup	Ounce	Scoop #	
Full Size 12" × 20"	2 ½ "	7 ½	30	1/4	2	16	120
				1/3	2.6	12	90
				3/8	3	10	80
				1/2	4	8	60
	4"	13	52	1/4	2	16	208
				1/3	2.6	12	160
				3/8	3	10	138
				1/2	4	8	104
	6"	19 ½	78	1/4	2	16	312
				1/3	2.6	12	240
				3/8	3	10	208
				1/2	4	8	156
				1	8		78
Half Size 12" × 10"	2 ½ "	3 ¾	15	1/4	2	16	60
				1/3	2.6	12	44
				3/8	3	10	40
				1/2	4	8	30
	4"	6 ½	26	1/4	2	16	104
				1/3	2.6	12	80
				3/8	3	10	69
				1/2	4	8	52
Third Size 12" × 7"	2 ½ "	2 qt + 12 ¾ oz	9 2/3	1/8	1	30	77
				1/4	2	16	38
				1/3	2.6	12	28
				3/8	3	10	25
	4"	3 qt+ 28oz	15 1/2	1/8	1	30	124
				1/4	2	16	62
				1/3	2.6	12	46
				3/8	3	10	41

Temperature Conversion

32° F=0° C	150° F=65.6°C
40° F=4.4°C	160° F=71.1°C
50° F=10°C	170°F=76.7°C
60° F = 15.6°C	180° F= 82.2°C
70° F = 21.1°C	190° F = 87.8°C
80° F = 26.7°C	200° F = 93.3°C
90° F = 32.2°C	212° F = 100°C
100° F = 37.8°C	250° F = 121°C
110° F = 43.3°C	300° F = 149°C
120° F = 48.9°C	350° F =177°C
130° F = 54.4°C	400° F = 205°C
140°F=60°C	450° F=233°C
	500° F = 260°C

Sous Vide Time and Temperature Chart

	Celsius	Hours		Celsius	Hours
Beef Brisket – Corned 3 lb	80°	8	**Halibut 10 oz**	50°	1
Beef Ribeye Rare 10 oz	54°	1 ¼	**Pork Belly 4 lb**	68°	24
Beef Short Rib 3 lb	75°	8	**Pork Chop 10 oz**	62°	1½
Beef Strip Steak Rare 10 oz	54°	1	**Pork Loin 3 lb**	54°	5
Beef Tenderloin 3 lb MRare	56°	3	**Salmon 8 oz**	45°	1
Chicken Breast 8 oz	65°	1½	**Sea Scallops 1 lb**	50°	½
Duck Breast 7 oz	58°	1½	**Shrimp 1 lb**	70°	¼
Duck Legs 12 oz	70°	17	**Tuna Loin 2 lb**	47°	1½
Eggs- Silky Texture	64°	1	**Turkey Breast 3 lb**	65°	3

These are suggested cooking times, refer to the FDA food code for time and temperature parameters regarding the period of time to check internal temperatures. Addition time is required for larger portions, colder products, and an increased number of pouches in the hot water bath.

Recommended Resources and Readings

100 Styles of French Cooking, Karl Wurzer. Grosset and Dunlap. 1981

150 Projects to Get You into the Culinary Arts. Mark Allison, Barron's Educational Series 2011

Ad Hoc at Home Thomas Keller, Artisan 2009

Bakewise Shirley O. Corriher, Scribner 2008

Baking, James Peterson, Ten Speed Press 2009

Bouchon, Thomas Keller, Artisan 2004

Classical Cooking the Modern Way, 2nd ed. Eugene Pauli. Van Nostrand Reinhold. 1989

Classical Indian Cooking, Julie Sahni, Morrow 1985

Classical Turkish Cooking, Gillie Basan, St. Martins Press, 1997

Cooking, James Peterson, Ten Speed Press, 2007

Culinaria, European Specialties, Volume 1&2. Joachim Romer , Konemann, 1995

Culinaria, France, Andre Domine, Konemann. 1999

Culinaria, Germany. Christine Metzger . Konemann. 1999

Culinaria, Italy, *Pasta Pesto Passion*. Claudia Piras, Konemann. 2000

Culinaria, Spain. Spanish Specialties, Marion Trutter, Konemann. 1999

Culinaria, Southeast Asian Specialties, Konemann. 1998

Culinaria, The United States, A Culinary Discovery. Peter Feierabend. Konemann. 1998

Desserts, Pierre Hermes, Little Brown and Company, 1998

Dictionnaire de l' Académie des Gastronomes, Prisma Paris 1962

Eating in America, A History. Waverly Root , Richard de Rochemont. Ecco Press 1995

elBulli (2005-2011) Ferran Adria, Albert Adria, Phaidon Inc Ltd, 2014

Eleven Madison Park: The Cookbook, Daniel Humm,2011

Essentials of Classical Italian Cooking, Marcella Hazan, Knopf Publishing Group, 1992

French Feasts, Stephanie Reynaud, Stewart Tabori 2009

How to Cook Everything Mark Bittman Wiley,2008

Italian Regional Cooking , Ada Boni,Bonanza Books, 1989

James Beards American Cookery, James Beard, Little, Brown and Company, 1972

Jeremiah Tower's New American Classics, Jeremiah Tower, Harper Row, 1986

Kitchen Science, Howard Hillman revised edition, 1989

La Technique: An Illustrated Guide to the Fundamental Techniques of Cooking, Jacques Pepin, Random House, 1976

Larousse Gastronomique(American Edition) Jennifer Harvey Lang, ed. Crown 1988

Le Guide Culinaire. A. Escoffier, Wiley and Sons, Inc 1979

Mastering the Art of French Cooking Julia Child, Knopf 1963

Meze Diane Kochilas , Harper Collins Publishers 2003

Modernist Cuisine: The Art and Science of Cooking, Myhrvold, Young, Bilet , The Cooking Lab 2011

On Food and Cooking Harold McGee , Simon & Schuster 2004

Pastries, Pierre Hermes, Abrams, 2011

Pastry, Michel Roux, Quadrille Publishing Ltd, 2008

Practical Baking, William Sultan, Director Books 1981

The Art and Science of Culinary Preparation, Jerald W. Chesser, ACF. 1992

The Art of Fine Baking, Paula Peck, Fireside Book, 1993

The Bakers Manual, Joseph Amendola, Van Nostrand Reinhold, 1992

The Boston Cooking School Cook Book. Fannie Merritt Farmer, Little Brown 1924

The Bread Baker's Apprentice Peter Reinhart , Ten Speed Press 2002

The Cook's Ingredients. Adrian Bailey, ed. Readers Digest Association, 1990

The Encyclopedia of Fish Cookery. A.J. McClane. H. Holt& Co. 1977

The Fat Duck Cookbook, Heston Blumenthal, Bloomsbury, 2009

The Flavor Bible, Karen Page, Andrew Dornenburg, Little Brown and Company 2008

The French Laundry Cookbook, Thomas Keller, Artisan 1999

The Hotel Butcher, Garde Manger, and Carver. Frank River. Hotel Monthly 1916

The Hungry Empire: How Britain's Quest for Food Shaped the Modern World, Lizzie Collingham Random House, 2018

The Oxford Companion to Food, Oxford University Press, Alan Davidson, 1999

The Oxford Companion to Wine, Oxford University Press, Jancis Robinson, 2015

The Oxford English Dictionary, Oxford University Press, 1986 Second Edition

The Professional Server. Marcella Giannasio, Edward Sanders, Paul Paz, Ronald Wilkinson. Prentice Hall 2012

The Whole Beast, Fergus Henderson, Harper Collins, 2004

The World Atlas of Food, Jane Grigson, Spring Books, 1988

The World of Wine, Hugh Johnson, Jancis Robinson, Octopus Publishing, 2007

U.S. Food and Drug Administration Food Code 2017

Additional resources can be found at www.chefreference.com

Frederick J. Tiess ME, WCMC, CEC, CCA, FMP is an Associate Professor at Johnson and Wales University. Fred was the former Executive Chef at the Founders Inn and Conference Center in Virginia Beach and the Sous Chef at the Greenbrier Resort in West Virginia. He has also worked in Palm Beach Florida, Hilton Head, South Carolina, and New York City. In 2017 he completed Master Chef courses at the University of Guelph and was certified by the World Associate of Chef Societies (Paris) and City and Guild (London) as a Certified Master Chef. He holds a master's degree in Entrepreneurship from of Western Carolina University and Undergraduate Degrees from Johnson and Wales University, the Culinary Institute of America, the State University of New York, as well as graduating from the Greenbrier Apprenticeship Program. He is a member of the Board of Directors for Mercy Chefs. He is thankful for the contributions of fellow faculty and colleagues from around the globe who have helped in the development and peer review of this guide.

Contributing Faculty - Johnson and Wales University Charlotte Campus

Susan Batten CEC, CCE
Brian Campbell CEC,CCE
Thomas DeRosa MBA, CEC
Jennifer Gallagher MS, CEC
Ashley McGee CEC

Jerry Lanuzza MS.Ed
James O'Hara PCEC
Harry Peemoeller MB, FMP
Paul Malcolm MS.Ed., CEC, CCE, CHE
Daina Soto MSc.

Editorial Advisors
Mark Allison MBA, FMCGB, MCFA
Ronald DeSantis CMC
Bruno Marti CCC, OBC (Order of British Columbia)
Peter Lehmuller Ed. D, CCC, CCE, CHE
Tobias McDonald CMC

Lawrence McFadden CMC
Steven Sadowski CEC, CCE
Judson Simpson CMC
Karl Stybe Ed. D
Peter Timmins CMC

Acknowledgment- Chef Travis Garrett, Cover Subject – Emeril Lagasse Lab JWU Charlotte

Please support the efforts of Mercy Chefs through with your talent and gifts. Mercy Chefs is a non-profit, faith based, charitable organization committed to serving free high quality professionally prepared meals, during local, state and national disasters and emergencies. www.mercychefs.com

"Serve God, Serve People, Serve Great Food" Fred Tiess